A Neolithic Ceremonial Complex in Galloway

A NEOLITHIC CEREMONIAL COMPLEX IN GALLOWAY

Excavations at Dunragit and Droughduil, 1999–2002

Julian Thomas

Oxbow Books

Oxford & Philadelphia

Published in the United Kingdom in 2015 by
OXBOW BOOKS
10 Hythe Bridge Street, Oxford OX1 2EW

and in the United States by
OXBOW BOOKS
908 Darby Road, Havertown, PA 19083

Paperback Edition: ISBN 978-1-78297-970-8
Digital Edition: ISBN 978-1-78297-971-5

A CIP record for this book is available from the British Library

Library of Congress Control Number: 2015945526

Printed in Malta by Melita Press

For a complete list of Oxbow titles, please contact:

UNITED KINGDOM
Oxbow Books
Telephone (01865) 241249, Fax (01865) 794449
Email: oxbow@oxbowbooks.com
www.oxbowbooks.com

UNITED STATES OF AMERICA
Oxbow Books
Telephone (800) 791-9354, Fax (610) 853-9146
Email: queries@casemateacademic.com
www.casemateacademic.com/oxbow

Oxbow Books is part of the Casemate Group

Front cover: Reconstruction of the Late Neolithic palisaded enclosure at Dunragit, looking toward the Droughduil mound. Image by Aaron Watson

CONTENTS

LIST OF FIGURES AND TABLES

List of Figures

List of Tables

LIST OF CONTRIBUTORS

DEREK HAMILTON
Scottish Universities Environmental Research Centre
Rankine Avenue
Scottish Enterprise Technology Park
East Kilbride
G75 0QF

ELIZABETH HEALEY
School of Arts, Languages and Cultures
University of Manchester
Oxford Road
Manchester
M13 9PL

JASON JORDAN
Geography, Environment and Disaster Management
Coventry University
Priory Street
Coventry
CV1 5FB

COLIN KERR
Scottish Universities Environmental Research Centre
Rankine Avenue
Scottish Enterprise Technology Park
East Kilbride
G75 0QF

MATTHEW LEIVERS
Wessex Archaeology
Portway House
Old Sarum Park
Salisbury
SP4 6EB

HELEN LEWIS
UCD School of Archaeology
Newman Building
University College Dublin
Belfield, Dublin 4

JACQUELINE MCKINLEY
Wessex Archaeology
Portway House
Old Sarum Park
Salisbury
SP4 6EB

DAVID SANDERSON
Scottish Universities Environmental Research Centre
Rankine Avenue
Scottish Enterprise Technology Park
East Kilbride
G75 0QF

DAVID SMITH
Oxford University Centre for the Environment
South Parks Road
Oxford
OX1 3QY

JULIAN THOMAS
School of Arts, Languages and Cultures
University of Manchester
Oxford Road
Manchester
M13 9PL

RICHARD TIPPING
Biological and Environmental Sciences
University of Stirling
Stirling
FK9 4LA

ACKNOWLEDGEMENTS

First and foremost, I should like to thank the landowners at Dunragit, Mr and Mrs J. McKie for their generosity in allowing the excavation to take place. Forest Enterprise kindly allowed investigation to take place on the Droughduil mound. The funding for the project was generously provided by Historic Scotland, the University of Southampton and the University of Manchester, and the former also contributed support for a period of teaching buyout, during which a substantial part of the writing of this report was completed. At Historic Scotland, Patrick Ashmore, Gordon Barclay, Deirdre Cameron and Rod McCullagh provided invaluable assistance and advice. In the years since the fieldwork concluded, Rod has contributed unstinting support, and answered innumerable questions. John Pickin of Stranraer Museum helped us out with computing and communications facilities, and access to collections during our time in the field. Jane Brann, Dumfries and Galloway regional archaeologist, gave support and information. Marilyn Brown and Kenny Brophy, then of the Royal Commission on the Ancient and Historic Monuments of Scotland, gave advice, and assistance both on site and above it. Trevor Cowie turned a welcome critical eye onto our ceramic assemblage. Dave Webb constructed and maintained the project website, and brought us to the attention of the international archaeological community. Julia Roberts cooked for the multitudes on site, and Rick Peterson managed the project and kept things from falling apart. David Aspden, Ange Brennan, Chris Fowler, and Matthew Leivers supervised the excavation, and generally kept order. Thanks are finally owed to the students from Southampton, Manchester and other universities, and the other volunteers and drivers who did all the hard work.

The site plans and maps were drawn by Jo Wright and Julian Thomas, the sections by Nick Overton, Jo Wright and Julian Thomas, often on the basis of pen and ink originals drawn by Matthew Leivers. The cover illustration was created by Aaron Watson.

This volume is published with the support of a subvention from Historic Scotland, which is gratefully acknowledged.

1

INTRODUCTION

Julian Thomas

Location, topography and geology

The modern village of Dunragit lies between Stranraer and Glenluce in Western Galloway, immediately to the north of Luce Bay (at approximately NGR NX 150576). The major road between Stranraer and Newton Stewart, the A75, runs ESE-WNW through the village, parallel with the railway that links Girvan with the ferry port at Stranraer. Both of these exploit the expanse of flat ground that lies at the foot of Challoch Hill, which borders on the sand dunes of Torrs Warren to the south. The road has been established since at least the eighteenth century, when it was constructed to serve the port of Portpatrick (MacHaffie 2001). The level ground is narrowest immediately to the east of Dunragit, at East Challoch, where Challoch Hill overlooks Luce Sands. Dunragit is thus located on a natural routeway, where the north-south axis of the Water of Luce turns westward to the isthmus between Loch Ryan and Luce Bay. Further west, the country opens up onto the Rhins of Galloway, while to the east the coast skirts the low uplands of the Machars. North beyond Challoch Hill, the land rises toward Cairnscarrow and Cairnerzean Fell. Overall, then, the location of Dunragit represents an area of gently rolling lowland sandwiched between the uplands to the north and Luce Bay to the south.

South from the village, the large mound of Droughduil Mote stands on the border of Torrs Warren sands. This is a major dune system covering an area of 1200 hectares, with a coastal frontage of approximately 7 kilometres (Cowie 1996: 14). The uplands to the north and west of Dunragit, and the northern part of the Rhins of Galloway

are composed of Ordovecian sedimentary rocks, while the southern Rhins and the country south of Glenluce are Silurian rocks of the Llandovery series. A broad strip running southward from Loch Ryan, however, is composed of more recent sediments, principally alluvium and glacial outwash gravel. This provides the subsoil at Dunragit itself. The place-name Dunragit may be derived from Din Rheged, meaning the fort of Rheged, which would refer to the Dark Age kingdom. This name probably does not relate to the prehistoric sites, but to Round Dounan, a fort located on a natural rock outcrop overlooking Dunragit village. The fort is stone built, with a containing wall and an entrance passage. It has been argued to be of fifth or sixth century AD date (Reid 1952).

Challoch Hill rises abruptly north of the village, but from the A75 southwards toward Piltanton Bridge the ground drops no more than 15 metres over a kilometre or so. Between the road and the railway running 150 metres to the south lies what was once the major employer in the village, Dunragit Creamery. The creamery was opened in 1882, and was one of the earliest of its sort in Scotland. It merged with the Valleyfield Dairy Company in 1891 to form the United Creameries Company, and later was operated by Nestlé. In recent years the creamery has closed down, and the building is now used by a light engineering company manufacturing motorbikes (Stell 1996: 55). The land between road and railway has largely been under pasture in recent decades, but the fields south of the railway have been under the plough, and have revealed spectacular results from air photography. South of these fields, Droughduil Mote is located in an area of woodland managed by Forest Enterprise. At this point the

Julian Thomas

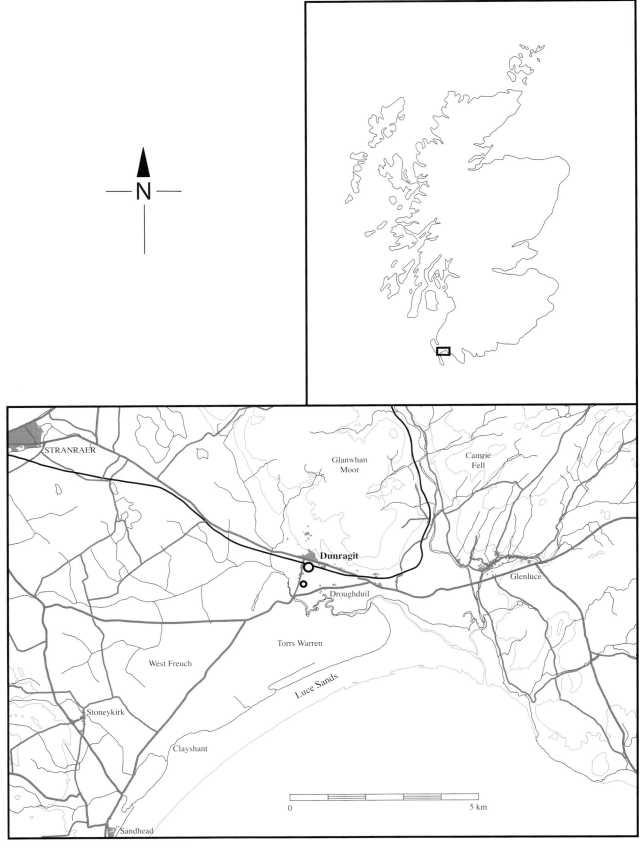

Figure 1.1 Dunragit, Galloway: location

Figure 1.2 Dunragit complex: central area of the palisaded enclosure, from the south-west

Figure 1.3 Dunragit complex: central area of the palisaded enclosure, from the north

subsoil is sandier, and the mound itself is set on an ancient sand dune. West from the A748 (which runs south from the A75) air photographic cover is far poorer, as the land bordering the road is taken up by a large nursery growing small conifers. South and east from the nursery a very flat expanse of land, the Freuch, is drained by Piltanton Burn and stretches toward West Freuch airfield.

Discovery

The complex of cropmark features at Dunragit (focused on NX 14805735), was first identified from the air by Marilyn Brown of the Royal Commission on the Ancient and Historic Monuments of Scotland in 1992. A second series of photographs of the complex was taken in 1995, and together these images provide evidence of a remarkable group of prehistoric structures, bisected by the modern railway line (Figs. 1.2 to 1.5). These images show a large enclosure, composed of three concentric rings of what are now known to be post-holes (numbers 1 to 3 on Fig. 1.6). The middle ring of the enclosure appears to be associated with an entrance avenue leading toward the south, while the outer ring is more irregular, and is in-turned at two or three points on the southern side, which may represent less monumental entrances. Inside the inner ring there is a ring-ditch (4), and a second lies between the middle and outer post-rings on the western side of the enclosure (5). Immediately to the south of this ring-ditch a series of lines of post-holes or pits cuts across the enclosure on a northeast to southwest axis (6). In a similar position on the eastern side is a post- or pit-ring with a diameter of about 20 metres (7). Between

the two innermost rings of the enclosure immediately to the west of the entrance avenue lies a small penannular enclosure, opening to the east (8). Two smaller enclosures of a similar kind, each with an apparent central feature of some form, are found north of the railway line and east of the outer post-ring of the enclosure (9 and 10). The outer ring of the enclosure can be identified to the west of these structures, and a further arc of features lies further west still (11). This is clearly not part of the palisaded enclosure, and was eventually identified as the terminal of a post-defined cursus, of earlier date (see Chapter 3 below). North of all of these elements is a line of large features running parallel with the A75 and now identified as road quarry pits (12). Two more penannular enclosures are found south of the railway line (13 and 14), the larger of them apparently forming the westerly termination of an alignment of post-holes or pits, which runs for some 150 metres. South of the eastern end of this alignment is an enclosure with five flattened sides, again formed of post-holes or pits (15). South of this in turn are two further pit- or post-alignments, in which the constituent features are closely-set, and perhaps intercutting (16 and 17). Finally, southwest of the enclosure lies a ring-ditch surrounded by a ring of posts or pits, with an overall diameter of about 25 metres (18).

Most of these features are better defined in the fields to the south of the railway line, and it was to be presumed that various elements projected north into the pasture fields, where they were not all visible from the air. On morphological grounds, comparisons can be made between the Dunragit enclosure and a group of later Neolithic palisaded enclosures in Scotland, Ireland,

Figure 1.4 Dunragit complex: area north of the railway line

Figure 1.5 Dunragit complex: area south-east of the palisaded enclosure, with a pit- or post-alignment and a hengiform enclosure

Wales and England, which include Meldon Bridge (Burgess 1976; Speak and Burgess 1999), Forteviot (St. Joseph 1978; Noble and Brophy 2011a), Ballynahatty (Hartwell 1998), Mount Pleasant (Wainwright 1979), Walton and Hindwell (Gibson 1999). The inner two concentric rings of possible posts at Dunragit are well matched at West Kennet, while the distinctive entrance structure is paralleled at Meldon Bridge, Forteviot and Walton. With the exception of Meldon Bridge, all of these large palisaded enclosures are associated with groups of lesser features, as appears to be the case at Dunragit. At the time when fieldwork was undertaken at Dunragit, of the Scottish sites of this type it was only Meldon Bridge that had undergone extensive excavation. Since 2007, excavations have been undertaken by the Universities of Glasgow and Aberdeen at Forteviot and Leadketty (Noble and Brophy 2011a).

The area surrounding the Dunragit monument is one that contains dense traces of prehistoric activity. Immediately to the south, the sand dunes of Luce Bay have provided considerable evidence of Neolithic and Bronze Age occupation, in the form of scatters of artefacts, hearths and burials (Davidson 1952; McInnes 1964; Cowie 1996). In the hills to the north, there are numerous Neolithic and Bronze Age cairns (e.g. Corcoran 1969a; b). Coastal southern Galloway also has an extensive distribution of rock art (Morris 1979; van Hoek 1986). It is conceivable that the Dunragit enclosure represents a focus for much of the Late Neolithic and Early Bronze Age activity, and that the central part of Luce Bay constituted a place of importance through much of prehistory.

Circumstances of the excavations

Between 1994 and 1998 the author had undertaken a series of excavations in the Dumfries area, investigating the Pict's Knowe henge, the Holywood cursus complex, and the post alignment at Holm Farm, with the support of Historic Scotland (Thomas 2007a). Following the success of these investigations, a campaign of work at Dunragit was proposed, in order to test the date and character of the features, and to assess the state of their preservation. Parts of the complex have been under the plough in recent years, and it was evident from the results of fieldwork that many of the cut features investigated were severely truncated.

Four seasons of excavation took place on the Neolithic ceremonial complex at Dunragit during 1999–2002. These investigations demonstrated that the large enclosure was of Late Neolithic date, and had been constructed using timber uprights in ramped post-holes. The largest of the post-rings had a diameter of around 300 metres, while the innermost had a diameter of perhaps 120 metres. Both the outer post-ring and the middle were composed of large uprights interspersed with smaller members, probably forming a continuous palisade and comparable with the structure of the Late Neolithic enclosure at Meldon Bridge in Peebleshire (Speak and Burgess 1999). Both of these post-rings had been single-phase structures, and in both cases the posts had eventually rotted out and been replaced by silting and collapsed gravel packing. These two outermost rings of post-holes also produced very little in the way of material culture. By contrast, the inner ring had largely been made up exclusively of large, free-

Figure 1.6 Dunragit complex: plot of features revealed on aerial photographs

standing posts, most of which had rotted away, but some of which had been deliberately removed, although in one short stretch smaller posts were present. The post-holes of the inner ring were considerably larger than those of the two outer rings, and it is possible that their digging had involved a conspicuous expenditure of effort. Where posts had been pulled out, a number of elaborate deposits had been placed in the crater left by the post-removal.

The enclosure had been preceded on the site by a post-defined cursus monument, one side and the terminal of which had been identified in the 1999–2001 seasons. The post-holes of the cursus were easily distinguishable from those of the enclosure, for in almost every case the post had been burned *in situ*. However, numerous other post-holes were located on the same axis as the cursus, extending beyond the monument itself. The coincidence of earlier Neolithic cursus monuments and later Neolithic enclosures on the same site is known from a number of other sites, including Dorchester on Thames in Oxfordshire, Llandegai in Gwynnedd, and Thornborough in Yorkshire (Atkinson, Piggott and Sandars 1951; Lynch and Musson 2004; Harding 2013). This suggests that the relationship is not fortuitous, and that the significance that a location achieved through the construction of a cursus was a significant factor in the positioning of later enclosures.

The aerial photographs taken by RCAHMS that were responsible for the identification of the Dunragit enclosure also show two possible sets of entrances, both located in the area immediately to the south of the modern railway line. It is notable that the entrance through the outer post-ring does not respect that which is connected with the middle ring. The outer entrance opens to the southwest, while the middle ring entrance is aligned to the south. Given that both of these palisade-rings are single-phase structures, while the central post-circle has two phases of construction, it may be that the three concentric circles are not all contemporary. On the contrary, an interpretation is preferred in which the monument as a whole had two phases of construction, in each of which a timber circle was surrounded by a palisade, and in which the middle post-ring succeeded the outer, or vice-versa.

The more elaborate of these entrances, connected with the middle post-ring, is composed of two parallel lines of features, which are presumably post-holes. It opens toward the south, and is aligned almost precisely on the large earthen mound at Droughduil, some 400 metres away. This mound presently stands in a plantation managed by Forest Enterprise, and had been cleared of trees shortly before fieldwork took place. It is located between the enclosure and the extensive dune systems of Luce Sands, and as such it stands in an area where the subsoil is much sandier than the outwash gravels on which Dunragit village has grown up. The mound is known as Droughduil Mote, and has been recorded as a medieval motte (Feachem 1956). However, the spatial relationship with the Dunragit enclosure is suggestive, and the site is

by no means representative of local castle mounds. Mottes such as Mote Slap at Sandhead are generally high-lying, and have a profile which is much more flattened than the Droughduil mound. Moreover, a number of large Late Neolithic mounds are known in Britain, and many of these are directly associated with henges or palisaded enclosures. The best-known example is Silbury Hill in Wiltshire (Whittle 1997a), but others include the Conquer Barrow in Dorset, perched on the bank of the Mount Pleasant henge and overlooking the palisade enclosure that it contains; The Marlborough mound (Wiltshire); the Hatfield Barrow, contained within the Marden henge (Wiltshire); and Duggleby Howe, which contained an important sequence of Late Neolithic burials, and is enclosed within a massive causewayed ditch (Kinnes *et al.* 1983). Excavation on the Droughduil mound in 2002 demonstrated that it had been constructed with stepped sides, and that a stone cairn had been constructed on its summit. A series of optically stimulated luminescence dates on the accumulated sand over the surface of the mound demonstrated that it was certainly not medieval, and was probably Neolithic in date.

Introduction to the report

In writing the report on the Pict's Knowe henge and other sites in the Dumfries area (Thomas 2007a: 4), a decision was made to present as complete as possible a record of the archaeological evidence, rather than limit the detailed description to the support of a particular narrative account of the sites. While it was recognised that any distinction between description and interpretation is artificial, since excavation is itself an interpretive practice (see Hodder 1999: 92; Lucas 2012: 215), the intention was to present a treatment which amounts to a 'handbook' of the set of deposits under discussion. The same philosophy is followed here. This approach arose from the author's frustration with excavation reports that presented only a summary of the stratigraphic information for a site, rendering the contents difficult to work with, and often mandating access to the site archive if the results were to be evaluated. As an observation, where a small site that may have produced only a few pits and post-holes is published, full details of all contexts are generally provided. Yet larger sites with numerous features are sometimes described in a more summary fashion. Ironically, it follows that the most important sites are occasionally published in least detail. The excavations at Dunragit and Droughduil were perhaps just at the upper limit of what can be fully addressed within a single-volume monograph. One particular justification for the fine-grained description attempted here is that the overall interpretation of the monumental complex rests to some extent on the cumulative effect of the individual stratigraphic histories of a great many separate cut features. Ultimately, rather than choose some of these features to discuss in detail while arbitrarily neglecting others, a uniform level of description was decided upon. Each feature is fully described, and the original context numbers are retained from the field records, with Munsell universal colour values quoted for each deposit (Munsell 2009). This latter inclusion is arguably an unusual decision to make, but at this particular site colour values are of some significance, as subtle variations in hue were observed across the monumental complex and within individual features, contributing significantly to interpretation. Many of the feature fills in the eastern part of the principal excavated area, largely in Trench A, fell into the 7.5 YR series, while those further west in

Trenches AA and J were more likely to gravitate around the more yellowish 10 YR hues. This was undoubtedly related to variation is the subsoil, but it provided the background to important differences within and between contexts, most notably the recuts of the inner post-ring of the Late Neolithic enclosure. In some cases, the details of individual features are complex and intricate, and this level of detail is essential in order to understand their formation. In others the information is admittedly unexciting and repetitive, and it is not imagined that the casual reader will wade through the entire descriptive text. However, the intention is to provide a definitive account of the evidence from the Dunragit excavations with a consistent level of detail.

2

CONTEXT: THE PREHISTORY OF LUCE BAY

Julian Thomas

Introduction

Luce Bay is a broad, shallow embayment located in the extreme southwest of Scotland, between the peninsula of the Rhins of Galloway to the west and that of the Machars, or the Whithorn-Wigtown area, to the east. The bay has an extent of 47,942 hectares, and is 31 kilometres wide at its outer margins, between Burrow Head and the Mull of Galloway. The headland of the Mull of Galloway is the southernmost point in the Scottish mainland. While the headlands are rocky, much of the bay is low-lying and sheltered from wave action. Toward the head of the bay there are extensive sandy inter-tidal sediments, while much of the remainder is no more than 20 metres deep below sea-level (Scottish Natural Heritage 2006: 10). As a result, the landward part of the bay is composed of a complex combination of sandbanks, sandy sediments and mud, with reefs and boulders. Although the bay was formerly a significant commercial fishery, the industry has declined in recent decades. In the northern apex of the bay lies Luce Sands, composed of imposing dunes together with scrub and saltmarsh. While some of the sand dunes are relatively stable, others are mobile, with the result that older land surfaces are continually being revealed and destroyed. The total extent of Luce Sands is around 1200 hectares, with a coastal frontage of 7 kilometers between Clayshant Burn and Piltanton Burn, the outflow of the Water of Luce (Cowie 1996: 12). Aside from its archaeological importance the dune system is a great natural significance, where over-wintering migratory birds roost, and where several rare species (including newts) are found. The sands were declared an Area of

Special Scientific Interest in 1955, and the bay and sands together were made a Special Area of Conservation by Scottish Natural Heritage in 2005. Between the 1930s and 1990s the sands were used as a training bombing range for RAF and allied aircraft based at West Freuch airfield. Several of the conical concrete bombing targets that date to this period are still visible. The sands represent one of the richest archaeological landscapes in Scotland, having produced over 8,500 artefacts held in the National Museum of Scotland alone (Cowie 1996: 14). Many of these have come from buried soil horizons periodically revealed by the ceaseless movement of the dunes.

Immediately to the north and west of the dunes lies an area of low-lying bog and moorland, known as the Freuch. Northward again is higher country, which rises eastward from the Water of Luce toward Cairnsmore of Fleet. Historically, much of the importance of this part of Scotland has lain in its role as a point of departure for Ireland, and during the eighteenth century ships sailed between Portpatrick and Donaghadee. At this time the Wigtownshire coast was notorious for the smuggling of brandy, tobacco and tea, and garrisons were established at Port William and Sinniness in order to combat this problem. At this time the Old Military Road was constructed between Stranraer and Newton Stewart, part of which has now become the A75 (MacHaffie 2001).

Mesolithic and Early Neolithic

The shores of Luce Bay and Loch Ryan have produced numerous flint scatters of Mesolithic date, with a

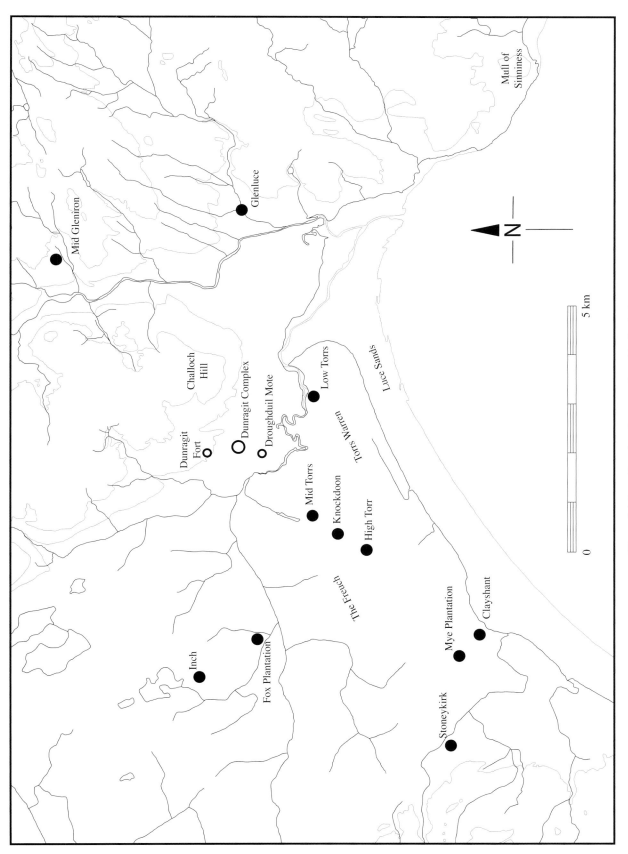

Figure 2.1 Luce Bay: locations mentioned in the text

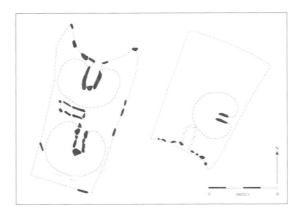

Figure 2.2 The Mid Gleniron chambered cairns, plans

particular concentration around the Water of Luce (Cherry and Cherry 1997; Coles 1963; Cummings 2001: 186). However, none of the sites in the Luce Sands area have been subject to the level of investigation seen further east at Starr on Loch Doon (Edwards 1996) or Low Clone and Barsalloch on the Machars (Cormack 1970; Cormack and Coles 1968). Traces of occupation in the Early Neolithic are equally extensive. McInnes (1964: 60) cited 92 Early Neolithic pots that had been recovered from Luce Sands. These included at least two fine, thin-walled, burnished, plain carinated bowls, which presumably date to the thirty-sixth century BC or earlier. Many of the other vessels are Cowie's 'heavy bowls' (1993: 16), with thicker walls and expanded rims, while some are shouldered bowls with an upright neck and sparse decoration. These probably date to the middle centuries of the fourth millennium BC. Other indications of Neolithic occupation are provided by stone axes, which are quite numerous in the Luce Bay area. Group VI axes from Langdale in Cumbria are the most common non-flint axe type in the former county of Wigtownshire. Williams cites 124 Group VI axes in the area, and seven Group IX axes from the source at Tievebulliagh in Antrim, while by 2011 Coles was able to refer to 240 stone axes in total (Coles 2011a: 142; Williams 1970: 111). Although the Antrim axes are less numerous, their presence suggests that the connection between Galloway and Ireland was already a significant one during the Neolithic. Twelve Group VI axes came from Inch parish, a little to the north of Dunragit, and 25 came from the parish of Old Luce. One axe of unknown source was found at Droughduil, and another at Dunragit schoolhouse, while a Group VI axe was discovered at Dunragit council scheme (Williams 1970: 118). Interestingly, the Star Site on Luce Sands produced forty-nine fragments of Group VI rock, suggesting the reworking of Langdale tuff axes amongst the dunes (Williams 1970: 120). Luce Bay has also produced a large collection of Arran pitchstone, including knapping debris (Coles 2011a: 145). Such an

extensive assemblage is rare elsewhere in Scotland, and as this material may have been valued for its aesthetic or symbolic qualities, it may be an indication that the area had already developed a particular importance during the earlier part of the Neolithic (Warren 2006: 37).

The principal monuments of Early Neolithic date in the Luce Bay area are chambered long cairns of the Clyde tradition, although the local examples are somewhat atypical, and potentially relatively early. At Mid Gleniron Farm, north of Glenluce and overlooking the Water of Luce, Corcoran excavated two long cairns with relatively complex structural histories. Mid Gleniron I was originally composed of two small oval cairns with simple orthostatic chambers, each with little or no discernable passage. These were minimal constructions, in which the surrounding cairn mass did little but provide support for the chamber (Corcoran 1972: 35). The two cairns were arranged one in front of the other, on the same axis. On the face of it, this would seem an unusual arrangement if the two structures were both to be used for interment and/or veneration, the southern chamber being hidden away behind the northern cairn. This would almost seem to imply that the positioning of the two cairns anticipated their later incorporation into a larger monument. This larger monument was a trapezoidal cairn 20 metres long, with a forecourt defined by a curved façade of upright stones and dry-stone walling, a surrounding kerb, and a third simple chamber in the western side of the cairn (Corcoran 1969a: 35). The construction of the façade a little to the north of the northern chamber had the effect of lengthening the chamber, and segmenting it into two spaces, on either side of the bracing stone (Noble 2005: 27). This might be understood as a deliberate means of creating a more divided space for deposition, in line with the segmented chambers more common amongst tombs of the Clyde group. Unfortunately, the only trace of a mortuary deposit within the cairn took the form of some scraps of urburnt bone in the southern chamber. The forecourt was later neatly blocked with a kerbed mass of stone, but it had originally contained three upright pillars of stone, and the surface showed traces of burning.

The second cairn, Mid Gleniorn II, was located a little to the southeast of the first. It contained a single small oval cairn, very similar to the two within Mid Gleniron I, with a simple chamber formed by two large upright slabs and a boulder kerb. Unlike the other two primary cairns, it was oriented toward the east. This was later encapsulated within a rectilinear cairn with a shallow forecourt defined by a façade composed of large stone uprights and sections of drystone walling (Corcoran 1969a: 60). A new, south-facing chamber had been added in the façade of the larger cairn, but this had been disturbed and several of the orthostats removed. In the upper layers of the chamber fill, sherds of Mortlake Ware and Food Vessel were present. The limited emphasis on segmentation

Figure 2.3 The Mid Gleniron chambered cairns

within the chambers at Mid Gleniron has been taken as an indication that the tombs may fall early within the Clyde sequence. The simple chambers of the primary oval cairns, composed of pairs of parallel orthostats, are characteristic of what Scott (1969: 181) defined as 'protomegaliths'. These were identified as the primary megalithic burial structures in Scotland, possibly modelled in the first instance on linear timber mortuary structures. Only later were chamber segmentation, trapezoidal cairns, façades and forecourts added to create the true Clyde long cairn.

Another site which may exemplify the same process of development is Cairnholy I, one of two long cairns located on the eastern side of Wigtown Bay. Although excavation did not reveal the plan of an earlier cairn, the section does appear to show two distinct phases of construction (Noble 2005: 28). This might potentially suggest that a first phase had consisted of a simple round or oval cairn with a single-cell chamber. In its final form, the chamber at Cairnholy I is divided by a massive upright slab, which impedes passage from the entrance to the back cell. The inner chamber is composed of a pair of massive parallel uprights, separated by smaller bracing stones, and very similar to the chamber in the primary cairn of Mid Gleniron II. The suggestion is that the 'antechamber', built of smaller slabs and communicating with the entrance and forecourt, is a later addition. The long cairn has a very distinctive façade with eight tall vertical stones, the tallest of which form the portals of the chamber entrance. A further tall stone had at one

point blocked this entrance (Piggott and Powell 1949: 116). In the forecourt, a stone socket below the blocking suggests an upright like those at Mid Gleniron I (Piggott and Powell 1949: 112). The similarity of the chamber and façade arrangement at Cairnholy I to the timber structures found beneath earthen long barrows in eastern Britain has been noted before, suggesting a translation from one medium of construction to another (Sheridan 2006: 109). If the monument were to have been a composite structure, this possibility takes on further significance, for like Mid Gleniorn I and II it would fall within a formative stage of the Clyde tradition. This much is hinted at by the pottery from the site. A fine Carinated Bowl was found next to the north portal of the entrance, together with a flake of Arran pitchstone. A further, s-profiled vessel was recovered from earth that had covered one of six hearths that had been burned on the forecourt surface. As Scott (1969: 193) pointed out, these pots are rather unusual finds in chambered tombs in southwest Scotland.

The Later Neolithic

The discovery of the Dunragit complex by aerial photography during the 1990s placed a major Neolithic monument into what might have been considered an archaeological vacuum up to this point. As Barclay (2009: 3) points out, our perception of southwest Scotland as a relatively 'unimportant' region during the Neolithic might have been entirely different had the complex been built of stone rather than timber. However, the dense evidence of prehistoric occupation on Luce Sands should perhaps have provided an indication of the significance of the area, and other hints had already existed. There are, for instance, a series of possible stone circles in the region. That at Glenjorrie may only amount to a single stone upright, but at Balmennoch a circle of six large stones was apparently destroyed by workmen at some time between 1760 and 1770. Futhermore, Clachanmore and Kirkmadrine Church (both south of Sandhead) have records of 'Druidical' circles or 'temples' (Murray 1981: 30). Rock art sites, however, are not known at the head of Luce Bay. A number of complex panels are located in the Machars (Morris 1979), but it is often the case that rock art and monumental complexes are to some extent mutually exclusive in spatial terms (Bradley 1997: 117). Traces of Late Neolithic occupation are extensive, if ambiguous. The dunes of Luce Sands have produced significant quantities of pottery of Late Neolithic date. McInnes (1964: 70) lists 53 vessels of Impressed Ware, a style that has affinities with Peterborough Ware, and which probably dates to the later fourth and earlier fifth millennia BC. She also notes 19 vessels of Grooved Ware from similar locations, most of which appear to be of Durrington Walls style (McInnes 1964: 68). Evidence from fieldwalking is to date minimal, but fieldwork in advance of the upgrading of the A75 produced some interesting results. A series of 147 test pits was dug along the route of the road, and those in the immediate vicinity of the Dunragit monumental complex were significantly more likely to produce small quantities of flint flakes or pebbles (Toolis 2005: 1).

One potentially important but poorly-understood site of Late Neolithic date is that at Mye Plantation, near Stoneykirk. This was originally identified as a series of five surface depressions, running on a NNW-SSE alignment over a distance of about 40 metres. The features were oval in plan, with their long axis at right angles to the overall alignment. Several of these were excavated by Ludovic Mann at the start of the twentieth century, and proved to be pits or shafts up to 3 metres deep and 3 metres across the long axis, at the surface. Pit number 3 contained flintwork, pottery and charcoal, together with a setting of 72 wooden posts or stakes in the base of the pit (Mann 1903: 375). These posts had been sharpened at one end, and the marks of a stone axe were still visible in their surfaces (Mann 1903: 382). Each was up to 1 metre in length, and examples of birch, hazel and alder were all noted. The timbers had been set into the clay at the base of the pit, jammed closely together in an elaborate pattern, involving a concentric ring of uprights surrounding an inverted cone at one end of the feature. The oval settings of posts had been surrounded by wattle-work, and the sides of the pits had apparently been revetted or lined with hazel rods and brushwood.

The site was reinvestigated by Atkinson and Ritchie in 1951, who noted that the five pits had been linked by a timber fence, and that this had cut off a small promontory within a marsh (Piggott 1954: 306). Mann implies that the posts were set pointed end down in the clay, and that their upper end supported a floor, which was represented by a horizon of burnt material containing flints and sherds (1903: 379). His interpretation was that the features had represented pit-dwellings, and that they had been access by entrance passages cut into their sides. By contrast, Atkinson and Ritchie suggested that the tops of the posts excavated by Mann had probably been eroded away, while the fully-preserved examples that they had observed had been sharpened at both ends (Sheridan 2005: 20). On this basis, they concluded that the features had been pitfall traps, intended to capture and kill large mammals. They further noted that the brushwood lining of the shafts had been renewed on a number of occasions. Archaeological interpretation has generally moved away from the notion that the prehistoric inhabitants of Britain ever lived in holes in the ground (e.g. Evans 1988: 52), and it is not clear why a pit with a suspended floor would represent a desirable dwelling. The pitfall argument is strengthened by the presence of the fence, which might have served to funnel animals that were being driven up the promontory into the pits. If large animals were being hunted in this way during the later Neolithic, parts of Galloway must still have represented a 'wildscape' at the time. Presumably the animals concerned would have been deer or aurochs. The bones of these animals are not common on many later Neolithic sites in Britain, but in Orkney Sharples (2000: 112) has noted the discovery of several sites where the carcases of deer had been butchered and consumed, or perhaps left to rot. These locations were quite separate from settlement activity, and it may be that the hunting of wild animals and the eating of their meat was segregated from domestic activities. If so, the kind of activity represented at Mye Plantation may have been more common than has often been imagined.

The ceramics recovered from pit number 3 seem to resemble Scottish Impressed Ware of Middle Neolithic date, although Mann's illustration of one sherd is certainly Grooved Ware. Sheridan (2005: 21) argues that the whole assemblage is Grooved Ware, and this certainly fits better with the radiocarbon date of 2500–2230 cal. BC (at 2σ; UB-3882) that has been acquired from one of the alder stakes from the pits. This potentially falls toward the end of the use of the enclosure at Dunragit, and the relationship between the two sites is intriguing. Other sites of Late Neolithic date have been identified on Luce Sands. In 1951 Richard Atkinson carried out investigations at Burnt Dune, exposing an area of an old land surface, which contained quantities of prehistoric pottery. A number of pits had been cut through this land surface and into the sterile sand below. The pits contained sherds of Grooved Ware, and Beaker pottery was present

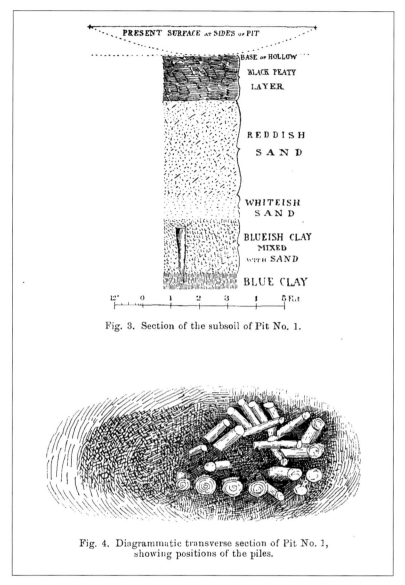

Fig. 3. Section of the subsoil of Pit No. 1.

Fig. 4. Diagrammatic transverse section of Pit No. 1, showing positions of the piles.

Figure 2.4 Pit number 1 at Mye Plantation

elsewhere on site. There were also unused clay and possible wasters at Burnt Dune, prompting the suggestion that ceramic manufacture might have taken place there (McInnes 1964: 41). A further assemblage of Impressed Ware was recovered from Atkinson's excavation at Pin Dune Site A, where three distinct horizons of occupation were identified, separated by phases of abandonment (McInnes 1964: 41). This is particularly interesting, as it suggests a cyclical pattern of inhabitation, which chimes with debates concerning settlement and mobility in the Neolithic (Whittle 1997b).

Further investigations amongst the dunes of Luce Sands were undertaken by Trevor Cowie during the 1970s. Cowie's excavation site C2 contained a hollow, a gully and a pit, with small finds being concentrated in the

hollow. A dump of burnt stones was also encountered, and the composition of the lithic assemblage indicated that flint-working had probably taken place at the site. The ceramics at C2 were exclusively Impressed Ware (Cowie 1996: 26). Cowie's Site E was located on High Torr, a large sand dune. It produced traces of agricultural activity and a depression containing worked flint and sherds of Impressed Ware (Cowie 1996: 51). Site J produced some sherds of Early Neolithic bowl pottery, while higher in the profile was a hearth or pyre containing fragments of burnt human and animal bones, the latter probably sheep or pig (Cowie 1996: 61). This finding might have some bearing on the excavated results from Dunragit, given the presence of the cremated remains of a woman and a sheep in Feature 215, and of possible pyre debris containing fine sand in Feature 579/619 (see Chapter 3 below). However, the deposit at Site J was relatively high in the profile, and it is unclear whether it might have dated to the Late Neolithic or much later. Cowie (1996: 96) offers the important caution that appreciable quantities of Neolithic pottery may have been trapped in sub-surface features and relict land-surfaces on Luce Sands, only to be released as the sand dunes migrate. Consequentially, we should be wary of assuming that the density of pottery finds is a reflection of the density of prehistoric occupation, rather than a reflection of taphonomic circumstances. However, in the light of discoveries at Dunragit and Droughduil, as well as the density of finds of fine artefacts of early Bronze Age date (many of them from funerary contexts), we can begin to edge toward the conclusion that the area represented a significant regional centre over a lengthy period of prehistory.

Beaker and Early Bronze Age

While the most elaborate monuments within the Dunragit complex are of Late Neolithic date, there are strong indications that the area retained its importance into the Early Bronze Age, a pattern that has often been identified elsewhere (see, for a classic example, Renfrew 1973). There is certainly a notable concentration of Beaker pottery in the Luce Bay area. Many of the Beakers in southwest Scotland are of David Clarke's All Over Corded, European Bell Beaker and Northern British styles (Ritchie 1970a: 123). The first of these two fall at the beginning of the insular Beaker series, and arguably provide an indication that the area was not a backwater, but was tied in to inter-regional contacts and networks during the mid-third millennium BC. In his corpus of British Beakers, Clarke (1970: 522) lists 28 vessels from the Luce Bay area, all of them from various locations within Luce Sands. Beakers had been recovered from Burnt Dune, Clayshant, Knockdoon, Pin Dune and Torrs Warren. Of these, 12 are All Over Corded, and four are European Bell Beakers. There is also a probable late Beaker burial from Stoneykirk. The vessel is lost, but descriptions suggest that it may have been a Beaker/Food Vessel hybrid. It was associated with 187 jet or lignite disc beads, which were graded in size to make a necklace, to which a triangular toggle or pendant may have been attached (Ritchie 1970a: 124; Ritchie and Shepherd 1973: 23). A further two necklaces of jet beads were found during recent investigations in advance of the A75 bypass at Dunragit (Munro 2014). The unusual concentration of this fine and exotic artefact type in the area provides an indication of the enduring importance of Luce Bay into the Early Bronze Age.

A small sherd of Beaker pottery was also recovered from the foot of the western orthostat in the northern chamber at Mid Gleniron I chambered tomb (Ritchie

1970b: 146). The same long cairn also contained eight cremations with cordoned urns. One of these had been placed into a recess in the cairn material and surrounded by a packing of water rolled pebbles before being covered by a stone slab. As well as cremated bone, this vessel contained fragments of a bronze pin (Corcoran 1969a: 49). These phenomena introduce the theme of the re-use of Neolithic monuments during the Beaker phase and subsequently, whether representing continuity or a form of appropriation of the past (see Bradley 2002: 17). There are strong indications that during the Early Bronze Age efforts were made to connect new cultural developments with places and structures that represented the established order of things, or distant ancestral pasts. Aside from the introduction of new burials into Mid Gleniron I, the two long cairns at this site became the focus for a more extensive cemetery. Two round cairns were constructed close to the Neolithic structures. Mid Gleniron A was a disturbed circular monument, with a capping of small stones over a basal layer of much larger boulders in an annular or pennanular setting (Corcoran 1969b: 91). At the centre of the round cairn were disturbed fragments of cremated bone and the broken sherds of a pottery vessel, probably representing an urned cremation deposit. Cairn A had been built onto a rock outcrop, and positioned very close to Mid Gleniron I. As Corcoran points out, the builders 'may have been prompted by motives comparable with those which led to the insertion of secondary cremations in the body of Mid Gleniron I' (1969b: 91). That is to say, a relationship between past and present was being asserted through spatial juxtaposition. Mid Gleniron A was remarkably similar in construction to the cairn on the summit of the Droughduil mound (see Chapter 4 below).

Like Mid Gleniron A, the second cairn, Mid Gleniron B was about 7 metres in diameter. It was slightly different in construction, however, being built of large boulders around a small closed cist or chamber composed of orthostats and drystone walling (Corcoran 1969b: 91). This raises the question of whether Mid Gleniron B was an Early Bronze Age structure, or a simple Early Neolithic tomb with closed chamber, comparable with Achnacreebeag (Ritchie 1970b). On balance the former is more likely, particularly given the 'paired' relationship with Mid Gleniron II long cairn, whose façade and chamber it stands immediately in front of.

Like Beakers, Early Bronze Age metalwork is concentrated in the area surrounding Dunragit. Narrow butted axes, daggers and halberds are clustered in the area between Luce Bay and Loch Ryan (Coles 1965: 65). A pair of daggers of probable Beaker date have been reported from Mid Torrs and Low Torrs amidst the Luce Sands dunes. Both may have been rhomboid daggers of Clarke's Class iii (Ritchie and Shepherd 1973: 27). A further dagger came from Dunragit itself, probably from a ruined cist, associated with a cremation burial, in a gravel pit near Dunragit railway station (Ritchie 1970a: 134). This would have placed it very close to the Late Neolithic palisaded enclosure, again suggesting an attempt to place new mortuary practices in locations of established importance. The dagger was triangular in shape, with three rivets (Whitelaw 1932: 19).

Four Food Vessels have been recovered from Luce Sands; it is only here in the whole of southwest Scotland that they occur in any context other than burial (Simpson 1965: 26). This prompts the question of exactly what kinds of activity might have been going on in the dune areas during the Neolithic and Bronze Age, in order to have attracted such an array of relatively fine material culture. Collared and Cordoned Urns are likewise concentrated around the head of Luce Bay, although the circumstances in which they are discovered generally suggest some kind of funerary practice. A total of nine urns have been recovered from the sands. For the most part they occur as groups or cemeteries, rather than as single finds (Morrison 1968: 81). Luce Sands Site D, for instance, was a small cairn of pebbles covering a pair of urns (Cowie 1996: 50). Not far distant was a small cemetery enclosed within a bank of gravel and pebbles one metre across, containing a number of urned cremations, one of which was accompanied by a knife-dagger. East of Clayshant, amongst the dunes, two urns and a fragment of a third were found with quartz pebbles strewn nearby (Davidson 1952: 46). In addition to cremated bone, one of the urns contained a jet bead, while some of the bones were stained green, probably indicating the former presence of a bronze object. In this same area, many sherds of Impressed Ware were noted, adding to the sense of its comparative ubiquity on Luce Sands.

Further inland, some of the Early Bronze Age burials appear to have been richer than those on the sands. At Stoneykirk, a cremation burial with a bucket-shaped urn was also accompanied by a jet or lignite necklace and a stone axe-hammer (Morrison 1968: 11). A Collared Urn cremation burial at Droughduil Farm, however, had only a flint scraper. Battle-axes and mace-heads are both scarce in the Luce Bay area, the latter more surprising given the Grooved Ware associations of the Dunragit complex. Axe-hammers are much more common, and are concentrated in the immediate area of Glenluce (Roe 1967: 67). Three axe-hammers have been found in Glenluce itself, three from Stoneykirk, one from Old Luce, one from New Luce, and one from Dunragit creamery (Roe 1967: 78).

While much of the evidence for Beaker and Early Bronze Age activity in the Luce Bay area has come from stray finds and antiquarian digging, one recent excavation has provided a useful index of the density of prehistoric features in the region. In 1995, Glasgow University Archaeology Research Division (GUARD) undertook investigations in advance of a Transco pipeline 0.75

kilometres long at Fox Plantation, north of West Freuch airfield. Eleven trenches were opened, revealing very numerous subsoil features. The majority of these appear to have been Late Bronze Age or Iron Age in date, but some were probably earlier. Trench 1 contained a pit alignment, with no artefactual associations. No mention is made of posts, so this structure would appear to have been composed of cut features alone (MacGregor *et al.* 1996: 11). At Holm Farm in Dumfries the pit alignments that post-dated the Neolithic post-structures were of probable Bronze Age date, although at Milton of Rattray near Blairgowrie a Neolithic cursus monument was composed simply of pits (Brophy 2000: 15; Thomas 2007a: 211). Trench 2 at Fox Plantation contained another row of pits, again with no indication that they had contained posts. Trench 9 revealed a series of pits containing coarse Beaker pottery. These were concentrated around a slot-built structure of some kind, in the vicinity of which flint-knapping appeared to have taken place (MacGregor *et al.* 1996: 37). As a more or less random sample of the landscape surrounding the Dunragit complex, the work at Fox Plantation indicates the potential richness of the prehistoric record.

Conclusion

While the group of monuments at Dunragit and Droughduil is both complex and extensive, and its initial discovery occasioned some surprise, in retrospect it can be seen to fit into a broader process of landscape development. The unique record of prehistoric inhabitation provided by Luce Sands indicates continuous if sporadic activity from the Mesolithic onwards, and is complemented by sparser evidence for further inland. The presence of a few sherds of primary Neolithic fine carinated bowl from the sands represents the scant evidence for a local content into which the post-defined cursus at Dunragit can be placed. Most striking is the widespread occurrence of Impressed Ware, both at numerous locations on the sands and at Mye Plantation, hinting at dense occupation in the period immediately before the construction of the Dunragit palisaded enclosure. Whether these document sporadic gatherings on the part of the communities who eventually built the enclosure is an open question, but it is worth considering whether the complex was a site of seasonal aggregation, as now appears to have been demonstrated for Stonehenge and Durrington Walls in Wiltshire (Parker Pearson *et al.* 2007: 628). Whether a short-lived settlement comparable with that at the eastern entrance at Durrington Walls ever existed in the vicinity of Dunragit is a tantalizing question. One of the recurring tendencies in the prehistory of the region is the way in which established locations retained their significance over long periods, attracting later activity and additional structures. The group of funerary monuments at Mid

Gleniron is a case in point, and this sheds further light on the relationship between the Early Neolithic cursus and the Late Neolithic enclosure at Dunragit, discussed below. Dunragit and Droughduil themselves became foci for later burials and deposits, in the form of the summit cairn on the mound and the various Beaker and Urn burials noted above. Indeed, the aerial photographs of Dunragit show numerous small circular structures, and while some of these may have been ancillary features contemporary with the enclosure, others will doubtless have been round barrows and ring-ditches containing burials of Early Bronze Age date.

3

DUNRAGIT: FEATURES REVEALED BY EXCAVATION

Julian Thomas and Matthew Leivers

Excavation procedure

The subsoil at Dunragit is composed of a series of glacial outwash gravels. When seen in section these appear as clearly sorted, but in plan they present a complex mass of patches of more or less coarse sand and gravel, dissected by frost wedges. The ploughsoil is largely composed of a well sorted 'A' horizon, which suggests that the gravel surface is severely truncated. For the most part, then, the archaeology of the site consists of the lower fills of features cut into an unforgiving subsoil. In the course of four years of investigation it was discovered that the most effective way of identifying these features was to employ a sequence of shovel-scraping, repeated trowellings, and finally brushing with soft brushes, following the removal of the topsoil by an earth-moving machine. The effect of this final stage was to remove the fine, dusty fragment of the gravel, leaving patterns in the sand and pebble fractions to reveal the fills of cut features. Features that contained silty or clayey upper fills were easier to identify, but the method was also successful in locating features whose fills were barely distinguishable from the subsoil. In the 2000 and 2001 seasons in particular, alternating periods of rain and sunshine meant that the site was being dug under rapidly changing conditions, and this provided the opportunity for features to be identified through patterns of differential drying. The gravel drained very swiftly, but some of the feature fills retained moisture for an appreciable period of time. Consequentially, the surface of the site was repeatedly cleaned using different methods (trowelling, brushing) throughout each season, and supervisory staff continually inspected the trenches in search of features that had not yet been identified, particularly after rain or in the early morning when dew was still on the ground. Even once identified, the features were often deceptive in character. In many cases, what appeared on the surface to be a diminutive pit or post-hole proved on excavation to be a much larger entity, whose true extent could simply not be recognised on the surface. Often, the silty material that had slumped into the top of a cut feature was visible in plan, but the more extensive gravel packing that surrounded it was not. The consequence of this was that it was often difficult to place a section line in the most advantageous position in relation to a feature that later 'exploded' outwards in an unpredictable fashion.

Given a series of discrete features whose interconnections were often only a merging of weathering cones, stratigraphic relations between different structures were often difficult to identify. The features are described below, grouped according to the structures to which they have been assigned. A single context recording system based on separate recording sheets was employed (*sensu* MoLAS 1994), with separate context numbers for cuts and fills. However, site diaries were also kept, and the recording system departed from a strict single-context one in that multiple-context plans were made. In this volume, individual features are identified by their cut numbers. In some cases features were excavated using a quadrant method, and where alternate segments were removed particular contexts were often given different numbers in different quadrants. It follows that some contexts were given more than one number. Where a complex sequence of features intersected, the whole is

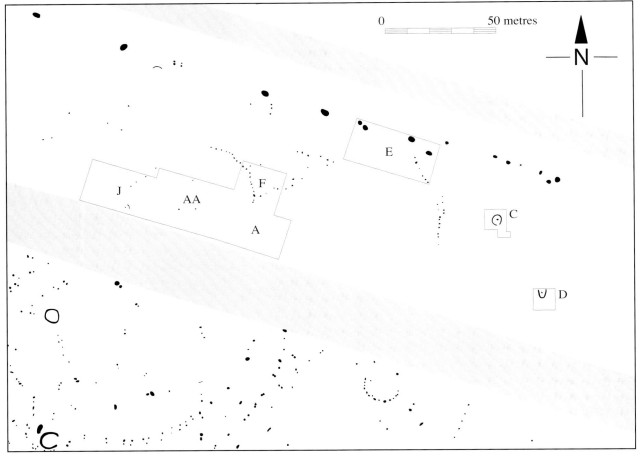

Figure 3.1 Dunragit excavations 1999–2002: location of trenches

identified by the earliest cut in the series (in stratigraphic terms), although in some cases where two distinct post-holes intercut, the resulting feature is identified by both of the two cut numbers concerned. Separate pre- and post-excavation plans were drawn of the site, and all finds were individually logged in three dimensions using a total station. Bulk samples were taken for flotation where evidence for burning or charcoal were present, and monoliths were removed from deep features for soil micromorphology and soil pollen analysis (see Chapter 9). Despite this, the environmental evidence recovered from the site was very meagre indeed. No soil pollen was discovered at all, while all of the flotation samples were unfortunately destroyed as a result of laboratory error.

Preservation

As noted above, the subsoil surface was extremely heterogeneous, ranging from patches of compact reddish-orange sandy material to coarse sandy gravel and areas of small loose pebbles with no soil or sand matrix. The challenging character of the subsoil was compounded by a series of post-depositional transformations of the

glacial and archaeological deposits. The southern side of Trench AA ran parallel with the modern railway cutting, and here the subsoil surface had dried out considerably. Moreover, rodent damage could be recognised, as the side of the cutting had provided an entrance for numerous rabbit burrows. Finally, the subsoil along the southern edge of Trench AA, and in its northeast corner, had been subject to extensive root penetration, which had had the effect of stirring up and homogenizing the gravel deposits. A sondage dug in the southern part of this trench demonstrated that this root action had been effective to a depth of more than twenty centimetres below the subsoil surface. Consequentially, it is very likely that cut features in these parts of the site had been obscured or destroyed.

Trenches A, AA, F and J

The contiguous trenches A, AA, F and J were excavated in 1999, 2000, 2001 and 2002 respectively, and represented a total area of approximately 2475 square metres. Trench A was initially located to reveal a stretch of the two innermost rings of the palisade enclosure, which were visible on a series of aerial photographs (Figs. 1.1–1.4), together with some of the mass of features cutting across the enclosure on a NNE–SSW axis. The area excavated was 30 × 20 metres, and the trench revealed an unexpected variety of features. Some of these eventually proved to represent a much earlier structure, an Early Neolithic post-defined cursus monument, although this was not immediately obvious from the fraction excavated in 1999. In addition to these features, there were a great number of smaller post-holes. One group of these, in the extreme south of the trench, appeared to make up a circular building, considered likely to be later in date than the enclosure. Others clustered along the line of the middle ring of large posts. It was conjectured that these latter might represent elements of a continuous palisade,

contrasting with the inner ring, which appeared to have been made up of free standing posts.

The addition of Trench AA in 2000 represented a change from the initial research design, and was intended to illuminate two phenomena: the line of burnt post-holes that were eventually attributed to the cursus, and the apparent 'doubling' of the posts of the innermost palisade ring, which was eventually attributed to the presence of two separate phases of post-holes, which did not always coincide precisely. Trench AA was a larger cutting, 35 × 25 metres, opened immediately to the west of Trench A. In Trench AA, the more compact subsoil allowed the identification of a greater number of the smaller post-holes that lay between the more substantial posts. However, it also became clear that although many of these had been large, ramped post-holes, they were considerably smaller than the post-holes of the innermost ring. The middle ring post-holes generally contained a rather straightforward stratigraphy, documenting a single phase of construction, followed by the rotting away of the post, and the silting and collapse of packing into the post void. Five posts of the inner post-ring were identified in the 2000 season. While the inner ring post-holes in 1999 Trench A had formed two distinct and parallel arcs, in Trench AA only one line of post-holes existed. It is suggested that at this point the two phases of construction of the inner ring coincided spatially, so that rather than constituting separate features the second phase took the form of recuts into the first phase post-holes. This much is confirmed by the sections of the 2000 features, several of which contain clear recuts filled with material which was darker and more loamy than the sandy gravel of the primary post-hole packing. Trench AA also revealed

Figure 3.2 Trenches A and C from the air

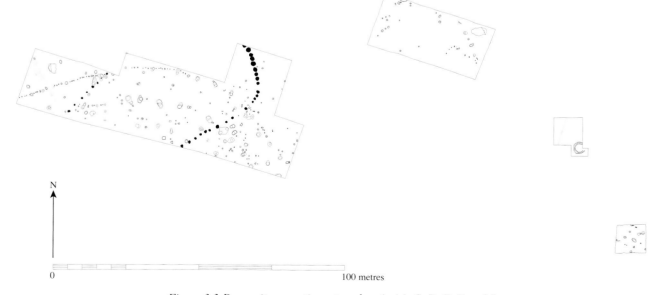

N

0   100 metres

Figure 3.3 Dunragit excavations: trenches A, AA, C, D, E, F and J

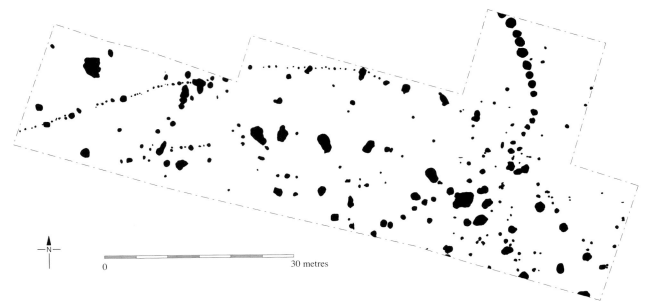

Figure 3.4 Dunragit excavations: Trenches A, AA, F and J

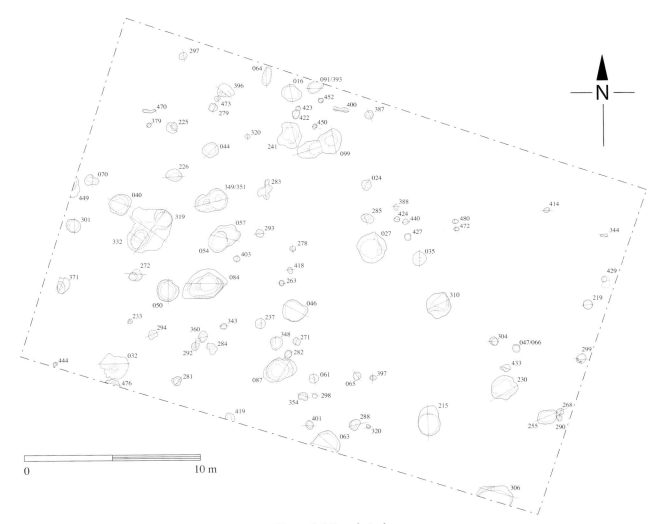

Figure 3.5 Trench A plan

a further portion of the two lines of posts identified as post-lines A and B in 1999. These features were smaller and shallower than those of the enclosure, and they often contained dark fills including a great deal of charcoal. It was in the course of the 2000 season that the possibility that these features might represent a structure separate from the Late Neolithic enclosure was first considered.

In 2001, Trench F was positioned to investigate an arc of very large post-holes, visible on the air photos for the site, which had initially been conjectured on the basis of the aerial photographic evidence to represent a post-circle. On excavation, it became clear that these formed a shallow arc, broken by a single entrance, and that they were graded in size, becoming deeper and larger to the north. Given the scale of these features, it seemed impossible that they formed part of a circle that had had left no trace at all on 2000 Trench AA, to the west. For this reason, during the 2001 excavation it was considered likely that these features formed some kind of cuspate façade structure. This, however, did not explain the size grading, and when the plan of Trench F was joined to that of Trenches A and AA it became clear that they were part of a larger structure which also included the linear arrangement of burnt posts that had been encountered in the two previous seasons. This then represented a line of posts which abruptly curved to the north, becoming more monumental in scale as it progressed. The obvious interpretation of this structure is that it represents a portion of a post-defined cursus, and with the benefit of hindsight the remainder of such a monument can be identified on the air photo plots, heading away to the southwest from the excavated area. The linear part of this arrangement had previously been identified as a post alignment, or as a radial entrance structure associated with the palisade enclosure. This was largely because further post-holes on the same alignment continue toward the northeast from the cursus, and had been identified on the air photo plots and in Trench E. Prior to the excavation of Trench F, it was thus easy to be misled into believing that a continuous alignment of posts ran across the entire field, from southwest to northeast. In the southwest corner of Trench F, a single large post of the middle ring of the late Neolithic enclosure (3024) was encountered, together with some smaller features, two or three of which are probably lesser elements of the fence or palisade. There were also a number of post-holes which may have formed part of a diffuse alignment, respecting the orientation of the southern side of the cursus, and two very rich Grooved Ware pits.

Trench J was added in 2002 to address the intersection of the western side of the cursus with the inner and middle rings of the palisade enclosure. In Trench J, the inner post-ring was unusual in that smaller post-holes were observed between some of the large ramped features, a phenomenon not seen elsewhere. It is possible that this represented a small area of screening. The middle

post-ring in Trench J contained many smaller posts, and middle ring post 4100 intersected with the western side of the cursus, cutting cursus post-hole 4157. It is interesting that post-hole 4110 contained one of the few artefacts recovered from the middle ring, a fine stone axe. Trench J also contained a large amorphous feature, 4206, similar to two others excavated in Trench E, and judged to represent a gravel quarry pit associated with road-building.

Features revealed by excavation

Posts of the cursus

During the 1999 season, a series of post-holes that could not be attributed to the palisade enclosure were identified within Trench A. At that time it was suggested that they represented as many as four different settings, some straight and some arced, but all running on a NNE–SSW axis across the inner and middle palisade rings. They were initially defined as 'post lines A–D', and were identified with lines of features that could be recognised on the aerial photo plots of the site. The most distinctive element was 'post line B', a set of very conspicuous features with dark charcoal-rich fills and generally containing packing-stones, now recognised as comprising the principal post-holes of the cursus. At the time, however, it was still considered possible that these features were contemporary with and integral to the Late Neolithic palisade enclosure, perhaps representing some form of post avenue or entrance structure. With the excavation of Trench AA in 2000, the other three conjectured post lines began to seem less substantial and coherent. Rather than a series of distinct structural entities, it now seems more likely that they represent a scatter of post-holes that broadly follow the line of the east side of the cursus, and extend beyond it. The significance of this will be discussed below. These features are now collectively described under the heading 'Other Features Possibly Associated With The Cursus'. In 2001, Trench F revealed the northern terminal of the cursus. Here the post-holes became progressively larger and deeper, indicating that the posts themselves had become taller and more substantial at the northern end of the structure.

Feature 016 (Figs. 3.15 and 3.16)

A steep-sided oval cut, contained a primary silting 018, which was composed of loose very dark brown sand (10 YR 3/3) and contained numerous small stones. Above this was 017, a friable brown (7.5 YR 5/4) sand with many stones, which included packing stones. This was presumably the original post-packing material of a post-hole. The uppermost and most extensive fill was 006, a friable loamy sand with small stones and charcoal flecks, which was dark brown/black in colour (7.5 YR 3/2). 006 probably represented the disturbed remains of a post-pipe, including the debris of a burnt post.

Feature 040 (Fig. 3.15)

A shallow, flat-based, cut with sides that were straight in places, 040, was packed with friable very dark brown loamy sand 039 (7.5 YR 2.5/2), which included packing stones. Above this fill was a silting of sandy clay loam

containing a great deal of charcoal, 038, (10 YR 2/1 black), and a lens of black (5 YR 2.5/1) sandy silt with much charcoal, 013, which is not visible on the published section. This was the much-eroded socket of a burnt post. A piece of hazel charcoal from context 013 provided a radiocarbon date of 3760–3630 cal. BC (at 95.4% probability; SUERC-2103), the only determination from the Dunragit cursus (see Chapter 10).

Feature 044 (Fig. 3.15)

An oval, bowl-shaped cut with gently sloping sides 044, was filled with a packing of loamy sand 043 (5 YR 2.5/2 dark reddish-brown). Above this was layer 015, a loose reddish-brown (5 YR 4/3) sandy fill, representing a disturbed post-pipe. This fill was less intensely burnt than others of the cursus.

Feature 091/393 (Fig. 3.15)

091 was the circular cut of a post-hole with near-vertical sides, and was filled with 072, a friable dusky red (2.5

Figure 3.6 Trench A during excavation, 1999

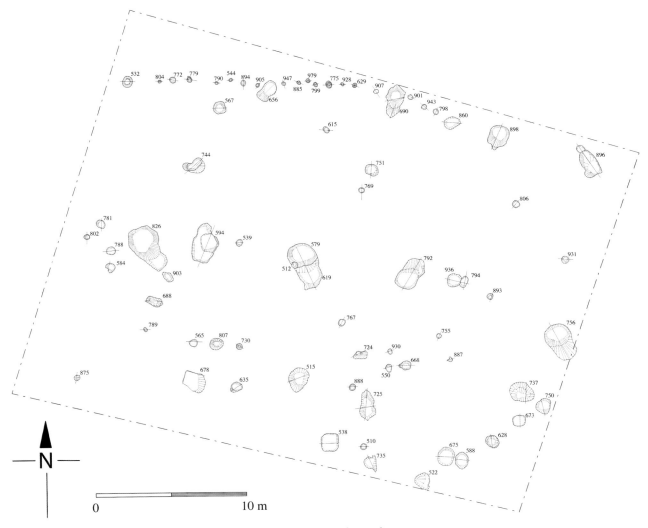

Figure 3.7 Trench AA plan

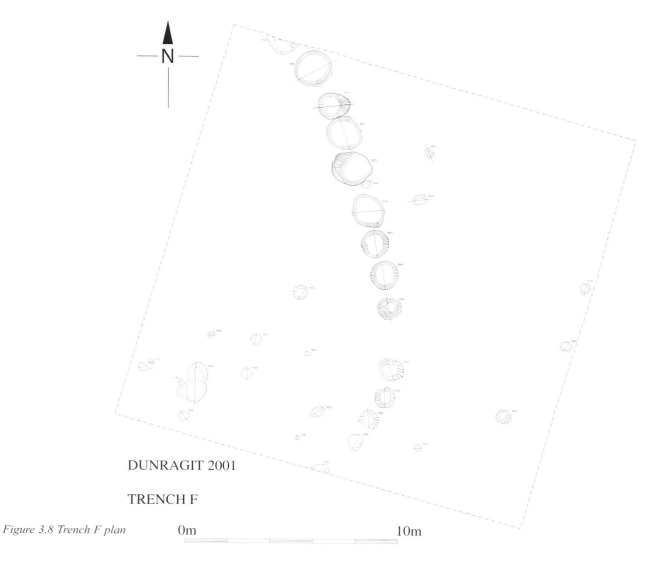

DUNRAGIT 2001

TRENCH F

Figure 3.8 Trench F plan

0m   10m

Figure 3.9 Trench AA after excavation

Figure 3.10 The cursus terminal in Trench F under excavation

Figure 3.11 Trench F after excavation, 2001 season

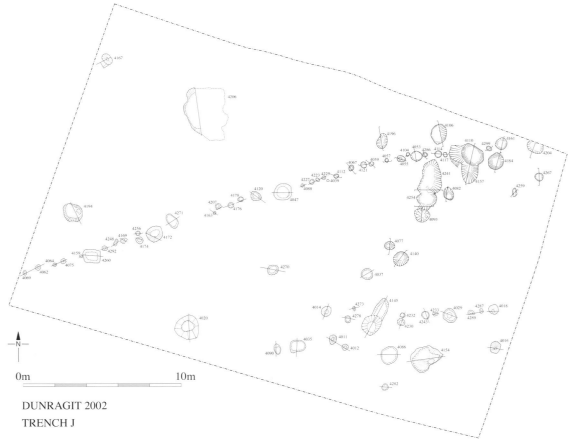

DUNRAGIT 2002

TRENCH J

Figure 3.12 Trench J plan

Figure 3.13 Trench J under excavation

Figure 3.14 Trench J after excavation

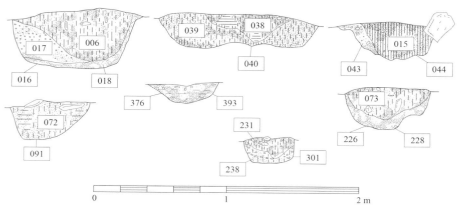

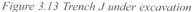

Figure 3.15 Post-holes of the cursus: sections

Figure 3.16 Cursus post-hole 016: section

YR 4/2) clay loam containing three large packing stones. This was cut by 393, another post-hole with sloping sides and a rounded base, which was filled with 376, a firm dark brown loamy sand (7.5 YR 3/3). They were drawn as two separate sections.

Feature 226 (Fig. 3.15)
The circular cut of moderately sized post-hole with concave sides and flat base 226, was filled with 073/247, a friable, very dark greyish brown loamy sand (10 YR 3/2), which contained a few large pebbles and much charcoal. This post had clearly been burned.

Feature 301 (Fig. 3.15)
A small vertical-sided post-hole cut with rounded base, 301, contained the primary fill 238, a loose strong brown sandy loam containing much fine gravel and packing stones (7.5 YR 4/6). The post-pipe fill of this feature was 231, a friable very dark brown sandy loam with 20% medium pebbles and charcoal flecks, suggesting that the post had been burned (7.5 YR 2.5/3).

Feature 522 (Fig. 3.17)
The irregular/oval cut of a post-hole 522, with steep sides and a flat base, contained basal fill 521, a thin lens of loose dark brown (10 YR 3/3) gravel. Above this lay 520, a friable, very dark brown (7.5 YR 2.5/2) silty loam. Above this in turn were 517, a friable loamy sand with pebbles (7.5 YR 2.5/3 very dark brown) and 519, a mass of friable loamy sand (10 YR 2/2 very dark brown), which were stratigraphically equivalent. 518, a patch of

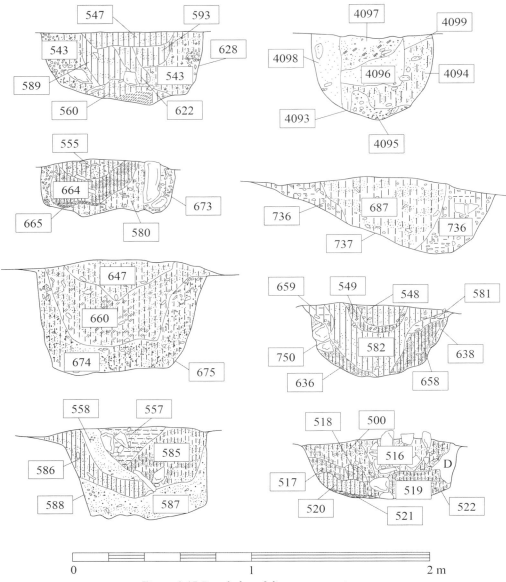

Figure 3.17 Post-holes of the cursus: sections

Figure 3.18 Cursus post-hole 737

Figure 3.19 (right) Cursus post-hole 750

very dusky red (10 R 2.5/2) friable sandy silt loam lay above these, suggesting burning. Above this was 500, a friable very dark brown (7.5 YR 2.5/2) loamy sand, evidently packing material, and on top of this was 516, a dark brown friable loamy sand containing dense angular packing stones, and which represented the collapsed remains of a burnt post-pipe. As a whole, the sequence represented a series of lenses surrounding the collapsed post-pipe and packing stones.

Feature 588 (Fig. 3.17)
588 was a circular post-hole, with steeply sloping sides and a flat bottom, which contained 587, a loose dark brown (7.5 YR 3/4) sandy gravel, representing a primary packing. Above this was 586, a friable very dark brown (7.5 YR 2.5/2) sandy loam with some charcoal. This lay below 558, a loose dusky red (2.5 YR 3/3) gritty sand, above which was 585, a loose very dark brown loamy sand (7.5 YR 2.5/3) with packing stones, which may have represented a burnt post-pipe. Above this in turn was 557, a friable very dusky red (2.5 YR 2.5/2) sandy clay containing further packing stones, presumably fire-altered material washed into the post void.

Feature 628 (Fig. 3.17)
The cut of a circular post-hole 628, whose lowest fill was 560, a tenacious dark reddish-brown (5 YR 3/2) sandy silt loam with 40% small stones. Above this lay 543, a loose reddish-brown loamy sand (5 YR 3/2), forming a packing around the edges of the cut feature. This lay below 589, a loose dark reddish-brown loamy sand (7.5 YR 3/2), which represented the lowest fill of the space formerly occupied by the post. Contiguous with this was 593, a friable dark reddish-brown (5 YR 3/3) sandy loam. Between 589 and 593 was 622, a friable dark brown (7.5 YR 3/2) sandy loam, which appeared to preserve the form of the displaced post. In the top of the feature, 547, a tenacious dark reddish-brown (5 YR 3/2) sandy loam, represented a settling or silting layer. There was less direct evidence of burning in this feature than in other nearby cursus post-holes.

Feature 673 (Fig. 3.17)
673 was the near-circular, flat-based, straight-sided cut of a post-hole, whose primary packing was 580, a friable dark brown (7.5 YR 3/3) loamy sand. This material contained several large packing stones, and appeared to have slumped as the post collapsed. Surrounded by this material, a charcoal lens (665) lay at the base of the post-pipe. The principal fill of the post-pipe, 664, was a friable very dark brown (10 YR 2/2) sandy loam, and a patch of friable very dark brown (7.5 YR) sandy loam had slumped or silted into the top of the post-pipe. The dark colouration of the fills suggested a post burnt *in situ*.

Feature 675 (Fig. 3.17)
The steep-sided, flat-based cut of a circular post-hole,

containing a thin layer of packing 674, which was a loose, dark reddish-brown (5 YR 3/3) loamy sand containing numerous pebbles. Above this was the more extensive layer 660, a friable, dark reddish-brown (5 YR 3/4) loamy sand with much charcoal, the disturbed post-pipe. Above this in turn was 647, a friable dusky red (2.5 YR 3/4) loamy sand with some charcoal, slumped into the top of the feature, and indicating an episode of burning.

Feature 737 (Figs. 3.17 and 3.18)
An amorphous cut with shallow sides and a sloping base, 737, contained the possible post-pipe fill 687, a loose, strong brown (7.5 YR 4/6) loamy sand with numerous medium angular stones, within packing 736, a friable dark brown (7.5 YR 3/3) loamy sand. This was probably a post-hole, although it appeared somewhat irregular by comparison with the others of the series. This feature was offline from the other cursus post-holes, and given that it was unburned where all of the cursus post-holes in the immediate vicinity were burned, it is possible that it is unrelated to the cursus.

Feature 750 (Figs. 3.17 and 3.19)
750 was the steep-sided cut of a round post-hole with a concave base, which contained two layers of friable, charcoal-rich black sandy loam (10 YR 2/1), 636 and 658. 658 had been preceded by 638, a small deposit of friable reddish-brown (5 YR 4/3) silty clay loam. Above the dark charcoally layers, 659 and 581 represented deposits of clayey material. 582, the principal fill of the post-hole, was a friable reddish-brown (5 YR 4/3) silty clay loam with gravel, while 549 and 548 represented layers of slumping and compaction into the top of the post-pipe. The presence of burnt material in the lower part of this feature is unusual, and it is possible that the clayey layers post-dated the burning of a post, and either filled a recut, or the crater left behind by the digging-out of the burnt post stump. If this were the case, 635 and 658 could be understood as mixtures of displaced packing and burnt material.

Feature 3009 (Figs. 3.28 and 3.29)
Cut 3009 was a post-hole located towards the southern end of the stretch of the cursus exposed in Trench F, just north of a suspected entrance. The cut was flat-based, with an abrupt break of slope at the top and sharply sloping sides. After the feature had been cut a post and packing had been inserted. This post had apparently decayed. Fills 3010, a loose brown sand (7.5 YR 4/4) with numerous medium pebbles and 3046, a loose strong brown sand (7.5 YR 4/6) with small to medium pebbles, represented packing that had slipped following the post decay. 3045 was a small deposit of very dark material (a fine black sand, 5 YR 2.5/1, with small pebbles) contained entirely within 3046 (not visible in the section), and may indicate the remains of organic material or burnt sand mixed in with the packing. 3027, a loose reddish-brown sand (5

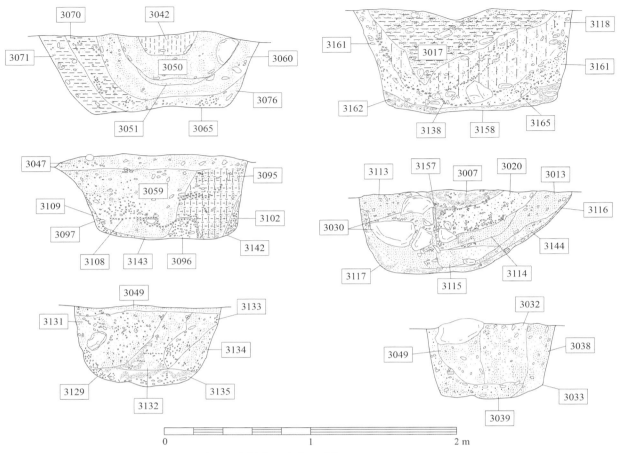

Figure 3.20 Post-holes of the cursus: sections

Figure 3.21 Cursus post-hole 3097 showing section

Figure 3.22 Cursus post-hole 3097 after excavation

YR 4/4) with numerous fine pebbles, was a mixture of packing collapse and silting filling the post-pipe void. Above this 3011, a loose dark reddish-brown (5 YR 3/2) medium sand containing a few fine pebbles, was the result of gradual silting and ploughing. There were some traces of charcoal in layer 3027, but there were not sufficiently extensive to indicate that the post had been burnt out. Instead, this probably represented burnt material from nearby washed into the post void as it rotted out.

Feature 3028 (Fig. 3.23)

Cut 3028 was a post-hole immediately to the north of the putative entrance in the post-defined cursus. The cut had an abrupt break of slope at the top and vertical sides with a gradual transition to a flat base. The friable strong brown sand with pebbles 3037 (7.6YR 4/6) represented slipped packing material, a layer partially penetrated by 3111, a group of large packing stones which extended into other layers as well. Overlying 3037 and again penetrated

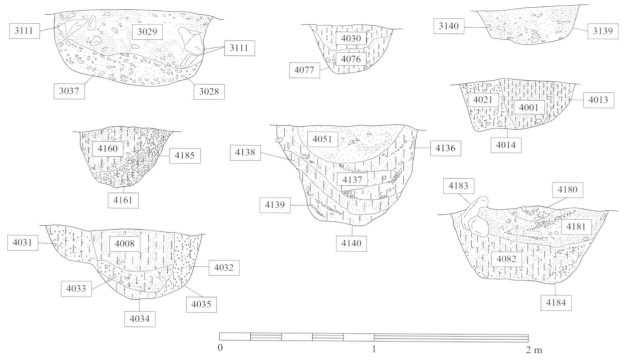

Figure 3.23 Post-holes of the cursus: sections

Figure 3.24 Cursus post-hole 3033

Figure 3.25 Cursus post-hole 3065

by 3111 was 3029, a friable dark yellowish-brown silty sand (10 YR 3/4) which would also appear also to have been slipped packing. This feature appeared to be heavily truncated, but there was some indication from the displaced packing that the post may have been withdrawn. There was certainly little indication of burning.

Feature 3033 (Figs. 3.20 and 3.24)

Cut 3033 was a post-hole with an abrupt break of slope at the top and gradually curving sides sloping toward a rounded base. A friable, dark yellowish-brown sandy silt (10 YR 4/4) with fine and medium pebbles, 3038, and a friable dark yellowish-brown coarse silty sand (10 YR 3/6) with packing stones, 3039, appeared to represent

collapsed packing. Above these, 3049, a loose, yellowish-brown (10 YR 5/6) fine sandy silt containing fine and medium pebbles, may also have been slipped packing. This may indicate that the post was withdrawn, as there was no clear post-pipe. 3032, a friable dark reddish-brown (5 YR 3/3) sandy silt with small pebbles and charcoal flecks (and one large charcoal fragment) was a tertiary silt into the post void, but might also have contained elements of packing. There was little trace of burning in this feature.

Feature 3040 (Fig. 3.28)

3040 was the cut of a relatively shallow post-hole, roughly square in plan with sloping sides and a flat bottom. The

Figure 3.26 Cursus post-hole 3117

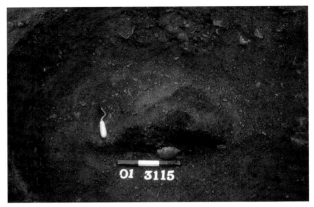

Figure 3.27 Cursus post-hole 3117, showing remains of the post in situ

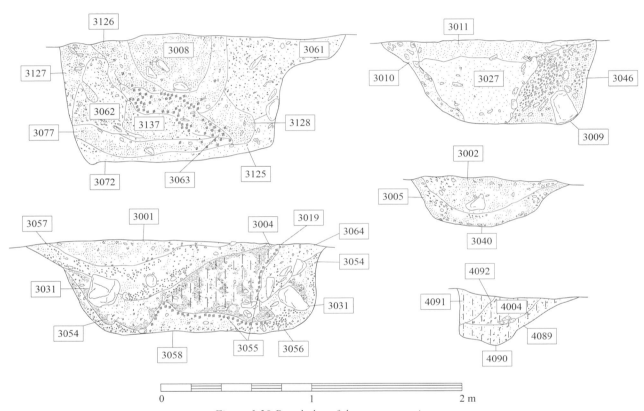

Figure 3.28 Post-holes of the cursus: sections

basal fill was 3005, a friable dark yellowish-brown (10 YR 3/6) sandy silt with pebbles and flecks of charcoal, representing a mass of slipped packing. The upper fill of the feature was 3002, a friable dark yellowish-brown (10 YR 3/4) sandy silt with fine pebbles and charcoal flecks, which contained a number of packing stones sitting around the edge of the fill, but also concentrated toward the centre of the feature, perhaps indicating that they had tumbled down into a post-pipe. There was little indication of burnt matter, and it may be that the post that had been held in this feature had been withdrawn.

Feature 3058 (Figs. 3.28, 3.30, 3.31 and 3.32)
Cut 3058 was an ovoid feature, with straight sides (weathered back as a result of collapse of the parent gravel) and a flat base. It contained a primary silting of a crumbly brown (7.5 YR 4/4) sandy gravel (3056). Above this was 3054, a friable dark brown (7.5 YR 3/2) silty sand, making up a primary packing. The packing contained a series of large packing stones, 3031 (Fig. 3.32). More disturbed or slipped packing was located above this, making up layers 3057 and 3064. The former, on the eastern side, had collapsed forward over the post-

Figure 3.29 Cursus post-hole 3009

Figure 3.30 Cursus post-hole 3058 showing remains of the post

Figure 3.31 Cursus post-hole 3058 showing section

Figure 3.32 Cursus post-hole 3058 showing packing stones

pipe fill 3004. The edge of the post-pipe was clearly visible, was in places vertical, and was defined as cut number 3019 (Fig. 3.31). This contained a band of solid charcoal, 3055, which covered the base of the post-pipe, and ran up the western side (Fig. 3.30). To the east, the collapse of the packing had displaced it. The fill of the post-pipe, 3004, was a friable loamy silt, black to dark brown in colour (7.5 YR 2.5/1 to 3/3). In the top of the feature, context 3001 represented a layer of silting, a compact to friable strong brown (7.5 YR 4/6) sandy silt, which had been deposited after the collapse of the packing into the post void. The post-pipe fill, 3004, contained burnt stones, while the charcoal 3055 represented the solid imprint of a collapsed post. 3054 showed signs of reddening from fire, as did the surrounding natural, particularly in its more clayey bands. This indicated that the post had been burned *in situ*, and had fallen or had been pulled over toward the south.

Feature 3065 (Figs. 3.20 and 3.25)

Feature 3065 was a circular post-hole containing the traces of a post that had been burnt out. Cut 3065 was a rounded and approximately flat-bottomed post-hole cut, with a rounded break of slope at the base running

up to almost vertical sides and an abrupt break of slope at the top. Initial silting of the cut had resulted in the formation of deposit 3076, a moderate brown (5 YR 4/4) silty sand with pebbles. A post and packing had apparently been inserted, and at some later point the post was burnt. The firm, yellowish red (5 YR 3/4) sandy clay 3071 and the firm yellowish red (5 YR 3/4) sandy clay 3070 had both been transformed by burning. This bright orange colouration was also noted in the natural subsoil surrounding the feature. A loose dark reddish-brown (5 YR 3/2) silty sand, 3060, directly above 3071 and underlying the burnt post stump 3051, contained a number of large packing stones which had shifted during the destruction of the post. This may indicate that the post was moved prior to its burning, or that packing was allowed to spill around the base of the post during its erection. 3051 consisted principally of charcoal in lumps of up to five centimetres in diameter in a matrix of loose, dark brown (7.5 YR 3/3) sandy silt with pebbles,

Figure 3.33 Cursus post-hole 3072 during excavation

Figure 3.34 Cursus post-hole 3072 showing post-pipe

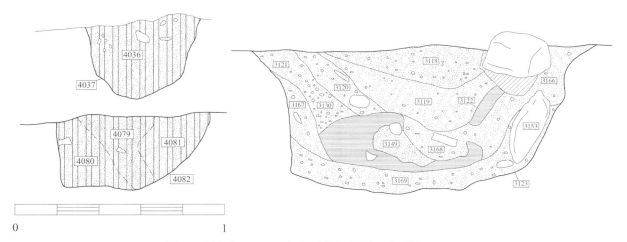

Figure 3.35 Cursus post-holes 3123, 4037 and 4082: sections

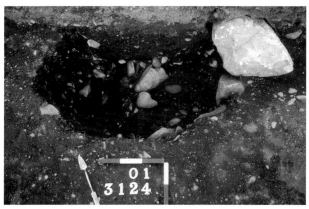

Figure 3.36 Cursus post-hole 3123

Figure 3.37 Cursus post-hole 4037

and would seem to represent the bottom and/or sides of the burnt post, slumped downward by the movement of packing from higher up in the feature. 3050, a loose, very dark brown sandy silt (7.5 YR 2.5/2) containing small pebbles and charcoal flecks, and one large packing stone, and 3042, a loose dark brown (7.5 YR 3/3) sandy loam, were the remains of subsequent packing collapse and later silting.

Feature 3072 (Figs. 3.28, 3.33 and 3.34)
Feature 3072 was the socket of a post within the northern arc of the cursus that had been both burnt and pulled over.

Figure 3.38 Cursus post-hole 4140

Cut 3072 was a circular post-hole with a ledge or shelf along the western side, very close the modern subsoil surface. There was an abrupt break of slope at the top, with near vertical sides running down to a distinct break of slope at the base, which was flat. The basal fill, 3125, was a loose reddish-yellow (7.5 YR 6/8) coarse sand, with small pebbles and occasional large stones. This material derived from the erosion of the sides of the feature prior to the insertion of post and packing. 3125 was all but covered by 3077, a loose, dark reddish-brown (5 YR 3/3) sandy silt with small pebbles and occasional charcoal fragments, which also contained burnt organic material. This layer was followed stratigraphically by a series of deposits associated with post erection and destruction (contexts 3127, 3062, 3061, 3034). 3062, a loose strong brown silty sand (7.5 YR 5/6) with fine and small pebbles, was a thick wedge of slipped packing, and was equivalent to 3061. 3127 was a friable dark reddish-brown sandy silt (5 YR 3/2), with occasional large stones, which also represented slipped packing. It is likely that these layers had been displaced during an event in which the post was pulled to one side (the north), either before or after being burnt. Context 3034 consisted of a group of large packing stones that had become interspersed through the other slipped packing during the loosening of the post (Fig. 3.33). 3063 represented what remained of the burnt post stump, composed of charcoal chunks in a matrix of firm reddish black sandy silt (10 R 2.5/1) (Fig. 3.34). During the burning of the post, several layers (3137, 3128, and 3048) were transformed by the intense heat that was generated even at some depth within the feature. 3137, a loose, silty dusky red sand (10 R 3/4) with fine pebbles, and charcoal flecks was proximal to 3063, and in every way resembled it with the exception that it had a bright orange appearance and contained small flecks of charcoal. 3128, a loose dusky red sandy silt (2.5 YR 3/2) with a few fine pebbles, shared a similar relationship with 3061. Finally, the friable red (2.5 YR 5/8) silt with charcoal lumps 3048 – which is not visible in section

– also appeared to have been altered by fire. Contexts 3126 (a friable dusky red sandy silt with occasional fine pebbles: 2.5 YR 3/3) and 3008 (a firm sandy weak red silt, containing three large stones: 10 R 4/4) represented the silting of the post-pipe void.

Feature 3097 (Figs. 3.20, 3.21 and 3.22)
The cut of this post-hole, 3097, was rounded with straight sides, and was packed with a dark reddish-brown (5 YR 3/3) silty sand, 3109, and a friable very dark brown (7.5 YR 2.5/3) silty sand, 3102. Above this were large packing stones 3084, and further packing in the form of a friable yellowish-brown (10 YR 5/6) sandy gravel, 3096. Within the latter was the post-pipe of a post (defined as interface 3142) filled with 3095, a firm very dark brown (10 YR 2/2) silty clay loam, which contained a good deal of charcoal. This material had been truncated by 3143, the removal of a second and larger burnt post, the base of which remained *in situ* as a mass of charcoal, 3108. Above this was 3059, a fill composed of silting and the collapse of packing into the post void, consisting of a very dark brown (10 YR 3/2) sandy silt. Finally, 3047 represented a final silting into the top of the feature, a firm dark brown (10 YR 3/3) silt. Of the two posts that had originally occupied the feature, 3143 was larger than 3142, and the larger packing stones appeared to respect the former. 3142 had been burned, but had seemingly not been removed, perhaps on account of its lesser size. It is possible that the two posts were contemporary, even though the removal of one truncated the remains of the other.

Feature 3117 (Figs. 3.20, 3.26 and 3.27)
Feature 3117 was a large post-hole, the post of which had been burnt and left to silt up. The cut (3117) was circular in plan, with an abrupt break of slope at the top, and gradually sloping sides that merged into a very rounded bottom. The east side had far a more vertical edge. There had been an initial silting or erosion of the sides, producing layer 3116, a firm dark brown (7.5 YR 3/4) silty sand, with a few very small pebbles. This fill extended across the base of the feature. The presence of 3144, a lens of friable, dark brown (7.5 YR 3/3) sandy silt, with charcoal and small pebbles demonstrated the inclusion of burnt or organic material in a pre-post layer of silting, after which it is presumed that the post and packing were inserted. 3115, a firm yellowish red (5 YR 4/6) sandy silt containing a great deal of charcoal, sat directly above 3116, towards the east side of the feature. 3115 seemed to represent the remains of a post that had been burnt *in situ* (see Fig. 3.27). Contemporary with 3115 were contexts 3114, 3113/3030, 3013 and 3157, each of these fills being implicated in the burning of the post and the subsequent settling of the packing. 3013 was slipped packing material, a loose very dusky red (7.5 YR 2.5/2) sand, with charcoal flecks and fine pebbles. Loose, very

dusky red (2.5 YR 2.5/2) sandy silt 3114 contained traces of the burnt post from higher up I the profile, which had slid down above the burnt stump. Loose dark reddish-brown (5 YR 2.5/2) sand 3113, which incorporated packing stones 3030, contained packing that had slipped from the southwest pushing some of 3157 before it. 3157 was a remnant of the side of the post itself, which remained *in situ* in some places and had been crushed in others, within a matrix of loose very dusky red (2.5 YR 2.5/2) sandy silt. 3020, an extremely loose brown (7.5 YR 4/3) sand, was a silting into the post-pipe void. Dark reddish-brown (5 YR 3/3) sandy silty clay with small pebbles and charcoal 3007 represented a tertiary silting.

Feature 3123 (Figs. 3.35 and 3.36)

Feature 3123 was a very large post-hole in the northern part of the cursus exposed in 2001, which extended into the northern edge of Trench F. Consequently it was only excavated to the extent of one half in section. This section demonstrated that the cut was abrupt at the top with sharply sloping sides to an abrupt break of slope near the base, and had a slightly concave flat bottom. The primary fill, 3169, was a friable, coarse medium brown (7.5 YR 4/4) sand with numerous fine pebbles, which indicated that there had been some erosion of the sides of the feature prior to the introduction of a post. This erosion may have been caused by human activity within and around the feature. This fill ran along the bottom of the post-hole, and up the sides. It was overlain by contexts 3167, 3124 and 3166, and partly interpenetrated by 3135. 3167 was a friable brown (7.5 YR 4/3) coarse sand with medium pebbles, and represented a slipped packing fill from the west side of the feature, while 3166 was a friable coarse brown (7.5 YR 4/3) sand with mixed pebbles, which had slumped in from the south and east. 3124, a friable black (10 YR 2/1) sand, containing a great deal of charcoal and some orange flecks, was a thick layer almost entirely composed of charcoal and burnt sand, and was identified as the remains of a burnt post (Fig. 3.37). In places the layer seemed to indicate the *in situ* burning of a post stump, while toward the top of the deposit the charcoal would seem to have derived from the collapse of the burnt material of a post from higher up, above ground level. This would also explain the complex intermixing of different gravel packing layers within the charcoal. Excavation demonstrated that the grain of the charcoal was easily distinguished and ran in a variety of different directions. 3149, a lens of intensely burnt reddish-yellow coarse sand (7.5 YR 6/8) lay immediately above 3124, although the latter had also slumped over it. Resting on top of 3149 was 3168, a lens of loose brown coarse sand (7.5 YR 4/3). On the western side of the feature, two lenses of collapsed packing had fallen over the remains of the post, and showed signs of having been intensely affected by fire. Of these, 3121/3130 was a loose, dark

brown coarse sand containing many small pebbles, while 3120 was a loose dark greyish brown coarse sand (7.5 YR 3/2) containing numerous small pebbles and some displaced packing stones. On the eastern side of the feature, 3122 represented a patch of charcoal from the burnt post, sealed beneath 3119, a spread of loose dark brown coarse sand (7.5 YR 3/2), which had filled much of the feature following the collapse of the post. Above this was 3119, a loose brown silty sand (7.5 YR 4/3), which represented a slow silting into the top of the feature.

Feature 3129 (Fig. 3.20)

3129 was the cut of a post-hole with an abrupt break of slope at the top, near vertical sides on the north, and undulating but sharp sides on the south. This feature contained a series of very gravelly fills: 3135, a loose brown silty sand (10 YR 3/4) with fine pebbles, ran along the base of the feature, while 3134, a loose dark reddish-brown sand (5 YR 3/2) with fine to small pebbles, and 3133, a loose red to reddish-brown sandy silt (5 YR 4/4) with small pebbles and charcoal flecks, ran down the edge of the feature on the north. 3132, a loose grey-brown sandy silt (10 YR 2/1) containing fine pebbles and charcoal, gave the appearance of a slumped post-pipe from a burnt post, while 3131, a loose dark reddish-brown silty sand (5 YR 3/2) with fine pebbles appeared to represent the slipped packing which had crushed it. It would appear that the post within this feature had first been burnt, and then left to decay further.

Feature 3139 (Fig. 3.23)

This feature was the most southerly of the post-holes of the post-defined cursus uncovered in Trench F. The feature extended into the section and was only partially excavated. Cut 3139 had an abrupt break of slope at the top and gradual sides onto a slightly concave vase. The single fill that was revealed in the excavated area was 3140, a friable very dark grey (5 YR 3/1) silt with medium pebbles. There was no indication of burning.

Feature 3158 (Fig. 3.20)

Cut 3158 was sub-oval with straight sides and an uneven bowled base. It contained 3162, a primary silting of friable yellowish-brown (10 YR 5/6) coarse sand, above which was a layer of burnt material, 3165, which suggested that an episode of burning had taken place in the pit before the insertion of the post. This layer of burnt sandy clay did not cover the whole of the post-hole base, and appeared to have been disturbed by the insertion of the post. The primary packing of the post-hole was 3161, a loose yellowish red (5 YR 4/6) sandy gravel, which contained only a few small packing stones. Above this were the scant traces of a burnt post, 3138, and collapsed friable dark reddish-brown (5 YR 3/4) gravel packing, 3018, which had clear tip-lines. It seems likely that the post had been burned out above ground level, but that some of the stump had rotted, leaving charcoal and packing to collapse into the post void. In the top of the feature, a firm dark brown (7.5 YR 3/2) clayey silt, 3017, dipped into the post void.

Feature 4014 (Fig. 3.23)
4014 was the cut of a shallow circular post-hole. It had sloping concave sides dipping onto a flat base. Its basal fill was 4013, a very loose dark yellowish-brown sandy loam (10 YR 3/4). This appeared to represent the packing around a central post, and was contiguous with 4021, which was also a loose dark yellowish-brown sandy loam (10 YR 3/4). Context 4001 was a loose, very dark brown sandy loam (10 YR 2/2) and appeared to constitute the fill of a post-pipe. The post is likely to have rotted out *in situ*, as there was no trace of burning.

Feature 4035 (Fig. 3.23)
Feature 4035 was a steep-sided, sub-circular post-hole with a concave base. On excavation the feature showed indications of having a post-ramp, although few of the other posts in the cursus sequence had any trace of a surviving ramp. This feature may have been over-cut, and if so contexts 4032 and 4034 actually represented natural subsoil. The basal fill would then be 4031, a loose very dark brown sandy loam (7.5 YR 2.5/2), which represented a stony fill or packing surrounding a central post-pipe. The lower fill of the post-pipe was 4033, a friable, very dusky red silty loam (2.5 YR 2.5/3) containing a number of large pebbles. The uppermost fill of the feature was 4008, a loose, dark reddish-brown silty loam (5 YR 2.5/2), material that had silted or slumped into the top of the feature. This contained large quantities of charcoal (which was taken as a series of samples) and one small piece of flint, find number 1459. The large quantity of charcoal in this feature and the colour of the deposits concerned suggests that the post had been burnt *in situ*.

Feature 4037 (Figs. 3.35 and 3.37)
4037 was the circular cut of a cursus post-hole. It was steep sided, flat based and retained diffuse traces of a burnt post. Its principal fill was 4036, a loose very dark brown sandy loam (7.5 YR 2.5/2). This contained large packing stones and a great deal of charcoal, representing the disturbed and undifferentiated remains of a burnt post and collapsed packing material.

Feature 4077 (Fig. 3.23)
4077 was the cut of a circular post-hole, with steep concave edges descending onto a flat, sloping base. This was filled with 4076, a friable dark yellowish-brown sandy loam (10 YR 3/4) containing a number of large packing stones. This deposit appeared to constitute packing, arranged around the sides and base of the post-hole. The upper part of the feature was filled with 4030, a friable dark brown loamy sand (10 YR 3/3),

which contained a dense concentration of small charcoal flecks, and which probably represented the remains of a burnt post.

Feature 4082 (Fig. 3.35)
Feature 4082 was the cut of an oval post-hole, which had a possible post-ramp on northern edge. The feature had steep straight edges, dipping toward a flat base. The feature was filled with 4080, a loose, strong brown sandy loam (7.5 YR 4/6) with medium-sized gravel fragments. This appeared to have been the packing deposit around a post. 4080 was similar to 4081, another loose strong brown sandy loam (7.5 YR 4/6), and both layers lay below 4079, a friable dark brown sandy loam (7.5 YR 3/2) which appeared to be the remains of a post-pipe. The post-pipe was at a distinct angle, indicating either the collapse and decay of post, or, perhaps less likely, its deliberate removal. There were traces of burning within 4079, including burnt stones, and this may indicate that the post had burned above ground level, but not down into the socket.

Feature 4090 (Fig. 3.28)
4090 was the cut of a post-hole, sub-oval in shape, with gradual straight sides sloping to a rounded base. The primary silting in the base of the feature was 4089, a friable brown sandy loam (7.5 YR 4/4) containing medium-sized pebbles. Above this was 4004, a friable dark red-brown sandy loam (5 YR 3/3) containing small pebbles, and with occasional charcoal staining, but no more extensive traces of burning. This feature lay slightly to the west of cursus alignment, but it was otherwise very similar to the other cursus post-holes. It was cut by modern drainage ditch 4092, and therefore survived in a disturbed condition.

Feature 4093 (Fig. 3.17)
Feature 4093 was the cut of sub-circular cursus post-hole. It had steep concave edges descending onto a rounded base. The primary fill was 4095, a loose red/yellow sand (7.5 YR 6/6) with mixed pebbles. This was apparently a product of collapse or silting when post-hole had first been cut. Above this was a deposit of loose red-brown sand (7.5 YR 7/6) with medium pebbles, 4098. This material represented *in-situ* packing, standing against one side of the feature. Its equivalent on the other side of the feature was 4094, a friable dark yellow-brown sandy loam (10 YR 3/6) with medium pebbles, presumably a rather more disturbed packing deposit. This lay beneath the loose red-brown sand 4099 (7.5 YR 7/6), which was similar in composition to 4098. 4099 butted up against 4096, a loose red/yellow sand (7.5 YR 7/6) with medium pebbles and much charcoal. This may have been the remains of a post that had burnt *in situ*. Above this was a friable, dark brown silt 4097 (7.5 YR 3/3), which contained some charcoal. This may also have been related

to the decay and collapse of the post, although it was more likely a silting into the top of the feature.

Feature 4140 (Fig. 3.23 and 3.38)

Context 4140 was the cut of a post-hole, a sub-rounded feature with the vestigial trace of a ramp on its southern edge. It had steep, straight sides grading on to a flat base. The primary filling was 4139, a friable dark reddish-brown sandy loam (5 YR 3/3) containing much fine gravel. This deposit represented collapsed packing material on the southern side of the feature. It lay below 4138, a loose/friable dark red-brown sandy loam (5 YR 2.5/2) containing frequent charcoal flecks, which might indicate the presence of a burnt post. This lay beneath 4137, a loose friable dark brown sandy loam (10 YR 3/3) with large pebbles, a spread of collapsed packing material, possibly fallen into the void created by a burnt or rotting post. Above this was 4136, a loose/friable red-brown sandy loam (5 YR 4/4) with gravel inclusions and a number of larger packing stones. This was also collapsed packing, lying below the loose friable brown sandy silt (7.5 YR 4/4) with small pebbles, context 4051. This deposit may indicate a stabilisation layer of silt above the collapsed remains of the post. This feature was located slightly to the east of the main cursus alignment, but was otherwise entirely comparable with the cursus post-holes in general.

Feature 4157 (Fig. 3.77)

Context 4157 was the cut of sub-circular post-hole, which had been cut by post-hole 4110 of the middle post-ring of the Late Neolithic enclosure. It had a shallow and gradual slope on southern side, was more bowled on the east and west, and had a rounded base. This feature was initially thought to be the ramp of post-hole 4110, but in the course of excavation it was identified as a separate feature. The primary filling of the feature was 4156, a loose/friable dark brown silty loam (7.5 YR 3/3) with small to medium pebbles. This was apparently a gravel packing within the post-hole. Above this packing was a layer of dark post residue, 4155, a friable very dark brown silty loam (7.5 YR 2.5/2) with a few small rounded pebbles and a great deal of charcoal. This post had apparently been burned.

Feature 4161 (Fig. 3.23)

4161 was the cut of a circular feature whose status as part of the cursus monument was initially indicated by its dark colour. The cut had steep straight sides sloping to a rounded base. The principal fill of the feature was 4185, a loose, dark brown sandy loam (7.5 YR 3/3) with small pebbles. There was a great deal of charcoal flecking within this material, probably indicating the burning of a post. The upper fill of the post-hole was 4160, a loose, reddish black sandy loam (10 YR 2.5/1) containing small pebbles and charcoal fragments. This appeared to represent the trace of the burnt post-pipe and post.

Feature 4184 (Fig. 3.23)

4184 was the cut of a sub-circular post-hole. It had steep concave edges sloping to a rounded base. The layers of collapse and silting in this feature suggested that the post had been removed at some point, rather than left to decay *in situ*. The basal filling of the feature was 4182, a loose to friable dark yellowish-brown sandy loam (10 YR 3/4) with fine gravel inclusions. This was a layer of gravel packing at the base of the post-hole. Above this was 4183, a discrete deposit of large packing stones, concentrated on the southern side of the feature. The packing stones were contained within the matrix of 4181, a friable, very dark brown sandy silt (10 YR 2/2) which contained small gravel fragments. This deposit appeared to be disturbed and collapsed. The final deposit in the feature was 4180, a friable to loose sandy yellowish-brown silt (10 YR 5/8) containing a number of mixed stones. This seems to have been a silting deposit, probably formed after the post had been removed and presumably truncated by ploughing. This feature showed no indication of a post having been burnt.

Other features possibly associated with the cursus

As noted above, a series of features were identified in the excavation of Trench A that could not readily be accommodated into the two innermost post-rings of the palisaded enclosure, and at the time it was conjectured that they might have formed elements of either post avenues or timber circles. Once larger areas of the site had been investigated, these possibilities began to recede. Many of these features were scattered on either side of the eastern side of the cursus, a few were present on the western side, and in Trench F they continued the line of the cursus on beyond the terminal. As we will suggest below, it is possible that these features indicate that the cursus itself was a multi-phase structure, which was remodelled or re-created on a number of occasions. This is consistent with results from other timber cursus monuments in Scotland, such as Holywood North and Holm Farm (Thomas 2007a). But equally, it is clear that some of these features were much later in date than the cursus, and that the orientation of the monument continued to influence acts of construction and deposition that took place for many generations after the burning of the cursus posts.

Feature 064 (Fig. 3.39)

The oval cut of a small post-hole with vertical sides 064 was filled with 041, a friable brown loamy sand (7.5 YR 5/4).

Feature 070 (Fig. 3.39)

The small, shallow, round cut 070 had a rounded base,

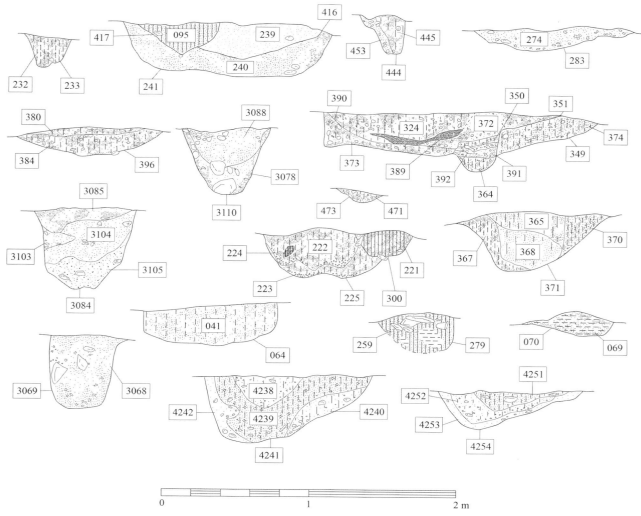

Figure 3.39 Features possibly associated with the cursus: sections

and was filled with friable dark reddish-brown sandy clay 069 (5 YR 3/4).

Feature 225/300 (Fig. 3.39)
The flat-based, steep sided cut of a post-hole, 225, contained the friable dusky red (2.5 YR 3/3) loamy sand 223, which lay below a friable dark reddish-brown (5 YR 3/4) loamy sand, 222. These layers were cut by 300, a further post-hole with rounded base, which contained 221, a compact dark brown loamy sand (7.5 YR 3/3).

Feature 233 (Fig. 3.39)
The steep-sided, round-based cut of a small post-hole, 233, contained a friable dark reddish-brown loamy sand (5 YR 3/3) with many stones and pebbles, 232.

Feature 241 (Fig. 3.39)
A steep-sided cut with a flat base, 241, had a principal fill of loose dark yellowish-brown sand 240 (10 YR 3/4).

Two small post-holes were cut into the top of this feature. Cut 416 was a post base filled with 239, a sticky brown to strong brown silt (7.5 YR 4/4 – 4/6) with a concentration of pebbles at its centre, while cut 417 contained a firm dark yellowish-brown (10 YR 3/4) silty loam, 095.

Feature 279 (Fig. 3.39)
The cut of a small post-hole with straight sides and a concave base, 279, was filled with 259, a compact dark brown sandy clay loam with eight packing stones (7.5 YR 3/3). Above this was a compact dark brown (7.5 YR 3/3) silty clay loam 311, which represented a silting into the top of the feature.

Feature 283 (Fig. 3.39)
A shallow, irregular cut with gradual sides, 283, which had probably been disturbed by animal burrowing. It was filled with 274, a tenacious, dark reddish-brown silty clay (5 YR 2.5/2) with angular and rounded pebbles.

Feature 349/351 (Fig. 3.39)

This was a complex feature, in which the earliest cut was 349, a gently sloping post-hole which contained the packing 374, a friable dark brown sandy loam (7.5 YR 3/3). Within the post-pipe was a series of fills. The earliest of these was 364, a loose dark yellowish-brown loamy sand (10 YR 4/6), above which was 391, a loose dark yellowish-brown sand (10 YR 4/4). This was followed by 392, another loose dark yellowish-brown sand (10 YR 4/6), and finally 350, a loose and slightly humic yellowish-brown loamy sand (10 YR 5/8). It is likely that these lenses of material had slumped into the void left by a withdrawn or rotted-out post. All of these fills were truncated by the broad shallow cut 351, the lower part of which was filled with 373, a friable brown loamy sand (7.5 YR 4/4). This might represent either a slump or a deliberate backfill. Above this was a loose strong brown sandy gravel fill (7.5 YR 5/6), 372, concentrated in the eastern part of the feature. These two fills were then in turn truncated by the smaller, shallower cut 390, an oval feature with a rounded base. This contained 389, a loose yellowish-brown sandy gravel layer (10 YR 5/6), and above this was 324, a loose, strong brown loamy sand with gravel (7.5 YR 5/6). Owing to its location, 349/351 was initially compared with the post-holes of the inner ring of the Late Neolithic palisaded enclosure. However, it was clearly not a part of that suite of features, and can perhaps be associated with other post-holes running to the south and east of the principal line of the cursus, such as 371 and 241.

Feature 371 (Fig. 3.39)

371 was the cut of moderately-sized post-hole with bowl-shaped sides and base, whose primary packing was composed of 369 and 370, friable dusky red sandy silt loams with small stones (2.5 YR 4/4). Between these two bodies of packing was a post-pipe, the lowest fill of which was 368, a friable yellowish-brown sandy loam (5 YR 5/6). Above this material was 365, a compact yet friable dark brown sandy loam (7.5 YR 3/3), presumably a silting into the top of the post void.

Feature 396 (Fig. 3.39)

396 was a shallow circular cut which deepened to the south, with a concave base. It contained 384, a friable reddish-brown loamy sand (5 YR 4/4) with a series of clear packing stones.

Feature 444 (Fig. 3.39)

A step-sided post-hole with a rounded base, 444, contained a lower packing, 453, of reddish-yellow friable sand (5 YR 6/6). Above this was a post-pipe, 445, a compact yellowish red loamy sand (5 YR 4/6) pitched at a near-vertical angle into the feature.

Feature 473 (Fig. 3.39)

A rather small circular post-hole cut with sloping sides and rounded base, 473, contained 471, a friable dark brown sandy clay loam (7.5 YR 3/3).

Feature 3026 (Fig. 3.44)

3026 was the roughly circular cut of post-hole, with uneven sides and a concave base. The feature contained only one fill, 3025, composed almost entirely of collapsed packing stones, which appear to have been smashed from a piece of sandstone, in a matrix of friable reddish-brown (5 YR 4/4) silty sand with a little charcoal. It was impossible to tell whether the hole had contained a post, and if so whether the post had been removed or had rotted *in situ*. There were no indications of burning, and the feature was not clearly associated with any known alignment.

Feature 3069 (Fig. 3.39)

Cut 3069 was a post-hole, circular in plan, with an abrupt break of slope at the top and vertical sides, the southern edge being slightly undercut, while the north was inclining beyond the vertical. There was only one fill, 3068, a friable dark brown sandy silt (7.5 YR 3/4).

Feature 3084 (Fig. 3.39)

Cut 3084 had an abrupt break of slope at top and vertical sides, with a gradual transition to a rounded bottom. The feature contained four rather similar fills, all thoroughly penetrated by root activity. 3105, a very loose very coarse dark yellowish-brown sand (10 YR 2.5/2), with fine and medium pebbles, contained three fairly large packing stones, and gave the impression of slipped packing. 3104 was a loose, very dark brown coarse sand (7.5 YR 2.5/2) with coarse and fine pebbles, which was perhaps the post-pipe void, but has been crushed by the collapse of other packing fills. The two remaining slipped packing fills above 3104 were 3103, a loose very dusky red coarse sand (2.5 YR 2.5/2) with fine, medium and coarse pebbles and 3085, a loose sandy dark reddish-brown silt (5 YR 2.5/2) containing a few fine pebbles.

Feature 3110 (Fig. 3.39)

3110 was the deep cut of a circular post-hole with an abrupt break of slope at the top and a gradual base of slope toward the rounded bottom. 3078, a friable dark yellowish-brown sandy silt (10 YR 3/6) containing charcoal and fine and medium pebbles, was the basal fill of the post-hole, which also contained a number of small packing stones. 3088, a friable dark yellowish-brown sandy silt (10 YR 3/6), with some charcoal flecks, some medium pebbles, and one cobble, was a silting in the post-pipe void which may have resulted from post extraction or decay.

Feature 3147 (Fig. 3.44)

3147 was a rather ephemeral scoop-shaped cut with a homogeneous fill of tenacious dark brown silty clay 3148 (7.5 YR 3/3).

Feature 4241 (Fig. 3.39)

4241 was a large, irregularly shaped feature with poorly defined edges and a diffuse interface with the natural subsoil, first identified in the course of excavating feature 4254. The relationship between these two features was unclear, although 4241 is likely to have been the later. It was located to the south of the middle post-ring of the palisaded enclosure and immediately to the west of the western side of the post cursus. It is conceivable that it was associated in some way with the latter. It had irregular, concave edges dropping onto a rounded base. The basal fill was 4240, a friable reddish-yellow sandy loam (7.5 YR 6/6) with numbers of medium pebbles. This fill was similar to 4242, a loose reddish-yellow sand (7.5 YR 7/6) with a few small stones. Both appear to have been packing deposits at the edge of the feature. Above these was 4239, a friable sandy loam (2.5 YR 2.5/3 very dusky red) with a few pebbles and some flecks of charcoal. This may have represented the remains of a charred post. Above this was 4238, a friable dark red sandy loam (2.5 YR 4/6) with numerous medium-sized pebbles, apparently a silting into the top of the feature. On the whole, 4241 is likely to have been a packed post-hole from which the post had rotted out, leading to the collapse of the surrounding gravel packing.

Feature 4254 (Fig. 3.39)

4254 was a sub-rounded feature which lay to the south of the middle post-ring of the palisaded enclosure, and immediately to the west of the western side of the post cursus. 4254 appeared to have been cut by 4241, although the relationship was not absolutely clear during excavation. 4254 may also have been clipped by post-hole 4093 of the post cursus, which would place it very early in the overall sequence, and perhaps mark it out as associated with an early phase of the cursus itself. It had steep concave sides dipping onto a rounded base. The basal fill of 4254 was 4253, a loose, reddish-yellow sand (7.5 YR 7/5) containing many medium-sized pebbles, which might represent redeposited natural subsoil used as packing. Above this was the rather similar material 4252, a friable reddish-yellow sandy loam (7.5 YR 6/6) with many small pebbles. The uppermost fill was 4251, a friable black sandy loam (7.5 YR 2.5/1) with a few medium pebbles and numerous charcoal fragments. It is not clear whether this feature had ever held a post.

Pits containing prehistoric pottery

Three features excavated in 1999–2002 stood out as containing unusually dense concentrations of finds. Each of these was located in the immediate vicinity of the cursus, although pit 050 was probably more intimately related to post-hole 084 of the inner palisade ring. In all cases the pottery found in these pits was Grooved Ware.

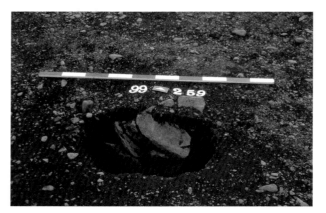

Figure 3.40 Feature 279, possibly associated with the cursus

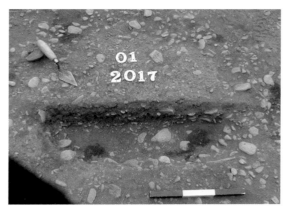

Figure 3.41 Feature 2016, possibly associated with the cursus

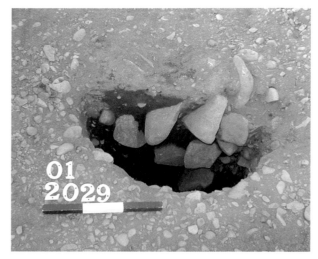

Figure 3.42 Feature 2028, possibly associated with the cursus

Feature 050 (Figs. 3.45 and 3.46)

Pit 050 was one of the more significant features excavated at Dunragit, producing one of the richest assemblages of prehistoric pottery from any single feature (44 sherds from six different vessels). 050 was located immediately to the west of inner post-ring post-hole 084, but was quite different in character. The two features were linked in that they each produced sherds from four of the same Grooved Ware vessels. 050 had a round, flat-based cut with slightly sloping sides, containing primary fill 049, a friable dark brown loamy sand with large packing stones (10 YR 3/3). Above this was 048, a friable dark yellowish-brown loamy sand (19 YR 3/4). Finally, a

silting of compact dark brown sand (10 YR 3/3) filled the top of the feature, context 004. There was no trace of a post-pipe, and it seems improbable that the feature had held a post. The pottery was distributed through all three layers of the fill, although it was especially dense in contexts 004 and 048. A few lithic objects were also present, including a fine hammerstone. Three radiocarbon dates were acquired from this feature, producing a calibrated date on a pooled mean of 2871–2623 Cal BC at 95.4% probability (see Chapter 10).

Feature 3074 (Fig. 3.45)
Like feature 050, pit 3074 was also rich in artefacts and other finds. Cut 3074 had an abrupt break of slope at the top and gradually sloping sides, with a slight shelf to the south and a rounded bottom. Fill 3082 consisted entirely of dense clay and was extracted whole for further investigation. This clay was located on the southern shelf of the cut. 3080, a friable, dark reddish-brown silty sand (5 YR 3/4) with fine and medium pebbles, composed the principal fill of the feature and contained two pot sherds, nine pieces of flint including one scraper, and five lumps of a material similar to shale. 3081, a friable, very dark brown silty sand (7.5 YR 2.5/2) with fine pebbles and charcoal sat as a distinct lens within the top of 3080.

Figure 3.43 Feature 2028 after excavation

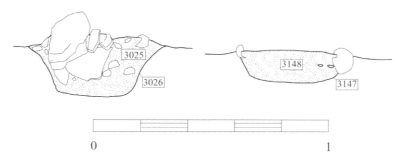

Figure 3.44 Features associated with the cursus in Trench F: sections

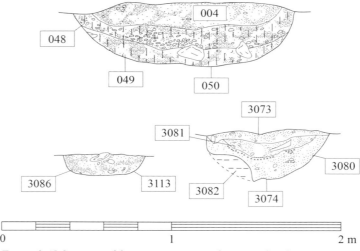

Figure 3.45 Sections of features containing deposits of prehistoric pottery

Context 3081 contained two quartz pebbles, two pieces of shale-like material, five pieces of flint, one hammerstone, and four sherds of pottery, including one large, flat rim sherd. Pot sherd FN1450 lay sandwiched between two large stones. 3073, a loose brown silt (7.5 YR 4/4), with fine pebbles and charcoal flecks, lay across the top of the feature as a silting and contained four flint flakes and two sherds of pottery. The feature appears to have been the base of a truncated pit, although the possibility that it is the bottom of a shallow post-hole cannot be entirely discounted. The pottery recovered from the feature came from two Grooved Ware vessels (FG3 Vessel 2 and FG7 Vessel 1), both of which were also represented in pit 3112 (see below). This suggests that the two pits were dug and filled within a single episode of activity.

Feature 3112 (Figs. 3.45 and 3.47)

3112 was a shallow cut with an abrupt break of slope at the top, and gradually sloping sides dipping onto a flat base. This feature contained only one fill, 3086, which was a firm very dark brown sandy silt (10 YR 2/2), with small pebbles and several large stones. This contained three sherds of pottery from two different vessels and six flint pieces and one hammerstone. Like 3074, feature 3112 can also be interpreted as the base of a heavily truncated pit. All of the pottery came from the same two vessels as that in feature 3074.

The inner post-ring of the palisaded enclosure

This group of features was first identified as two converging arcs of very large post-holes, some of them with the vestiges of post-ramps remaining. Many of the posts appeared to have rotted *in situ*, leaving a clear post-pipe visible in section, although an appreciable number had either been rocked and withdrawn, resulting in the disruption of the post-hole profiles, or dug out. In Trenches A and AA there were few obvious traces of smaller posts interspersed between these uprights, unlike the middle post-ring (see below). However, in Trench J, a number of smaller posts were present. It is open to interpretation whether this indicates that there were smaller posts, presumably now entirely truncated, throughout the inner ring, or whether there was simply a limited area of screening of some kind within Trench J. Certainly, it is difficult to explain why smaller posts of the *middle* ring should have survived in Trenches A and AA, but those of the *inner* ring did not, and this supports the view that they had never existed. If so, we have to accept the possibility that the appearance of the enclosure was not uniform throughout its circuit.

In Trench A it was noted that there appeared to be two distinct arcs of inner ring post-holes, which grew further apart from each other toward the east, while converging

Figure 3.46 Pit containing pottery deposit 050 after excavation

Figure 3.47 Pit containing pottery deposit 3112

on Feature 319/332. These are referred to as the 'eastern' and 'western' arcs of post-holes, and are presumed to relate to two separate phases of construction, although it is not easy to identify which was earlier or later. It is notable that the 'eastern arc' continued the gentle curve of the rest of the inner post-ring, but that it ran very close to the middle post-ring in the eastern part of the excavated area. The 'western arc', by contrast, described a more acute curve, perhaps intended to maintain a set distance between the two innermost post-rings. Feature 319/332 contained two distinct post-sockets, and appeared to represent two overlapping post-holes – presumably one from each of two phases of construction. Unfortunately, within the complicated stratigraphy of this feature it was not easy to judge which had been the earlier cut. In most cases, the post-holes of the 'eastern arc' were shallower than those of the western, although it must be remembered that all of the excavated features represented the lower portion of sockets that had been severely truncated by erosion. Moreover, post-hole 215 of the 'eastern arc' was as deep as any of those of the 'western arc', so depth alone cannot necessarily be used as a criterion for distinguishing between the two series of post-holes. To the west of feature 319/332, in Trenches AA and J, only one set of inner ring post-holes was present. It is suggested that within this area the two phases of construction of the inner ring coincided spatially, so that rather than constituting separate features the second phase took the form of recuts into the first phase post-holes. Certainly, in this part of the site the majority of the major inner ring post-holes had been recut, and it was evident that the post had been replaced in some cases. However, it is also clear that some of the inner ring post-holes were single-phase features, and it may be that the posts that they had originally contained survived to form part of the second phase enclosure. Post-holes 579/619 and 792 may not have received a second post at all, although each contained major recuts that had presumably removed the post stump. These recuts may have been contemporary with the reconfiguration of the inner post-ring, and formed part of the general 'tidying up' of the site before reconstruction began, but they might equally have been later. In that case, the original posts in the two post-holes might actually have formed part of the second-phase enclosure, and the recutting might form part of its decommissioning.

As we have noted, it is difficult to judge whether the 'eastern' or 'western' arc of post-holes within Trench A was the earlier set of features, corresponding with the primary cuts of the post-holes in Trenches AA and J. The western set of inner ring post-holes had all rotted out, whilst all those of the eastern arc had apparently been withdrawn. In Trenches AA and J, some (but not all) of the posts may have been withdrawn before the recuts had truncated the primary features. However, it is not easy to correlate these with the post-holes further to the west. In features 756/449 and 825/826 the second post had rotted out, and it is possible that the first post in 756/449 had been withdrawn. However, the primary posts in 825/826 and 4145/4173 appeared to have decayed. It is perhaps logical to suggest that the 'eastern arc' was earlier, and that its posts were removed before they were replaced by those of the 'western arc', which were left to decompose naturally. In this case, the rebuilding of the inner post-ring would have had the function of correcting the distance between the two post-rings, and replacing a set of post-holes that may have been judged too shallow.

None the less, this hypothesis is not proven, and it leaves us with two possible sequences of events, with significant implications. If the 'western arc' of posts had been the earlier, the fact that they had had time to decay before being replaced implies that an appreciable period (perhaps more than a century) had elapsed between the two phases of construction. Conversely, if the 'eastern arc'

were earlier, the withdrawal of posts (also seen in some of the two-phase post-holes) would indicate a rather shorter sequence. The removal of one of the 'eastern arc' of posts was accompanied by an act of deliberate deposition: in the case of Feature 215 a deposit of cremated human and sheep bone had been placed in the crater left behind by the post removal before it was backfilled. In Trench AA, four of the large post-holes (579/619, 755, 756 and 826) had been recut, although feature 594 was a single-phase feature. Interestingly, in Trench J only Feature 4145/4173 had clearly been recut. The presence of smaller post-holes between the larger uprights in this area, and indeed the relatively modest size of the main post-holes here (to the point that the distinction between the two begins to break down) indicates that the construction of the circle was far from homogeneous around its circuit.

'Western arc' of the inner post-ring

Feature 063 (Figs. 3.48 and 3.49)
063 was the cut of a large round post-hole with slightly sloping sides and flat base, with a primary packing fill of friable dark reddish-brown sandy gravel, 244 (5 YR 3/2). Context 244 contained a large piece of fragile carbonised wood, which appeared flat in section. Set within 244 was a post-pipe of loose dark brown sandy material 058 (7.5 YR 3/2). Above this was a silting into the top of the feature, 022, composed of friable dark reddish-brown sandy clay (5 YR 3/3). The presence of the clear, undisturbed post-pipe suggests that the post rotted out, rather than having been removed.

Feature 084 (Figs. 3.48 and 3.50)
084 was the oval cut of a large palisade post with a rounded base, almost vertical on three sides but more gradual on the west, and this probably represented the remains of a post-ramp. Soil micromorphology samples 014, 105 and 016 were taken from this feature (see Chapter 9). The profile of this feature was very striking, the various layers apparently dipping in toward the middle of the post-hole. The primary packing was a loose, brown sandy gravel, which made up contexts 003 and 086 (7.5 YR 4/3). On the western side of the feature, layer 082 (above 086) was a firm, dark reddish-brown loamy sand, which had probably been thrown in as part of the packing within the post-ramp (5 YR 3/4). These various packing deposits gave the impression of having been truncated, although it is actually more likely that they had been packed up against the original post within the feature, which had subsequently rotted out. The material that these layers were now pitched against was 081, a loose, brown sand containing numerous small and medium-sized pebbles (7.5 YR 4/4). This was one of the bodies of material that had replaced the decayed post. Two further layers, 079 and 085, both tenacious dark brown

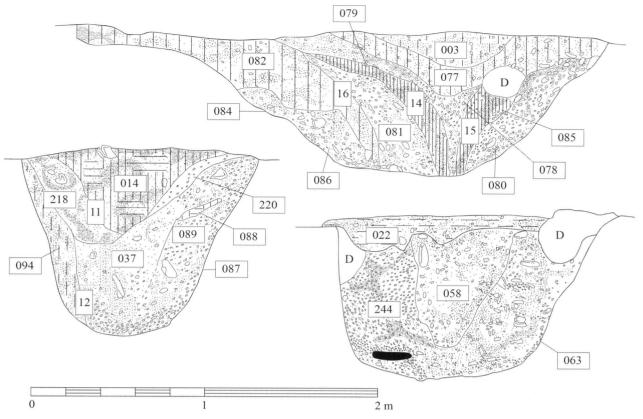

Figure 3.48 Post-holes of the inner post-ring: sections

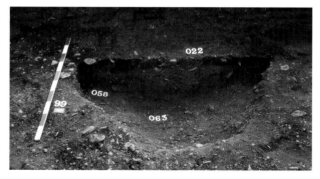

Figure 3.49 Post-hole of the 'western arc' of the inner post-ring 063

Figure 3.50 Inner ring post-hole 084

loamy sands (7.5 YR) represented further deposits that had tumbled into the space left by the rotted post, while 078, composed of loose brown sandy gravel (7.5 YR 4/4), filled the central part of the post-pipe. In thin section, this material appeared particularly gravel-rich. This could be explained as material that had dropped down into the core of the post stump before the edges of the post had rotted away, resulting in a distinctive v-shaped section. Under the microscope, context 079 appeared steeply bedded, which accords with this interpretation (see Chapter 9).

Above these layers, 077 represented a stabilisation layer, composed of firm brown silty loam (7.5 YR 4/3). Finally, 003 above this was a friable dark brown sandy clay loam (7.5 YR 3.3), a further natural silt or slump into the settled feature. Overall, the profile of feature 084 constitutes a classic example of the decay of an earthfast timber, as described by Reynolds and Barber (1984: 100). Because the post-stump is likely to rot from the inside outward, sediment and artefacts from higher in the profile can penetrate the developing void and ultimately occur low in the section. Reynolds and Barber caution that this situation may be mistaken for recutting, and it is worth pointing out that the distinctive section of 084 was quite different from the recut post-holes at Dunragit, such as 215. 084 was also one of the features at Dunragit that produced the greatest quantities of prehistoric pottery, all of it Grooved Ware. This was most densely concentrated in the uppermost contexts, 003 and 077, but sherds also came from layers 078, 079, 082, 085 and 086. Fragments from many of the same vessels represented in these contexts were also recovered from pit 050, which was situated immediately to the west of 084. Significantly, sherds from these pots were distributed *throughout* the stratigraphy of post-hole 084. Individual pieces of pottery may have moved down the profile through various post-depositional processes, but it is evident that the insertion, packing, rotting-out and collapse of the post represented an integral suite of events, and that no recutting or digging-out needs to be invoked to explain the distribution of pottery through the stratigraphy.

Feature 087 (Fig. 3.48 and 3.51)
087 was the cut of a steep-sided oval post-hole with a flat base. This feature produced soil micromorphology samples 011 and 012. The primary packing of the post-hole was a friable, strong brown loamy sand and gravel, 094 (7.5 YR 4/6). 089, a friable dark reddish-brown silty sandy gravel (5 YR 3/2) was probably contiguous with this material. 088, above 089, was a lens of firm brown clay loam (10 YR 4/3). Between 094 and 089 was a steeply pitched post-pipe, composed of 037, a friable dark reddish-brown silty sand (5 YR 3/2). In thin section, this material was more horizontally bedded toward the top, perhaps indicating that the filling of the post void was more gradual at this point. Two lenses of silty brown sand, 218 and 220, lay above 037, while 014 was a silting into the top of the post void, made up of firm dark reddish-brown loamy sand (5 YR 2.5/2). Microscopically, context 014 contained a good deal of fragmentary charcoal, although not enough to suggest the burning of a post *in situ* (see Chapter 9). It is more likely that charcoal from fires burned nearby had been washed into the feature during the process of silting. The post in this feature had presumably rotted out.

Two-phase post-holes, and other post-holes in trenches A, AA and J

Feature 319/332 (Fig. 3.52, two sections)
This complex series of intercutting features was initiated by two large cuts, 332/413 and 246/319. Both of these can be identified as post-holes of the palisaded enclosure. The precise stratigraphic relationship between the two cuts was unclear, and their relative sequence could not be

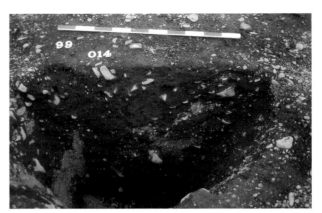

Figure 3.51 Post-hole of the 'western arc' of the inner post-ring 087

identified. The southernmost cut (413/332) had a primary fill of loose, very dark greyish brown sand with a very high gravel content, 336 (10 YR 3/2). This was sealed by 254, a layer of dark brown loamy sand, which probably represented weathering and/or silting (7.5 YR 3/2). In the more northerly cut (319/246) the primary fill was a friable dusky red loamy sand with much gravel, 406, which seemed to have been generated by the weathering of the sides of the feature (2.5 YR 3/2). Immediately above this was 328/367, a run of loose dark brown loamy sand and gravel (7.5 YR 3/3), and above this was a layer of slumped dark reddish-brown sandy loam, 405 (5 YR 3/4), which contained 315, a possible decayed turf composed of loose, very dark brown loamy sand (7.5 YR 2.5/3). This was sealed by 376/411, a friable dark brown loamy sand, constituting a further layer of collapse (7.5 YR 3/3). All of these layers of packing were truncated by a wide shallow cut (098/327/331/357/412). The principal fill of this cut was 097/333, a friable brown sandy silty loam with limited gravel content (7.5 YR 4/2), which appeared to have contained a small post. A very shallow layer of fine, sorted dark brown gravel, 346 (7.5 YR 3./3), lay over this fill in the central portion of the cut. Sealing this in turn was a thick layer of friable brown sandy silt loam containing appreciable amounts of gravel and pebbles (7.5 YR 4/3) (contexts 314/318/334/410). At the northern end, this was capped by 096/313, a friable, very dark brown loamy sand with small pebbles (7.5 YR 2.5/3). Three separate features cut into these fills, none of which were stratigraphically related to each other. Cut 355 was broad and shallow, at the southern end of the complex, and was filled with the collapsed packing 335, a loose very dark brown loamy sand with a few pebbles (7.5 YR 2.5/3), above which was a weathering layer of loose brown loamy sand 347 (7.5 YR 4/3). 235 was a post-pipe, descending through these fills. Cut 352 was a much smaller post-hole, with a single fill, 353, a friable brown sandy silt loam with some brown pebbles

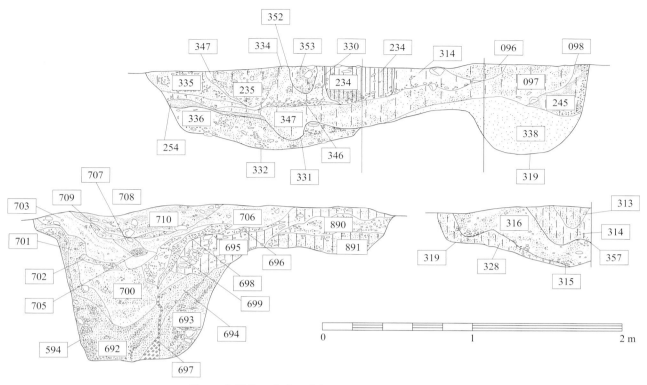

Figure 3.52 Post-holes of the inner post-ring: sections

(10 YR 4/3). Cut 415 was similar to 355, being broad and shallow. Its fills, 409, 408 and 407 were successive layers of packing, all brown sandy loams with small pebbles, while 234 was the fill of a post-pipe, a compact reddish-brown silt loam with coarse pebbles (5 YR 3/2), containing a darker patch which may have represented the trace of the post. Another small feature cut into the top of the complex was cut 460, which was small and shallow, and filled with layer 461, which held a small fragment of glass. The feature was presumably a modern intrusion.

Feature 579/619 (Figs. 3.53, 3.54, 3.55, 3.56, 3.57, 3.58)
579/619 was one of the most complex features on the site, and the process by which its character was identified is worth recounting in some detail. After the initial cleaning of Trench AA, the first element of the complex to be recognised was 512, a small dark post-hole. The cut of this feature was sub-circular and on excavation showed to be a shallow bowl-shape with concave edges, descending onto a steeper sloping base. 512 was filled with 506, a very dark greyish brown silty sand and charcoal deposit (10 YR 3/2) and 513, a dark yellowish-brown silty sand (10 YR 3/6) (not visible in section). In the course of excavation it became clear that 512 was cut into a much larger feature, whose fill was initially difficult to differentiate from the parent subsoil. This larger feature was of an appropriate size, morphology and location to

be one of the ramped post-holes of the inner palisade. The principal characteristic that facilitated its recognition was the presence of appreciable quantities of charcoal in its upper layers. The ramp of the large post-hole was filled with 537, an eroded yellowish-brown silty sand deposit (10 YR 5/4), and this contained several abraded sherds of Grooved Ware pottery (FG3 Vessel 2). Sherds from the same vessel were also recovered from pits 3074 and 3112. On excavation, the larger feature initially conformed to the expected character of a post-hole, although one with a disturbed and collapsed post-pipe. This impression was supported by the discovery of a large piece of charcoal at the base of the putative post-pipe. During excavation, this was conjectured to represent the remains of a burnt post, which might have snapped off as the rest of the upright was removed from its setting. The fills above the 'post' were very similar to the deposits encountered when a post had been removed by pushing it from side to side to loosen it from its setting: small lenses of interwoven deposits.

However, it was rapidly recognised that the feature was defined by two distinct cuts (579 and 619), and that the principal fills of the post-hole were loose and mixed, suggesting backfill rather than packing. 619 had been the first cut of the feature, and was initially filled with packing layers 611, a mixed yellowish-brown sand and charcoal layer (10 YR 5/4), and 686, a very dark brown sand and charcoal deposit (10 YR 2/2), presumably supporting an upright post. The ramp fills 601 (a dark yellowish-

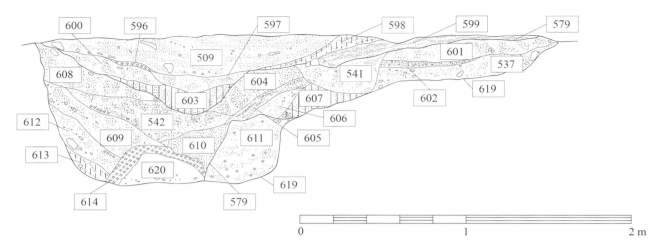

Figure 3.53 Post-hole 579/619 of the inner post-ring: section

Figure 3.54 Inner post-ring post-hole 579/619 after excavation

Figure 3.55 Inner post-ring post-hole 579/619 during excavation

Figure 3.56 Inner post-ring post-hole 579/619 during excavation

brown silty sand: 10 YR 4/4), 602 (a loose silty sand lens made up of dark yellowish-brown pea gravel: 10 YR 4/6) and 537 (a friable yellowish-brown silty sand: 10 YR 5/4) also belonged to this initial phase of activity. At some point, the feature had been extensively recut (cut 579), removing most of the initial fill. This activity can be assumed to have resulted in the removal of the post itself, whether it had been intact or rotted by this stage. Moreover, what had initially been identified as a possible post-pipe resolved itself into a distinct mound of charcoal, 614, whose grain ran in multiple directions, while the layers of backfill actually ran uninterrupted over the surface of this deposit: there was no true post-pipe (Fig. 3.58). The charcoal contained many tiny fragments of cremated bone (more likely to have been animal than human, but otherwise unidentifiable), and made up a dense layer rather than a single piece of burnt wood. The possibility was initially entertained that this deposit might have represented pyre material, and the presence of small grains of fine sand within the matrix suggested that it might have been burned at a location some distance from

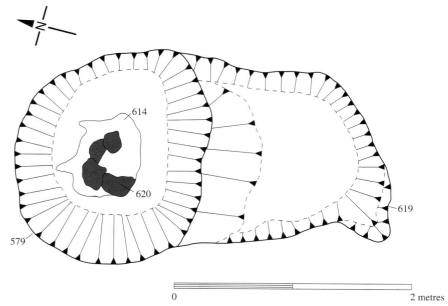

Figure 3.57 Plan of inner post-ring post-hole 579/619, showing sand mound 620

Figure 3.58 Inner post-ring post-hole 579/619 showing deposit 614/620

the Dunragit enclosure. A piece of prehistoric pottery was found directly underneath the charcoal layer (FN 1258, part of Fabric 3 Vessel 2, see Chapter 6). This sherd of plain Grooved Ware was in very good condition and showed little evidence of abrasion, by contrast with the sherds of the same vessel recovered from the post-ramp. The charcoal layer proved to have been deposited on a small mound of clean, very coarse light yellowish-brown sand (10 YR 6/4) (context 620). Immediately above the charcoal layer was 613, a loamy yellowish-brown sand layer with small gravel pieces (10 YR 5/6). This may have been a natural silting or collapse from the side of the feature, immediately before the purposeful backfilling of the entire post-hole began.

The deliberate backfill of the feature was made up of 14 layers of material, which probably accumulated in

a short space of time. There were, in sequence: 612, a yellowish-brown silty sand with various gravels (10 YR 5/6); 609, a silty dark yellowish-brown sand with medium gravel (10 YR 4/4); 610, a silty dark yellowish-brown sand with small pea grit, gravel and charcoal (10 YR 3/4); 607, a dark grey brown silty loam with medium gravel pieces (10 YR 4/2); 606, a yellowish-brown silty sand with pea grit gravel (10 YR 5/4); 605, a dark brown silty sand with small gravel pieces (10 YR 3/3); 542, a dark yellowish-brown silty sand with charcoal (10 YR 3/6); 608, a brown sandy silt with medium gravel pieces (10 YR 4/3); 604, a silty dark yellowish-brown sand with pea grit gravel (10 YR 3/6); 603, a dark yellowish-brown sandy loam with medium to large gravel pieces and charcoal (10 YR 3/6); 541, a yellowish-brown silty sand with small gravel pieces (10 YR 5/4); 600, a brown sandy silt with medium gravel pieces (10 YR 4/3); 597, a greyish-brown sandy silt (10 YR 5/2); 596, a very dark greyish-brown silty sand with charcoal (10 YR 3/2). It was at this point that the backfilling ceased and the feature was left open to weather and to silt up naturally. The natural silt deposits consisted of: 599, a very dark brown silty sand with large gravel pieces (10 YR 2/2); 598, a dark yellowish-brown loamy sand (10 YR 4/4); 509, a brown sandy silt with small gravel pieces and occasional larger pieces (10 YR 4/3).

Overall, then, the sequence for this feature was one in which a ramped post-hole was dug, and a post secured in place with packing deposits. The post was removed and the fill of the post-hole scoured out, before a small mound of clean sand was placed on the base of the resulting cut. A sherd of pottery was positioned on this mound, before a mass of wood charcoal containing fragments of burnt animal bone was poured onto its surface. The recut was

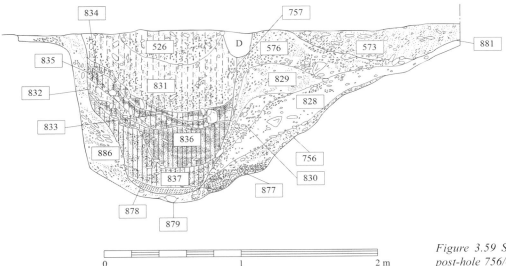

Figure 3.59 Section of inner post-ring post-hole 756/449

then backfilled with a series of heterogeneous layers, and as these began to settle, silting began to accumulate above them. Eventually, post-hole 512 was cut into the top of the feature.

Feature 594 (Fig. 3.52)
Feature 594 was a large, deep post-hole with a pronounced ramp on the southern side, and a slight lip on the northern. The post-hole was sub-circular, with steep sides and an abrupt break of slope on the upper edge. The base was relatively flat. In stratigraphic terms the earliest fills in the feature were the two layers of backfill in the ramp, 891, a loose, yellow-brown silty sand with many medium-sized pebbles (10 YR 5/6), and 890, a loose, dark yellowish-brown sandy loam with many small rounded pebbles (10 YR 3/6). On the southern side of the post-hole, context 693, a loose, dark yellowish-brown sandy loam (10 YR 3/4) with many pebbles and cobbles of various sizes, appeared to represent a block of undisturbed packing. This was butted up against 697, the burnt base of an oak post. This was probably a timber that had been charred before insertion in order to retard rotting, rather than one that had been burned *in situ*, as there were few more extensive traces of fire in the feature. Context 694 was a sandy loam essentially similar to 693 below it, but had slumped forward and become somewhat disturbed. 692, to the north of the post-base, was a more displaced deposit of post-packing and weathering material, composed of friable dark yellowish-brown (10 YR 3/6) sandy silt with many small and medium pebbles. Layer 701, a tenacious dark yellowish-brown (10 YR 3/4) silt, dipped across the surface of 692, representing a rapid weathering event immediately after the collapse or removal of the post, leaving the burnt trace in place. The remainder of the post void was filled by 700, a friable dark brown (7.5 YR 3/4) sandy silt. Loose dark yellowish-brown (10 YR 4/3) sandy silt 702 formed a lens across the surface of this

Figure 3.60 Feature 756/449 under excavation

material. At the base of the ramp, 695 consisted of a slump of loose dark yellowish-brown (10 YR 4/4) sandy loam with many pebbles. This material rested unconformably on the ramp-fills 890 and 891, and it might be argued that 695 and 694 represented the fill of a recut, which also truncated the primary post-packing deposit, 693. This would make feature 594 a two-phase post-hole, like others immediately nearby. However, on balance it seems likely that the truncation of the ramp-fills was actually a consequence of the collapse and slumping of the various layers of packing as the post rotted out. Further lenses of gravel, 696, 698 and 699, slid across the surface of 695, before loose sandy silts 703, 705, 706, 707, 708 and 709 effectively filled the top of the feature. These may simply have been the product of weathering and erosion, but it is more probable that they represented a deliberate backfill of the uppermost part of the post-hole. The loose, dark yellowish-brown (10 YR 3/4) sandy silt 710 represented a silting into the settled basin at the top of the post-hole. It seems that unlike feature 826 close by it, 594 may have been a single-phase post-hole. If so, it is possible that the posts of the inner ring structure were more closely set in one of its two phases of construction.

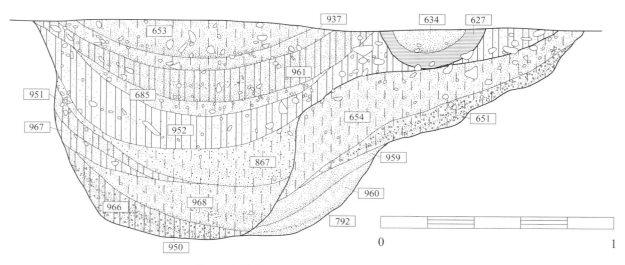

Figure 3.61 Section of inner post-ring post-hole 792

Figure 3.62 Inner post-ring post-hole 792, showing section

Feature 756/449 (Figs. 3.59, 3.60 and 3.65)

Feature 756/449 was one of the post-holes of the inner post-ring in which the recutting and replacement of the original post was most plainly marked. 756 was the cut of a large ramped sub-circular post-hole, with an abrupt break of slope and near-vertical, slightly stepped edge on the northern side, and a gradual ramp descending to the base of the feature on the south. The basal fill of the feature was 879, a loose, strong brown sand (7.5 YR 5/8), which represented silting or collapse immediately after the initial cutting of the post-hole. The ramp was packed with 877, a loose dark yellowish-brown sand (10 YR 3/6), stratigraphically equivalent with the slumped primary packing of the main post-hole, 880, a loose dark yellowish-brown sand (10 YR 4/6) containing many coarse pebbles and larger cobbles. A series of slumps of material similar to 880 lay in lenses over the ramp fill, varying only slightly in their composition: 828, 829, 830 and 576. There represented slipped and disturbed packing deposits. A poorly defined feature of some kind, 881, later cut through the ramp deposits, filled with 573, a friable yellowish-brown silt with a few cobbles and charcoal flecks (10 YR 3/6). All of the earlier fills were

truncated by the major recut 757, a bowled or U-shaped cut without a clear ramp, which descended almost to the base of the original feature. In the very bottom of this recut was a layer of charcoal, 878, and it was conjectured that this might have been connected with the insertion of a previously charred post.

Above the charcoal lens, the principal lower packing of the secondary post-hole was 837, a friable dark brown sandy silt loam (10 YR 3/3). Above this, the friable very dark brown sandy silt loam 836 was probably a collapsed post-pipe (10 YR 2/2). This material was covered by 835, a friable dark brown sandy loam with many fine pebbles and much charcoal (7.5 YR 3/4). Other lenses of collapsed packing, 832, 834 and 833 lay beneath the more substantial deposit 831, a friable dark yellowish-brown loamy sand with many fine pebbles (10 YR 4/6). This deposit contained numerous clear tip-lines, indicating the collapse of the upper layers of packing following the rotting-out of the post. This material was cut by rabbit burrow 882, with fill 827. The uppermost layer in the main post-hole was 526, a friable, dark yellowish-brown loamy sand (10 YR 4/4), representing slumping and silting into the post void of the recut post-hole. In 1999, the end of the ramp of this feature had been identified extending into Trench A, and given the cut number 449.

Feature 792 (Figs. 3.61 and 3.62)

792 was the cut of a large, ramped sub-circular post-hole, which had clearly been recut on a single occasion. Its southern side was near vertical and undercut, while on the northern side the ramp descended through two distinct breaks of slope. The base was flat, and the feature was rather shallower than other post-holes of the inner palisade ring. The primary fill was 960, a loose strong brown sand with fine pebbles (7.5 YR 4/6), and above this were 959, a loose dark brown sand with many

pebbles (7.5 YR 3/4), 651, a loose dark reddish-brown loamy sand with fine pebbles (5 YR 3/3), and 654, a friable dark reddish-brown loamy sand (5 YR 3/2). The latter two deposits extended into the post-ramp. These deposits together constituted the packing of the primary post-hole. They were all concentrated on the northern side of the feature, for on the southern side all of the primary packing had been removed by a major recut, 950, which had truncated all of the layers described above. In the base of the recut, concentrated on the southern side was 966, a friable dark yellow sandy silt loam with many small pebbles (10 YR 3/6), probably representing an initial silting into the newly cut feature. The subsequent layers of fill suggest a series of lenses of backfill, thrown in from different directions. The earliest of these was 968, a loose brown sandy loam with small pebbles (7.5 YR 3/3), a body of fill that was concentrated on the northern side of the recut. This in turn lay below 967, a friable dark brown silt loam with a few pebbles (10 YR 3/3), and 951, a lens on the northern side of the feature composed of loose dark grey-brown sandy silt with many small pebbles (2.5 Y 4/2). 867, a loose dark brown loamy sand with many small pebbles and much charcoal (7.5 YR 3/3) lay above this. 867 was sealed by the more extensive deposit 952, a friable dark greyish brown silt (2.5 Y 4/2) containing many fine pebbles, which extended into the post-ramp. Layer 685 was a loose, dark reddish-brown loamy sand with much charcoal (5 YR 3/3), with a notably greasy organic texture. It contained thirty-four sherds from three Grooved Ware vessels (FG3 Vessel 4, FG7 Vessel 1 and FG9 vessel 2) and flints including a core, numerous flakes and a fabricator (see Chapter 6). There was also a great deal of burnt flint in context 685, including a number of conjoining burnt flakes, which would appear to represent a deliberate deposit (see Chapter 7). There was no obvious trace of a post or post-pipe in this recut, and its morphology may suggest either that the post was withdrawn, or than no post had ever been inserted into the recut feature. If the latter, then this feature should be compared with 579/619, in which the recut of the post-hole received not a post but an elaborate deposit. A probable weathering surface, 937, was composed of loose dark yellowish-brown sandy gravel (10 YR 4/4), and resting above this thin layer was a silting into the top of the feature, 653, a compact very dark brown sandy loam (7.5 YR 2.5/2). These final fills were cut by a small bowl-shaped feature, 939, with a primary fill of friable black charcoal, 627, and a main fill of friable very dusky red silty sand with small pebbles, 634. This latter contained a fine oblique arrowhead, FN1214.

Feature 825/826 (Figs. 3.63 and 3.64)
826 was a large ramped post-hole of the first inner post-ring, with an edge that was somewhat weathered back at the top, was near vertical on the north, and had a gradual ramp on the southern side. The northern end of the feature

was nearly circular, and the base was flat. The primary fill was 824, a loose mottled brown (10 YR 4/3) sandy gravel. This was an extensive deposit of packing material, remarkably clean and recognisably bedded. In the south of the post-hole this material was compact and had a very straight and abrupt interstice with the layers above. It is possible that this was a result of the original post having been laid on this surface immediately prior to its erection, with backfill having been immediately thrown in on top. However, in places layer 824 lay above 949, a body of loose dark yellowish-brown (10 YR 4/4) sand and gravel, which apparently represented an early collapse of material from the edge of the feature. The post-pipe for this post was represented by 820, a friable to loose dark yellowish-brown (7.5 YR 3/4) sandy loam with pebbles, into which a patch of gravel from the packing, 833, had slid. Further layers of packing thrown in around the post were represented by 822, a loose dark yellowish-brown loamy sandy gravel (10 YR 4.6), which was distinctly bedded and contained lenses of less stony material, and 648, a loose to friable yellowish-brown (10 YR 5/6) sandy loam/gravel, which extended into the post-ramp. The uppermost lenses of gravel packing in the post-hole (821, 642 and 640) were interspersed with layers of charcoally material (641 and 650). All of these packing deposits above 824 appeared to be somewhat disturbed, slipping towards the centre of the feature, perhaps as a consequence of the rotting out of the first post.

These packing layers were cut through and truncated by 825, the cut of a second post-hole, which had no ramp. This recut feature is considered to have been an element of the second inner post-ring. The cut was deep and straight-sided, and somewhat splayed back at the top. It was circular in plan, with a slightly bowled base. The primary filling of the recut was 817, a loose to friable dark yellowish-brown (10 YR 4/6) sandy loam, above which was the gravelly packing 814, a very loose strong brown sandy gravel, and 643, a dense, friable very dark brown (7.5 YR 2.5/2) sandy loam, much less stony than 814. These layers butted up against the post-pipe of the second post. 819, a thin layer of charcoal, defined the outer surface of the post itself (not visible in section), and it is imagined that this represented the charred end of the post, which had been burned prior to insertion in order to preserve it from rotting. The subsequent fills of the post-pipe can be understood as having slipped into the post void as it rotted from the inside outward. Of these, 818 and 815 were both loose to friable bodies of dark brown sandy loam (10 YR 3/3), which bracketed 816, a lens of charcoal-rich dark brown sandy loam. Above these were 813 and 827, patches of loose, gritty yellowish sandy gravel (10 YR 5/6) that had collapsed into the post void. These in turn were sealed by 812, a loose dark yellowish-brown (10 YR 4/4) silty loam, and the charcoal lens 811. All of these units had clearly slipped from north to south, and into the space left by

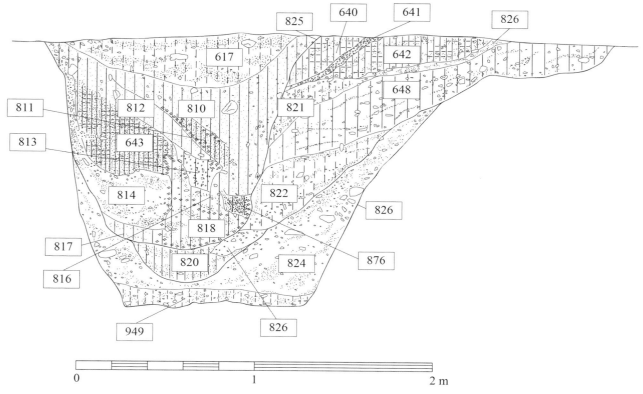

Figure 3.63 Section of inner post-ring post-hole 825/826

Figure 3.64 Inner post-ring post-hole 825/826

the rotting post. Much of the upper part of the post-hole was then filled by 810, a friable brown (10 YR 4/3) silty loam, which was considerably less stony than any of the collapsed packing. Finally, 617, a friable to compact dark brown (7.5 YR 3/3) loamy sand, represented a lens of settling and compaction into the top of the feature.

Feature 4011 (Fig. 3.65)

Feature 4011 was a shallow sub-rounded post-hole. It had concave sides dipping to a flat base. The single packing fill of the feature was 4009, a loose dark brown loamy sand (10 YR 3/3). This feature was notably similar to

4012, which was located beside it. In both cases the fill of the feature was unitary and homogeneous, so that it is not easy to say whether the post had rotted or been withdrawn. In this part of Trench J, smaller post-holes including 4011 and 4012 were located between the larger posts of the inner palisade ring, a phenomenon that had not been observed in Trenches A and AA. This may mean that there were lesser posts, now entirely eroded away, throughout the inner circuit, or, perhaps more likely, that there was a screen framed by lesser posts in this short stretch, and free-standing large posts elsewhere.

Feature 4012 (Fig. 3.65)

Feature 4012 was a very shallow, and presumably truncated, sub-rounded post-hole. The cut had steep sides and a flat base. The principal packing fill was 4010, a loose dark brown sandy loam (10 YR 3/3). This feature was similar to the nearby 4011, another 'lesser post'.

Feature 4018 (Fig. 3.65)

4018 was the cut of sub-circular post-hole, with steep straight sides descending to a rounded base. In size, it appeared intermediate between the 'major' posts of the inner post-ring and the very small posts such as 4011 and 4012. The basal fill of the feature was 4024, a loose to friable dark brown silty sand (7.5 YR 3/4) with some gravel. This deposit was probably the product of collapse and natural silting within the feature soon after

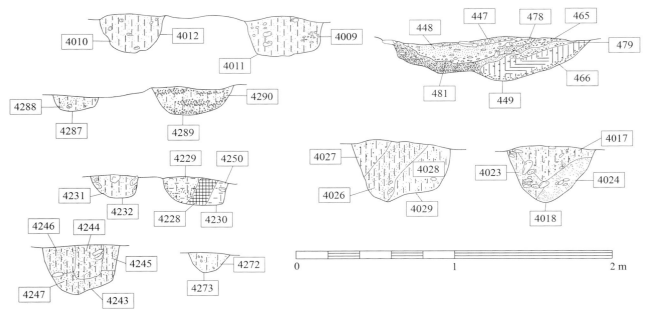

Figure 3.65 Post-holes of the inner post-ring: sections

it was opened. This was sealed beneath 4023, a friable dark yellow-brown loamy sand (10 YR 3/4) containing large pebbles, which probably represented the remnant of collapsed packing material. Above this was 4017, a friable dark yellow-brown loamy sand (10 YR 3/4) with medium/ small pebbles. This deposit may have represented material that filled the post-pipe of a post that had rotted out, although it did appear somewhat disturbed, and it is possible that the post had been withdrawn.

Feature 4029 (Fig. 3.65)

4029 was the cut of a rounded post-hole, with steep straight sides dropping to a flat base. Like post-hole 4018, it appeared to be intermediate in size. The basal fill was 4027, a friable dark yellowish-brown sandy loam (10 YR 3/6) containing small pea gravel. This was probably the principal packing around a post. 4028, a friable dark yellowish-brown sandy loam (10 YR 3/6) with small pea gravel was very similar in character. 4026 was evidently the post-pipe, composed of a dark-coloured friable sandy loam (10 YR 2/1) with a few small gravel pieces. The timber had probably decayed *in situ*, as the post-pipe was quite clear, and the deposits lacked the degree of disruption associated with post withdrawal.

Feature 4145/4173 (Figs. 3.66 and 3.67)

4145 was the original cut of very large inner ring post-hole, which was ramped on its northern edge. The feature had two distinct phases, with 4145 succeeded by 4173, a clear recutting episode. The primary feature had a distinct post-pipe and the possible remains of a charred post, but the later cut appeared to have had its post removed. 4145 had steep straight edges and a gently bowled base. It was

filled with 4141/4142, a friable dark yellow-brown sandy loam (10 YR 3/6) containing a few pebbles. This was probably a deposit of packing material. It was similar to 4135, a loose dark yellow-brown sandy loam (10 YR 3/6) containing some mixed pebbles. Within these packing fills were two vertical charcoal deposits, which appeared to represent the remains of post. These were 4143, a loose/ friable black charcoal within matrix of burnt soil (5 YR 2.5/1) and 4144, an identical deposit on the southern edge. 4132 was a loose dusky red sandy loam (2.5 YR 3/3) with many small pebbles and occasional flecks of charcoal, which lay above these packing deposits. 4132 had apparently slumped from the northern side of the feature into the post void, and presumably itself represented displaced packing. On the southern side, slump deposits were represented by 4134, a loose dark red-brown sandy loam (5 YR 3/4) with numerous mixed pebbles and 4133, a loose red-brown sandy loam (5 YR 4/4) with medium-sized pebbles. This latter is likely to have been re-deposited natural subsoil, which had eroded into the feature.

The ramp for the first phase of the post-hole had a gradual, irregular slope running north/south. Its primary fill was 4129, a loose red-brown sand (5 YR 4/4) with profuse tightly packed small to medium pebbles. Other, later ramp deposits were 4131, a loose dark brown sandy loam (7.5 YR 3/4) with many small pebbles, and above this 4130, a loose dark red sand (2.5 YR 4/6) with numerous mixed pebbles. These both appeared to be deliberately backfilled deposits intended to fill in the ramp and support the post, as both flowed into the post-hole and overlay the primary packing deposits. Above these ramp packing deposits was 4128, a compacted black charcoal

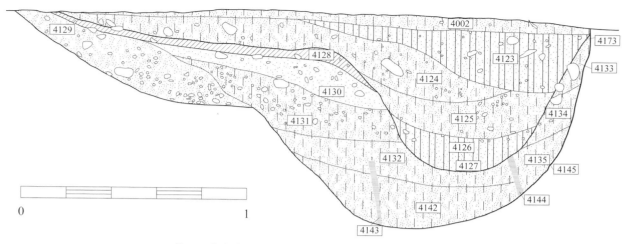

Figure 3.66 Section of inner post-ring post-hole 4145/4173

Figure 3.67 Inner post-ring post-hole 4145/4173

layer (5 YR 2.5/1). It was not clear whether this was in some way connected with the charred post, or related to the preparation of the ground for the construction of the second phase of the post-ring.

The second phase of the feature began with cut 4173, which also took the form of a ramped post-hole (with its ramp aligned north/south). If the second feature had contained a post, it appeared to have been removed by rocking it out of place. This was suggested by the disturbed character of the fills within the post-hole. The secondary feature had a more rounded profile than 4145. The layers of disturbed packing or backfill within the post-hole were 4127, a loose reddish black sandy loam (2.5 YR 2.5/1); 4126, a loose dark yellow-brown sandy loam (10 YR 3/4) with medium pebbles; 4125, a friable dark reddish-brown sandy loam (5 YR 3/2) with numerous small pebbles; 4124, a loose dark yellow-brown sand loam (10 YR 3/4); and 4123, a friable dark brown sandy loam (7.5 YR 3/4) with a few pebbles. These five deposits were interdigitated and slumped inward from the edges of the feature, giving the impression that they

had collapsed when the post had been removed. Deposit 4124 extended into the ramp, possibly suggesting that its disposition was connected with the dragging out of the post. Above these layers was 4002, a natural silting deposit that had accumulated after the post had been removed, and this indicates a stabilisation of the feature.

Feature 4230 (Fig. 3.65)
4230 was the sub-circular cut of a small post-hole, with steep straight edges dipping to a rounded base. The principal fill was 4229, a friable brown sandy clay loam with occasional pebbles (10 YR 5/3). This was probably a packing deposit, and was contiguous with 4250, a friable dark brown sandy clay loam (10 YR 3/3). Between these two deposits lay 4228, a compact black sandy clay loam (10 YR 2/1) principally composed of charcoal. This probably represented the remains of a charred post.

Feature 4232 (Fig. 3.65)
4232 was the cut of a small sub-circular post-hole situated close to 4230, with steep straight sides and a rounded base. Its single fill was 4231, a compact dark grey sandy loam with frequent small pebbles (10 YR 4/1).

Feature 4233 (Fig. 3.83)
4233 was a small sub-circular post-hole, with steep straight edges and a rounded base. The basal fill was 4237, a loose very dark brown sandy loam (7.5 YR 2.5/3) containing many small pebbles. This layer was probably packing material at the base of the feature. Above this was a further packing deposit, 4235/4236, a hard, dark yellowish-brown sand (10 YR 3/6) containing a great deal of gravel. 4234, a loose, very dark greyish-brown loamy sand (2.5 YR 3/2) with a few pebbles, represented the truncated remains of a post-pipe, indicating that the post had rotted out.

Feature 4243 (Fig. 3.65)

4243 was the cut of circular post-hole feature of intermediate size, with steep straight edges on to a rounded base. The basal fill was 4247, a loose dark brown sandy loam containing a number of large stones (10 YR 3/3), probably representing packing or stabilising material at the base of the feature. Above this was 4245, a friable dark yellowish-brown sandy loam containing numerous medium-sized stones (10 YR 3/4), probable packing material. This material was similar to 4246, a friable very dark brown sandy loam with many medium-sized pebbles (7.5 YR 2.5/3). Between these two deposits lay 4244, a friable olive loamy sand with occasional small pebbles (5 YR 4/4). This is likely to have represented the remains of the post-pipe, indicating a post that had rotted out.

Feature 4273 (Fig. 3.65)

4273 was the cut of a very small irregular post-hole, lying slightly to the north of the inner palisade ring. It had steep sides that dipped toward a concave base. Its single fill was 4272, a friable dark greyish brown sandy loam with a few medium-sized pebbles (10 YR 4/2).

Feature 4287 (Fig. 3.65)

4287 was the cut of a small sub-oval feature, with concave edges descending to a flat base. It was clearly heavily truncated. Its fill was 4288, a friable brown sandy loam with occasional medium pebbles (10 YR 4/3).

Feature 4289 (Fig. 3.65)

4289 was the cut of a shallow sub-oval feature close by 4287, with concave edges descending to a rounded base. This feature was heavily truncated. Its fill was 4290, a friable dark yellowish-brown sandy loam with frequent small gravel pieces (10 YR 4/6).

'Eastern Arc' of the Inner Post-ring

Feature 046 (Fig. 3.68)

046 was the oval cut of large but relatively shallow post-hole with gradual sides and a concave base, whose primary fill was 020, a friable dark brown sandy clay (7.5 YR 3.3), which contained a number of packing stones. A further layer of packing, 042, a friable dark brown sandy clay (7.5 YR 3/3) with more stones overlay this. The top of the feature was filled with 008, another friable very dark brown sandy clay (7.5 YR 2.5/3), containing fewer stones than 042, but including fragments of charcoal. This was clearly a single-phase feature, with no indication of recutting. The bedding of the fills suggests that if the feature had held a post, it may have been withdrawn, as there was no trace of a post-pipe.

Feature 054/057 (Figs. 3.68 and 3.69)

The primary cut of this feature, 057, was shallow and ragged, with a flat base. It was packed with loose brown sandy gravel 056 (7.5 YR 4/5), above which was a silting of loose to friable dark brown silty sand, 055 (7.5 YR 3/2). The whole was cut by the deeper, more regular cut 054, which appeared to be a palisade post-hole, and was packed with 053, a loose to friable dark brown sandy gravel (7.5 YR 3/4). Above this was a layer of silting, 052, a friable yellowish red sandy silt (5 YR 4/6), which contained a single sherd of Grooved Ware pottery (FG3 V1). Immediately above this was a collapse of gravel from the unstable east edge of the feature, 051, a loose to friable brown sandy gravel (7.5 YR 4/4). Finally, a dark silting of friable brown silty clay loam (7.5 YR 4/4), 023, capped the feature. This could potentially represent a sequence of two withdrawn posts, one cutting the other, although the character of the primary feature is less clear, and may not have been related to the palisade enclosure at all.

Feature 215 (Figs. 3.68, 3.70 and 3.71)

215 was the primary cut of a large post-hole, round to oval in plan with straight sides which had weathered back at the top. The north side was more gradual, perhaps suggesting that it had formed a ramp for the insertion of the post, or had been battered back by post removal. Soil micromorphology samples 021 and 022 were taken from this feature. The primary fill 251/253 was a loose, yellowish-red, slightly silty sand (5 YR 4/6), probably representing a single event of silting immediately after the cutting of the post-hole. Above this was a residual gravel packing 250/252, of loose to friable, strong brown to dark brown sandy gravel (mottled 7.5 YR 4/6 to 3/4) containing many small rounded pebbles. This was cut by 217, the ragged surface of disturbance caused by the digging out of the post, into which a number of layers of material had collapsed. In thin section, this cut was represented by a change in soil density (see Chapter 9 below). The lowest of the fills within this cut was 216, a friable dark reddish-brown sandy loam (5 YR 2.5/2), which slumped down over the northern side of the post-pull. Within this matrix, and resting on the underlying gravel was a deposit of cremated bone (defined as context 227), in a compact mass 40 by 20 centimetres in extent. The cremation deposit appeared to consist entirely of burnt bone, without ashes and with only a small quantity of possible pyre material. The cremated remains were later identified as those of a young woman, aged over 16, together with the fragmentary burnt remains of a sheep-sized animal (see Chapter 8 below). The burnt bone produced a radiocarbon date of 2869 to 2580 Cal BC (at 95.4% probability). It is possible that context 216 represented a deliberate throw of backfill to cover the cremated bone. The main body of the post-pull fill was 214, a loose to friable dark reddish-brown dirty sandy gravel, which contained patches and lenses of more loamy or gravely material (5 YR 3/3) (this material was sampled for soil micromorphological analysis, Samples 021 and 022, see

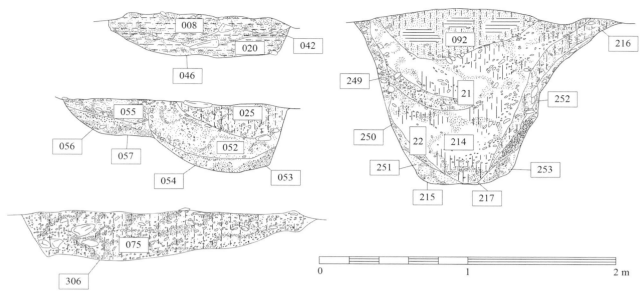

Figure 3.68 Post-holes of the 'eastern arc' of the inner post-ring: sections

Figure 3.69 Post-hole of the 'eastern arc' of the inner post-ring 054/057

Figure 3.70 Post-hole of the 'eastern arc' of the inner post-ring 215, showing section

Figure 3.71 Post-hole of the 'eastern arc' of the inner post-ring 215

Chapter 9). Several clear tip-lines seemed to be evident, although subsequent analysis suggests that these may have been the consequence of post-depositional leaching. One lens of gravel was defined as a separate context, 249, a loose to friable dark reddish-brown sandy gravel (mottled 5 YR 3/2 to 3/4). However, this simply represented a part of the overall collapse of material into the post-pull, which might have represented a deliberate backfill. Above the stabilisation of 214 was a layer of silting, 092, a friable dark brown silty clay loam with a few small rounded pebbles and charcoal flecks (7.5 YR 3/4).

Feature 306 (Fig. 3.68)

306 was the cut of a large shallow post-hole with sharp break of slope, vertical sides and a flat base. The single

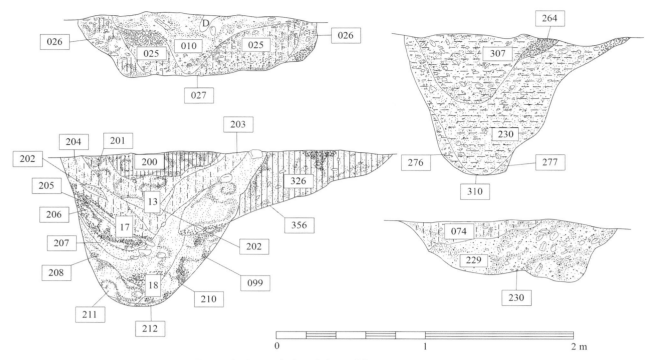

Figure 3.72 Post-holes of the middle post-ring: sections

fill 075 had been heavily disturbed by root penetration and animal burrowing, and consisted of a loose, very dark brown loamy sand with small and medium-sized stones (7.5 YR 2.5/2). There was no sign of a post-pipe, and it is possible that the post had been withdrawn.

The middle post-ring of the palisaded enclosure

The major middle ring post-holes were more likely to be associated with smaller features than those of the inner ring. These were generally smaller than the lesser post-holes present in a short stretch of the inner post-ring within Trench J. The smaller middle ring post-holes were particularly evident in Trench J and the western part of Trench AA. It is probable that the presence of these more diminutive features indicates that the middle ring was, throughout much of its length, a continuous feature of some sort, perhaps with horizontal elements held in place by the smaller posts and forming a screen or fence. Some of the larger posts of the middle ring had been withdrawn, but a slightly larger proportion had rotted out. A few of the smaller post-holes had clear post-pipes, and their posts had therefore rotted, but none had obviously been withdrawn. However, the great majority of the smaller post-holes had homogeneous single-context fills, which might equally denote a post that had been pulled out or one that had decayed *in situ*. Indeed, in some cases only the lowest portion of the post-hole had survived the erosion

of the subsoil, and little trace of any post-pipe may have existed at this depth. Some of the larger post-holes of the middle ring had vestigial post-ramps, but the features were generally somewhat smaller than the post-holes of the inner ring, particularly those in Trenches A and AA. It was also notable that none of the middle ring post-holes had the very complex stratigraphic sequences found on the eastern side of the inner ring. Several of the features contained clear post-pipes, or even the charred ends of posts, and some posts had apparently been withdrawn. However, none of the post-stumps appeared to have been dug out, and none of the post-holes had recuts containing placed deposits of any kind. The evidence for post-removal was therefore more equivocal than for some of the inner ring post-holes, and took the form of disturbed, homogenised packing deposits and layers of backfill. The middle post-ring was therefore a single-phase construction, in contrast with the inner ring, and was at least partially dismantled, with some of the larger posts having been withdrawn, probably by rocking and pulling rather than digging-out. With the conspicuous exception of a stone axe from feature 4110 and two sherds of pottery from post-hole 896, few of the post-holes of the middle ring contained any artefacts at all, whether deposited by accident or by design. In this respect the middle ring post-holes again contrasted with the inner ring.

Feature 027 (Fig. 3.72)
A large, round cut of moderate depth with relatively rounded sides and a flat base, 027, contained the primary

Figure 3.73 Middle post-ring post-hole 099

first fill above this was 210, a loose, dark yellowish-brown sand on the southern side of the feature, represented an undisturbed packing deposit (10 YR 3/4). 211, on the northern side of the section was a deposit of packing, a loose reddish-brown silty sand (5 YR 4/4), which may have collapsed into the post-pipe after the post had rotted out. Above 210 was 209, a fill which extended into the post-ramp, made up of firm dark brown silty sand with pea grit and a number of large stones (7.5 YR 3/5). It is possible that this material had also slumped forward out of the ramp after the post had rotted out. Fill 208, in the centre of the feature above 209 was a loose, reddish-brown silty sand (5 YR 4/3), which probably represented disturbed or slumped packing, which had again tumbled into the post void. 207, the lens above this was a loose, dark reddish-brown silty sand (5 YR 3/3), and above this was 206, a friable dark brown sandy silt (7.5 YR 3/3). Above this in turn was 205, a loose brown sandy loam with fine gravel (10 YR 4/3). These lenses, and the more extensive 204 (a friable dark greyish brown silty loam: 2.5 YR 4/2) had all collapsed from north to south, into the post void. Much the same could be said for 203, a friable dark greyish-brown silty loam (2.5 YR 4/2), while 202 was a small lens of loose reddish-brown sand (5 YR 6/4). Above this, 201 was a loose dark yellowish-brown loamy sand (10 YR 3/4), and the final fill was 200, a firm dark yellowish-brown loamy sand (10 YR 3/4). The sequence as a whole suggests the packing and rotting out of a post, followed by a series of collapses from the sides of the feature into the resulting cavity, and finally by the silting of 201 and 200 into the top of the feature. Microscopic study of the silting deposits in the upper part of 099 revealed appreciably less small charcoal than in the post-holes of the inner ring, and this may be an important indication of the distribution of activity within the enclosure (see Chapter 9).

Feature 230 (Fig. 3.72)
Context 230 was the cut of a post-hole of moderate depth with a slanting base and steep sides, with a primary fill of loose brown stony sand, 229 (7.5 YR 3/4). Above this was a fill of friable yellowish-red sandy loam flecked with charcoal 064 (5 YR 4/6). It is unclear whether the latter represented the fill of a post removal or a silting into the top of the feature, but there was no clear evidence of a post-pipe.

Feature 255 (Fig. 3.74)
255 was the cut of an oval, medium-sized post-hole with sides a little off vertical and a flat base, with a primary packing of friable dark greyish-brown sandy clay loam 267 (10 YR 4/2). Two lenses of brown sand, 265 and 266 lay above this (both 10 YR 4/3). The principal fill of the feature was 243, a friable, dark reddish-grey loamy sand (5 YR 4/2). This may have been a silting into the void of a withdrawn post.

fill 026, a friable dark brown silty sand (5 YR 3/4), a comparatively organic deposit concentrated around the edge of the feature. This was probably material thrown in as part of the packing, although it may have been altered subsequent to its deposition. Above this was 025, a friable dark brown silty clay loam containing a good deal of gravel (7.5 YR 3/3), concentrated in the southern part of the cut. The uppermost fill was 010, a friable, dusky red silty sand (2.5 YR 3/4), which dipped in toward the centre of the feature. This would seem to have been a silting into the top of the feature following the decay of the post. The dip in the surface of 025 suggests a post the rotted out, but it is possible that the upright had been rocked out of its position.

Feature 099 (Figs. 3.72 and 3.73)
The cut of large, deep post-hole, 099, had sides weathered from the vertical and a rounded base, and had a clear ramp on the western (inner) side. Soil micromoroplogy samples 013, 017 and 018 were taken from this feature. The primary fill, 212, was a patch of firm, dark brown silty sand with many small pebbles (7.5 YR 3/3), concentrated in the very bottom of the post-hole, and represented an event of silting soon after the cutting of the feature. The

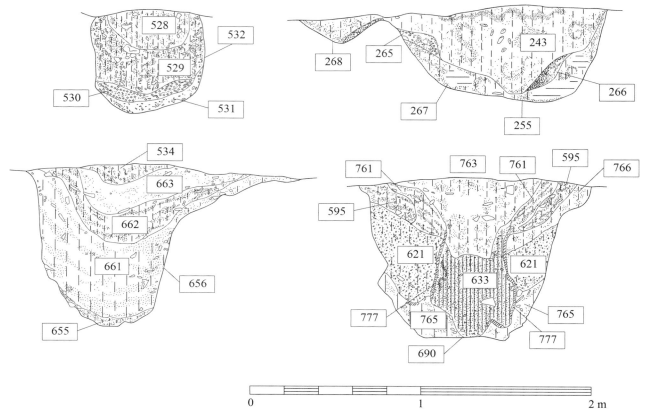

Figure 3.74 Post-holes of the middle post-ring: sections

Feature 310 (Fig. 3.72)

310 was the cut of a large, steep-sided oval post-hole, which contained two layers of packing material. 276/277 was a friable, dark brown sandy clay (7.5 YR 3/3). Above this was 312, a mass of friable dark brown silty clay with a great deal of fine to coarse gravel (7.5 YR 3/3). This probably represented the filling of a post-removal feature. Above 312 was a small lens of loose dark brown loamy sand and gravel 264 (2.5 YR 3/3), which presumably resulted from a collapse from the side of the feature. The uppermost fill was 307, a friable, dark olive-brown sandy clay (2.5 YR 3/3), which constituted a silting into the top of the post void.

Feature 532 (Fig. 3.74)

532 was a deep round cut with an abrupt edge and bowled base, which was slightly undercut in places, and which contained the primary filling 531, a compact dark brown gravel (7.5 YR 3/3). This was probably the primary packing of the post-hole. Above this was 530, a compact layer of black charcoal and loamy sand (7.5 YR 2.5/1). This may have represented the remains of a post that had been partially charred before being inserted into the ground. Above this was 529, a compact and very dark brown loamy sand (7.5 YR 2.5/2), which probably constituted a collapsed packing. Its homogeneity suggests

that the post may have been withdrawn, leaving only the charred tip behind, although it is also possible that the post rotted away leaving no trace as the packing slumped forward to replace it. Finally, 528 was the uppermost fill, composed of a compact dark yellowish-brown (10 YR 3/4) loamy sand. This suggests that packing material had settled into the top of the feature after the post had rotted out or been removed.

Feature 656 (Fig. 3.74)

656 was the cut of a ramped post-hole, with a graded break of slope and vertical sides. This contained a primary fill of friable black (10 YR 2/1) loamy sand (655) probably representing silting or collapse from the sides of the feature before or during the erection of the post, above which was 661, a friable brown (7.5 YR 4/4) loamy sand with flecks of charcoal, which appeared to represent a slumped post packing. Above this was 662, a friable very dark brown (10 YR 2/2) loamy sand, which in turn lay beneath 663, a friable dark brown sandy loam (7.5 YR 3/4). In the top of the cut feature was 534, a friable dark brown (7.5 YR 3/2) loamy sand with charcoal flecks. This single-phase post-hole lacked a clear post-pipe, and the most extensive body of fill, 661, was relatively homogeneous, with subsequent layers dipping down toward the centre of the feature. It may be that a

Figure 3.75 Middle post-ring post-hole 690

rotted post had left no appreciable sign of its presence, and the packing simply collapsed as it decayed. But it seems equally likely that the post was withdrawn, leaving a deflated pass of homogenised packing whose surface was filled by later deposits.

Feature 690 (Figs. 3.74 and 3.75)

690 was the cut of a large post-hole, with a flat base, sloping sides, and a clearly defined ramp. The primary fill was 765, a tenacious dark yellowish-brown (10 YR 5/4) sandy loam with numerous pebbles, above which was 621, a loose, yellowish-brown (7.5 YR 4/6) loamy sand with many small rolled pebbles. These, together with lenses 595 (friable yellow-brown loamy sand, 2.5 YR 2.5/3), 761 (compact dark brown loamy sand, 7.5 YR 3/2) and 766 (compact dark yellowish-brown loamy sand, 10 YR 5/4) represented the packing of the post-hole, surrounding the post-pipe. Within the post-pipe itself, 777 was a dense layer of charcoal, interpreted as the trace of a post that had been charred before insertion. Within this post-shadow was 633, a hard brown (2.5 YR 2.5/2) silt loam containing numerous pebbles, evidently material that had filled the rotting post. 763, above this, was a hard, strong brown loamy sand (7.5 YR 4/6), which represented silting and compaction into the top of the post void.

Feature 860 (Fig. 3.76)

860 was an oval post-hole cut, with near-vertical sides and a concave base. In the western side of the feature,

861 represented a patch of friable, very dark brown silty clay loam (7.5 YR 2.5/3), beneath 862, a loose strong brown sand containing numerous small pebbles (7.5 YR 5/6) and 868, a friable very dark brown sandy silt loam containing a few small stones (7.5 YR 2.5/3). All of these layers tipped from west to east, but 868 above them was concentrated in the eastern part of the feature, and represented a patch of tenacious strong brown silty clay with very little gravel (7.5 YR 5/8). This lay beneath 865, a tenacious, very dark brown silty clay with much charcoal (7.5 YR 3/2). These two deposits probably attest the presence of a charred post, although the fill above them, 770, was a homogeneous backfill of friable brown sandy silt loam (7.5 YR 4/4). This suggests the removal of a post, before the feature was deliberately refilled.

Feature 896 (Fig. 3.76)

896 was the cut of an irregular ramped post-hole, with a near-vertical edge on the south, and an edge that sloped gradually from the ramp on the northern side. A series of distinct patches of fill were identified within this feature, giving an impression of disturbance, and perhaps of deliberate backfilling. In the base of the feature, deposit 927 represented a mass of loose dark yellowish-brown loamy sand containing many pebbles and flecks of charcoal (7.5 YR 3/3), apparently material of various kinds that had collapsed into the space left behind by the withdrawn post. The various layers of packing had slumped forward over this material. Of these, 926 was a patch of loose dark brown sandy loam (7.5 YR 3/3), beneath 925, a loose dark brown loamy sand packed with many pebbles (7.5 YR 3/4). 924 was a lens of sandy loam on the surface of 925, beneath 921, a more extensive wedge of loose dark yellowish-brown loamy sand with many pebbles (10 YR 3/4). 919 and 920 were soily lenses above 921, and below 917, a loose dark brown sandy loam with many small pebbles (10 YR 3/3), the uppermost body of post-packing on the northern side of the feature. 917 contained two sherds of Grooved Ware (FG3 Vessel 3). On the southern side, 923 was a loose dark yellowish-brown loamy sand with many angular pebbles (10 YR 3/6), which appeared to extend beneath 927, and predate it. Above 923 was a tightly packed patch of cobbles, 922, and this in turn lay below 918, a loose dark brown sandy loam that formed the uppermost packing deposit in the southern part of the feature. These various packing deposits appeared to be truncated, so that layer 916 rested on them unconformably. 916 formed a disturbed mass of fine stony gravel in a loose, dark brown loamy sand with charcoal flecks (7.5 YR 3/3). This seems to have been disturbed material that filled the space left by the removal of a post. A lens of charcoal, 785, seems to have been deposited at much the same time as this removal, and may have been derived from the charred end of the post. This lay beneath 915, a friable dark reddish-brown sandy loam (5 YR 3/3), and 914, a

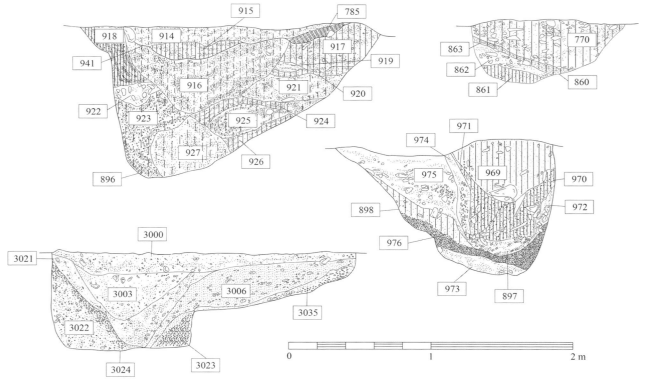

Figure 3.76 Post-holes of the middle post-ring: sections

friable dark brown loamy sand with a few pebbles (7.5 YR 3/3). These deposits represented stabilisation and silting following the post-removal.

Feature 898 (Fig. 3.76)

898 was the cut of an oval post-hole, with a near-vertical and undercut edge on the northern side, and a ramp that descended steeply into the base of the feature from the south. In the bottom of the post-hole, 973 was a layer of friable gritty dark yellowish-brown loamy sand (10 YR 3/4), perhaps material eroded from the sides. Above this was 897, a friable dark yellowish-brown loamy sand containing many pebbles and charcoal flecks (10 YR 3/6), and 976, a friable dark reddish-brown silty loam, with fewer pebbles (5 YR 3/3). These layers, together with 975 (a loose brown sand, 7.5 YR 4/4), made up the original packing of the post-hole. These were packed up against 974, a dark yellowish-brown loamy sand with numerous pebbles (10 YR 4/6), which appeared to trickle down the outer edge of the post-pipe. Its equivalent on the northern side was 972. Another body of loose to friable dark yellowish-brown loamy sand (10 YR 4/6), 897, lay at the base of the post-pipe, while the post-pipe was principally filled by two masses of friable dark reddish-brown silt loam (7.5 YR 3/2), 970 and 971. A silting into the top of the post void was represented by 969, a friable dark yellowish-brown silt loam (10 YR 4/4). This was apparently a post that had been left to rot out.

Feature 3024 (Fig. 3.76)

Cut 3024 formed a sub-circular pit with a deep ramp towards the north extending to the surface. Three initial fills 3022 (loose dark yellowish-brown sand: 10 YR 3/6), 3023 (loose dark yellowish-brown sand: 10 YR 3/6) and 3035 (loose dark reddish-brown sand: 5 YR 3/3) lay against the cut as lenses of gravel packing. There was no sign of any erosion beneath these fills. The packing of the post-ramp, 3006 (friable very dark brown sand 7.5 YR 2.5/3), was quite similar to these deposits. These packing deposits defined a v-shaped space that had originally been occupied by the post. Its primary filling was fill 3021, a friable dark brown sand (7.5 YR 3/3), but immediately above this was 3003, a slightly redder friable dark brown sand containing a few pebbles (7.5 YR 3/4). It is probable that this was material that had slipped into the core of the post as it rotted out. Above this was a layer of slower silting and stabilisation, 3000, a loose strong brown silt (7.5 YR 4/6).

Feature 4047 (Fig. 3.77)

4047 was the circular cut of post-hole, with very steep sides and a flat base. The profile is quite difficult to interpret, as there was no clear post-pipe. The earliest fill in the feature was a silting, 4046, composed of friable dark yellowish-brown silty loam (10 YR 3/4) containing frequent large pebbles. This probably indicates that the post-hole was left open for a while before a post was

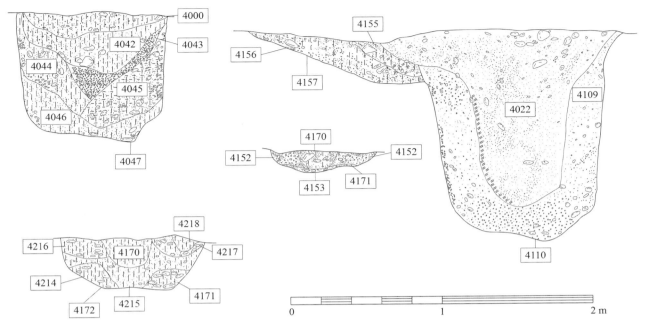

Figure 3.77 Post-holes of the middle post-ring: sections

introduced. Above this was 4045, a loose very dark brown sandy clay loam (7.5 YR 2.5/2) containing a few small pebbles. This deposit appears to have been a slumped packing deposit. 4044 was a further deposit of slumped packing, made up of friable dark brown clay loam (7.5 YR 3/3) with a number of small pebbles. Above this was a gravel layer, 4043, made up of loose dark yellowish-brown sandy loam (10 YR 3/6) with very numerous small pebbles. Above this was 4042, a friable dark brown sandy silt loam (7.5 YR 3/3) with a few small pebbles, representing a silting into the post void. It may be that the packing collapsed as the post was withdrawn. However, it is equally possible that 4043 represented material that had penetrated into the core of the post as it rotted, and that the subsequent collapse of the packing inward removed any trace of the post-pipe. The uppermost fill was context 4000, a loose very dark brown sandy loam (7.5 YR 2.5/3) with infrequent small pebbles, constituting a further layer of silting and stabilisation deposits. On balance, it is probable that this post decayed *in situ*, although it is possible that it was withdrawn.

Feature 4053 (Fig. 3.77)

4053 was the cut a of relatively shallow and truncated middle ring post-hole, with gradual concave sides coming down onto a rounded base. The basal fill was 4071, a loose brown sand (7.5 YR 5/2) with numerous mixed pebbles. 4071 was probably a primary silting at the base of the feature. Above this layer was 4052, a friable yellowish-brown sandy silt (10 YR 5/4) with much mixed gravel, representing the principal packing of the feature. 4070 was the fill of the post-pipe, made up of a brown loose

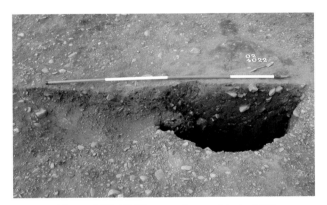

Figure 3.78 Middle post-ring post-hole 4110

sand (7.5 YR 5/2). The coherence of this entity suggests that the post had rotted out *in situ*.

Feature 4110 (Figs. 3.77 and 3.78)

4110 was the cut of a large, deep sub-circular middle ring post with a distinct ramp on the western side. This feature cut the cursus post-hole 4157, which had initially been identified as the ramp of the later feature. The post-hole had vertical sides, somewhat undercut on the northern side, and a slightly bowled base. The ramp was wide and steep in form. The basal fill of the feature was 4109, a loose strong brown sandy gravel (7.5 YR 4/6) with numerous small pebbles. This deposit appeared to be a relatively undisturbed gravel packing within the main body of the post-hole, and extending into the ramp. It contained a series of tip lines, presumably relating to its having being shovelled into place around the post. Above this was 4022, a friable strong brown silty sand (7.5 YR 4/6). This deposit probably constituted a post-pipe, although during excavation it was difficult to distinguish this from context 4109. There was a concentration of charcoal at the southern edge of the feature, which seemed to follow the boundary between the two fills. There was no evidence of direct burning, so the charcoal is much more likely to have derived from the charred tip of a post. The post itself appears to have rotted out *in situ*. Context 4022 produced a distinctive wacke sandstone axe (FN 1462, see Chapter 7).

Feature 4172 (Fig. 3.77)
4172 was the cut of a large but comparatively shallow post-hole, presumably representing only the base of a deeper feature. It had concave edges descending to a flat base. Its primary fill was 4171, a loose to friable dark red sandy loam (2.5 YR 4/6) containing many pebbles. This represented a packing deposit, and was straigraphically equivalent to 4214, also a loose to friable dark red sandy loam (2.5 YR 4/6). Above this was 4215, a loose to friable dark brown sandy loam (7.5 YR 3/4) with fewer pebbles. This was a slumped packing deposit. 4216 was a further packing deposit, a loose to friable reddish-brown sandy loam (5 YR 4/4) with many small pebbles. This was very similar material to 4217 and 4218, and although these could be distinguished on excavation they probably represented no more than separate bodies of packing thrown into the post-hole, rather than discrete stratigraphic events. The uppermost fill was 4170, a loose reddish-brown sandy loam (5 YR 4/3) with a few pebbles. This deposit appears to have been the remains of a truncated post-pipe, suggesting that the post had rotted out *in situ*.

Feature 4204 (Fig. 3.79)
4202 was the cut of a sub-rounded post-hole, with steep straight edges descending onto a rounded base. Its basal fill was 4200, a friable strong brown sand (7.5 YR 4/6). This was a very sandy deposit, probably packing material, which was capped by 4197, a very loose red-brown sand containing many small pebbles (5 YR 4/4). These bodies of material were packed in between the edge of the feature and an apparent large post-pipe, in the bottom of which was 4203, a friable dark red-brown sandy loam (5 YR 3/4), constituting a 'soily' organic matrix. Overlying this was 4201, a loose black sandy loam (7.5 YR 2.5/1) filling much of the post-pipe. Much of this deposit was composed of charcoal, and probably represented the remains of a charred post. Above this in turn was 4198, a friable dark red-brown sandy loam (5 YR 3/2) with a few small pebbles. This deposit was very dark, and contained a concentration of charcoal, perhaps also derived from the post. This was separated from 4199, a friable dark red-brown sandy loam (5 YR

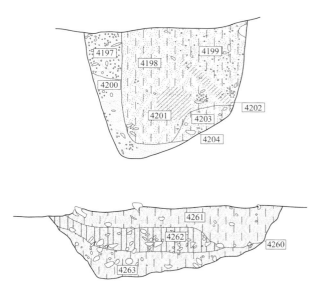

Figure 3.79 Sections of middle post-ring post-holes 4204 and 4260

2.5/2) representing a silting into the settled feature by a lens of loose very dark brown sandy loam (7.5 YR 2.5/2) with occasional small pebbles, 4202. The charcoal in this feature was very extensive, but on balance it seems that a charred post had been inserted into this feature, and had rotted out, leaving behind the charcoal fraction.

Feature 4260 (Fig. 3.79)
4260 was the cut of a large sub-oval middle ring post-hole, with irregular sides descending to a rounded base. Its primary fill was 4263, a friable dark brown loam (10 YR 3/4) containing occasional small gravel pieces. This was a silting or collapse that had accumulated when the post-hole was first opened. It lay beneath 4262, a loose to friable brown sandy loam (10 YR 4/4) containing large quantities of gravel, representing a slump of packing at the side of the feature. Above this was 4261, a friable dark brown sandy loam (10 YR 3/3) with a few small pebbles. There was no direct evidence of a post, but it may have been withdrawn, creating the displaced and layered deposits revealed in the section.

Middle post-ring, minor posts

In Trench A, a number of smaller features had been identified located between the major post-holes of the middle post-ring. Although the coherence of their pattern was not immediately appreciated, it was nonetheless suggested that they might constitute part of a palisade structure of some kind. These features were clearly very

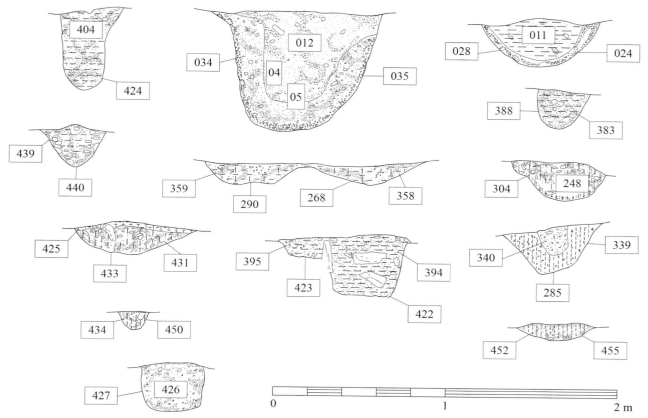

Figure 3.80 Minor post-holes of the middle post-ring: sections

truncated. In Trenches AA and J the evidence for minor post-holes running in lines between the major uprights was far more extensive, although their recognition was easier in some areas than others, owing to variations in the character of the subsoil. Further to the east, smaller post-holes may originally have existed, and might either have been removed by the abrasion of the subsoil, or obscured by root and rodent activity. This slightly patchy distribution highlights the problem of the small number of diminutive posts found in the inner ring, and the possibility that more may once have existed.

Feature 024 (Fig. 3.80)
024 was a small circular post-hole, with gradual sides and a rounded base, which contained basal fill 028, a gritty dark brown sand (10 YR 3/6) with many small pebbles. The uppermost fill was 011, a friable brown silty clay (7.5 YR 4/3), containing a few small stones, and which represented a silting into the top of the feature. So little remained of the original fill that it is difficult to come to any conclusion concerning the history of this feature.

Feature 035 (Fig. 3.80)
Feature 035 was a deep, narrow circular post-hole that probably formed part of the middle post-ring. It was off-line from post-hole 027, but lay between post-holes 099

and 310. It was somewhat larger than the other 'minor' post-holes of the middle post-ring. Soil micromorphology samples 004 and 005 were taken from this feature. The cut of the feature, 035, was straight-sided, with a flattened base. The principal fill was 034, a friable dark reddish-brown sandy gravel (5 YR 3/2), representing a primary packing. Within this was a post-pipe, 012, of silty dark reddish-brown sand loam (5 YR 3/3). Micromorphological study of the fills from this feature revealed organic material, and charcoal in particular, to be very scarce (see Chapter 9). This post had probably rotted out *in situ*.

Feature 268 (Fig. 3.80)
Post-hole 268 intersected with palisade post-hole 255, although no clear stratigraphic relationship could be established. The small bowl-shaped cut 268 was filled with dark greyish-brown sandy clay loam 358 (10 YR 4/2).

Feature 285 (Fig. 3.80)
The oval cut of a post-hole with vertical sides and a flat base, and with weathered edges, 285, contained the packing 339, a friable, very dark brown loamy sand (7.5 YR 2.5/2), which surrounded 340, a clear post-pipe of friable dark brown silt (7.5 YR 3/3). This small post had presumably rotted *in situ*.

Feature 290 (Fig. 3.80)
The cut of a small, bowl-shaped post-hole, 290, intersected with palisade post-hole 255, although no stratigraphic relationship could be established. It was filled with 359, a friable dark greyish brown sandy clay loam (10 YR 4/2).

Feature 304 (Fig. 3.80)
An oval, steep-sided cut with a distinct weathering cone and flat base, 304, was filled with 248, a friable very dark brown loamy sand with many small pebbles (7.5 YR 2.5/3).

Feature 388 (Fig. 3.80)
The cut of a small round post-hole, 388, which contained 383, a firm very dark greyish brown sandy clay (10 YR 3/2) with numerous small stones.

Feature 422/423 (Fig. 3.80)
This feature was composed of two related elements. The earliest cut was 422, a round, steep-sided post-hole with a concave base, filled with 394, a friable dark reddish-brown silty clay (5 YR 3/2), containing small gravel, packing stones and flecks of charcoal. This was cut by 423, a smaller, round, steep-sided post-hole with a concave base. 423 was filled with 395, a friable dark reddish-brown silty clay (5 YR 3/2).

Feature 424 (Fig. 3.80)
A circular post-hole cut with sloping sides and flat base, 424, which contained 382/404, a friable dark brown sandy clay (10 YR 3/3), containing packing stones and a block of charcoal.

Feature 427 (Fig. 3.80)
A step-sided concave based cut, 427, was filled with 426, a friable, very dark brown gravelly sand (10 YR 2/2). Above this was 402, a friable very dark brown loamy sand (7.5 YR 2.5/5).

Feature 433 (Fig. 3.80)
The shallow, bowl-shaped cut of a small post-hole, 433, was filled with 431, a friable, dark reddish-brown loamy sand (5 YR 3/2) containing a number of large packing stones, some of these tipped upward. Between the packing stones was a clear post-pipe, 435, composed of friable dark reddish-brown loamy sand (5 YR 3/2).

Feature 440 (Fig. 3.80)
The circular cut of a post-hole with steep sides and concave base, 440, which contained 339, a friable dark brown sandy clay with packing stones and pebbles (7.5 YR 3/3).

Feature 450 (Fig. 3.80)
The oval cut of a post-hole with flat base and distinct post socket, 450, which contained 434, a friable very dark brown sandy loam (7.5 YR 2.5/2), with one possible packing stone.

Feature 455 (Fig. 3.80)
The circular cut of a post-hole with a rounded base, 455, contained packing 452, a friable dark brown sandy loam with numerous small pebbles (7.5 YR 3/3).

Feature 544 (Fig. 3.83)
The circular cut, 544, of a small post-hole with a rounded base, which contained 536, a friable dark reddish-grey loamy sand (5 YR 4/2), with a few small stones as inclusions.

Feature 629 (Fig. 3.83)
The cut of a small circular post-hole with rounded base 629, containing 626, a compact and homogeneous dark brown (10 YR 3/3) sandy loam.

Feature 772 (Figs. 3.83 and 3.84)
A small post-hole 772, whose cut was sub-circular and bowled, which contained 771, a firm to friable dark brown (10 YR 3/3) loamy sand.

Feature 775 (Fig. 3.83)
The deep, bowled cut of a post-hole, 775, contained a friable dark brown (7.5 YR 3/4) sandy loam with small to large stones, 762.

Feature 779 (Fig. 3.83)
The truncated cut of a small concave post-hole, sub-circular in plan, 779, contained 778, a loose dark yellowish-brown (10 YR 3/4) loamy sand.

Feature 790 (Fig. 3.83)
The cut of a small shallow post-hole 790, with straight sides and a bowled base, which contained 791, a friable dark brown (7.5 YR 3/4) loamy sand with two packing stones.

Feature 798 (Fig. 3.83)
The cut of a small round post-hole with a bowled base, 798, with a basal fill of compact dark yellowish-brown sandy loam containing a great deal of gravel (10 YR 3/4), below a packing of compact dark brown sand (7.5 YR 3/4) and medium-sized stones, 796, which surrounded a post-pipe, 795, composed of friable dark reddish-brown sandy loam (10 R 3/4). This post had apparently rotted out *in situ*.

Feature 799 (Fig. 3.83)
A small oval post-hole with vertical sides and a flat base, 799, contained 793, a loose yellowish red loamy sand with inclusions of a few pebbles (5 YR 3/4).

Feature 804 (Fig. 3.83)
The shallow, sub-circular cut of a post-hole with a bowled

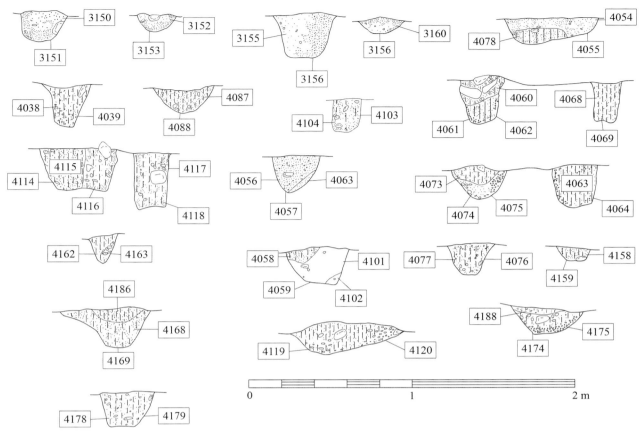

Figure 3.81 Minor post-holes of the middle post-ring: sections

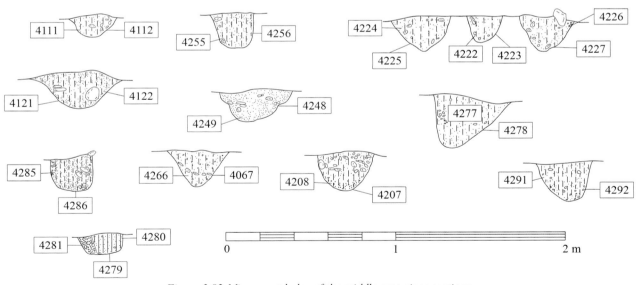

Figure 3.82 Minor post-holes of the middle post-ring: sections

base, 804, which contained 803, a loose dark yellowish-brown (10 YR 4/4) sandy loam. This feature was clearly very truncated.

Feature 885 (Fig. 3.83)
A small oval post-hole with steep sides and a flat base, 885, contained 884, a friable dark reddish-brown loamy sand which included a few small rounded pebbles (5 YR 2.5/2).

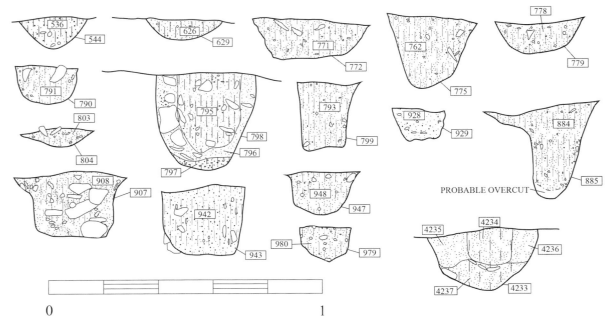

Figure 3.83 Minor post-holes of the middle post-ring: sections

Feature 907 (Fig. 3.83)
907 was the cut of an oval post-hole with near-vertical sides that were weathered back toward the top, with a flat base. The fill was 908, a loose, dark brown loamy sand containing several medium-sized stones (7.5 YR 3/3). The stones appear to have represented packing, surrounding a central post-pipe, which could not be differentiated from 908. If so, then the post may have rotted out.

Feature 929 (Fig. 3.83)
929 was a small, shallow and presumably truncated post-hole, sub-circular in plan with a flattened base. The fill, 928, was a loose dark reddish-brown silt loam containing a few pebbles (5 YR 3/2).

Feature 943 (Fig. 3.83)
943 was a near-circular post-hole with abrupt sides curving to a flat base. The single fill was 942, a loose brown silt loam with numerous pebbles and traces of charcoal (7.5 YR 4/3).

Feature 947 (Fig. 3.83)
947 was a small oval post-hole with steep sides curving to a rounded base. The fill was 948, a friable dark brown loamy sand with a few pebbles (7.5 YR 3/4).

Feature 979 (Fig. 3.83)
979 was an irregularly-shaped post-hole with a bowled base, filled by 980, a loose dark brown loamy sand with a few small pebbles (10 YR 3/3).

Feature 3151 (Fig. 3.81)
Cut 3151 was a rather heavily truncated post-hole, with an abrupt break of slope at the top, funnel-shaped sides and a flat bottom. There was a single homogeneous fill 3152, which was a firm reddish-brown sandy silt containing a few small pebbles (5 YR 4/4).

Feature 3153 (Fig. 3.81)
3153 was the scoop-shaped cut of a small post-hole with a pointed base, with a homogeneous fill 3154, composed of a firm reddish-brown sandy silt containing some charcoal flecks (5 YR 4/4).

Feature 3156 (Fig. 3.81)
3156 was a small, slightly squared post-hole with a flat base. The single homogeneous fill, 3155, was a friable reddish-brown sandy silt (5 YR 4/3), containing a few small pebbles.

Feature 3159 (Fig. 3.81)
3159 was a very ephemeral and heavily truncated circular post-hole, only the very base of which survived. The fill was 3160, a friable reddish-brown sandy silt (5 YR 4/4).

Feature 4039 (Fig. 3.81)
4039 was a small sub-circular post-hole, with steep straight edges descending to a flat base. Its fill was 4038, a loose very dark brown sandy loam (10 YR 2/2) with a few small pebbles.

Feature 4055 (Fig. 3.81)
4055 was the cut of a small, truncated oval post-hole, with irregular/straight sides dropping to a rounded base. The basal fill was 4078, a tenacious yellowish-brown sandy silt loam (10 YR 5/6) with a few small stones, representing a silting at the base of the feature. Above this was 4054, a tenacious yellowish-brown sandy silt (10 YR 5/4) with a few small pebbles.

Feature 4057 (Fig. 3.81)
4057 was a small post-hole with steep straight sides descending onto a rounded base. The primary fill was 4083, a loose yellow-brown sand (10 YR 5/8), representing primary silting at the base of the feature. Above this was 4056, a friable dark yellow-brown sandy silt (10 YR 3/6) with frequent small gravel pieces.

Feature 4059 (Fig. 3.81)
4059 was the cut of a small circular post-hole, with steep concave edges dipping onto a flat base. The fill was 4058, a loose to friable very dark brown sandy loam (10 YR 2/2) with numbers of small to medium sized pebbles.

Feature 4062 (Fig. 3.81)
The circular cut of a small post-hole, with steep straight sides dropping to a rounded base. The basal fill was 4061, a compacted dark yellowish-brown sandy loam (10 YR 3/4) with numerous stones, possibly a silting at the base of the feature. Above this was 4060, a friable dark yellowish-brown sandy loam (10 YR 3/6) containing further stones. This was probably packing material. This feature had been heavily disturbed by animal burrowing.

Feature 4064 (Fig. 3.81)
4064 was the cut of shallow post-hole with steep straight sides and a flat base. The single fill was 4063, a friable dark yellowish-brown sandy loam (10 YR 3/4).

Feature 4067 (Fig. 3.82)
4067 was a small circular post-hole, with steep straight sides and a flat base. The single fill was 4066, a loose dark red-brown sandy loam (5 YR 3/3) with a few small to medium pebbles.

Feature 4069 (Fig. 3.81)
4069 was the cut of a small circular post-hole with steep straight sides descending to a flat base. The single fill was 4068, a friable dark yellowish-brown sandy loam (10 YR 3/4) containing a small number of medium pebbles.

Feature 4075 (Fig. 3.81)
4075 was the cut of a small sub-circular post-hole. It had steep concave edges and a rounded base. The basal fill was 4073, a friable dark brown sand (10 YR 3/3) with occasional medium pebbles, and which represented

erosion or silting at the base of the feature. Above this was 4074, a friable yellowish-brown sandy loam (10 YR 3/6), representing a packing deposit.

Feature 4088 (Fig. 3.81)
4088 was the cut of a small, sub-circular, very truncated post-hole, with concave sides dipping to a flat base. The fill was 4087, a loose to friable very dark brown sandy loam (10 YR 2/2) with several large stones.

Feature 4104 (Fig. 3.81)
4104 was the cut of a small sub-circular post-hole, with steep straight sides descending to a rounded base. The fill was 4103, a friable brown sandy silt (7.5 YR 4/3) containing a great many small stones.

Feature 4112 (Fig. 3.82)
4112 was the cut of small, truncated post-hole, circular in plan with steep, straight sides descending to a flat base. The single fill was 4111, a loose to friable dark yellowish-brown sandy loam (10 YR 3/6) with small to medium pebbles.

Feature 4114 (Fig. 3.81)
4114 was the cut of a post-hole, which was circular in plan with steep, straight sides descending to a flat base. 4116, a loose, dark yellowish-brown sandy silt (10 YR 4/4) with a concentration of large stones at the top, was a packing deposit around post-pipe 4115, a loose dark brown sandy silt (10 YR 3/3).

Feature 4117 (Fig. 3.81)
4117 was the cut of a small circular post-hole, with vertical edges descending to a flat base. Its fill was 4118, a loose dark yellowish-brown sandy silt (10 YR 4/4) containing small to large stones.

Feature 4120 (Fig. 3.81)
4120 was a heavily truncated post-hole. It was oval in plan with shallow concave edges, descending onto a rounded base. Its single fill was 4119, a loose dark red-brown sandy loam (5 YR 2.5/2) with occasional medium to large pebbles.

Feature 4121 (Fig. 3.82)
4121 was the cut of a circular post-hole, with gradual concave edges dipping to a rounded base. Its fill was 4122, a loose to friable very dark brown silty loam (7.5 YR 2.5/3) with occasional small to medium pebbles.

Feature 4159 (Fig. 3.81)
4159 was a very small shallow sub-circular post-hole. It had steep straight sides dropping to a rounded base. Its fill was 4158, a friable dark brown sandy loam (10 YR 3/3) with very occasional small pebbles.

Feature 4163 (Fig. 3.81)

Feature 4163 was a very small shallow post-hole. It was probably part of the middle post-ring, but it lay somewhat to the south of other associated post-holes. It was poorly defined and indeed might possibly have been a natural feature. It had a sub-circular cut with steep irregular sides dropping to a flat base. Its fill was 4162, a friable sandy very dark greyish brown loam (10 YR 3/2) with mixed gravel.

Feature 4169 (Fig. 3.81)

4169 was the cut of a shallow post-hole, sub-oval in shape and slightly splayed on the eastern side. The western edge was steep and concave, descending to a rounded base. The packing of the post-hole was 4168, a friable very dark brown sandy loam (7.5 YR 2.5/3) containing some small to medium pebbles. The traces of a post-pipe were represented by 4186, a friable dark brown sandy loam (10 YR 3/3) with a few pebbles.

Feature 4174 (Fig. 3.81)

4174 was the cut of a circular post-hole. It had shallow concave edges leading to a flat base. It was filled with 4175, a friable sandy loam (7.5 YR 2.5/3 dark brown) with a high proportion of small to medium pebbles.

Feature 4176 (Fig. 3.81)

4176 was the cut of circular post-hole, with steep straight sides dropping to a rounded base. Its fill was 4177, a loose to friable very dark brown sandy loam (7.5 YR 2.5/3) with frequent small pebbles.

Feature 4178 (Fig. 3.81)

4178 was the circular cut of a post-hole with steep concave edges dipping to a rounded base. Its fill was 4179, a loose to friable dark brown sandy loam (10 YR 3/3) with frequent small pebbles.

Feature 4207 (Fig. 3.82)

4207 was a small sub-circular post-hole. It had steep straight sides above a rounded base. Its fill was 4208, a loose to friable dark brown sandy loam (7.5 YR 3/4) with mixed pebbles.

Feature 4223 (Fig. 3.82)

4223 was the cut of a small sub-rounded post-hole. It had concave edges dipping to a rounded base. The fill was 4222, a loose brown sandy loam (7.5 YR 4/3) with small pebbles.

Feature 4225 (Fig. 3.82)

4225 was the cut of a small oval post-hole. It had steep edges descending to a rounded base. Its fill was 4224, a loose brown sandy loam (7.5 YR 4/4) with numerous pebbles.

Feature 4227 (Fig. 3.82)

4227 was the cut of a rounded post-hole. It had steep straight sides above a rounded base. Its fill was 4226, a loose dark brown sandy loam (7.5 YR 3/2) with a few pebbles and one large packing stone.

Feature 4248 (Fig. 3.82)

4248 was an irregularly shaped feature. It had steep straight but irregular sides, descending to a flat base. Its fill was 4249, a loose dark yellowish-brown sandy silt (10 YR 3/4) with occasional medium pebbles.

Feature 4256 (Fig. 3.82)

4256 was the cut of a circular post-hole. It had steep straight sides descending to a rounded base. Its single fill was 4255, a friable black loamy sand (7.5 YR 2.5/1) containing many medium-sized stones.

Feature 4278 (Fig. 3.82)

4278 was the cut of a small circular post-hole. It had steep straight sides dipping to a flat base. Its single fill was 4277, a loose brown sandy loam (7.5 YR 4/4) with numerous medium-sized pebbles and occasional flecks of charcoal.

Feature 4279 (Fig. 3.82)

4279 was the cut of a sub-rounded post-hole. It had concave edges leading to a rounded base. It was filled with packing deposit 4281, a tenacious dark reddish-brown sandy loam (5 YR 3/2) with frequent small pebbles. The post-pipe was 4280, a tenacious dark reddish-brown sandy loam (5 YR 3/3).

Feature 4286 (Fig. 3.82)

4286 was the cut of a small circular post-hole. It had steep straight sides falling to a rounded base. Its packing fill was 4285, a friable dark brown silty loam (10 YR 3/3) with occasional large pebbles concentrated around the edge of the feature.

Feature 4292 (Fig. 3.82)

4292 was the sub-circular cut of a shallow post-hole. It had steep edges dropping to a rounded base. The packing fill was 4291, a friable dark yellowish-brown sandy loam (10 YR 3/4) with occasional medium pebbles.

Features of a late prehistoric round house

In the central southern part of Trench A, a series of evenly spaced post-holes of roughly similar size made up a particularly clear circle of roughly eight metres diameter. Most of the fills were composed of loamy sand, and many of the post-holes contained packing stones. Three further post-holes may have formed elements of the same structure. They appeared similar to the outer ring in

Figure 3.84 Middle post-ring minor post-hole 772

terms of size, form, and filling. They could form an arc concentric with the outer ring, and it is open to conjecture whether other, now vanished posts also formed part of this structure. Four post-holes located immediately to the east of posts 061 and 401 of the outer ring of the post structure formed an entrance structure or 'porch' aligned due east. When these features began to be excavated it was conjectured that they might have represented a diminutive post circle associated with the Late Neolithic enclosure, but their small size, and the presence of the porch structure soon caused them to be reinterpreted as a later prehistoric house. This was the first of two or three such structures to be identified at Dunragit.

Feature 061 (Fig. 3.85)
A straight-sided post-hole cut with a bowled base, 061, with a packing of loose reddish-brown loamy sand with packing stones, 009 (5 YR 4/3), contained a post-pipe of friable dusky red humic sandy clay, 029 (2.5 YR 3/2).

Feature 065 (Fig. 3.85)
The shallow, bowl-based cut of post-hole, 065, contained 062, a firm very dark brown loamy sand with small stones (10 YR 2/2).

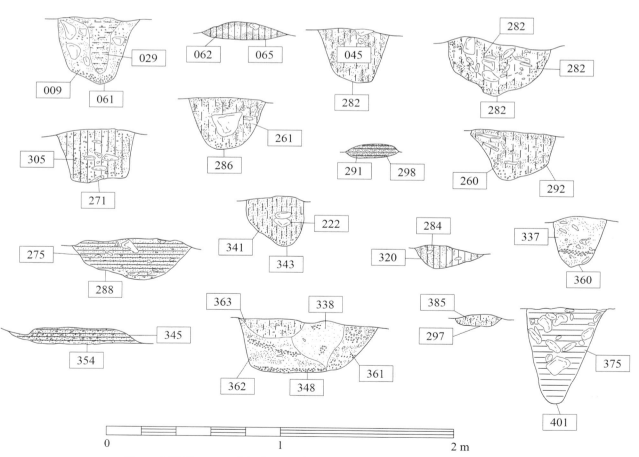

Figure 3.85 Features of the later prehistoric round house in Trench A: sections

Feature 237 (Fig. 3.85)
The cut of a circular post-hole with a sharp break of slope and bowled base, 237, contained a primary packing of loose dusky red loamy sand, 090, with inclusions of pebbles and stones (10 YR 3/2). Above this was a dusky red loamy sand, 236, which was not very distinct from the lower fill, but more stone-free (10 YR 3/2).

Feature 271 (Fig. 3.85)
The round, slightly sloping-sided, flat-based cut of a small post-hole 271, contained 305, a firm dark yellowish-brown loamy sand packed with pebbles clustered at the centre of the feature, perhaps collapsed into the post void (10 YR 3/4).

Feature 281 (Fig. 3.85)
The small, bowl-shaped post-hole cut 281 was filled with 280, a friable dusky red sandy loam with a few medium rolled pebbles and two packing stones (2.5 YR 3/3).

Feature 282 (Fig. 3.85)
The cut of a small oval post-hole with straight sides and bowled base, 282, was filled with a loose to friable dark reddish-brown loamy sand 045, containing a number of large packing stones (5 YR 2.5/2).

Feature 286 (Fig. 3.85)
The cut of a small post-hole with straight sides and rounded bottom 286, was filled with a friable loamy sand, 261, with one possible packing stone (10 YR 3/3 dark brown).

Feature 288 (Fig. 3.85)
The oval cut of a post-hole with sloping sides and flat base, 288, was filled with 275, a tenacious dark reddish-brown silty clay with numerous medium pebbles, burnt stones and charcoal flecks (5 YR 2.5/2).

Feature 292 (Fig. 3.85)
292 was a circular post-hole cut with vertical sides and a concave base, filled with friable dark brown loamy sand 260, which contained a group of packing stones (10 YR 3/3).

Feature 298 (Fig. 3.85)
The vestigial cut of a severely eroded post-hole 298 contained 291, a tenacious very dark brown silty clay with 25% small stones (7.5 YR 2/2).

Feature 320 (Fig. 3.85)
The oval cut of a small shallow post-hole with a rounded base 320, contained a compact dark brown loamy sandy gravel, 284 (3/3 7.5 YR).

Feature 343 (Fig. 3.85)
343 was the cut of a small deep post-hole with steep sides

and a pointed base, which contained 341, a friable dark brown silty loam with one packing stone (7.5 YR 3/2).

Feature 348 (Fig. 3.85)
An oval cut with vertical sides and flat base, 348, contained 361 and 362, similar layers of friable brown sand (both 7.5 YR 4/2), which probably represented the packing of the post-hole. These contexts were divided by 338, a friable pale brown silty material (10 YR 6/3), which was presumably a silting into the former post-pipe. Cutting across the top of this was 363, a friable brown loamy sand (7.5 YR 4/4).

Feature 354 (Fig. 3.85)
A shallow, elongated cut with one steep side, 354, contained 345, a tenacious, very dark brown silty clay with small stones (10 YR 2.5/2).

Feature 360 (Fig. 3.85)
The oval cut of a post-hole with steep sides and flat base, 360, was filled with 337, a friable dark brown sand with packing stones (10 YR 3/3).

Feature 397 (Fig. 3.85)
The shallow truncated cut of a small round post-hole 397 contained 385, a loose dark reddish-brown sandy loam (5 YR 2.5/2) with numerous small packing stones.

Feature 401 (Fig. 3.85)
The cut of a narrow post-hole whose sides tapered toward a flat base, 401, was filled with 375, a firm very dark brown clay (10 YR 2/2) with many packing stones.

Road quarry pit

Feature 4206 (Fig. 3.92)
4206 was a large cut feature that is likely to have been a gravel quarry pit associated with the construction of the historic road immediately to the north of the site. It was very comparable with two further features excavated in Trench E (see below). It was not fully excavated, and instead a slot was cut into its western edge. 4206 was irregularly shaped, with equally irregular edges descending to a flat base. It was approximately 3.5m wide, and within the excavated slot it reached a depth of 0.66 m. The basal fill was 4221, a friable dark yellow-brown sandy silt loam (10 YR 4/4). Above this were a series of layers representing the natural filling of the large feature by silting and collapse. These were, in sequence: 4211, a tenacious strong brown sandy loam (7.5 YR 4/6) with many pebbles; 4213, a tenacious brown sandy loam (7.5 YR 4/4) with many pebbles; 4212, a tenacious very dark brown sandy silt loam (7.5 YR 2.5/3) with a few pebbles; 4220, a friable dark yellow-brown sandy silt loam (10 YR 4/4) with very many pebbles; 4209, a tenacious

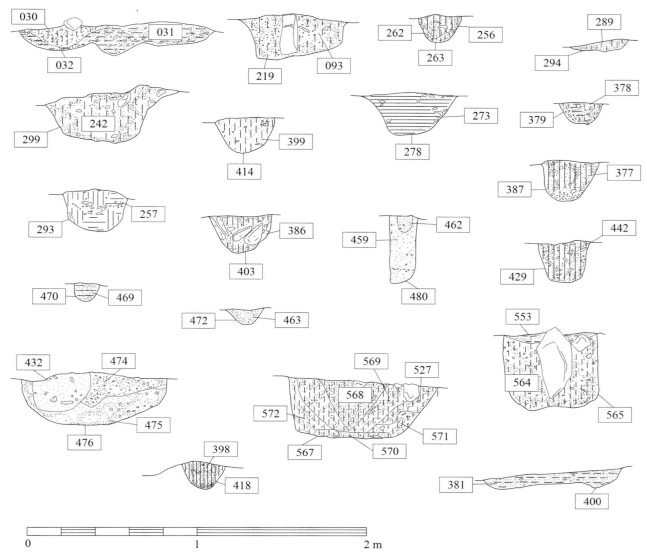

Figure 3.86 Miscellaneous features, Trenches A, AA, F and J: sections

dark yellow-brown sandy clay loam (10 YR 3/6); 4219, a tenacious dark yellow-brown sandy silt (10 YR 3/6) with few pebbles; 4210, a tenacious very dark brown silt loam (7.5 YR 2.5/2) with occasional pebbles; and 4205, a friable dark yellow-brown sandy silt loam (10 YR 4/4) with more numerous pebbles.

Miscellaneous features

While many of the features in Trenches A, AA, F and J could readily be identified as elements of the structures described above, there were numerous other features that were not so easy to attribute to the cursus or the Late Neolithic enclosure. Most of these contained no diagnostic finds to fit them into the history of the site. Some would appear to have been associated with each

other, and it is likely that they represented fragments of further constructions, providing additional evidence for the long history of construction on the site. For the sake of completeness they are described here at the same level of detail as the features of the monumental structures.

Feature 032 (Fig. 3.86)
A shallow, splayed dip in the subsoil 032 contained a thin deposit of compact, crunchy dark reddish-brown (5 YR 2.5/2) sandy gravel containing a few small rolled pebbles, 005 (not visible on section), which contained flakes of charcoal and three sherds of Beaker pottery (FG4 V1), as well as sherds of another vessel (FG1 V1), which was Grooved Ware. This lay above a friable dusky red (2.5 YR 3/2) silty loam, 030. The basal fill of the feature was 031, a friable dark reddish-brown (5 YR 3/4) sandy clay. Presumably this was the truncated base

of a rather deeper feature. It was the only feature on the site to produce Beaker pottery.

Feature 219 (Fig. 3.86)
219 was a circular post-hole cut with an abrupt break of slope, concave sides and a flat base, whose fill was 093, a fairly loose dark reddish-brown loamy sand (5 YR 3/2) with four large packing stones but no clear post-pipe.

Feature 263 (Fig. 3.86)
A small, round, flat-based post-hole cut, 263, contained a primary fill of fairly loose dark brown loamy sand with much small stone 262 (7.5 YR 3/3). Above this was 256, a firm dark reddish-brown sandy loam with many pebbles and one large stone (5 YR 3/2).

Feature 278 (Fig. 3.86)
278 was the cut of a small oval feature with an abrupt break of slope at the top, steep sides and a rounded base. Its fill was 273, a firm reddish-brown clay (2.5 YR 3/3), containing a few small pebbles.

Feature 293 (Fig. 3.86)
A small circular post-hole cut with steep sides and rounded base, 293, was filled with 257, a tenacious dark brown clay loam with numerous small and larger packing stones (10 YR 3/3). This feature contained sherds of the probable Food Vessel FG6 V1 (see Chapter 5 below).

Feature 294 (Fig. 3.86)
294 was the very shallow cut of a small saucer-shaped feature. It was filled with a friable dusky red loamy sand, 289 (2.5 YR 3/3).

Feature 299 (Fig. 3.86)
299 was the cut of a small post-hole with vertical sides and flat base, containing 242, a fairly loose dark reddish-brown loamy sand with two large packing stones (5 YR 3/3).

Feature 379 (Fig. 3.86)
The cut of a very small round post-hole with vertical sides and rounded base 379, was filled with 378, a friable to compact sandy clay loam, with pebbles concentrated in the centre of the feature (7.5 YR 3/4 dark brown).

Feature 387 (Fig. 3.86)
The circular cut of a small post-hole with steep sides and flat base 387, contained 377, a firm dark brown loamy sand with a few stones (7.5 YR 3/3).

Feature 400 (Fig. 3.86)
A linear cut with two distinct lobes, one at either end, 400, contained 381, a friable dark reddish-brown humic silty clay (5 YR 3/2).

Feature 403 (Fig. 3.86)
The steep-sided cut of a post-hole with a rounded base, 403, contained a compact dark reddish-brown loamy sand, 386 (5 YR 3/3), with packing stones which tipped in toward the centre of the feature.

Feature 414 (Fig. 3.86)
A round post-hole cut with vertical sides and a flat base, 414, contained 399, a friable brown silty loam (7.5 YR 4/4).

Feature 418 (Fig. 3.86)
418 was the cut of a small, shallow oval feature, possibly a post-hole. It had sloping sides and a flat base. This fill was context 398, a friable dark brown sandy loam (10 YR 3/3), containing a few small and medium-sized stones.

Feature 429 (Fig. 3.86)
The small, round cut of a post-hole with steep sides and flat base, 429, contained 442, a firm dark reddish-brown loamy sandy gravel with some packing stones (5 YR 3/3).

Feature 470 (Fig. 3.86)
The cut of a small linear feature with a rounded profile 470, which contained 469, a friable dark brown sandy clay (7.5 YR 3/2). Above this was a compact brown sand (7.5 YR 4/3), 468, which contained a small fragment of modern glass.

Feature 472 (Fig. 3.86)
The small circular cut of a post-hole with concave sides and base, 472, contained 463, a friable reddish-brown sandy loam (5 YR 4/4) with some quite large packing stones.

Feature 476 (Fig. 3.86)
476 was the round cut of a post-hole with steep sides and flat base, whose primary filling was the packing 475, a fairly loose yellowish-red sandy gravel with very many pebbles (5 YR 4/6). Above this was 474, a fairly loose brown sandy gravel (7.5 YR 4/4), which also appeared to have been part of the post-packing. Both of these layers butted up against 452, a distinct post-pipe of loose yellowish-brown silt (10 YR 5/8).

Feature 480 (Fig. 3.86)
The cut of a small oval post-hole with vertical sides and a flat base 480, contained 459, a friable strong brown silt with charcoal flecks and small stones (7.5 YR 4/6).

Feature 510 (Fig. 3.87)
The cut of a small oval post-hole with an abrupt break of slope at the top and a rounded base, 510, was filled with 501, a friable dark brown (7.5 YR 3/4) silt, which contained context 505, a packing of angular large to medium stone fragments.

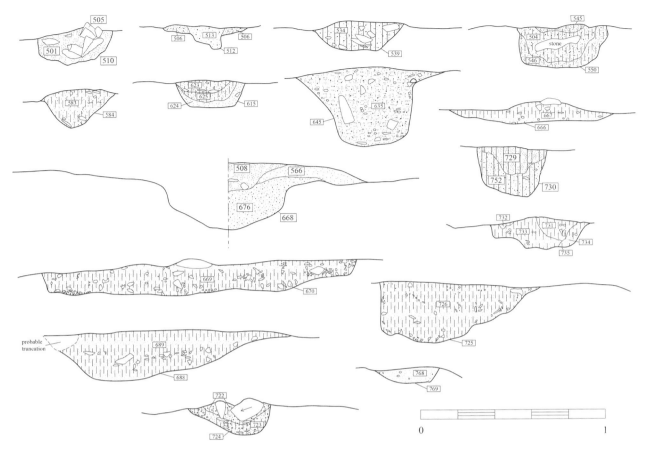

Figure 3.87 Miscellaneous features, Trenches A, AA, F and J: sections

Feature 512 (Fig. 3.87)
512 was the cut of a sub-circular post-hole, which intersected with the larger feature 579/619 (see above). 512 was shallow and bowl-shaped, with a steeper central portion. It was filled with 506, a very friable dark brown (10 YR 3/2) silty sand. A possible post-pipe was represented by 513, a loose dark yellowish-brown (10 YR 3/6) silty and with small rounded stones.

Feature 515 (Fig. 3.90 – two sections)
515 was the cut of an irregularly ovoid feature, with a clearly defined break of slope around its upper edges, which descended gradually to an uneven base. The earliest fill in the feature was 554, a patch of mottled yellowish-red (5 YR 4/6) loose sand that covered only a part of the base of the feature. This lay beneath 507, a more extensive patch of compact yellowish-red (5 YR 4/6) loamy sand. 562, which lay above this, was another small lens of compact brown (7.5 YR 4/3) loamy sand, above which was 503, a compact black (7.5 YR 2.5/1) silt containing charcoal flecks. Above this in turn was the compact dark reddish-brown silty loam 561, which also contained charcoal flecks. A dark patch within this material, 616,

may have represented a small post-hole cut into the feature. Although very irregular in form, it was evident that 515 had had a complex stratigraphic history. It is probable that the feature had been deliberately backfilled, with contexts 554 and 562 thrown in from different sides. Contexts 503 and 561 presumably represent siltings into the top of the feature following this backfilling.

Feature 539 (Fig. 3.87)
The cut of a small circular post-hole with sides sloping to a flat base, 539, which contained 535, a friable dark reddish-brown (5 YR 3/2) silty clay, with a series of large rounded packing stones.

Feature 550 (Fig. 3.87)
The oval cut of a post-hole 550 with a flattish base, which contained 546, a compact yellow-brown (5 YR 4/3) sandy loam, above which was 504, a tenacious black/grey silt loam (7.5 YR 2.5/2) with small rounded pebbles and charcoal flecks and a number of packing stones. Above this was 545, a compact brown/grey silt loam (5 YR 2.5/1) with charcoal flecks. A post-pipe was not evident.

Feature 565 (Fig. 5.86)
The cut of a circular post-hole with concave base 565 was filled with 564, a loose dark brown (5 YR 3/3) loamy sand with packing stones, above which was 553, a friable dark reddish-brown (2.5 YR 3/3) sandy clay, which represented a layer of compaction in the top of the feature.

Feature 567 (Fig. 5.86)
567 was the cut of a circular post-hole with concave sides, which contained a basal deposit of loose dark reddish-brown loamy sand with pebbles (5 YR 2.5/2), 570. The lowest fills above this primary silting were 571, a loose dark brown loamy sand (7.5 YR 3/4) and 572, a loose reddish-brown (5 YR 3/2) loamy sand. These were stratigraphically equivalent. Above these was 527, a loose dark red (2.5 YR 3/2) loamy sand with packing stones, evidently material that had slipped into the post void. Above this was 569, a loose dark brown (7.5 YR 3/4) loamy sand, also collapsing into the post void, and having a 'v' shape in section. In the top of the feature, 568 represented a layer of compaction, a loose dark yellowish-brown (10 YR 2/2) loamy sand.

Feature 584 (Fig. 3.87)
A shallow bowl-shaped cut of a roughly circular post-hole, 584, contained 583, a friable dark red loamy sand (2.5 YR 3/3) with a few rounded pebbles, which represented a single homogeneous fill.

Feature 615 (Fig. 3.87)
The cut of a circular post-hole with a concave section, 615, was filled with 625, a friable dark yellowish-brown (10 YR 3/4) sandy loam, above which was a lens of slumped material or compaction, 623, a friable brown (10 YR 4/3) sandy loam.

Feature 645 (Fig. 3.87)
The cut of an oval post-hole with steep sides and concave base, 645, contained 635, a friable, dark reddish-brown (5 YR 3/3) silty clay loam with charcoal flecks and large packing stones.

Feature 666 (Fig. 3.87)
The shallow cut of a circular feature with a rounded base, 666, contained 667, a coarse black loamy sand (10 YR 2/1), which appeared to include a certain amount of burnt material.

Feature 668 (Fig. 3.87)
The shallow cut of an oval feature 668 contained 676/511, a loose, dark yellowish-brown coarse sandy silt (10 YR 3/4). Above this was 566, a loose, dark reddish-brown silty sand (5 YR 3/4), which represented the principal packing of the feature. This underlay 508, a friable, very dark brown (10 YR 2/2) sandy silt with flecks of charcoal.

Feature 670 (Fig. 3.87)
The cut of a shallow oval feature with sloping sides, 670, was filled with 669, a compact very dark brown (7.5 YR 2.5/3) loamy sand with charcoal flecks. This was possibly the base of a very truncated feature.

Feature 688 (Fig. 3.87)
The shallow-sided cut of an elongated oval feature, 688, contained 689, a compact yellowish-red (5 YR 4/6) loamy sand. This was possibly a natural feature.

Feature 724 (Fig. 3.87)
The cut of an amorphous feature, 724, which was filled with 723, a friable dark reddish-brown (2.5 YR 3/4) loamy sand, above which was 722, a friable very dark brown (7.5 YR 2.5/2) silty clay loam with fragments of charcoal, and a number of packing stones.

Feature 725 (Fig. 3.87)
725 was the irregular oval cut of a feature which had been heavily disturbed by animal burrowing. It was filled by 726, a compact dark reddish-brown (5 YR 2.5/2) silt and silt loam mixture.

Feature 730 (Fig. 3.87)
The cut of a small rounded post-hole with steep sides and rounded base, 730, contained 752, a loose to friable dark yellowish-brown (10 YR 3/4) sandy loam with gravel, above which was 729, a friable dark olive brown (2.5 Y 3/3) loamy sand, which represented compaction or settling into the top of the feature.

Feature 735 (Fig. 3.87)
A steep-sided post-hole cut, 735, which contained 734, a friable dark brown (7.5 YR 3/4) sandy loam with numerous small rounded pebbles. Above this was 733, a friable brown (7.5 YR 4/4) sandy loam with flecks of charcoal. Above this in turn were 731, a friable strong brown (7.5 YR 4/6) sandy loam with flecks of charcoal, and 732, a similar matrix which may have represented a truncated fragment of the same deposit.

Feature 744 (Fig. 3.88)
744 was the elongated oval cut of a feature with slanting sides and a concave base, which contained 746, a friable dark brown (7.5 YR 3/3) loamy sand, above which was 745, a friable, strong brown loamy sand (7.5 YR 4/6) which evidently represented a silting or slumping into the top of the feature.

Feature 751
The cut of a sub-circular post-hole with slanting sides and flat base 751, which contained 533, a friable, very dark greyish-brown (10 Y 3/2) loamy sand with many small pebbles and some packing stones. Above this was

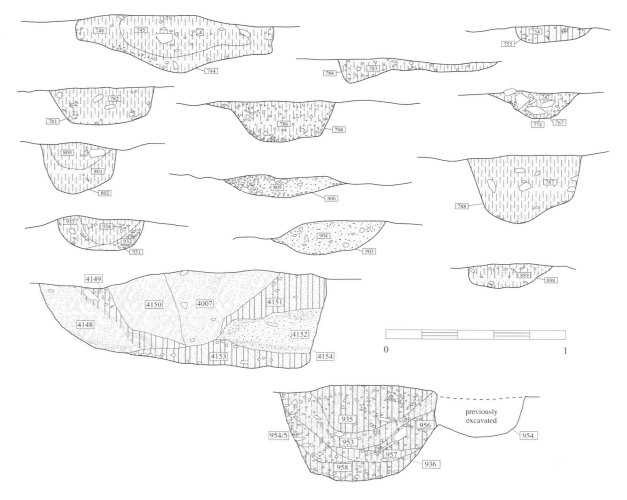

Figure 3.88 Miscellaneous features, Trenches A, AA, F and J: sections

514, a compact very dark grey (2.5 Y 3/1) loamy sand, which represented a post-pipe.

Feature 755 (Fig. 3.88)
The shallow, bowled cut of a sub-circular post-hole, 755, which contained 754, a friable dark brown (5 YR 3/4) sandy clay with small pebbles and charcoal staining.

Feature 767 (Fig. 3.88)
767 was an irregular sub-circular cut with a concave base, the lowest fill of which, 774, was a loose very dark grey (2.5 Y 3/1) sandy loam, and may represent a post-pipe. Above this, fill 747 was a friable, very dark brown (10 YR 2/2) loamy sand.

Feature 769 (Fig. 3.87)
The cut of a small round post-hole with bowled base, 769, which contained 768, a friable dark reddish grey (5 YR 4/2) loamy sand, with numerous small pebbles.

Feature 781 (Fig. 3.88)
The cut of a sub-circular post-hole with flattened base, 781, which contained 782, a friable dark yellowish-brown (10 YR 3/6) sandy loam: a homogeneous fill with large pebble inclusions.

Feature 784
784 was a circular cut with a sharp break of slope at the top and straight sides, rounded at the base, which contained a fill, 783, of compact to friable dark yellowish-brown sandy loam with numerous pebbles (10 YR 4/4).

Feature 788 (Fig. 3.88)
788 was the cut of a small, near-circular feature with vertical sides and a rounded base. Its single fill was 787, a friable brown loamy sand with a few medium pebbles (7.5 YR 4/4).

Feature 794 (Fig. 3.88)
794 was the cut of an oval-shaped feature with sides that

were more gradual at the two ends, and a flat base. The fill was 786, a friable yellowish red loamy sand with numbers of small to medium pebbles.

Feature 802 (Fig. 3.88)
The steep-sided, round-based cut of a circular post-hole, 802, which contained 801, a friable dark brown loamy sand (7.5 YR 3/2) with some charcoal staining. Above this was 800, a friable dark reddish-brown (5 YR 3/3) loamy sand with pebbles, perhaps representing a post-pipe.

Feature 806 (Fig. 3.88)
The shallow, truncated cut of a circular post-hole 806,

Figure 3.89 Miscellaneous feature 788

filled with 805, a loose, coarse dark yellowish-brown (10 YR 3/6) silt.

Feature 807 (Fig. 3.90)
807 was the cut of a substantial oval-shaped feature with steep sides which bowled down to a flat base. It contained a series of interdigitated fills, concentrated on alternate sides of the feature. The basal fill, 869, was a lens of pure, friable dark brown sand with small rounded pebbles (7.5 YR 3/4). This and the layer above, 870, a loose dark brown gravel (7.5 YR 3/3) were banked up at the eastern end of the cut. 871, concentrated in the west, was a friable dark brown sand with a few rounded stones (7.5 YR 3/4). The loose dark brown gravel 872 (7.5 YR 3/3) was also banked in the eastern part of the feature, while 911, a loose brown sandy loam with numerous small rounded stones (7.5 YR 4/4) lay above 873. 912, by contrast, was concentrated in the middle of the feature, a loose yellowish-brown sandy loam with a high proportion of small pebbles and two larger stones. The uppermost fill was 913, a compact dark greyish-brown sandy loam with small rounded stones (10 YR 4/4). It is unclear whether 807 was a post-hole from which the upright had been withdrawn, or simply a small pit with a series of layers of deliberate backfill.

Feature 888 (Fig. 3.88)
888 was the shallow concave cut of a circular post-hole, which contained 889, a compact to friable dark yellowish-brown (10 YR 4/6) sandy loam.

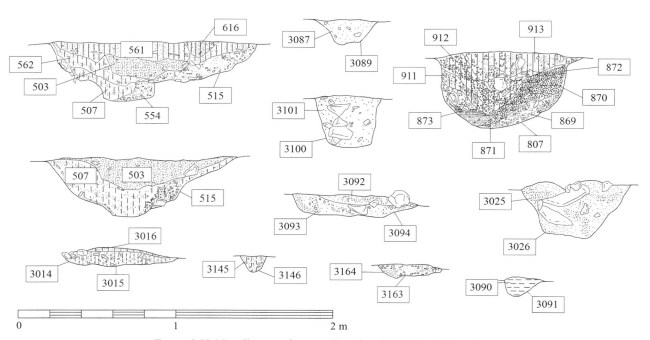

Figure 3.90 Miscellaneous features, Trenches A, AA, F and J: sections

Feature 903 (Fig. 3.88)

903 was the cut of a small irregular feature on the southern edge of a large inner ring post-hole, 825/826. It was shallow, with a bowled base, and held a fill of loose dark yellowish-brown silty sand (10 YR 4/6) with numerous medium-sized pebbles, 904.

Feature 931 (Fig. 3.88)

931 was the cut of an oval-shaped feature, with steep sides except on the south, which was more gradual, and with a rounded base. The basal fill, 932 was concentrated toward the east, and was a friable strong brown loamy sand with small pebbles (7.5 YR 4/6). Above this, skewed toward the west of the feature, was 933, a friable strong brown loamy sand (7.5 YR 5/6). The uppermost fill was 934, a friable reddish-brown loamy sand (5 YR 4/4).

Feature 936 (Fig. 3.88)

936 was an irregularly-shaped feature which intersected with the earlier feature 794. It had steep sides and a gently curving base. Its basal fill was 958, a friable olive brown loamy sand with many small pebbles (2.5 YR 3/2), above which were a series of inter-mixed lenses of loamy sand, 954, 955, 956 and 957. It is debatable whether these really represented separate stratigraphic episodes. All of these layers appear to have been disturbed post-hole packing. They were sealed beneath the more coherent layer 953, a friable dark olive loamy sand with many gritty small stones (2.5 YR 2.5/2). The uppermost fill was 935, a friable dark reddish-brown loamy sand with small pebbles (5 YR 2.5/2), with a lens of charcoal at its base. This probably represented the base of a disturbed post-pipe.

Feature 3014 (Fig. 3.90)

Cut 3014 was a shallow and flat bottomed feature with an abrupt break of slope at the top, and a gradual break of slope at the bottom. 3015, a loose dark brown sandy loam (10 YR 3/3) containing many pebbles was the primary silting within the cut. Fill 3016, a friable brown sandy loam (10 YR 4/3) with a few rounded pebbles, was the only other fill remaining in this feature. Feature 3014 can be interpreted as a heavily truncated post-hole or a small pit.

Feature 3089 (Fig. 3.90)

Cut 3089 was a shallow, heavily truncated feature which may have been a small post-hole, with gradual breaks of slope at top and bottom and an irregularly bowled profile. There was a single fill, 3087, a friable fine yellowish red sand (5 YR 4/6), which contained a few small pebbles.

Feature 3091 (Fig. 3.90)

Cut 3091 was a small scoop with shallow sloping sides, with a single fill of friable dark reddish-brown (5 YR 3/3) humic material 3090, and may have represented the truncated base of a post-hole.

Feature 3094 (Fig. 3.90)

3094 was a shallow oval cut, with a flat base and a near-vertical edge on one side. There were two fills: 3093, a loose, yellowish-brown sandy silt (10 YR 5/6) with numerous pebbles, and 3092, a friable brown sandy silt (10 YR 4/3) with a few fine pebbles. These appear to have been silting layers in what was a very heavily eroded feature.

Feature 3100 (Fig. 3.90)

Cut 3100 was a small roughly circular feature, with sloping sides breaking to a fairly flat base. There was only one fill, 3101, a hard, dark reddish-brown silt (5 YR 3/3), with numerous medium-sized pebbles and several large angular stones, which appeared to have been burnt. However, there were no other signs of burning within the feature, and it follows that the stones had been subjected to burning before they were introduced to the pit.

Feature 3146 (Fig. 3.90)

Cut 3146 was a very small, scooped feature, either a post-hole or stakehole, with a very homogeneous fill, 3145, a friable dark reddish-brown silty sand (5 YR 3/3), containing a few fine pebbles.

Feature 3164 (Fig. 3.90)

3164 was the circular cut of very small post-hole with a single fill, 3163, a friable dark reddish-brown silty sand (5 YR 3/3) with many fine pebbles.

Feature 4016 (Fig. 3.91)

4016 was a shallow rounded feature located to the south of inner post-ring of the Late Neolithic enclosure. It had very gradual concave edges dipping to a rounded base. The basal fill was 4015, a loose red-brown sandy loam (5 YR 4/4) with a few small rounded pebbles. This appeared to be a natural silting at the base of the feature. Above this was 4025, a friable strong brown sandy loam (7.5 YR 4/6). This represented a thin lens of darker material, possibly caused by natural silt accumulation.

Feature 4020 (Fig. 3.91)

4020 was a large irregular feature, located to the south of the middle post-ring, but not apparently associated with it. The sides had a gradual irregular slope onto a rounded base. The basal fill was 4019, a compact dark yellow-brown sandy loam (10 YR 3/4) with very large numbers of small pebbles. It is conceivable that the feature was of natural origin, and that this lower fill was not anthropogenic. The upper fill, 4005, was a compact very dark brown sandy loam (10 YR 2/2). This was equally full of pebbles but contained appreciable numbers of charcoal flecks, and if the feature was not of human origin this material had become trapped in the top of a natural hollow.

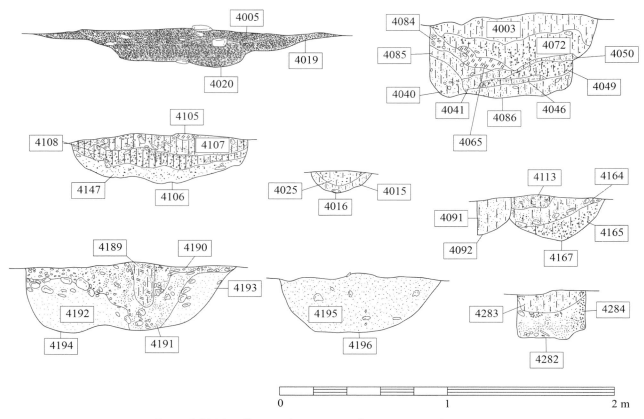

Figure 3.91 Miscellaneous features, Trenches A, AA, F and J: sections

Feature 4086 (Fig. 3.91)

4086 was the cut of a well-defined circular post-hole lying to the south of the inner post-ring of the Late Neolithic enclosure, and immediately to the east of the western side of the cursus. It had steep straight sides descending to a flat base. The basal fill was 4040, a friable dark brown sandy loam (7.5 YR 3/2), which appeared to represent redeposited natural subsoil. Above this was 4041, a friable dark yellowish-brown sandy loam (10 YR 3/4) with a few small pebbles. Above this in turn was 4048, a friable very dark brown sandy loam (10 YR 2/2) with a few small pebbles. This band of dark material may have represented the charred base of a post. Above this was 4049, a loose reddish-yellow sandy loam (7.5 YR 6/8) with a few medium pebbles. This formed part of a horizon of interwoven deposits, suggesting that the post was possibly removed leading to collapse on either edge of the feature. 4050 was a loose dark red sandy loam (2.5 YR 3/6) with numbers of medium pebbles. This appears to have been a burnt soil, indicating that burning had taken place in or nearby to this feature. 4085 was a loose dark yellowish-brown sandy loam (10 YR 3/6) with a few small pebbles, seemingly a collapse deposit. Above this was 4084, a loose dark yellowish-brown sandy loam (10 YR 4/4) with a few medium pebbles, and this layer was probably affected by the slippage of the post. 4065 was a

lens of dark charcoally material. Above this was 4072, a loose dark yellowish-brown sandy loam (10 YR 3/6) with a few mixed pebbles, apparently a stabilisation layer. The uppermost fill was 4003, a loose yellowish-brown loamy sand (10 YR 5/8) with a few mixed pebbles. This was a natural silting at the top of the feature. It is possible that a post that had stood in this feature had been at least partially burned before its removal, since the profile gives little indication of a surviving post-pipe. There was no indication of the date of this feature, but the evidence for burning might indicate that it was in some way related to the cursus.

Feature 4092 (not illustrated)

4092 was the cut of a straight modern drainage feature running NW/SE across the site. It was filled with 4091, a dark humic deposit.

Feature 4106 (Fig. 3.91)

4106 was a large oval cut feature that occurred north of the middle post-ring of the Late Neolithic enclosure, and immediately to the west of the line of the cursus post-holes. Steep concave sides descended to an irregular base. The basal fill of the feature was 4147, a loose brownish-yellow sand (10 YR 6/6). This was apparently a natural accumulation of material generated when the feature

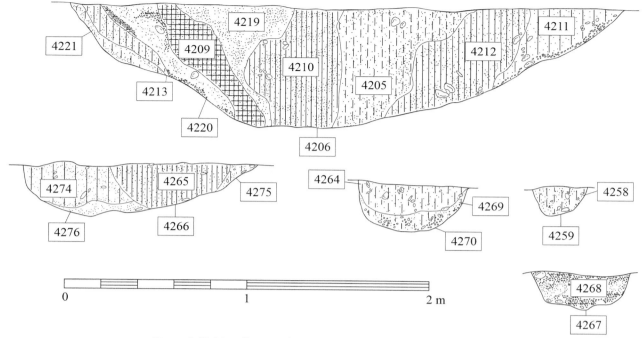

Figure 3.92 Miscellaneous features, Trenches A, AA, F and J: sections

was first cut. Above this was 4108, a tenacious dark red-brown sandy silt loam (5 YR 3/4) with many mixed stones and occasional flecks of charcoal. This material may have been subjected to burning, since it contained occasional fired stones and burnt soil. It lay below 4107, a tenacious strong brown sandy silt loam (7.5 YR 5/6) with a few mixed stones and occasional charcoal flecks. The uppermost fill was 4105, a compacted charcoal layer. This may have constituted the remains of a charred post, or evidence for other burning activities. As in the case of 4086, it is possible that the evidence for burning in this feature links it to the cursus rather than the Late Neolithic enclosure.

Feature 4154 (Fig. 3.88)
4154 was the cut of a large irregular feature, located to the south of the inner post-ring of the Late Neolithic enclosure. It was poorly defined. The edges were steep, straight and concave, with a flat sloping base. The basal fill was 4153, a compact to hard strong brown sandy loam (7.5 YR 4/6) with extremely numerous medium pebbles. This might have represented packing at the base of the feature. Above this was 4152, a loose strong brown silty sand (7.5 YR 4/6) with frequent small pebbles, another potential packing deposit concentrated on the eastern edge of the feature. Above this in turn was 4151, a friable dark reddish-brown sandy loam (5 YR 3/4) with occasional small pebbles, a final packing deposit on the eastern edge of the feature. On the western edge of the feature the principal fill consisted of 4148, a loose strong brown silty sand (7.5 YR 4/6), which may have been

equivalent to 4152. Above this was 4149, a loose dark yellowish-brown sandy loam (10 YR 3/4). This contained distinct tip lines, suggesting the descent of the material from the western edge of the feature. Deposit 4150 lay above the various packing deposits and was composed of friable dark brown sandy silt (7.5 YR 3/3). During excavation, it was conjectured that this might have been a post-pipe. The uppermost fill of the potential post-pipe was 4007, a friable yellowish red silty sand (5 YR 5/6) with frequent large pieces of charcoal. This might have been the remains of a charred post. In section, the layers of fill within 4154 dip and converge toward the centre of the feature in a fashion that does not conform with expected patterns of sedimentation. It is possible that they represent a disrupted profile generated by the removal of a burnt post stump, but given the splayed character of the cut of 4154, it is perhaps more likely that the feature was actually a tree-throw hole, and that 4007 and 4151 represented a silting of burnt material into the top of the feature.

Feature 4167 (Fig. 3.91)
4167 was a small feature that had been cut and partially destroyed by the drainage trench, 4092. Only about a half of the feature remained. It had concave edges on to a rounded base. Its basal fill was 4165, a friable strong brown sandy loam (7.5 YR 3/4) with frequent small pebbles, representing redeposited natural gravel on the base of the feature. Above this was 4164, a friable yellowish red silt loam (5 YR 4/6) with occasional large stones. This was probably a collapsed packing deposit.

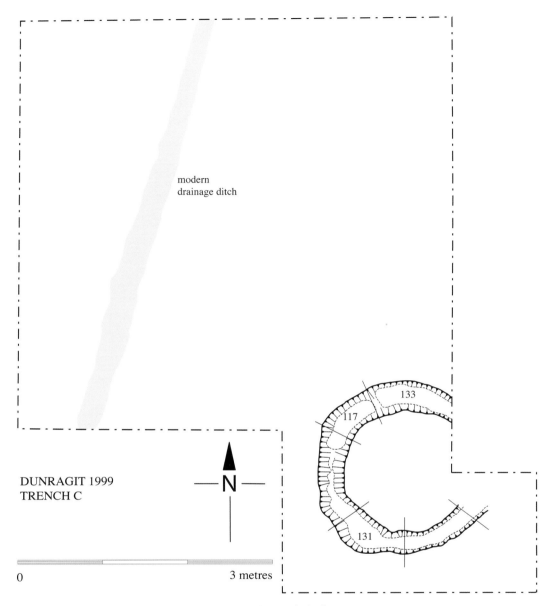

Figure 3.93 Trench C plan

The uppermost fill was 4113, a friable very dark brown silty loam (7.5 YR 2.5/3) containing frequent flecks of charcoal. This probably constituted the remains of a post.

Feature 4194 (Fig. 3.91)

4194 was a large irregular cut located to the north of the middle post-ring in the western part of Trench J. During excavation the feature was difficult to distinguish from the natural subsoil, and it might arguably have been a geological feature, such as solution hollow. Its fills comprised of 4193 and 4192, both of which were loose dark brown sands (10 YR 3/3). Both appeared to represent slumped edge material. Above these was 4191, a friable dark yellow-brown sandy silt (10 YR 3/4) with mixed

Figure 3.94 Trench C showing the ring-ditch

stones. This was a product of silting within the feature. It was in turn capped by 4190, a friable dark reddish-brown sandy silt (5 YR 3/4), representing a further phase of silting. The uppermost fill was 4189, a friable black sandy silt (5 YR 2.5/2). This deposit contained frequent flecks of charcoal, and may have represented an anthropogenic layer that had slumped into the top of an otherwise natural feature.

Feature 4196 (Fig. 3.91)
4196 was the cut of a sub-oval feature that lay to the north of the middle post-ring. Like 4194 above, it may have been a natural feature, judging by the mixed character of the infill. It had steep, straight, concave sides on to a flat base. Its single fill was 4195, a friable dark yellow-brown sandy loam (10 YR 4/6) containing pebbles of various sizes.

Feature 4259 (Fig. 3.92)
4259 was the cut of a small, irregularly shaped feature located to the south of the middle palisade ring of the Late Neolithic enclosure. It had steep concave sides dipping to a rounded base. Its single fill was 4258, a loose to friable very dark brown sandy loam (10 YR 2/2) with numerous medium pebbles. It may have represented no more than a rodent burrow.

Feature 4266 (Fig. 3.92)
4266 was located a little way to the east of road quarry pit 4206. It was an irregular sub-oval feature with steep sides descending to an irregular base. Its primary fill was 4276, a friable, yellowish-brown sandy silt (10 YR 5/6) with numerous small pebbles, apparently representing redeposited natural at the base of the feature. Above this was 4274, a tenacious strong brown sandy silt loam (7.5 YR 5/8) containing four large stones. 4275 was a tenacious strong brown sandy silt loam (7.5 YR 5/6), with occasional large stones. Above these was 4265, a tenacious dark brown sandy silt loam (10 YR 3/3) with a few large large stones and frequent charcoal flecks. This feature was probably a large post-hole, although its relationship with the palisade enclosure is unclear.

Feature 4267 (Fig. 3.92)
4267 was the cut of a circular feature lying to the south of the middle palisade ring, and east of the western side of the post cursus. It was appreciably removed from either of these alignments, so any association is tenuous. It had steep straight sides, descending to a flat base. The uniform fill was 4268, a tenacious dark reddish-brown sandy silt (5 YR 3/4) with numerous medium pebbles, and there was no clear post-pipe.

Feature 4270 (Fig. 3.92)
4270 was the cut of a circular feature that lay between the middle and inner rings of the palisade enclosure. It was a

well-defined cut, although there were no features in the immediate area that it could be obviously associated with. It had steep straight edges, descending onto a rounded base. It was filled with 4269, a loose brown sandy loam (7.5 YR 4/4) with occasional large stones, which appeared to be a packing deposit around the base and sides of the feature. Above this was 4264, a friable very dark brown sandy loam (7.5 YR 2.5/3) with a series of large packing stones. This is likely to have been a post-pipe, into which the packing stones had collapsed.

Feature 4271 (not illustrated)
4271 was a small ovoid pit with a relatively pointed base, containing the dark humic fill 4257. As it lay on the line of the middle post-ring, it was initially considered that this was a prehistoric post-hole. However, on excavation it became clear that it was a modern feature, and for this reason it is not illustrated.

Feature 4282 (Fig. 3.91)
4282 was the cut of a circular post-hole lying to the south of the inner palisade ring. Like 4270, it was clearly defined yet had no direct association with any other feature. It had steep, vertical straight sides leading to an irregular flat base. The fill in the base of the feature was 4284, a loose dark brown sandy loam (7.5 YR 3/4) with very many medium pebbles, probably a packing of redeposited natural gravel. Above this was 4283, a friable dark brown silt (7.5 YR 3/3) with occasional medium pebbles, representing a silting into the top of the feature.

Trench C

Trench C was laid out in order to investigate a small ring-ditch, one of a number that are visible on the aerial photographs of Dunragit. An area of 10 × 10 metres was stripped, cleaned, trowelled and brushed, and left to weather after the ring-ditch had not proved immediately evident. After some days, a small portion of the ditch was identified in the extreme southeast of the trench, and it was clear that for one reason or another the cutting had not been located precisely over the cropmark feature. The trench was consequentially extended, and the whole of the structure was excavated (Figs. 3.93 and 3.94).

The ring-ditch consisted of a single shallow cut 133 (also identified as 116, 177, 131, 136, 135 and 138 in different sections), which had gradually sloping sides and a flat base. It contained two distinct fills (Fig. 3.95). The uppermost of these was 121 (also 113, 119, 120, 125, 127 and 134), which was a friable, very dark grey loamy sand (5 YR 3/1). Below this was 128 (also 112, 115, 122, 128, 132, 140, 141, and 142), a friable dark reddish-brown sandy loam (5 YR 3/2). There was nothing about these fills to suggest anything beside a normal silting process. Cutting through the ditch deposits were two possible

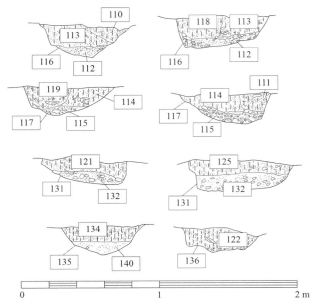

Figure 3.95 Trench C: sections of the ring-ditch

post-holes, cut 118, filled with 110, a firm dark brown sand loam (10 YR 3/3), and cut 114, filled with 111, a firm reddish-brown sandy loam (2.5 YR 2.5/1). Although the aerial photographs had suggested the presence of an internal feature within the ring-ditch, none was identified save for a small rabbit burrow.

The ring-ditch provided disappointingly limited information. Two possibilities presented themselves for the interpretation of the structure. At the Late Neolithic palisaded enclosure at West Kennet in Wiltshire, small enclosed structures with Grooved Ware associations formed integral elements of the monumental complex (Whittle 1997a: 76). However, these were considerably more substantial features than the Trench C ring-ditch. Alternatively, the feature might have represented a small funerary structure. At many other sites in Scotland, Wales and England, Late Neolithic to Middle Bronze Age structures were 'attracted' by the presence of already ancient and venerated sites, whose precise significance might already have been partially forgotten by the time of their construction. Since the Trench C feature was clearly a ring-ditch rather than a small palisaded enclosure, the latter would seem more likely, though the absence of any funerary deposit renders this view conjectural. Certainly, a burial might have been laid out on the old land surface and a small mound raised above it, in which case no trace need have survived ploughing in recent times.

Trench D

The Trench C ring-ditch had been rather ephemeral, and had contained no central feature. The inconclusive character of this investigation made the excavation of a

further minor structure a priority, and with this in mind another suitable feature had been identified on the aerial photo plots for the site, and identified as Trench D. Trench D was an area of 10 × 10 metres, located immediately to the north of the railway line, in the eastern part of the field, a little way to the southeast of Trench C (Fig. 3.96).

However, while the air photo plots had indicated the presence of a continuous ditch surrounding a central feature, no trace of a ditch was located in Trench D. One large pit containing a mass of burnt matter was located (1015), and this may be the presumed 'central feature'. While a number of other features were excavated, it is not clear that they were all contemporary, or that any of them were necessarily prehistoric. Many of the features in this trench were very heavily truncated and difficult to interpret. In many cases the fills closely resembled re-deposited natural material that was clean, did not contain material culture or charcoal, and was generally well sorted. These fills may indicate the erosion of open features that had been heavily truncated since, or may indicate that the features were insubstantial cuts, and not all of these were necessarily of anthropogenic origin. However, 1002, 1008, 1013, and 1021 were organised in a rough arc, and may have formed some kind of integral structure. Certainly, the fills and morphology of this group of features were relatively homogeneous, and we might choose to compare the structure with the later prehistoric round houses found in Trenches A and E.

Feature 1002 (Fig. 3.97)
Feature 1002 was an oval cut with shallow sloping sides breaking to a scooped base. It contained two fills: 1003 (a loose greyish-brown coarse sand, 10 YR 5/2, with many small pebbles) and 1004 (another loose dark greyish-brown coarse sand, 10 YR 3/2, with a higher concentration of small to medium pebbles). Both these deposits closely resembled the natural subsoil.

Feature 1005 (Fig. 3.97)
Cut 1005 was a small circular cut, the western edge of which was steep while the eastern edge was shallow, breaking to a steep slope half way down; the base was flat. This cut contained two fills. The basal deposit was 1006, a loose brown sand (7.5 YR 4/3) with many fine pebbles, which was quite similar to the natural subsoil. 1007, a friable dark greenish-grey silty sand (10 YR 2.5) contained many fine pebbles, and appeared to represent a silting into the top of the feature.

Feature 1008 (Fig. 3.97)
A shallow, oval cut, 1008, with gradual sloping sides breaking to a scooped base, contained two fills. The lower, 1010, was a loose, dark yellowish-brown sand (10 YR 3/4) with numerous medium pebbles, while 1009 was a loose dark brown coarse sand (10 YR 3/3) with many medium pebbles.

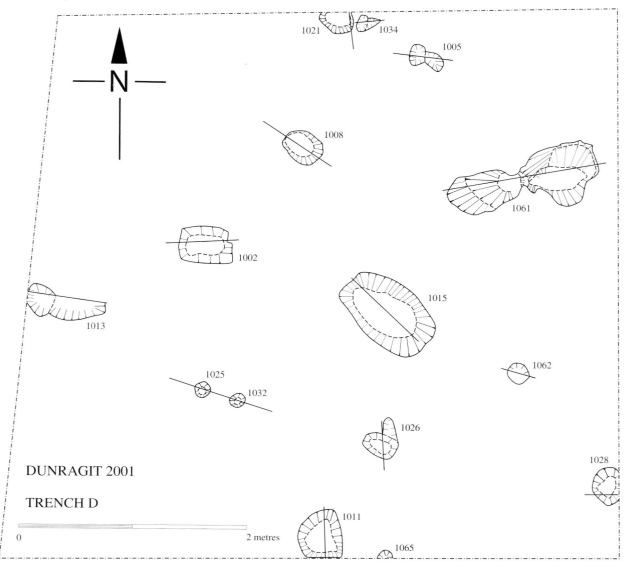

Figure 3.96 Trench D plan

Feature 1011 (Fig. 3.97)

Cut 1011 was not fully exposed within the trench. It appeared as a semi-circular feature extending north from the southern boundary of the site. The profile was stepped with steep sides at the surface breaking to more a more shallow slope at the bottom, and a flat base. 1011 contained a single fill, 1012, a loose very dark greyish-brown sand (7.5 YR 3/2), with many small pebbles.

Feature 1013 (Fig. 3.97)

1013 was a small circular cut, extending east from the western boundary of the trench; the greater part of the feature appeared to be exposed. It had moderately sloping sides breaking to a rounded base. It contained a single fill, 1014, a compact very dark greyish-brown sand (10 YR 3/2) with many small pebbles.

Feature 1015 (Fig. 3.97)

1015 was a roughly oval feature, with sides descending gradually to an uneven base, which was deepest in the northwest. Contained within the cut were 1016, a loose dark yellowish-brown sand (10 YR 3/4) with many small rounded pebbles to the northwest, and 1020, a loose dark brown coarse sand (7.5 YR 3/4), with very numerous medium pebbles. Above 1020 to the southeast lay 1019, a loose yellowish-brown sand (10 YR 5/8). Above these were two further fills, 1017, a friable very dark greyish-brown sandy silt (10 YR 3/2) and 1018, a friable black sandy silt (10 YR 2/1) with numerous rounded pebbles and occasional charcoal fragments. The edges of this feature were poorly defined, but did not resemble a tree throw hole, and is more likely to have been anthropogenic in character.

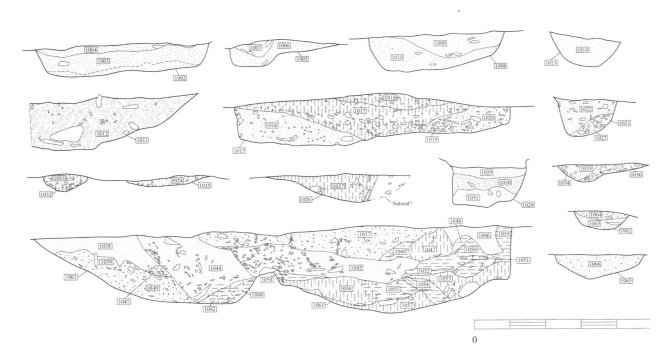

Figure 3.97 Trench D: sections of features

Feature 1021 (Fig. 3.97)

1021 was a small circular feature extending from the north of the trench, and almost entirely excavated. Cut 1021 had moderately sloping sides and a scooped base. There were two consecutive fills which were both quite similar to the natural subsoil; 1023, a loose dark yellowish-brown coarse sand (10 YR 3/4), with very many medium pebbles, and 1022, a loose dark reddish-brown coarse sand (5 YR 3/3) with many small pebbles.

Feature 1025 (Fig. 3.97)

Cut 1025 was very shallow, but was clearly a circular cut with a scooped base, and with a single fill, 1024, a compact very dark greyish-brown sandy silt (10 YR 3/2), containing some small pebbles. 1025 was similar to feature 1032, which was located half a metre to the southeast. The two features might have represented a pair of very truncated post-holes.

Feature 1026 (Fig. 3.97)

Cut 1026 was a most ephemeral feature, cutting into a frost-wedge, with a gradual break of slope along the eastern side, and a sharper slope to the north. The single fill was 1027, a loose dark brown sandy silt (5 YR 3/3) with numerous small pebbles, another fill that closely resembled the natural subsoil.

Feature 1028 (Fig. 3.97)

A circular feature extending west from the eastern wall of the trench, cut 1028 had steep sides which dipped gradually to a roughly flat base. It contained three consecutive fills in the following order: 1031, a loose strong brown fine sand (7.5 YR 4/6) with occasional large pebbles; 1030, a compact light olive brown coarse sand (2.5 YR 5/6) with small rolled pebbles; and 1029, a loose dark yellowish-brown fine sand (10 YR 4/6), with occasional small pebbles. All of these deposits appeared to represent redeposited natural subsoil that had not been altered in any appreciable way.

Feature 1032 (Fig. 3.97)

A very small, circular scooped cut, 1032, had steep sides breaking to a very rounded base. The feature contained a single fill, 1033, a friable, dark olive brown sandy silt (2.5 YR 3/3) with many small pebbles. This feature was too truncated to be readily understood, but may have been associated in some way with the nearby 1025.

Feature 1034 (Fig. 3.97)

The small roughly circular cut 1034 had gradually sloping sides breaking gently to a scooped base. The feature had two fills, 1036, a loose strong brown sand (7.5 YR 4/6) with many medium pebbles and above that 1035, a loose brown sand (7.5 YR 2/5) with a few pebbles small pebbles. This feature was heavily truncated.

Feature 1061

This was by far the most complex feature in Trench D, and seemed to represent the remains of two, and perhaps three intercutting features. In plan, the feature represented a 'figure of eight', formed by two intersecting craters, although at the time of excavation only one cut number was assigned to the feature as a whole. To the west, in a broad cut with shallow sloping sides lay a series of gravelly fills (1038, 1039, 1045) which overlay the siltier primary fill 1040, a friable very dark brown silt (10 YR 2/2) with a few medium pebbles. These layers of fill had apparently been truncated by a further cut, which contained two basal lenses of gritty yellow-brown sand, 1060 and 1042. 1044, a loose dark yellowish-brown sand (10 YR 3/4), with numerous medium pebbles and occasional coarse pebbles, had settled into the cut above these lenses. Further to the east, another probable cut had truncated 1044, and was filled by a chaotic series of lenses of sandy gravel fills (1037, 1043, 1057, 1055, 1056, 1058, 1054, 1053, 1052, 1059, 1050, 1047). Of these, 1043, a loose dark yellowish-brown sand (10 YR 4/4) with numerous fine pebbles and a few medium-sized pebbles, and 1037, a firm brown silt (7.5 YR 4/2) with a few medium-large pebbles, were notable in that they extended across much of the feature, and ran across the high point of the cut in the centre of the feature. The jumbled character of these fills suggests that they may have represented layers of backfill shovelled in from various directions, or perhaps distinct deposits of collapsed packing, which had tumbled into the feature as a post was withdrawn. Although no clear post-pipe was observed I this feature it is possible that the sequence can be understood as a large post that was removed and replaced on a number of occasions.

Feature 1062 (Fig. 3.97)
A small and shallow circular cut, 1062, contained two fills. The basal deposit was 1063, a loose very dark brown silty sand (7.5 YR 2.5/3), with occasional pebbles near the base of the cut. 1064, above this, was a friable dark reddish-brown sandy silt (5 YR 2.5/2) with occasional small pebbles. Both fills were easy to distinguish from the natural subsoil, but the cut was too shallow to support a definitive interpretation.

Feature 1065 (Fig. 3.97)
A small scoop-shaped cut, 1065, extended from the southern boundary of the excavated area. Its sides were even and moderately sloped, breaking to a very scooped base. There was one fill, 1066, a loose, very dark brown silty sand (7/5 YR 2.5/2), with occasional small pebbles, which was quite similar to the surrounding natural subsoil.

Trench E

Trench E was located to the north and east of the large excavated block composed of Trenches A, AA, F and J (Fig. 3.98). The purpose of this trench was to investigate the relationship between the outermost post-ring of the Late Neolithic enclosure and an alignment of posts running southwest/northeast across the enclosure, which represents an extension of the eastern side of the post-defined cursus, beyond its northern terminal. What was not clear was whether these represented one element of a multi-phase monument, or whether the orientation established by the cursus was maintained over a longer period of time, through later episodes of post-erection. A number of features in the western part of Trench E could be taken to represent part of this continuation of the cursus axis. Perhaps the most interesting were 3028, 2036 and 2042, which consisted of a cremation burial deposit flanked by two very large posts. Given that these have proved to be of Bronze Age date, their relationship with the cursus orientation may have been fortuitous, or may demonstrate that this axis retained its significance for an extraordinarily long period of time.

On the eastern side of Trench E, six major posts of the outer palisade ring were encountered, together with a number of smaller posts (Fig. 3.99). The very loose and stony character of the gravel in this part of the site has probably had the effect of making very small features hard to recognise, but enough were identified to confirm that the outer ring of the enclosure was a fence or palisade, like the middle ring, and not composed of free-standing posts, which may have been the case with the innermost ring, for part of its extent or at one stage in its history.

Immediately to the west of the outer post-ring was a group of small post-holes, the majority of which made up a semicircle (2069, 2072, 2091, 2096, 2099, 2102, 2105, 2107 and 2111). This suggests a structure very like the later prehistoric house located in Trench A, with 2072 and 2069 representing the remains of a porch structure, oriented to the east (Fig. 3.98).

There were also two very large oval features, 2067 and 2161, which had showed up on the aerial photographs as elements of a more extensive arrangement of features running parallel with the modern road, the A75. Trench E was located a little to the south of the road between Stranraer and Newton Stewart. This is also known as the Old Military Road, and in this guise it was originally constructed in 1765, terminating at Portpatrick, where ships sailed for Donaghadee in Ireland. The string of large features visible on aerial photographs running immediately to the south of the road are likely to represent gravel quarry pits associated with road-building. In practice, the two large pits excavated contained homogeneous fills, and cut through the gravel to stop abruptly at the sand beneath. While no artefactual evidence was recovered from these features, this would appear to confirm their status as gravel quarries.

Discounting the later features (house and quarry pits), only five cut features were located in the area between the outer post-ring and the post alignment. That is to say, the southern and central parts of Trench E were remarkably

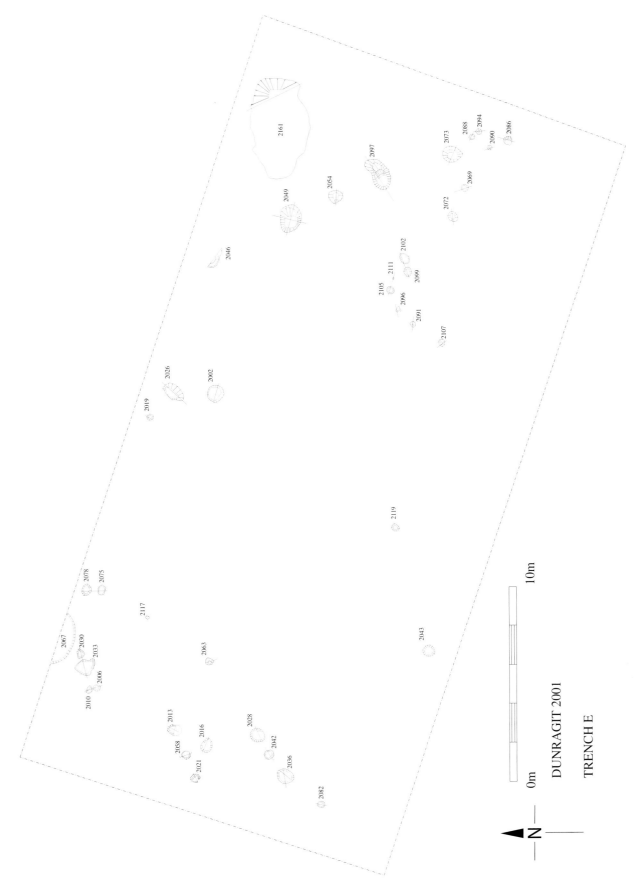

Figure 3.98 Trench E plan

DUNRAGIT 2001

TRENCH E

0m   10m

free of features, when compared with Trenches A, AA, F and J. This is an important observation, because it supports the reality and coherence of the group of features that have been argued to extend the line of the eastern side of the post-defined cursus.

Figure 3.99 Trench E after excavation

Features of the outer post-ring of the palisaded enclosure

Feature 2046 (Fig. 3.100)

2046 was a deep post-hole cut, oval at the surface dropping to a circular, rounded base. It contained packing 2047, a loose very dark brown silty sand/gravel with charcoal flecks (7.5 YR 2.5/2), and post-pipe fill 2048, a friable dark brown sandy silt (7.5 YR 3/3). This feature was notably narrow toward the base, suggesting a socket into which a post had been wedged, and contrasting markedly with the large post-holes of the inner post-ring. The post-pipe did not descend to the base of the cut, but it is considered that the post had rotted out rather than having been withdrawn.

Feature 2049 (Fig. 3.100)

2049 was the cut of a well-defined, deep, ramped post-hole. It was steep-sided on the north and south edges, with a ramp on eastern edge. The basal fill was 2050, a loose, very dark brown silty sand, (7.5 YR 2.5/2). This contained a few small stones, and constituted redeposited natural sand that had collected at the base of the feature before the introduction of the post. Above this was 2051, a friable black sandy silt (10 YR 2/1), with a few small stones. This may have constituted the remains of a decayed post, and did not appear to represent an episode of burning, as charcoal was absent. 2051 lay below 2052, a friable dark brown silty sand (7.5 YR 3/3) containing a few small stones. This was a silting into the top of the post-hole, postdating the rotting-out of the post. 2052 was rather mixed and mottled, indicating a degree of disturbance or settling. Finally, in the top of the feature

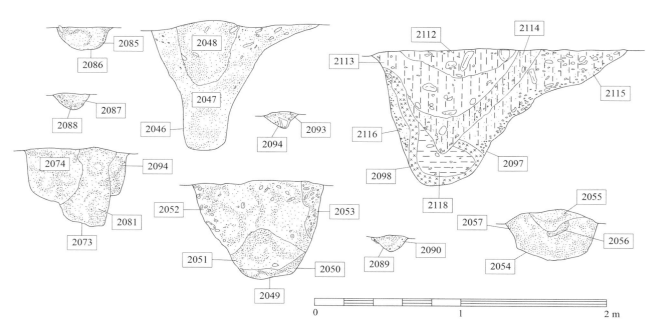

Figure 3.100 Trench E: features of the outer post-ring

at one side, 2053 was a friable dark brown silty sand (7.5 YR 3/4) containing numerous small and medium stones, and probably resulting from a collapse of the southern edge of the post-hole, subsequent to the silting episode.

Feature 2054 (Fig. 3.100)

Cut 2054 was a shallow post-hole feature, sub-rounded in plan with gentle concave edges dipping onto a rounded base. The basal fill was 2057, a loose dark brown silty sand (7.5 YR 3/3) with sparse gravel inclusions, probably representing a packing deposit. This lay beneath 2056, a loose, very dark brown sandy silt (7.5 YR 2.5/2) with sparse gravel inclusions and a little charcoal, probably representing the base of a post-pipe. Above this was 2055, a loose dark brown sandy silt (10 YR 3/3) containing a few small pebbles: a silting into the top of the feature.

Feature 2073 (Fig. 3.100)

2073 was the cut of a well-defined post-hole with clear evidence of a post-pipe visible in the section. The cut had an abrupt break of slope at the top, slightly concave sides and a base that stepped down into the post-pipe. The packing of the post-hole was 2074/2094, a loose, very dark brown silty sand (7.5 YR 2.5/2) with a moderate quantity of gravel fragments. This material surrounded the post-pipe, 2081, which was composed of loose very dark brown sandy silt (10 YR 2/2), with a few small stones. 2074 had apparently slipped forward, partially crushing the post-pipe, subsequent to the rotting out of the post.

Feature 2086 (Fig. 3.100)

2086 was the cut of a shallow post-hole, one of a series of smaller features between the larger post-holes of the outer palisade ring. It had concave edges descending onto a rounded base. The single fill was 2085, a compact dark brown silty sand (10 YR 3/3) containing numerous small pebbles, with occasional charcoal flecks.

Feature 2088 (Fig. 3.100)

2088 was the cut of shallow post-hole similar to 2086, which had concave edges descending onto a rounded base. The single fill was 2087, a friable very dark brown sandy silt (7.5 YR 2.5/2), which contained a few small pebbles.

Feature 2090 (Fig. 3.100)

2090 was a small post-hole of the outer post-ring. It had concave edges, which descended to a rounded base. The single fill was 2089, a compact dark brown silty sand (10 YR 3/3), containing many small pebbles.

Feature 2094 (Fig. 3.100)

2094 was a small post-hole of the outer post-ring. It had concave edges grading onto a rounded base. Its fill was 2093, a friable very dark brown silty sand (7.5 YR 2.5/3), containing numerous small stones and two larger stones, which may have been packing stones.

Feature 2097 (Fig. 3.100)

2097 was the cut of a large ramped post-hole, with relatively straight sides descending to a slightly bowled base, and a rather stepped ramp. The surrounding natural subsoil surface was scorched, suggesting that a post may have been burned *in situ*, and indeed the charred remains of a post were present in the feature. This was represented by context 2098, composed of black charcoal (7.5 YR 2.5/1), and retaining the form of the outer surface of the lower part of the post. The post was flanked by two bodies of packing material, 2116 and 2115, which were probably contiguous. Both were composed of friable strong brown sandy clay (7.5 YR 3/2) containing small and medium pebbles. 2115 extended into the post-ramp. The void of the post, inside the charred fragment, was filled with 2118, a friable dark brown sandy clay (7.5 YR 3/4). 2114 lay above this, a friable dark brown sandy clay (7.5 YR 3/3), containing a few medium rounded pebbles. This may simply have been generated in the slumping of the packing following the collapse of the burnt post, but the deposit appeared to fill a distinctly 'V'-shaped cut, possibly a recut following the burning-out of the post. Above 2114 were 2113, a friable brown sandy clay (7.5 YR 4/4), and 2112, a friable very dark brown sandy clay (7.5 YR 2.5/2), which seem to have represented successive phases of silting into the top of the feature as it settled.

Features located on the axis of the cursus

As noted above, these features might have been constructed at a relatively late date, and need not have been contemporary with each other. Collectively, they extended the established line of the eastern side of the cursus. Alternatively, some of these features might have been integral to the cursus itself in one of its phases of construction, implying that the terminal revealed in Trench F was only the end of the structure in one phase. Certainly, there were a small number of features on this axis within Trench F itself (3069, 3084, 3110 and 3147), which does support the notion that the cursus was renewed or commemorated at some point.

Feature 2006 (Fig. 3.104)

Cut 2006 was a small post-hole, which was reasonably deep, with well-defined sloping edges and a pointed base. The basal fill was 2009, a friable dark brown silty sand (7.5 YR 3/4), containing a few angular stones. Above this was 2008, a friable dark brown sandy silt (7.5 YR 3/4), which contained more numerous angular stones. The uppermost fill was 2007, a loose dark yellow-brown silty sand (10 YR 4/4), with a few angular stones.

Feature 2010 (Fig. 3.104)

2010 was a shallow, poorly defined, irregular feature,

located close to 2006. Its basal fill was 2015, a loose strong brown sandy silt (7.5 YR 4/6), with many rounded pebbles. Above this was 2012, a loose dark yellow-brown silty sand (10 YR 3/4), containing very many small angular stones and one substantially larger stone. The uppermost fill was 2011, a loose dark brown sandy silt (7.5 YR 3/4), with a few small pebbles.

Feature 2013 (Fig. 3.104)
2013 was a heavily truncated feature, and rather difficult to interpret. It had diffuse edges, which were poorly defined. Its fill was 2014, a friable strong brown silty sand (7.5 YR 4/6), with numerous pebbles.

Feature 2016 (Fig. 3.104)
2016 was a shallow, poorly defined feature, similar to 2013. It was probably highly truncated. The lower fill was 2018, a loose dark yellow-brown silty sand (10 YR 4/4), containing large numbers of very small stones. Above

Figure 3.101 Outer post-ring post-hole 2049

this was 2017, a loose strong brown coarse sand (7.5 YR 4/6), with a few medium and small pebbles.

Feature 2021 (Fig. 3.104)
2021 was the well-defined sub-circular cut of a probable post-hole with steep sides and a rounded base. The basal fill, 2022, swept down the eastern side of the feature from the surface, and was composed of a friable, very dusky red silty sand (7.5 YR 2.5/2) which contained many small rounded stones. Above this was 2023, a looser very dusky red sandy silt (7.5 YR 2.5/2) with a very few small rounded stones. The uppermost fill was 2024, a loose very dusky red sandy silt (7.5 YR 2.5/2) with large numbers of small to medium stones. There was no obvious sign of a post-pipe, and if a post had been present it is likely that it had been withdrawn.

Feature 2028 (Fig. 3.102)
Feature 2028 was one of two deep post-holes that flanked cremation burial pit 2042. Cut 2028 was a deep, well-defined post-hole, with a single fill. Fill 2029 was a friable sandy silt (7.5 YR 2.5/2) containing numerous small stones and some larger (possibly packing) stones. This deposit was somewhat mottled and disturbed. The concentration of the larger stones in the centre of the feature suggested that the contents of the post-hole had collapsed when the post was removed.

Feature 2030 (Fig. 3.104)
2030 was a small sub-circular feature with sloping sides and a rounded base, which appeared to be severely truncated. The thin basal fill was 2031, a friable very dusky red silty sand (2.5 YR 2.5/3) containing very numerous pebbles. Above this was 2032, a tenacious dark red-brown sandy silt (5 YR 3/3), which contained a few angular stones.

Feature 2033 (Fig. 3.104)
2033 was a large irregular feature. Its edges were ragged,

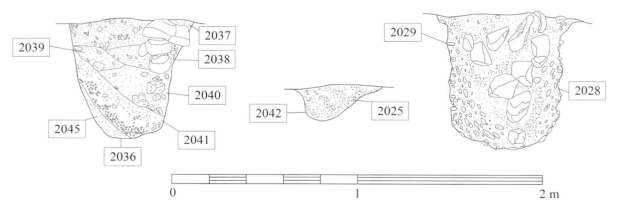

Figure 3.102 The cremation burial pit 2042 and its two flanking post-holes

undulating and poorly defined, suggesting that it might have been of natural origin. The basal fill was 2034, a loose dusky red sandy silt (10 YR 3/4) containing a few angular medium stones. A second episode of silting was represented by 2035, a friable very dusky red silty sand (2.5 2.5/4) with a few angular stones.

Feature 2036 (Fig. 3.102)

Feature 2036 was the second of two deep post-holes that flanked cremation burial pit 2042. The very deep, round post-hole cut 2036 contained primary silting 2045, above which was 2041, a slumped packing of loose dark

brown coarse sandy gravel (10 YR 4/6). Above this was a very loose dark brown sandy gravel, 2040 (7.5 YR 2.5/3), which represented further disturbed packing, with packing stones on its eastern side. Two further layers of disturbed packing, 2039 and 2038, were above this, a loose dark brown coarse sand with small pebbles (7.5 YR 3/4) and a loose dark yellowish-brown fine sand (10 YR 3/6). Finally, the top of the feature was filled with 2037, a friable, very dark brown coarse sand (7.5 YR 2.5/3), representing a layer of silting. This very deep post-hole contained slipped packing stones, and gave the impression that the post had been rocked out of position. It is therefore likely that both of the posts that had bracketed the cremation burial had been deliberately removed.

Figure 3.103 Feature 2036, one of the post-holes flanking cremation burial pit 2042

Feature 2042 (Fig. 3.102)

This small feature lay between the large, deep post-holes 2028 and 2036, and the three together represented a coherent structure. A shallow, sub-circular cut with rounded base, 2042, contained a deposit of cremated bone, closely packed together in the matrix of 2025, a loose, very dusky red silty sand (7.5 YR 2.5/2). Although the feature was not deep, it appeared that little of the burial deposit had been lost to erosion. The cremation burial was probably that of a woman aged 25–45, together with some cremated animal bone, from a medium to large sized creature (see McKinley, Chapter 8). The cremated bone produced a radiocarbon determination of 1397 to 1132 Cal BC, at 95.4% probability, a date in the Middle Bronze Age (see Chapter 10).

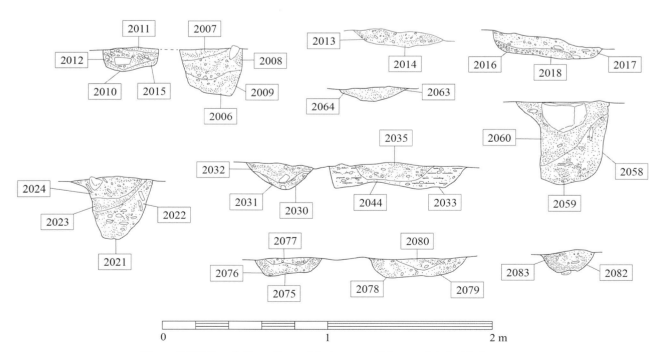

Figure 3.104 Trench E: sections of features possibly associated with the cursus

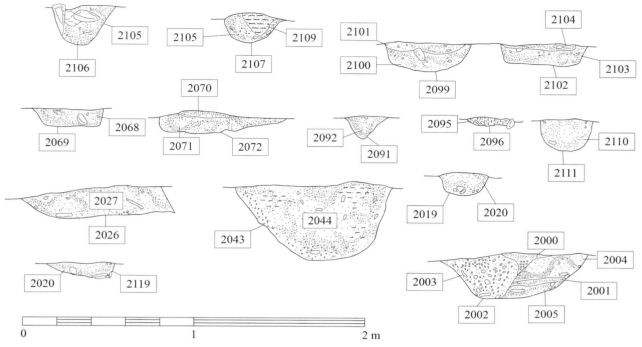

Figure 3.105 Trench E: features of the later prehistoric round house, and miscellaneous features

Feature 2058 (Fig. 3.104)
2058 was a well-defined post-hole cut with steep vertical sides descending onto a rounded base. At the base of the feature was a layer of natural silting, 2059, composed of friable very dusky red sandy silt (7.5 YR 2.5/2), with a few small stones. Above this, context 2060 was a loose, very dusky red sandy silt (7.5 YR 2.5/2) with many medium-sized stones and two large stones, which can reasonably be interpreted as packing stones. There was no clear sign of a post-pipe in the section, and it is most likely that this was a post-hole from which the timber had been withdrawn, causing the disruption of the packing.

Feature 2063 (Fig. 3.104)
The small, shallow feature 2063 was probably a sub-rounded post-hole, although interpretation was hindered by the degree of truncation. It had moderately concave edges, descending onto a rounded base. The single fill was 2064, a very loose dark reddish-grey silty sand (5 YR 4/2). This contained a few small to medium-sized rounded pebbles.

Feature 2075 (Fig. 3.104)
2075 was a shallow, poorly defined feature in the northern corner of Trench E. It was severely truncated, and had steep concave sides descending to a flat base. The basal fill was 2076, a loose dusky red sandy silt (2.5 YR 3/3), with a few small angular stones. Above this was 2077, a loose dark reddish-brown silty sand (5 YR 3/4) with a

very few small pebbles. This might possibly have been the very bottom of a post-pipe.

Feature 2078 (Fig. 3.104)
2078 was a shallow, irregular feature located close to 2075 above, and was equally truncated. Cut 2078 had steep, concave edges descending onto an irregular base. The single fill was 2079, a loose dark reddish-brown silty sand (5 YR 3/4) which contained a very few small angular stones. Above this was 2080, a friable, reddish-brown silty sand (5 YR 4/4), with a few small angular stones.

Feature 2082 (Fig. 3.104)
2082 was a small, shallow feature with steep concave edges descending onto a rounded base. Its single fill was 2083, a loose very dark brown sandy silt (7.5 YR 2.5/3) containing a few small to medium stones.

Features of a later prehistoric house

Trench E revealed traces of a circular later prehistoric building, similar to that discovered in Trench A, although rather smaller with a diameter of around seven metres. Only the northern half of the structure survived owing to the extensive truncation of the subsoil surface in this part of the site. Feature 2069 probably represented part of a porch structure, in which case the building faced to the east, like that in Trench A.

Feature 2069 (Fig. 3.105)
2069 was a shallow, circular feature lying to the west of the outer palisade ring. It had steep concave sides descending onto a flat base. The fill was 2068, a compact dark brown sandy silt (10 YR 3/3) with a few small pebbles and one large stone. This context contained flecks of charcoal, and a few flakes of burnt bone.

Feature 2072 (Fig. 3.105)
2072 was a well-defined sub-circular cut with vertical sides and a pointed base, containing post-pipe 2081 of loose, very dark brown sandy silt (10 YR 2/2) and packing 2073/2074, a loose very dark brown silty sand with small stones (7.5 YR 2.5/2).

Feature 2091 (Fig. 3.105)
Cut 2091 was a somewhat disturbed feature, sub-oval in plan and with gradual sides descending to a pointed base. Its fill was 2092, a loose very dark brown silty sand (7.5 YR 2.5/2), containing a little small gravel.

Feature 2096 (Fig. 3.105)
The small, bowl-shaped cut 2096 contained 2095, a compact dark brown sandy loam (10 YR 3/3).

Feature 2099 (Fig. 3.105)
2099 was the shallow base of a small post-hole, with lower fill 2100, a friable dark reddish-brown (5 YR 2.5/2) sandy silt, above which was 2101, a friable dusky red (2.5 YR 3/2) sandy silt.

Feature 2102 (Fig. 3.105)
Cut 2102 was a small post-hole with irregular sides dropping onto a rounded base. Its basal fill was 2104, a friable dark reddish-brown sandy silt (5 YR 2.5/2) which contained a few small pebbles. Above this was 2103, a friable dusky red sandy silt (5 YR 3/2), containing a few small, angular stones and one larger stone, which may have been a packing stone.

Feature 2105 (Fig. 3.105)
2105 was the well-defined cut of a circular feature, with steep concave sides descending onto a rounded base. The fill was 2106, a friable very dark brown sandy silt (7.5 YR 2.5/2), containing a few small pebbles and three large packing stones, making up a packing deposit.

Feature 2107 (Fig. 3.105)
2107 was the cut of a truncated post-hole, with steep concave sides descending onto a rounded base. Its fill was 2108, a loose very dark brown sandy clay (7.5 YR 2.5/2), containing a little small to medium gravel, representing a packing deposit. The truncated post-pipe was 2109, a loose dark red sandy silt, (5 YR 2.5/1), containing a little small gravel.

Feature 2111 (Fig. 3.105)
2111 was the cut of a shallow, irregular feature, smaller than the other components of the later prehistoric house but situated on the line of the northern wall. It was filled with 2110, a compact dark grey sand (10 YR 4/1) containing a large quantity of small pebbles.

Road quarry pits

Feature 2061 (Fig. 3.106)
2061 was a very large, sub-circular feature (roughly 5 metres in length) with shallow concave sides sloping to a flat base. It was very notable that the feature cut through the natural gravel, but did not dig into the sand that lay beneath it, supporting the interpretation as a gravel quarry. The basal fill was 2062, a loose dark yellowish-brown sandy silt (10 YR 4/4), with quantities of small to medium pebbles. This appeared to represent a natural silting into the bottom of the feature, indicating that it had not been deliberately backfilled. The gravel within this layer was patchy, and was probably generated by weathering or collapse from the edge of the feature. A further layer of silting above this, 2056 (not visible in section), was a loose, very dusky red sandy silt (7.5 YR 2.5/2), with fewer pebble inclusions. There were considerable quantities of charcoal dispersed through this layer, suggesting an episode of burning in the pit or nearby. Finally, 2055 was a loose dark brown sandy silt (10 YR 3/3) containing a few pebbles (also not visible in section). The overall sequence indicates a feature that had been allowed to silt up naturally following the removal of gravel. As with 2067, 2061 was void of finds.

Feature 2067 (Fig. 3.106)
2067 was a large, rounded feature caught in section against northern baulk of Trench E. It had a steep, straight-sided cut descending onto a rounded base. The basal fill was 2066, a compact greyish brown sandy silt (10 YR 3/2) containing numerous small pebbles. This appeared to represent a natural silting in the base of the feature. It lay beneath 2065, a compact brown sandy silt (10 YR 3/3). This contained still more numerous small and medium pebbles. No dating evidence was recovered from the pit.

Miscellaneous features
Feature 2002 (Fig. 3.105)
2002 was a well-defined circular feature, with an abrupt break of slope at the top, near-vertical sides, and a flat base. The basal fill was 2005, a friable very dark brown silty sand (7.5 YR 2.5/3) containing numbers of small rounded pebbles. This material had probably fallen from the sides shortly after digging. Above this was 2001, a thin layer of friable black silty sand (5 YR 2.5/1), which contained appreciable quantities of small fragments of charcoal, as well as a few small rounded stones. This may

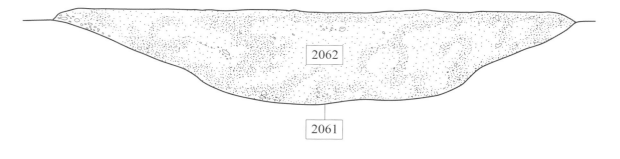

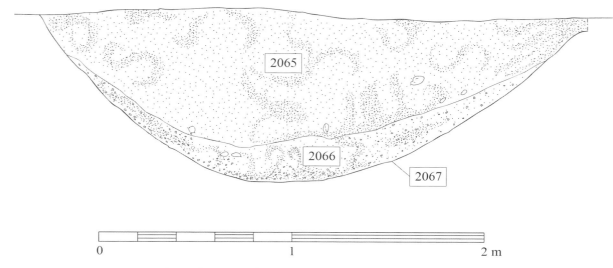

Figure 3.106 Trench E: road quarry pits 2061 and 2067

have been the trace of a burnt post. 2001 lay below 2004, a friable dusky red sandy silt (2.5 YR 3/3), containing a very few small rounded pebbles, which represented a silting into the top of the feature. 2005, 2001 and 2004 appeared to have been truncated, and it is probable that the feature had been recut. The principal fill of this recut was 2003, a loose dark yellow-brown sandy silt (10 YR 3/6), containing many medium-sized rounded pebbles. This deposit appeared to have suffered a considerable degree of slumping. The uppermost fill in the feature was 2000, a loose very dusky red sandy silt (2.5 YR 2.5/2), a silting into the uppermost part of the profile. Curiously, this material appeared to have penetrated down the side of the recut, beside 2003.

Figure 3.107 Road quarry pit 2067

Feature 2019 (Fig. 3.105)
2019 was a small, shallow, circular feature, with shallow sloping sides, possibly associated with features 2002 and 2026. It was probably a small post-hole. Its single fill was 2020, a loose dark yellowish-brown sandy silt (10 YR 3/6), containing a few rounded pebbles.

Feature 2026 (Fig. 3.105)
2026 was a shallow oval feature, with gradual sides from a poorly defined break of slope, owing to its evident truncation. The feature had been disrupted by animal disturbance on its northeast edge. It was perhaps associated with Features 2002 and 2019, although

the shallow character of all of these features hindered interpretation. The fill of 2026 was 2027, a loose dark yellow-brown sandy silt (10 YR 4/4) with a few small rounded stones.

Feature 2043 (Fig. 3.105)
2043 was a shallow but well-defined post-hole, with sloping sides and a rounded base, from a gradual break of slope. The single homogeneous fill was 2044, a compact very dark grey-brown sandy loam (10 YR 3/2), containing numerous medium pebbles and occasional small flecks of charcoal.

Feature 2119 (Fig. 3.105)
2119 was a shallow, sub-circular cut with poorly defined edges. It was possibly a post-hole, but may simply have been a natural feature. Its fill was 2120, a friable to loose very dark brown sandy silt (7.5 YR 2.5/2) containing a few small pebbles.

4

DROUGHDUIL MOTE

Julian Thomas, David Sanderson and Colin Kerr

Introduction

Droughduil Mote is located at approximately NX14805685, in a plantation situated to the west of Droughduil Primary School, 400 metres south of the Late Neolithic enclosure at Dunragit. The mound is flat-topped, approaching 10 metres in height, and roughly 60 × 50 metres in extent. It is markedly oval rather than circular in plan, with a long axis running north-south (Fig. 4.1). The mound stands in an area of woodland managed by Forest Enterprise, and had recently been cleared of trees at the time of investigation in 2002. It stands at the point where the rolling fields south of Dunragit begin to give way to the sand dunes of Luce Sands. It had been noted that the entrance avenue that connects with the middle ring of the Dunragit enclosure was aligned on the mound, which has a commanding view across the monumental complex (Fig. 4.2) and this prompted the speculation that the latter might be Neolithic in date, rather than representing a medieval motte (or castle mound), as had been suggested at the time when the site was scheduled as an ancient monument. The most obvious Neolithic parallel for such a mound would be Silbury Hill (Whittle 1997a; Leary 2010), but other large mounds of certain or possible Neolithic date include the Marlborough Mound, the Conquer Barrow, Duggleby Howe, Wold Newton, the Hatfield Barrow and Courthill (Barber *et al.* 2010; Gibson and Bayliss 2010; Linge 1987; Sheridan 2010). Several of these are closer in scale to the Droughduil mound than is Silbury Hill, which might be understood as a uniquely elaborate example of a more general monumental form. The immediate objective of

the fieldwork at Droughduil in 2002 was to determine whether the mound was medieval or Neolithic in date, by investigating its morphology and identifying dating material. While suitable samples for radiocarbon dating would be ideal, it was judged that obtaining dates through optically stimulated luminescence dating ('OSL') would be very acceptable. While this method has a high margin of error, it should be entirely possible to distinguish between a date in the early second millennium AD and one in the third millennium BC. The site was especially well suited to the method, since it was largely composed of sand, which would provide the quartz grains necessary for dating.

A complete section of the Droughduil mound would have involved severe logistical problems, for a trench deep into large mound composed of sand would have required substantial shoring, and this was not considered practicable in the context of a university excavation. Instead, it was decided to excavate a trench up the side of the mound, bottoming on the original mound surface and revealing its morphology and construction (Trench G) (Fig. 4.3). Silbury Hill, in its final form, was composed of a series of stacked drums, revetted by walls of chalk blocks (Leary 2010: 146). If the Droughduil mound were Neolithic in date, it was conceivable that a comparable structure might have existed. It was agreed with Historic Scotland that a limited part of this section would cut into the tail of the mound, to enable the structure of the monument to be revealed to some extent, and to allow samples to be taken for environmental analysis and OSL dating. A second trench, 3 × 3 metres in extent was opened on the summit of the mound, allowing a depression there

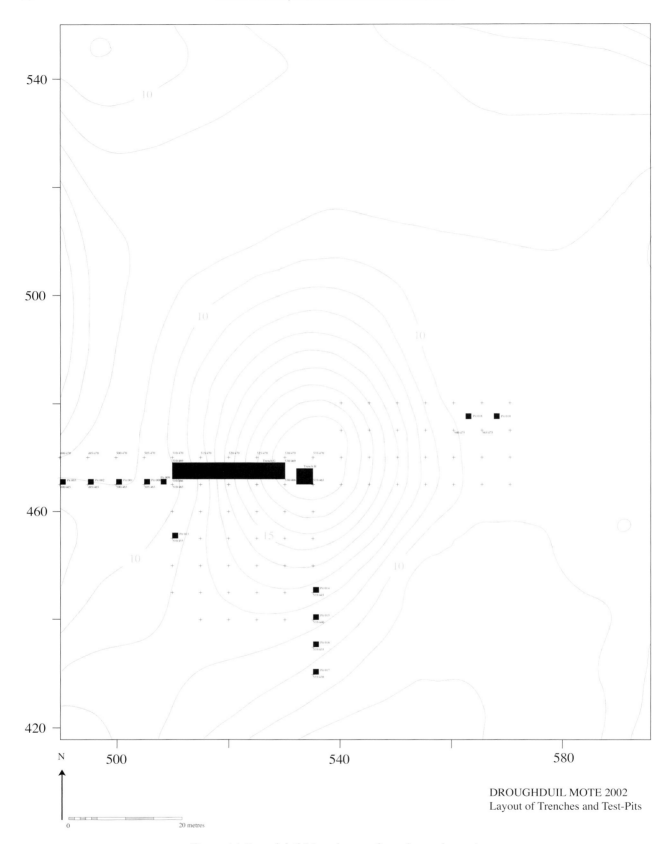

DROUGHDUIL MOTE 2002
Layout of Trenches and Test-Pits

Figure 4.1 Droughduil Mote: layout of trenches and test-pits

Figure 4.2 The view northwards from the Droughduil mound, over the Dunragit complex

Figure 4.3 The Droughduil mound under excavation, from the west

to be investigated (Trench H). This, it was speculated, might have been the location of an antiquarian trench, excavated at some time in the eighteenth or nineteenth centuries. The third trench was to be cut over the presumed quarry ditch surrounding the mound. In order to locate this trench to the best advantage, a transect of shovel-pits was laid out running due west from the mound at 5 metre intervals for a distance of 55 metres (Fig. 4.1). Although several of these were dug to a depth of around 2 metres, none produced any evidence for the presence of a ditch. The exercise was then repeated with transects of pits to the east and south of the mound. These too were unsuccessful, and it was eventually concluded that no ditch had ever existed.

This circumstance proved more comprehensible when Trench G had been fully excavated (Fig. 4.4). At the base of the sequence lay a deposit of finely bedded sand (context 5013). This material was dark yellowish-brown (10 YR 4/4) and clearly laminated. It was concluded that this might represent a naturally accumulated deposit. However, it was not easy to identify a clear boundary between this and context 5022, another dark yellowish-brown sand (10 YR 4/6) which made up the principal build of the mound. There was not, for instance, any clear turf-line or other land-surface separating the two. The best way to explain this circumstance is to argue that the mound had been constructed by scarping and adding to a natural sand mound that had existed on the site at the time of building.

On the upper part of the mound the profile of the monument was clearly stepped (Fig. 4.5). The original mound had been more obviously flat-topped than the structure now appears, and a series of three or four distinct ledges ran down from the summit (Fig. 4.6). There was no obvious evidence of any revetment of these ledges, although the slope of the side of the mound is relatively gentle. However, given that the material from which the mound is composed is compacted sand, it seems highly likely that a revetment of turf or timber had

originally existed. Immediately above the original sand surface of the mound, deposits of wind-blown sand were identified. On the summit of the mound a thick wedge of friable dark yellowish-brown sand (10 YR 4/4) could be recognised (context 5018/5017), while filling the ledges and extending down the western slope of the mound was context 5021, another compact dark yellowish-brown sand (10 YR 4/8).

Immediately above these windblown sand deposits, an entirely unexpected stone cairn was encountered on the western summit of the mound (Fig. 4.7). At its base the cairn included a number of large angular rock fragments (5011), several of which appeared to form a curved kerb (Fig. 4.8). The same large stones could be identified in Trench H, and it seems likely that the structure had been a round cairn, around 8 metres in diameter (Fig. 4.9). The main core of the cairn was composed of rounded cobbles (context 5010/5008) (Fig. 4.10). In the northeast part of Trench G, where the cairn was highest, there were voids between the cobbles, but much of the cairn material had been pressed down into the windblown sand deposit below by gravity (Fig. 4.11). The body of the cairn produced two small flint scrapers and some tiny crumbs of burnt bone (much too small, unfortunately, to allow radiocarbon dating).

The round cairn appeared to have been capped with further large angular stones (5019/5023). The cairn had evidently been quite tall, and relatively unstable, for a scatter of collapsed stones in a matrix of strong brown (7.5 YR 4/6) loose to friable sand (5003) spread down-slope across the whole of Trench G. Above this layer in Trench G there were further patches of windblown sand (5001 and 5020), and a darker layer at the foot of the mound (5012), which may have represented a stabilisation horizon.

However, in Trench H the presumed prehistoric deposits were cut through by a more recent set of features. The wall of a small stone building (5007) was set in a foundation trench (5015), which cut through the stone

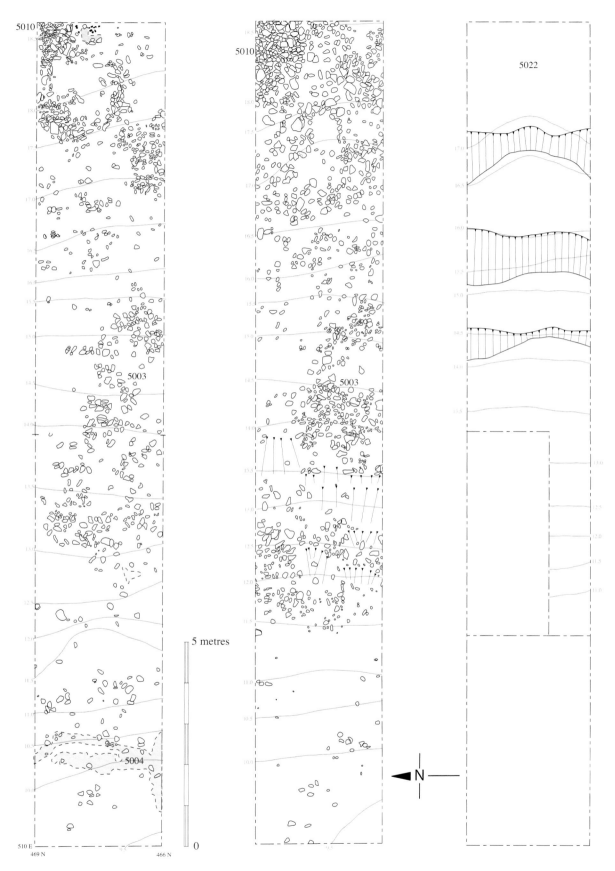

Figure 4.4 Drougduil: successive stages in the excavation of Trench G

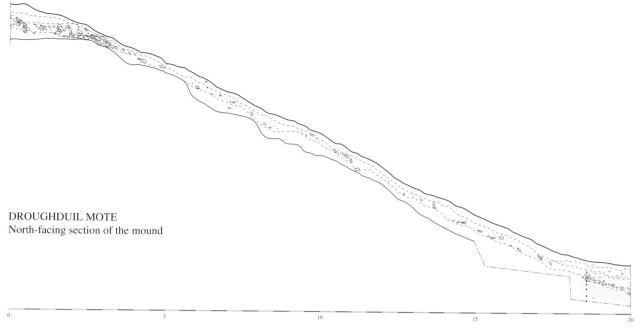

DROUGHDUIL MOTE
North-facing section of the mound

Figure 4.5 North-facing section of the mound in Trench G

Figure 4.6 The steps or ledges on the Droughduil mound from above

Figure 4.7 The cairn in Trench G from above

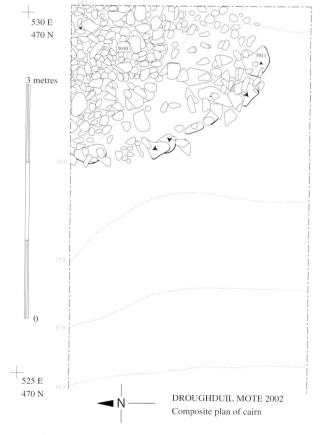

DROUGHDUIL MOTE 2002
Composite plan of cairn

Figure 4.8 Composite plan of cairn in Trench G

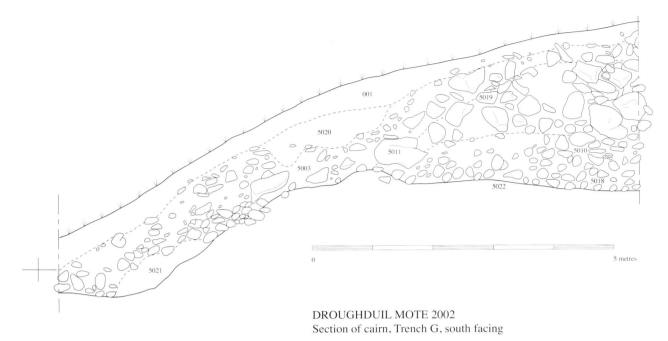

DROUGHDUIL MOTE 2002
Section of cairn, Trench G, south facing

Figure 4.9 Section of cairn in Trench G, south facing

Figure 4.10 Section of the cairn in Trench G from the south

Figure 4.11 The cairn in Trench G

mass of the cairn (Fig. 4.12). It was this building that had been the cause of the depression in the top of the mound that had been observed prior to excavation. Within the trench the structure was roughly 2 metres from north to south, and to the east the fourth wall of the building could be seen through the rubble infill that formed the section, indicating that it was no more than 1.5 metres wide (Fig. 4.13). Although no medieval finds at all were recovered from any part of the mound, a concentration of nineteenth century bottle fragments and china sherds was found in and around the building, and in the upper part of the cairn, which had been heavily disturbed by animal burrowing and bracken and tree roots. A door opened westward from the structure, seemingly leading

directly into the cairn, so that it is to be presumed that enough of the stone had been cleared aside to allow access to the building (Fig. 4.14).

At the base of the building were traces of a wooden floor (context 5016). Beside the wood a glass bottle was located, and inside the bottle was a small scrap of paper, which was quite wet. However, on one side of the paper the following message could be made out, in pencil:

"The Hut"
Demolished
Oct 14, 1908
By Robert Broadfoot
Droughduil

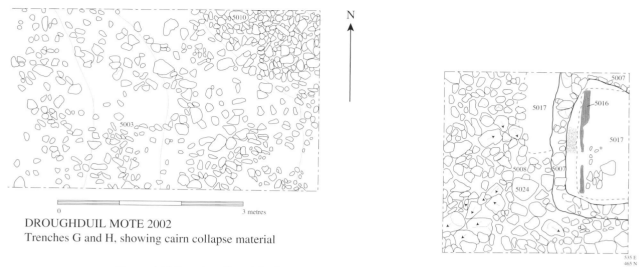

DROUGHDUIL MOTE 2002
Trenches G and H, showing cairn collapse material

Figure 4.12 Trenches G and H, showing cairn collapse material and plan of 'the hut'

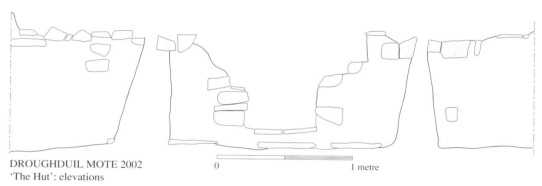

DROUGHDUIL MOTE 2002
'The Hut': elevations

Figure 4.13 'The hut': elevations

On the other side, in another hand and less distinct (in pen):

------------ present
agree to serve Charles Broad------
farm servant from -----------
I am to receive £--
--------- to set
and to cut from good

This would appear to represent part of an agricultural labourer's contract, torn up and used for the note in the bottle. The Charles Broadfoot mentioned in the text is almost certainly the subject of an obituary in the *Wigtown Free Press* for 2 July 1914:

Old Luce Farmer

By the death, which occurred on Saturday last, the parish of Old Luce has lost one of its oldest inhabitants, and the Dunragit estate its oldest tenant farmer. The deceased, who was in his ninety-second year, was for over fifty years tenant at Droughduil, and was reckoned as an agriculturalist

Figure 4.14 'The hut' from above

of outstanding ability. For over a quarter of a century Mr Broadfoot was an elder in Glenluce Parish Church and continued to carry out the duties pertaining to that position until incapacitated by the infirmities of age. Mr Broadfoot, who was of a quiet and kindly disposition, leaves a large family of sons and daughters.

Charles Broadfoot thus farmed at Droughduil as a tenant of the Dunragit estate, and is buried in Old Luce Churchyard. The tomb also contains the body of his son Robert, who died in 1952 at the age of 90. At the time when he demolished 'the hut' he would have been aged around 35. The note was handed over to Stranraer Museum for conservation.

Optically Stimulated Luminescence dating

D.C.W. Sanderson and C. Kerr

Introduction
A sampling visit to Dunragit mound was undertaken on 28 August 2002 to facilitate luminescence dating of sediments (Fig. 4.15). The mound has a spatial alignment with the entranceway to the middle circle of the Late Neolithic enclosure in a nearby field, identified from aerial photography, and partially excavated. It had been postulated that the mound might also be of prehistoric (i.e. Late Neolithic/Early Bronze Age) origins, rather than a medieval motte-like structure, in which case it might have had a role connected with the activities in the henge-like monuments to which it appears linked. The

Figure 4.15 OSL dating samples being taken at Droughduil

purpose of the sampling trip was to identify opportunities for optically stimulated luminescence (OSL) dating of sediments which might be helpful in clarifying the formation chronology of the monument.

OSL dating records the luminescence levels induced by exposure to natural background radiation during periods of enclosure and protection from daylight. Quartz and feldspars, which are both common components of most sands and sediments are capable of accumulating luminescence signals. For dating purposes we require a depositional history which deposited the sediment with negligible residual levels of luminescence. OSL signals from quartz and feldspars are rapidly depleted by exposure to daylight. Typical bleaching rates result in 3 orders of magnitude signal reduction in 10^6–10^7 J m^{-2} exposure to daylight, which can be readily achieved at UK latitudes in less than a single day. Therefore sedimentary deposition processes which result on significant exposure to daylight immediately prior to deposition, or to enclosure of sediments whose recent environmental history of erosion and transport has already resulted in negligible residuals, can provide the basis for meaningful dating. In practice Aeolian sediments are normally expected to be well bleached. Other classes of sediments may experience more complex depositional histories, which can lead to mixed age material, or to partially bleached samples. While luminescence characterisation of such re-deposited materials may also be of value in understanding the formation history of archaeological sites, dating may be problematical in the absence of a well constrained depositional event.

At the time of the visit, the excavation had progressed to the extent of revealing two structures in the upper area: (i) the remains of a mortared structure which contained a document indicating demolition of a small hut in the early twentieth century, (ii) a stone cairn presumed to be of prehistoric origins and containing quantities of burned bone. A section from the top to the bottom of the site in the lee side showed extensive evidence of wind-blown sand. Indeed the cairn was set on relatively clean sand, and a layer of stones, presumed to be associated with the collapse of the cairn could be seen in section particularly at the top and bottom of the mounds. This collapse layer was also enclosed above, and below by windblown sands. At the base of the mound the sand layers continued with vestigial remains of possible weathered landscape surfaces (revealed by oxidation stains) and darker layers that may have represented older vegetation layers. While it was difficult to identify a palaeolandscape surface that predated the original mound, opportunities were identified for sampling Aeolian sands that should represent (i) the landscape evolution in the earlier formation stages of the mound, (ii) layers that predate the construction of the cairn, (iii) layers that predate the cairn collapse, and layers that post date the major collapse of the cairn.

These samples provided a useful means of confirming

the developmental sequence of the major units which could be observed in the excavation.

Sampling details

Eleven samples for OSL dating were collected during the fieldtrip from selected locations. In each case the area was cleaned back immediately prior to sampling to remove layers which may have been bleached by excavation. Samples were collected in opaque 4 cm diameter tubes, which were removed by overcutting the sampling location with a 10 cm diameter black pipe. The sample tubes were transferred to lightproof bags, endcapped, labelled and sealed to retain moisture. Gamma ray spectra were recorded in the sampling location using a 50 × 50mm NaI detector and Rainbow 1000 channel spectrometer. Integral count rates above 450 keV were converted to gamma dose rates using conversion factors determined at the SUERC gamma ray calibration facility in East Kilbride. The samples were registered in the SUERC luminescence laboratory and weighed to establish a traceable water content history. They were then dark stored pending selection for measurement. Site coordinates for each sampling location were recorded, and the locations transcribed to site records.

Of the 11 samples, four represented the material under the edges and centre of the cairn. One mid-slope sample predated the collapse of the cairn and should record a period associated with the construction of either the main mound, or the cairn. At the base of the mound a set of six vertically stratified samples had also been assembled which represented the full sequence of events revealed by the excavation. The set contained sufficient replicates to provide internal consistency checks on dating assumptions. A small quantity of sand was also collected from superficial areas around the excavation for use as a modern bleaching control.

The site appeared to be well suited to OSL dating. The samples collected represented important indicators of the site chronology, and it was understood that there was little independent age control available from other evidence. The gamma dose rates implied a sand with a significant U,Th and K content; therefore both quartz and feldspars were expected, from a system with moderate dosimetry. Providing the luminescence sensitivities of the quartz phase in this sand were sufficiently high the prospects for successful OSL dating using the Single Aliquot Regenerative (SAR) method appeared to be good.

The standard SAR procedure involves independent determination of stored dose from 16–20 subsamples. The stored-dose distribution can provide supporting information to identify heterogeneities. Where necessary supplementary measurements of a large number of small aliquots (typically 96 subsamples) can be conducted to resolve mixed age components.

In the case of these samples the sand appeared to be aeolian in nature, in which case homogeneous dose distributions and data sets following the internal logic of the site stratigraphy were to be expected. While there was evidence of root invasion, and animal burrows in parts of the site, these areas were avoided in so far as possible in selecting samples. It was expected that dose distributional analysis, as described above, would be capable of identifying perturbations of this type. Similarly the comparison of results from samples OSL 1–3, 11 and 4–10 could reveal whether or not there had been anthropogenic interference with the built surfaces on which the cairn was constructed.

Results

The six vertically sequenced samples shown at the western end of the north-facing section were respectively identified as samples OSL 5, 6, 7, 8, 9 and 10, from top to bottom. The OSL ages for these are give in Table 4.1.

The modern date from the upper tumble implied some recent disturbance in the layers above the stone tumble. The entire series were in stratigraphic order, and appeared to confirm a prehistoric rather than a medieval date for the mound as a whole. The implication of OSL 6 and OSL 7 is that the cairn on the summit of the mound had at least partially collapsed by about 1200 BC.

Higher up on the mound, OSL 4 from the layer beneath the stone tumble gave a date of 2640±400 BC, which was broadly in line with the sequence, yet not related to the construction of the cairn in any conclusive way.

Sample OSL 11 from the quarter section under the cairn gave a date of 1810±240 BC, probably constituting a *terminus post quem* for cairn construction.

Samples OSL 1, 2 and 3 came from the middle of the trench in the vicinity of the cairn. All gave dates in the later first millenium BC, and may not have been in perfect stratigraphic sequence. The measured beta dose rate from one of them was a poor match for the calculated beta dose rate obtained by high resolution gamma spectrometry. It is possible that the material covering samples OSL 1, 2, and 3 might itself result partially from cairn collapse, or was disturbed by roots or burrowing animals. In any case, the dates are not late enough to challenge the prehistoric character of the mound as a whole.

Table 4.1 OSL dates from the north-facing section of the Droughdil mound

OSL 5	1900±170AD
OSL 6	1200±240BC
OSL 7	1310±200BC
OSL 8	1520±200BC
OSL 9	2310±220BC
OSL 10	2520±250BC

5

RELATIVE SEA-LEVEL CHANGE AND EXPERIENCING THE DROUGHDUIL MOUND

Richard Tipping, David Smith and Jason Jordan

Introduction

The Droughduil Mound has a rather ambiguous location, connected to the land and yet at the coast (Fig. 5.1). In the Neolithic period the sea was much closer than it is now because it was markedly higher than today. The lie of the land between the ceremonial complex and the mound suggested to us that the relation between sea, mound and monument complex was intimate, and that the sea became part of how the cultural landscape was experienced. This chapter describes the extant topography of the Dunragit monument complex before defining the regional context of Holocene relative sea-level change in southwest Scotland. Our data at and near Dunragit is then described, and these lead to an exploration of the dynamic interaction between tides and people in the late Neolithic and early Bronze Age.

The topography and superficial geology of the Dunragit monument complex

Figure 5.1 is a map of the present-day topography and superficial geology around the monument complex. Steep hills north of the present A75 are in bedrock, mantled in thin till. The A75 marks the break of slope to much gentler terrain below *c.* 20 metres Ordnance Datum OD. The highest and oldest surfaces, those above *c.* 10 metres OD, are in Devensian glaciofluvial sands and gravels. The southern side of the Piltanton Burn valley, including Droughduil Wood, is almost entirely composed

of blown sand, which forms dunes along the coast but tapers northward to form a sand sheet. The Burn becomes tidal just south of Droughduil Wood, reaching the Solway Firth at Luce Bay some 3 kilometres east. The Piltanton Burn valley is occupied by estuarine silty clay, similar to the "carselands" widely present along Scottish estuaries, contrary to British Geological Survey mapping (Fig. 5.1) which records all the low ground, below *c.* 9.5 metres OD, as alluvium, implying a fluvial origin. North and east of the Droughduil Mound is a second, seemingly isolated patch of estuarine silty clay in a shallow valley from No. 2 Holdings to the west, pinching out to the east at Whitecrook. This patch of alluvium is called here the Whitecrook Basin. It is connected to the Piltanton Burn through a north–south trending gorge directly east of the Schoolhouse. The alluvial fills are not riverine. They are estuarine, relating to one or more periods when relative sea-level was higher than now. This recognition, and the observation that estuarine sediments almost wrap around Droughduil Wood and its mound, led to an investigation to define the time when these estuarine sediments were deposited and whether this was contemporaneous with the use of the ceremonial complex.

The regional context of relative sea-level change in southwest Scotland

Southwest Scotland was covered by the British-Irish Ice Sheet during the maximum of the last glaciation, and only became ice-free sometime around 11,000 cal BC. With

Figure 5.1 Present-day topography showing major locations mentioned in the text

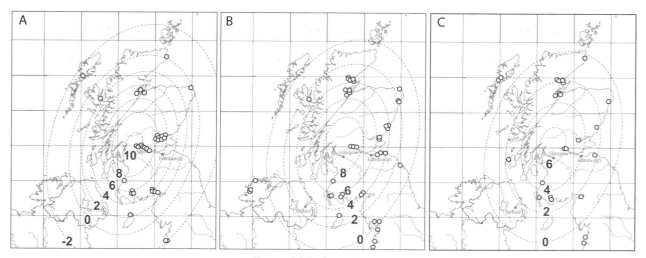

Figure 5.2 Isobases in metres

the withdrawal of the ice, the area was initially widely occupied by sea, perhaps up to an altitude of around 20 metres OD. However, although the sea surface was rising at that time, land uplift was also occurring with the removal of the ice load, and within a short time land uplift outpaced sea surface rise and the relative level of the sea fell, probably in stages revealing a staircase of shorelines. By c. 7550 cal BC in the Cree estuary, relative sea-level lay at c. 1 metre OD (Smith *et al.* 2003a). With the passage of time, the rate of land uplift fell so that the continuing rise in sea surface level now outpaced the rise in the land and a widespread transgression of the sea occurred, the Main Postglacial Transgression (Sissons 1974). This event is evident throughout southwest Scotland and illustrated in the estuaries of the Water of Girvan to the north and the Cree estuary to the east (Smith *et al.* 2007), and in the Nith estuary further east (Smith *et al.* 2003b). However, the rise fluctuated, and as the sea surface rise slowed but the land rise continued, albeit more slowly with time, a suite of shoreline terraces

resulted. The oldest terrace is only present at the heads of the estuaries, where it is covered by peat; it is termed the Main Postglacial Shoreline and is dated to c. 5550 cal BC. The second terrace is slightly higher and occurs above the oldest terrace and its cover of peat; it is termed the Blairdrummond Shoreline and is dated to c. 2550–3050 cal BC. Below these shorelines a lower shoreline is widely present. This is termed the Wigtown Shoreline. It is dated to c. 50–1050 cal BC. Below these shorelines the modern saltmarsh, known locally as Merse, lies at c. 4 metres OD along the Solway Firth, rather lower on the more open coastline in the Girvan area.

Isobase maps (Fig. 5.2) depict land uplift in southwest Scotland as increasing towards the north-north-east (Smith *et al.* 2012). In the Luce Bay area, the isobase trend is nearly east–west, with relatively little difference in the altitude of a given shoreline in this direction across the area. In a north-north-east to south-south-west direction there is a greater difference, but still relatively small, reflecting the pattern of glacial loading and unloading.

Methods and results

Relative sea-level change in the Dunragit area was analysed from civil engineering borehole logs (http://www.bgs.ac.uk/GeoIndex/boreholes.htm) and hand-sunk borehole logs, levelled to OD. Sediments were described in the field. Organic-rich sediment was sampled for AMS ^{14}C dating with closed-chamber Russian and Abbey piston cores. All ^{14}C assays were on the humic acid fraction of organic sediment. Brief summaries of diatom analyses only are provided here. The results of analyses at three locations are presented.

1. The Piltanton Burn

The Piltanton Burn extends some 4 kilometres west of the Dunragit monument complex. Holocene estuarine clays and silts penetrate either side of the farm at Barsolus (Fig. 5.1). A transect of radiocarbon-dated boreholes showed that peat at 4.85 metres OD was buried by laminated silty clay after 6653–7025 cal BC (SUERC-38782: Table 5.1). In some localities, peat continued to accumulate until it reached 7.04m OD when it was buried by laminated silty clay after 6031–6212 cal BC (SUERC-38783: Table 5.1). The diatom species found in the underlying peat are a freshwater assemblage of *Diploneis ovalis, Eunotia exigua, Fragillaria construens, Fragillaira construens* var. *venter, Fragillaria ulna, Gomphonema acuminatum* and *Melosira islandica*. The overlying laminated silty clay has a brackish/marine diatom assemblage contained within it consisting of *Cocconeis sublittoralis, Coscinodiscus nitidus, Diploneis didyma, Diploneis interrupta, Diploneis smithii, Navicula ancilla, Nitzschia punctata, Paralia sulcata* and *Podosira stelliger*. The clay rises to *c*. 8.8 metres OD in most boreholes at Barsolus. The basal layer of a peat bed lying on estuarine clay at 8.39 metres OD at Barsolus was AMS ^{14}C dated to 1025–1158 cal BC (SUERC-38784: Table 5.1). Relative sea-level fall commenced before this time as is indicated by a diatom assemblage transitional from brackish to freshwater.

East of Barsolus, levelling of terrace surfaces to OD shows that discrete terrace surfaces fall eastward, related to sea-level fall after 6250–6040 cal BC. There are currently not enough levelled points to define these with precision. At Mineral Plantation, *c*. 2km east of Barsolus, the highest estuarine clay, at 6.4m OD, was overlain by peat, the basal 0.5 centimetres ^{14}C dated to 420–270 cal BC (SUERC-39067: Table 5.1): this boundary may, however, be an eroded surface. South of the Mote Wood the highest preserved terrace surface has an altitude of *c*. 4.7 metres OD.

2. Eastern part of the Whitecrook Basin

A 440 metre long transect of boreholes east of the Sewage Works at Borehole 1031/01 (Figs. 5.1, 5.3). Till is seen in Borehole 9554/115 to 4.8 metres OD. West of this and below -9.2 metres OD in Borehole 1031/01 is fine to coarse gravel with coarse sand, with well-sorted fine-medium sand, to -8.8 metres OD: till was not recorded. At -8.8 metres OD rising to 3.3 metres OD are 12.1 metres of soft, grey laminated clay separated by silt partings and bands of sand which are more frequent at depth, with traces of fine gravel. Around 150 metres east of Borehole 1031/01, laminated clays overlie gravel and sands at around -1 metres OD in Borehole 1031/08 and rise to 3.1 metres OD. Some 385 metres east of Borehole 1031/01 laminated clays again lie on coarse gravel at 1.95 metres OD and rise to 4.0 metres OD (Borehole 02).

In Borehole 1031/01 these clays are overlain between 3.3 metres and 4.4 metres OD by coarse to medium structureless sand. Immediately east the hand-sunk boreholes 02 and 14 stopped at impenetrable material close to this depth, the surface of which consistently rises east from 4.4 metres OD in Boreholes 8 and 14 to 7.0 metres OD in Borehole 9554/115. A north–south transect of hand-sunk boreholes every 5 metres replicates the stratigraphy further west. All boreholes on this transect stopped at impenetrable material at *c*. 6.7 metres OD. This material at Borehole 1031/08 is coarse angular gravel, from 3.1 metres OD to 5.2 metres OD, probably the deposit that prevented hand-coring to the west. This angular gravel forms a broad ridge in the landscape.

Organic matter (peat or organic-rich sand) directly overlies this impenetrable material in almost all boreholes eastward to Borehole 1031/08 (Fig. 5.3). The uppermost 1.0 centimetre of peat in Borehole 8 at 4.57 metres OD, immediately below well-sorted fine-medium sand, was ^{14}C dated to 6083–6328 cal BC (SUERC-38788: Table 5.1). The diatom assemblage is largely brackish/marine in origin, dominated by *Caloneis westii, C. sublittoralis, D. didyma, D. smithii, Navicula marina, Navicula digitoradiata* and *P. sulcata*, but also includes some freshwater species, namely *F. construens* var. *venter, Fraglilaria pinnata* and *F. ulna*. This mixing of the assemblage to include freshwater species could be explained by the geomorphological setting of the Whitecrook Basin, where streams would be expected to contribute a significant freshwater component. Laminated clays with sand then accumulate to *c*. 5m OD in Boreholes 103/01, 8 and 14 but are not seen further east, on and beyond the broad ridge, probably because they are confined to a narrow channel.

Above 5 metres OD in Borehole 1031/01 and rising to 8.3 metres OD are structureless sands and silts with occasional fine gravel. These can be correlated with similar sediments in hand-sunk boreholes 8–9 over 40 metres eastward. Within these is a 20 centimetre thick, laterally continuous horizontally bedded peat at *c*. 7.5 metres OD. Peat directly over silts and sands in Borehole 8 at 7.51 metres OD was dated to 2300–2560 cal BC (SUERC-38789: Table 5.1). The diatom data from the silts and sands once again exhibits a mixed assemblage,

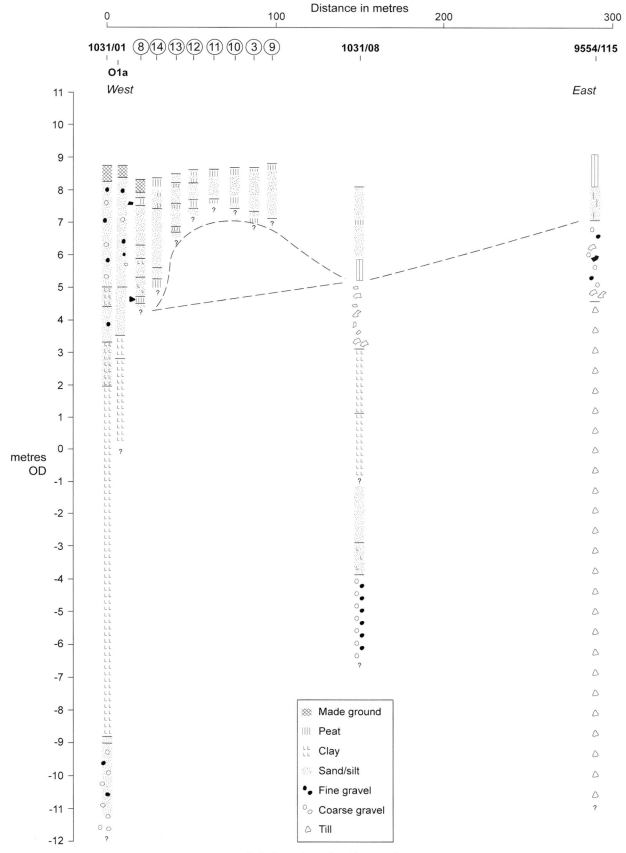

Figure 5.3 Borehole logs along the Whitecrook East transect

though predominantly brackish/marine. Brackish and marine species recorded include *C. westii, Cocconeis scuttellum, C. sublittoralis, D. interrupta, D. smithii,* and *P. sulcata.* The freshwater species recorded included *Pinnularia viridis, Pinnularia major, F. pinnata* and *F. ulna.* Deposition of structureless sands and silts then resumed to the present ground surface at *c.* 8.2–8.7 metres OD. Around the basin the glaciofluvial sands and gravels rise to *c.* 10 metres OD.

3. Western part of the Whitecrook Basin

The deep stratigraphy seen east of the Sewage Works is not seen to the west because there are no borehole data below *c.* 9 metres OD on the valley floor. Three commercial borehole logs (NX15NW3061/252, /251 and /250) lie along the northern edge of Mote Wood (transect 2: Fig. 5.1) at *c.* 10.3 metres OD. Till is recorded below 6.8 metres OD in Borehole 252 at the northwest corner of the wood. Sandy gravel, probably glaciofluvial, lies over the till at 6.8 metres OD. Borehole 251 has 0.25 metres of wood-rich peat at its base, below 8.3 metres OD. Borehole 250 has organic matter in sand at this depth. All boreholes then have 2.3 metres of sand, probably wind-blown, overlying peat to the ground surface at *c.* 10.5 metres OD. This sediment stratigraphy was confirmed by a hand-sunk borehole using an open-chambered corer *c.* 4 metres south of Borehole 252. The uppermost 5 centimetres of peat directly beneath wind-blown sand at 238–243 metres depth was ^{14}C dated to cal AD 662–744 (SUERC-39066: Table 5.1), clearly in error, probably through contamination, since wind-blown sand lies directly under the Droughduil Mound, its surface dated by OSL to *c.* 2500 cal BC. No wind-blown sand is found a significant distance north of Mote Wood.

Aerial photographs and areas exposed during excavation in 2012–13 by GUARD Archaeology along the line of the Dunragit bypass show the western head of the Whitecrook Basin to contain a series of small and shallow anastomosing channels incised into well-sorted fine gravel, probably glaciofluvial but water-winnowed. At *c.* 10.3 metres OD is a break of slope interpreted as a degraded cliff eroded by coastal processes. What is probably the same break of slope also cuts into the wind-blown sand at the northern edge of Mote Wood. Some 10 metres east of this, lying on glaciofluvial gravel is a 9 centimetre thick sequence of pale brown clay, highly organic at its top, covered by a thin, white, bleached well-sorted medium-coarse sand. The altitude of this former ground surface is around 8.7–9 metres OD. The sedimentology is suggestive of deposition of deposition in estuarine conditions. Diatoms that could demonstrate this are not preserved. The clay is thought to represent the highest deposit of estuarine mud in the Whitecrook Basin, overlain by well sorted wave-winnowed sand. Organic-rich clay at 5–7 centimetres depth was ^{14}C dated to 1740–1915 cal BC (SUERC-44834).

Interpretation and discussion

The data indicate the following sequence of events:

1. as the British-Irish Ice sheet decayed, glaci-marine and marine surfaces above *c.* 15 metres OD
2. after a period when relative sea-levels fell to levels as yet unknown, a terrace at *c.* 9–9.5 metres OD was formed, probably during the brief climatic deterioration of the Younger Dryas (Loch Lomond Readvance) (*c.* 11,000–9700 cal BC).
3. further incision in the earliest Holocene to depths exceeding -9 metres OD.
4. during the subsequent rise in relative sea-level, formation of terrestrial peat to a surface at 4.57 metres OD in the Whitecrook Basin and its burial after 6083–6328 cal BC by a water-lain well-sorted fine-medium sand. Diatom assemblages above, though poorly preserved, are strongly brackish/marine. Terrestrial peat also formed at this time in the Soulseat Burn at Barsolus to a surface at 4.85 metres OD. Peat was then buried after 6653–7025 cal BC by laminated silty clay with an estuarine diatom assemblage, with a freshwater component distal to the sea.
5. penetration of estuarine clay continued at Barsolus as relative sea-level rise continued, sealing peat at 7.04 metres OD after 6031–6212 cal BC, continuing to rise to *c.* 8.5 metres OD. This is a minimum altitude of the water surface at that time. Diatom data from higher-energy sand within the Whitecrook Basin continue to show a strong brackish influence to 7.5 metres OD at 2300–2560 cal BC with a strong freshwater component also. Again, this is a minimum altitude of the water surface at that time.
6. near No. 2 Holdings in the western arm of the Whitecrook Basin an organic clay accumulated at around 8.7–9.0 metres OD at 1740–1915 cal BC. The context and sediments surrounding this clay suggest this was very close to the tide at, perhaps, Mean High Water Springs (MHWS)
7. terrestrial peat covered sand with clay in the Whitecrook Basin at 7.5 metres OD after 2300–2560 cal BC. There are no diatom assemblages from which to characterise the environment but below this altitude diatom assemblages have an increasing freshwater component. Sea-level had fallen in a relative sense to 7.5 metres OD by 2300–2560 cal BC.
8. at Barsolus, terrestrial peat formed over estuarine clay at 8.39 metres OD at 1025–1158 cal BC. This contact is very likely to be unconformable.

It is clear that a very high relative sea-level, slightly higher than 8.7–9.0 metres OD was either maintained, or was reached on more than one occasion between the Mesolithic period and the early Bronze Age. Relative sea-level in the Whitecrook Basin within the Mesolithic can be constrained further by archaeological sites discovered

Table 5.1 Details of the AMS ^{14}C assays mentioned in the text

Site	Borehole	Depth (cm)	SUERC	^{14}C BP (2σ)	δ^{13}C ‰	Cal BC/AD (2σ)
Barsolus	BH1	398.0–485.0	-38782	7910 ±30	-26.9	6653v7025 BC
Barsolus	BH5	190.0–190.5	-38783	724 ± 35	-28.9	6031–6212 BC
Barsolus	BH5	55.0–55.5	-38784	945 ± 30	-29.3	AD 1025–1158
Whitecrook Basin	BH8	372.0–372.5	-38788	7430 ± 30	-27.2	6083–6328 BC
Whitecrook Basin	BH8	78.0–78.5	-38789	3930 ± 30	-28.5	2300–2560 BC
Mote Wood		238.0–243.0	-39066	1295 ±30	-29.8	AD 662–774
Mineral Plantation		88.5–90.0	-39067	2320 ±25	-29.0	262–411 BC
No. 2 Holdings		5.0–7.0	-44834	3497 ± 33	-28.9	1740–1915 BC

in 2012–13 by GUARD Archaeology in advance of the Dunragit bypass. These are as yet not fully analysed, but Site 7, a Mesolithic complex at the edge of the eastern arm of the basin at around 8.7 metres OD, with apparently no natural deposits sealing it, was ^{14}C dated from four assays with an overlap at 7001–6867 BC (Hurl pers. comm. 02/2013). If this interpretation is correct, then tidal conditions that left a sediment record did not subsequently exceed 8.7 metres OD.

A recent isobase model (Smith *et al.* 2012) estimates the altitude of the Main Postglacial Shoreline in the Dunragit area at 8.5 metres OD, the altitude of the Blairdrummond Shoreline at 8.8 metres OD and the altitude of the Wigtown Shoreline at 6.6 metres OD. The mean absolute residuals are, respectively, 0.50 metres, 0.44 metres and 0.33 metres. The morphological and stratigraphical relationships of the features emphasise that the Blairdrummond Shoreline is the highest in this area, with the Main Postglacial Shoreline below that and the Wigtown Shoreline the lowest. With the culmination of the Main Postglacial Transgression, relative sea-levels lay at about the same altitude for *c.* 3000 years. This is fundamental to understanding the landscape contexts of the Dunragit ceremonial complex and the Droughduil Mound.

Present-day tidal range values for Kirkcudbright Bay, a macro-tidal embayment comparable to Luce Bay (Smith *et al.* 2003b), have a MHWS altitude of 3.8 metres OD and a MHWN altitude of 1.9 metres OD. The Spring Tide range is 6.7 metres and the Neap Tide range is 3.5 metres. The highest astronomical tides (HAT) are *c.* 1 metre greater and the lowest astronomical tides (LAT) are *c.* 1 metre lower (Admiralty Hydrographic Department 1996). It is unlikely that the tidal prism during the Holocene in the area would have been greatly different. Hence, during particularly high tides, the Droughduil Mound would have appeared as an island when viewed from the Dunragit complex. The visual effect of the lowest tides might have been equally striking, with the Whitecrook Basin almost entirely emptying of water.

Acknowledgements

We thank Julian Thomas for his patience. We are grateful to Rod McCullagh (Historic Scotland) for part-funding the project and providing the funding for the ^{14}C assays presented here. Declan Hurl and Amey plc were most generous of their time and data during the 2012–2013 excavation, as were the excavators of GUARD Archaeology. We thank Julian Thomas for encouraging this contribution. Bill Jamieson and John McArthur (Stirling University) drew most of the figures.

6

PREHISTORIC POTTERY

Matthew Leivers with Julian Thomas

Introduction

The prehistoric pottery assemblage studied from Dunragit consists of 196 sherds recovered during four seasons of fieldwork. As each of these seasons was concerned with small parts of the same complex of features the pottery assemblage is treated as an integral whole and no further reference is made to the separate episodes of excavation. Overall, the pottery was concentrated in a relatively small number of features, principally the post-holes of the innermost ring of the palisade enclosure, the shallow pits in Trench F, and a variety of features concentrated within the innermost post-ring, most notably the small pit 050. Several of these features contained sherds of the same fabric, and even from the same vessels, suggesting that they were in use at much the same time. A substantial proportion of the sherds are small and relatively featureless, but some of those that have been illustrated are more substantial. The proportion of each vessel that is represented varies very considerably. In some cases, numerous fragments of a single pot are present, but often only a single sherd from a given vessel was found. These circumstances together raise the possibility that some of the pottery may have been curated for a period in a surface context, such as a midden, between use, breakage, and subsequent deposition (Beadsmoore, Garrow and Knight 2010: 130). Small quantities of Early Neolithic bowl, Beaker and perhaps Food Vessel ceramics are present within the assemblage, but the whole is dominated by Late Neolithic Grooved Ware pottery.

Although large quantities of prehistoric ceramics have been recovered from the sand dune complex at the head of Luce Bay, most of this material consists of collections of sherds without provenance, quantities of unstratified material from eroding sand dunes and surfaces, or nineteenth and early twentieth century investigations for which records are scant or lacking (Callander 1911; 1929; 1933; Stevenson 1946; Davidson 1952; McInnes 1964; Simpson 1965; Clarke 1970; Penney 1975; Selwyn 1976; Gibson 1982). Even the most recent excavations in the area suffer from the problems of decontextualisation caused by material eroding from variously shifting dune systems (Cowie 1996). As a result, the material from the Dunragit excavations represents the first instance of a substantial ceramic assemblage from this important location for which secure contexts have been established, with the attendant possibilities of elucidating not only a chronological sequence, but also the relationships between different ceramic traditions.

Methods

The material was examined using a hand lens of ×10 magnification, with selected sherds re-examined using a binocular microscope at ×20 magnification. Clay matrices and tempers were identified, and fabrics defined on those bases. The analysis was based on the system suggested by Orton, Tyers and Vince (1993: 231–41), modified slightly in line with elements of the nationally recommended guidelines proposed by the Prehistoric Ceramics Research Group for later prehistoric pottery, and to take account of the more variable nature of early prehistoric pottery.

Condition

Condition of sherds was assessed on the basis of the degree to which edges and surfaces were abraded. The assemblage is dominated by sherds in moderate condition, with much smaller proportions of good, poor and very poor sherds. Profiles, proportions and diameters are largely unreconstructable, owing to the low numbers of diagnostic sherds (rims and bases especially). In no case is a complete vessel profile available, and many of the vessels are represented by only a very few sherds. Consequently, all forms are partial and inferred.

Table 6.1 Prehistoric pottery fabrics by chronological period

Date	Fabric	No. sherds
Early Neolithic	FG6	2
Sub-total EN		*2*
Late Neolithic/ Early	FG1	34
Bronze Age	FG2	22
	FG3	46
	FG4	3
	FG5	6
	FG7	54
	FG8	2
	FG9	6
Sub-total LN/EBA		*173*
Unassigned crumbs	FG99	21
Total		*196*

Individual vessels can however be identified for the most part on the basis of fabric, wall thickness, rim form and decoration. One or more surfaces of many of the sherds are obscured by apparently burnt deposits, and there is sooting on some sherds, suggesting that many of the vessels had been extensively used.

Pottery by chronological period

A total of nine fabric groups have been defined, which have been grouped into three chronological periods. The breakdown of ceramics by fabric group and chronological period is given in Table 6.1. Fabric descriptions are listed in Table 6.2.

Early Neolithic

Only two sherds of Early Neolithic pottery were recovered, representing Fabric Group 6. One sherd is a very small portion of a heavy, thickened and out-turned rim, while the other is a featureless crumb. Both were recovered from topsoil contexts, and they have no association with any archaeological feature encountered during excavation.

It is difficult to draw conclusions from such a limited quantity of pottery. The similarity of the temper to that of

Table 6.2 Pottery fabric descriptions

FG1	Fairly hard, fine, thin–moderately thick fabric; moderate, well-sorted, coarse to very coarse grog; sparse, well-sorted coarse to very coarse crushed quartzite; moderate, fairly well sorted coarse to very coarse sandstone fragments
FG2	Soft, irregular, thin to moderately thick fabric; moderate, well sorted, coarse voids; sparse well sorted medium grog; abundant fairly well sorted coarse to very coarse angular sandstone fragments.
FG3	Fairly hard, irregular, thin to moderately thick fabric; moderate, poorly sorted, sub-angular coarse to very coarse rock fragments; moderate, fairly well sorted, coarse to very coarse grog; moderate, fairly well sorted, angular, coarse to very coarse quartzite. Frequent voids give a corky appearance.
FG4	Fairly hard, fine, thin fabric; moderate, fairly well sorted, coarse to very coarse grog; sparse, well sorted, sub-angular very coarse quartzite; sparse, fairly well sorted, sub-angular coarse to very coarse rock fragments; moderate, fairly well sorted, sub-angular to angular, coarse to very coarse sandstone.
FG5	Fairly hard, irregular, thick fabric; abundant poorly sorted sub-angular to angular coarse to very coarse rock fragments; sparse well sorted coarse grog.
FG6	Soft fine thin to moderately thick fabric; sparse, well-sorted, coarse sandstone fragments, crushed quartzite and mica.
FG7	Soft irregular thin to moderately thick fabric; moderate, poorly sorted, coarse to very coarse grog; sparse, well sorted, coarse mica; sparse well sorted coarse sub-rounded rock fragments.
FG8	Soft irregular thin to moderately thick fabric; sparse, well sorted coarse to very coarse sub-angular rock fragments; moderate poorly sorted very coarse sub-angular quartzite; moderate, fairly well sorted coarse to very coarse grog.
FG9	Soft fine thin fabric; sparse well sorted coarse to very coarse sub-rounded to sub-angular rock fragments; sparse fairly well sorted sub-angular to angular very coarse sandstone fragments; sparse well sorted very coarse grog.

later ceramic traditions may suggest local manufacture. McInnes (1964: 60–66) notes local parallels for the form and fabric, and quantities of contemporary ceramics in a similar fabric were recovered from High Torr (Cowie 1996). The decontextualised character of this material precludes further discussion however.

Late Neolithic/Early Bronze Age

Late Neolithic ceramics of the Grooved Ware, Beaker and perhaps Food Vessel traditions were recovered from features forming elements of the palisade enclosure, and from a number of isolated pits.

Grooved Ware

There are portions of at least nine Grooved Ware rims within the assemblage, which fall into a basic division of more-or-less rounded and inturned from closed vessels and more-or-less upright and flat from neutral vessels. Some of the former seem to be from smaller bowls, but there are also larger jars or tubs. All identified bases are flat, with no foot or a minor protrusion. Rim diameters cannot be reliably reconstructed.

The Grooved Ware pottery accounts for six of the fabrics identified. All are basically similar, with inclusions consisting of various combinations of grog, rock, quartzite and mica, with some fabrics more or less vesicular. However, it should be noted that Fabric Group 1 was initially identified as coarse Beaker pottery, and only the reconstruction of the vessel forms distinguished this pottery as relatively fine, hard Grooved Ware. All of the fabrics are what may be termed detrital, and little interest seems to have been shown in the preparation of the clay prior to potting. This is particularly interesting if McInnes is correct in her identification of pits containing clay at Pin Dune (associated with broken sherds, charcoal, daub and worked and unworked flint) as a 'pot-making station' (1964: 40). She records the clay as "of good quality, cleaned and in a soft, pliable condition" (*ibid.*). At least some of the associated pottery seems to have been Grooved Ware (her Nos. 107 and 109), suggesting that not all of the pottery manufactured in the locality conformed to a single type. It would be unwise to attempt the identification of structuring pairs within the tempering traditions of this ceramic type, but a number of possibilities present themselves. It may be that certain materials were selected for inclusion in ceramics manufactured for use in certain situations. Alternatively, vessels known to be tempered with certain materials may have been selected for use in particular situations (remembering that the temper is often clearly visible in the vessels outer surface). Different tempers may

reflect variations in manufacture amounting to different traditions subscribed to by different potters. The colour of the outer surfaces tends to be reddish-brown to brownish-grey, with dark grey cores and inner surfaces the norm.

Both of the basic Grooved Ware vessel forms identified appear in both plain and decorated examples, although the small number of sherds belonging to many vessels again makes the definite identification of plain vessels impossible. Decorative techniques include applied cordons, incision and impression.

Stylistically speaking, the Dunragit assemblage is closest to Longworth's Durrington Walls style (Wainwright and Longworth 1971: 240–2). The combination of tubs, jars and bowls (and particularly 'bucket' forms with a closed mouth), applied ribs or cordons, incised horizontal and herringbone grooves, and twisted cord decoration all support this attribution. Particular vessels can be paralleled in Durrington Walls style assemblages. Thus FG1 V2 and FG2 V1 are similar to the simple undecorated closed-mouthed bucket-shaped vessels at Durrinton Walls itself (P478–89, Wainwright and Longworth 1971: 142). While the rim of FG7 V1 is atypical (and perhaps more in keeping with north Scottish assemblages), the parallel diagonal grooves lapping onto to vertical cordon could be compared with P172 or P191 at Durrington Walls (Wainwright and Longworth 1971, 102–6). Undecorated open bowls similar to FG3 V2 are found at Grimes Graves, N24–6 (Longworth, Ellison and Rigby 1988: 20). The Dunragit Grooved Ware is therefore relatively distinct from that found in Ireland (Brindley 1999a: 30) or northern Scotland (Cowie and MacSween 1999: 49), although Durrington Walls style assemblages are known elsewhere in the Scottish lowlands, as at Hillend and Wellbrae in Lanarkshire (Alexander and Armit 1992; Armit, Cowie and Ralston 1994). Indeed, the Hillend sherds have some points of similarity with some of the Dunragit material: vertical cordons, parallel diagonal incisions and cross-hatches, but with more of an emphasis on finger-tip impressions and lines of dots, and no cord impressions.

CATALOGUE

Neolithic

FG6 Vessel 1 is represented by a fragment of a simple rim, and a further tiny fragment of pottery, both from topsoil contexts. These were identified as potentially Early Neolithic on the basis of a hard fabric with small grits. Not illustrated.

FG 1 Vessel 1 (not illustrated) is a pot represented by nine sherds, and is too poorly preserved to allow a reconstruction of its form. The vessel may have been

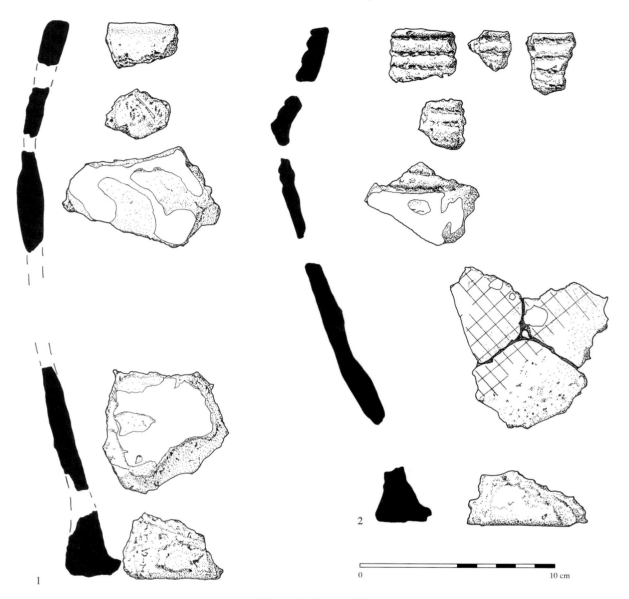

Figure 6.1 Grooved Ware

a slightly closed form with a thick lower wall thinning towards a noticeable shoulder, giving a biconical form. If this form is correct, then the lower body and the zone above the shoulder are smoothed, while the shoulder itself has a coarse surface which almost amounts to rustication. One of the lower body sherds has a thick deposit on the outer surface. Sherds from this vessels were recovered from the upper fill of miscellaneous feature 032, and from the pit associated with the innermost post-ring, 050, which produced appreciable quantities of pottery. Although this vessel has a similar fabric to other Grooved Ware pots, it might not be out of place in a coarse Beaker assemblage.

FG1 Vessel 2 (Fig. 6.1, 1) is a large jar-like vessel of weakly biconical form. A rim diameter cannot be

reconstructed from the single surviving simple, flat, slightly inturned rim sherd and the vessel appears to be undecorated except for a single instance of what appears to be grass-wiping. This occurs above the shoulder, below which the vessel is heavily encrusted with a thick deposit which obscures much of the surface. All of the sherds from this vessel were recovered from pit 050.

FG1 Vessel 3 (Fig. 6.1, 2) is a second large jar-like vessel, with a slightly more angular profile that Vessel 2. The rim diameter cannot be estimated. From the rim, through the only very slightly concave neck, to immediately beneath the weak shoulder the vessel is decorated with lines of coarse twisted cord. The remainder of the vessel appears to be plain, although again much of the surface is obscured

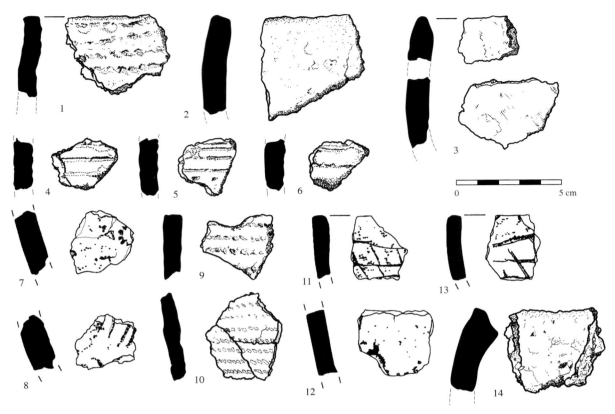

Figure 6.2 Prehistoric pottery

and sooted. Sherds of this vessel were found in inner ring post-hole 084, and the nearby pit 050.

FG1 Vessels 2 and 3 were represented by 14 sherds recovered from the fills of feature 050, the flat-bottomed pit adjacent to post-hole 084 of the inner post-ring. It has not proved possible to assign all plain body sherds to one or other vessel.

FG1 Vessel 4 (Fig. 6.2, 1) is a large neutral jar. A single surviving rim sherd bears four lines of coarse twisted cord impressions. The 11 sherds of this vessel were recovered from the fills of post-hole 084 of the 'western arc' of the inner post-ring.

FG2 Vessel 1 (Fig. 6.2, 2–3) is a slightly closed pot with a plain rim, flattened in places. None of the 17 sherds are decorated, but the form and fabric are appropriate for Grooved Ware. The vessel is probably a large bowl or jar. It was found in the fills of pit 050.

FG2 Vessel 2 (Fig. 6.2, 4–6) consists of five sherds. There are no rims, but four body sherds bear incised grooves or lines. One of these sherds also has a pair of triangular jabs. Given the generally straight and flat nature of the surviving sherds it is not possible to be absolutely certain

whether the decoration would form horizontal, vertical or diagonal designs. This vessel falls most comfortably within Class II of McInnes' catalogue of Luce Sands pottery (1964, 66–8). Three of the sherds came from fills of pit 050, while two came from the fills of post-hole 084 of the inner post-ring.

FG3 Vessel 1 (Fig. 6.3, 1–3) is of uncertain form: one large sherd with a pronounced shoulder may be from the upper part of a large open bowl, with diffuse decoration below the shoulder. Lower portions of the vessel are grass wiped, and one sherd bears eight jabbed impressions. 10 sherds were recovered from the fills of pit 050, in association with Grooved Ware of FG1 and FG2, while a further 16 sherds came from the fills of post-hole 084 of the inner post-ring. A single sherd in the same fabric came from post-hole 054 of the 'eastern arc' of the inner post-ring; it is not possible to determine whether this sherd belongs to Vessel 1 or is the sole survivor of an otherwise unrepresented vessel. It is none the less interesting that related sherds should have been recovered from features belonging to the two separate phases of the inner post-ring.

FG3 Vessel 2 (Fig. 6.3, 4–6) consists of 11 sherds from a plain Grooved Ware bowl or jar: the angle of

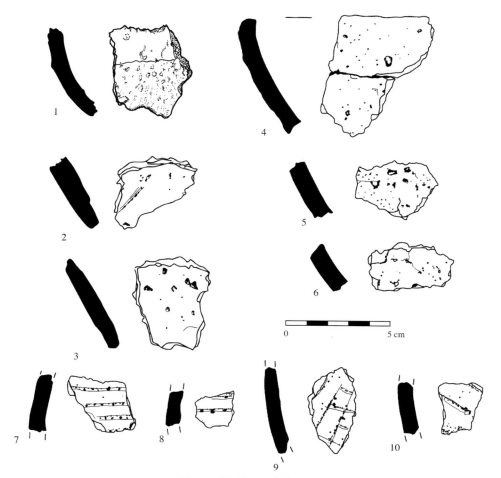

Figure 6.3 Grooved Ware

the vessel wall is difficult to define on the basis of the surviving fragments. Three sherds are from an irregular but predominantly pointed rim. One joining and one detached body sherd are distinctly curved, suggesting a rather small vessel. Four sherds came from context 537, the ramp fill of post-hole 579/619 of the inner post-ring. Seven sherds, almost certainly from the same vessel came from small pit 3074 (a rim; four plain body sherds, in contexts 3073 and 3081) and small pit 3112 (a rim and body sherd in context 3086).

FG3 Vessel 3 (Fig. 6.2, 7) consists of two sherds and some crumbs from a vessel of unreconstructable form. The sherds are all plain and from the body, and could in fact be fragments of FG3 Vessel 2, so alike are they. They were recovered from context 917, a layer of post-packing in feature 896, a major post-hole of the middle post-ring. These sherds are the only ceramics recovered from any feature of this post setting in any season of excavation.

FG3 Vessel 4 (Fig. 6.3, 7–10) consists of six sherds from a thin-walled vessel. One sherd is decorated with shallow grooves arranged in a diagonal lattice pattern. A

single horizontal groove is present on the interior. Two sherds are plain, one more has a single shallow groove with perpendicular grooves appended to it that are so faint as to be little more than wiping. The remaining two sherds have shallow horizontal grooves along which are irregularly-spaced pin pricks. These may have come from the upper half of the vessel. The sherds were all recovered from recut fill 685 and weathering surface 937 within post-hole 792 of the inner post-ring.

FG7 Vessel 1 (Fig. 6.4, 1–6) Fabric Group 7 was represented by three vessels. 23 sherds belonged to a Durrington Walls type Grooved Ware tub. 10 sherds were plain body fragments; 11 sherds had applied ribs and/or diagonal incisions. Two sherds were rims: the rim turns inwards at the very top and both the outside of the rim above the angle and the internal bevel are decorated with diagonal incised lines. Another sherd is from the portion of the vessel immediately below the rim. The sherds of this vessel came from recut fill 685 of post-hole 792 of the inner post-ring.

A further 25 sherds were recovered from the fills of feature 3074, a pit containing three sherds of FG10 Vessel

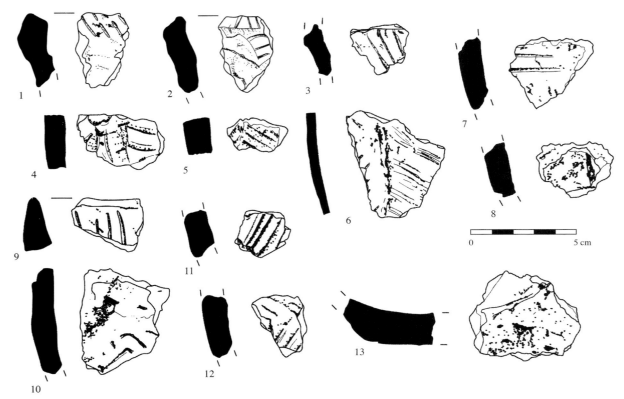

Figure 6.4 Grooved Ware

1 and a suite of other cultural materials. These 25 sherds *may* belong to FG7 Vessel 1: the fabric identification is certain, the vessel assignation less so. Certainly, some of these sherds are thinner than those from context 685, suggesting that this is indeed another vessel. A single sherd has an applied cordon and diagonal incisions; the rest are plain body sherds or (in at least four instances) fragments from the angle between the flat base and near-vertical wall. Two small featureless sherds in this same fabric came from feature 3112 (also containing a sherd from FG10 Vessel 1, lithics and a hammerstone). These may also be a part of this vessel.

FG7 Vessel 2 (Fig. 6.4, 9–12) Four sherds in FG7 represent a second vessel. It is impossible to reconstruct a form, but the pot has a simple rim and a relatively neutral profile. The rim is decorated with a thin horizontal groove, below which are thicker vertical grooves. It is not possible to estimate the diameter from this single small sherd, but the vessel is perhaps a bowl, probably somewhat smaller than Vessel 1 of this Fabric Group. This rim sherd came from feature 756/449 of the inner post-ring. A body sherd in poor condition came from recut fill 685, also within 756/449, while a second abraded body sherd (probably belonging to the same vessel) with incised lines was recovered from the fill of 881, a small pit cut into the upper fills of this same feature.

FG7 Vessel 3 (Fig. 6.4, 13) was represented by a single sherd of a flat base. It was recovered from a fill of post-hole 825/826 of the inner post-ring.

FG8 (Fig. 6.4, 7–8) was represented by two sherds from a vessel of unreconstructable form. Both are body sherds decorated with a pair of faint grooves on an otherwise plain exterior. Both came from recut fill 685 in feature 792 of the inner post-ring.

FG9 was represented by two vessels. Vessel 1 (Fig. 6.2, 8) was represented by two body sherds, one of which was decorated with incised lines. The sherds were recovered from the fills of miscellaneous features 515 (the decorated sherd) and 668.

FG9 Vessel 2 (Fig. 6.2, 11–13) is represented by four sherds. Two are joining plain upright rim sherds decorated with a diagonal lattice of incised line; a third is a fragment of the body just below the rim bearing the same design. The fourth sherd is plain. All sherds of this vessel came from recut fill 685 of feature 792 of the inner post-ring.

Beaker

FG4 Vessel 1 (Fig. 6.2, 9–10) Fine Beaker pottery was represented by three sherds of a single vessel of Fabric

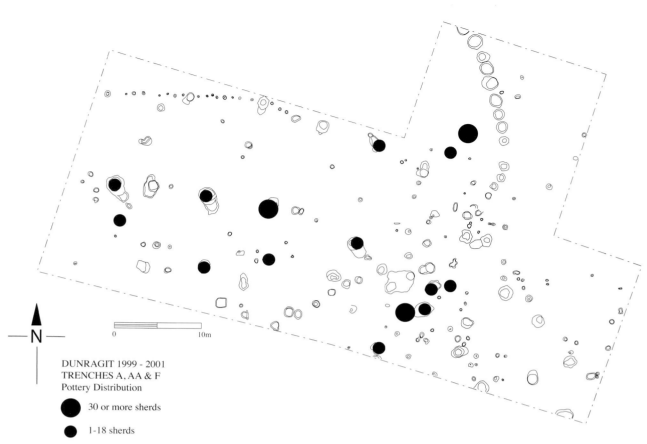

Figure 6.5 Pottery distribution in Trenches A, AA and F.

Group 4. No rim survives and the surviving sherds are too fragmentary to allow a form to be reconstructed. A sherd from the lower portion of the vessel bears seven lines of fine twisted cord; an upper portion (perhaps from the neck of the vessel) bears four coarser lines, more broadly spaced. This vessel finds parallels in those listed by Gibson (1982 i, 145; ii, 377) under Dunragit, Torrs Warren and under Luce Bay (Glenluce) (*ibid.*, i, 192–4; ii, 410–9) as AOC Beakers. All the sherds came from the shallow, splayed feature 032.

Food Vessel

FG5 Vessel 1 (Fig. 6.2, 14) Fabric Group 5 consisted of six sherds and a number of small crumbs belonging to a single vessel. Sherds of this vessel were recovered from context 257, the fill of small post-hole 293. The single rim sherd bears an internal bevel which suggests Food Vessel affinities, although too little of the vessel survives to allow certainty. The form, while uncertain, would appear to be globular. There are no immediate local parallels for this vessel. McInnes notes that pots in the Food Vessel tradition are rare in the locality (1964, 56), although Food Vessel and Grooved Ware were found in association at Pin Dune A (*ibid.*, 41; Wainwright and Longworth 1971: 306).

Distribution

Prehistoric ceramics were concentrated in the post-holes of the inner post-ring, and in a group of pits that fell in the immediate vicinity of the eastern side of the cursus, where it coincided with the two innermost post-rings. Ceramics of any kind were notable by their absence from Trench J. Two particular clusters of pottery-rich features were formed by post-holes 084 and 054, and pit 050, and by the pair of small pits 3112 and 3074. As some of these features share sherds from the same vessels it is likely that these concentrations relate to distinct episodes of activity. Amongst the Grooved Ware there appears to be two mutually exclusive sets of vessels, each of which are found in mutual association in a distinct set of features. Thus FG1 V1, FG1 V2, FG1 V3, FG1 V4, FG2 V1, FG2 V2 and FG3 V1 are found exclusively in pit 032, pit 050, post-hole 084 and post-hole 054, all located in the south-west part of Trench A. By contrast, FG3 V2, FG3 V4, FG7 V1, FG8 V1 and FG9 V2 are found in post-hole 579/619, post-hole 792, pit 3074 and pit 3112, all in the centre of Trench AA and the south of Trench F. These results might be explained in two different ways. It is possible that the two sets of vessels were fired and used at different times in the site's history. This picture

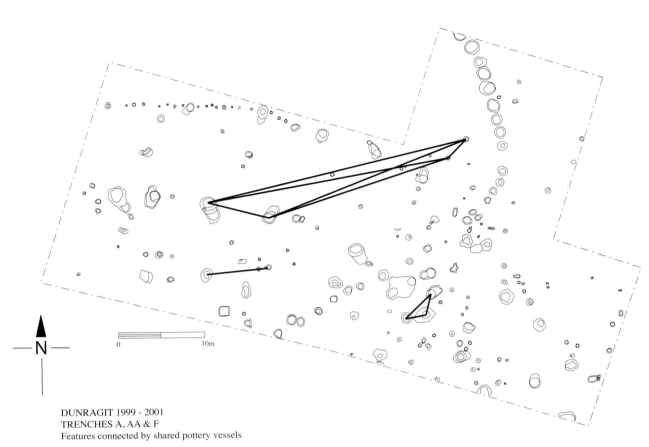

DUNRAGIT 1999 - 2001
TRENCHES A, AA & F
Features connected by shared pottery vessels

Figure 6.6 Features connected by shared pottery vessels in Trenches A, AA and F.

is complicated by the possibility that sherds may not have found their way into features immediately after use and breakage, but may have been curated in above-ground contexts such as middens for a period prior to deposition. Alternatively, the distinction may be primarily spatial. This may mean no more than that particular vessels were used, broken and disposed of in specific areas of the site. But it also carries the faint implication that certain sets of pots were made and used by distinct groups of people, whose activities were localised within the enclosure. This chimes with the suggestion that the monument may have been constructed in radially ordered segments, each built by a separate work gang (see Chapter 11 below). Importantly, the two groups of vessels are largely made up of mutually exclusive fabrics, with only Fabric Group 3 shared by the two areas of the site. This provides a further indication that the two

groups of pots might indeed have been made by different potters, who might have been exploiting separate sources of raw materials in order to make their vessels. These results might be compared with the spatial distribution of Grooved Ware fabrics observed by Andrew Jones at the Neolithic settlement of Barnhouse in Orkney. Here it was suggested that the differences could be attributed to micro-traditions of potting associated with particular groups of houses (Jones 2002: 128).

In general there was a contrast at Dunragit between contexts that included a small number of sherds, which might have being introduced into the deposits fortuitously, and larger concentrations of nine to 44 sherds, which may represent deliberate deposits. The former include the packing deposits of the inner post-ring, while the latter are generally recut fills and pit contents. The significance of this pattern will be discussed in Chapter 11.

7

LITHICS FROM DUNRAGIT

Elizabeth Healey

Introduction

A total of 180 objects of flint and two of non-flint stone were recovered during the excavations at Dunragit. Quite a high proportion of these (58.2%) are burnt chips and fragments, and the total also includes some large lumps of burnt flint and other vitrified material that were found on the surface of the site. The context of the artefacts and the composition of the assemblage is summarised in Table 7.1. The majority of the lithics come from post-holes and pits, most notably feature 792, a post-hole in the inner post-ring of the Late Neolithic enclosure and features 3074 and 3112, both pits containing Late Neolithic Grooved Ware pottery (Table 7.2).

Raw materials

A variety of lithic raw materials were exploited but by far the most usual are small pebbles of flint. They are small in size, the largest is only 54 millimetres in maximum dimension, and most are just over 30 millimetres and weigh 25–55 grammes. The flint is mainly opaque, light grey-brown or yellow-brown in colour sometimes with mottles or blotches; many have a smooth, water-worn cortex. A few pieces are more transparent and appear to have a fresher cortex. Some pebbles also have patinated scars from previous flake removals. It is highly probable that this pebble flint was collected locally, most likely from Luce Bay where flint pebbles are abundant or from

Table 7.1 Composition of the lithic assemblage from Dunragit

Contexts	Core & struck pieces	Flake	Retouched		Calcined chunk/ core	Calcined flake	Calcined chip/frag unid	Total flint
Inner palisade ring								
Inner palisade ring post holes	3	22	4		10	46	38	123
Second inner palisade post holes							2	2
Middle palisade ring post holes		1	1	axe				2
Cursus post holes		1						1
Features with pottery	7	16	9		0	0	0	32
Misc features			1					1
Top soil and unstratified	1+1	9			8		2	21
Total	12	49	15		18	46	42	182

Table 7.2 Lithic assemblage by context

Context	Core	Flake	Retouched		Calcined chunk/core	Calcined flake	Chip/frag unid	Calcined sub total	Total flint
Inner palisade ring									
F792									
627						1		1	1
978=627							1	1	1
634		1		oblique arrowhead				0	1
651							1	1	1
653		2			1	6	1	8	10
654		1						0	1
685	1	5	1	fabricator	7	21	24	52	59
867		1			2	4	3	9	10
883=967						4	1	5	5
937						2		2	2
951		1		fabricator				0	1
961						8	1	9	9
Total	1	9	3		10	46	32	88	101
F63		2							2
F84	1	4					1		6
F319/332		2	1	microlith					3
F579/619		1							1
F756	1 (indet struck piece)	2							2
F825/826		1							1
F898		1							1
F306							2		2
Middle palisade ring									
F27		1							1
F4110				Axe					1
Cursus post holes									
F44		1							1
Features with pottery									
F50									
48	1	2							3
4		3							3
Total	1	5							6
F3074									
3073		4							4
3080	3	4	2 + 2	2 scrapers, 2 edge chipping/retouch					11
3081	2	1	2	1 scraper, 1 notched					5
3082	1								1
Total	6	9	6						21
F3112	1	2	1 +2	1 scraper, 1 ret. edge & pebble with battering on edge					6
Misc features									
F32		1							1

the glacial gravels near Dunragit railway station (Coles 2011a and b). A few flakes have thick unrolled cortex like FN 1380 and may also be of different origin, but more likely reflect the mix of flint available.

In addition to the pebble flint there are six pieces of markedly different flint, most notably a scraper FN 1444 (from context 3080) and an oblique arrowhead 1214 (from context 634), which are made of a dark grey lustrous

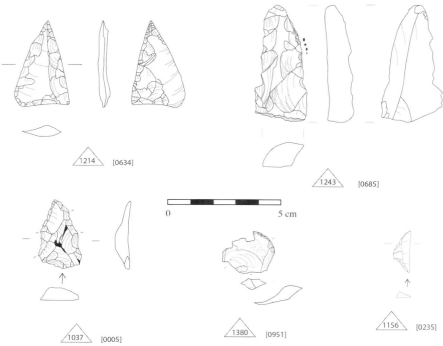

Fig. 7.1 Lithic items from post-holes 319/332 and 792, and feature 032

flint, and four flakes of macroscopically similar flint (find numbers 1259, 1225, 1217 and 1310). The size of some of the pieces of calcined flint also suggest that they may also be of non-pebble origin.

Non-flint material includes an edge retouched blade, FN 1481 from feature 3112, made of a muddy greeny-grey coloured fine grained, opaque material which is unique. There is also an axe of a coarse sandstone or greywacke from a post-hole, feature 4110, in the inner post-ring of the palisade enclosure.

Condition

The majority of the classifiable artefacts are in a fresh condition, but three have a distinct patina; although patina is unreliable as a chronological indicator it does suggest that there might have been at least two phases of activity on the site. One artefact, a fabricator FN 1243 from the same context in feature 792 as the calcined pieces (see below), and a scraper from pit 3112, have been heated, the scraper quite intensively.

Apart from the above, just over 58% of the stratified assemblage consists of highly calcined pieces including cores and struck pebbles (10), flakes (46) and small chips and other indeterminate fragments (40) (often under 0.1g in weight). They were all (except for three chips) found in post-hole 792, although in a series of different contexts (Table 7.2). Some of the flake fragments are large (Fig. 7.5) and three groups can be refitted across contexts. The

size of these flake fragments suggests that they are made of non-pebble, probably imported flint. However, many of these pieces are so highly calcined that they are no longer identifiable.

Technology

Cores and struck pebbles
Pebbles have been worked either by splitting the pebble and forming a striking platform, as for example finds numbers 1416 and 1445 (Fig. 7.3), from which to strike flakes, or by splitting the pebble on an anvil as FN 1417, a technique associated with the reduction of small pebbles which are hard to hold (Vergès and Ollé 2011). Most pieces are undirectionally worked, but FN 1453 is flaked from two separate platforms.

A large lump of calcined flint, FN 1275, weighing 82 grammes, appears to have originally been a core but it is too damaged by heat fractures to ascertain its original form. There are also a number of unclassifiable fragments which have been struck.

Flakes
Among the flakes are several pieces with cortex on the surface, which have been struck from pebbles (for example FN 1442: Fig. 7.3). They are generally quite small and squat, usually under 40 millimetres in length, the majority being 18–36 millimetres. Striking platform remnants are either plain, cortical or shattered; apart from

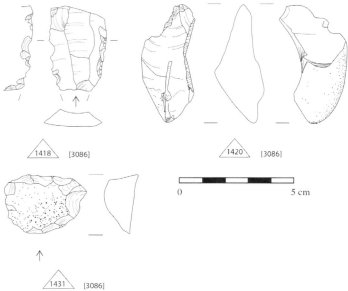

Fig. 7.2 Lithic items from small pit 3112

the shattered examples bulbs of percussion are generally resolved with the occasional ring crack visible, or more diffuse if struck from a platform with cortex, attributes which suggest the use of hard hammers; profiles tend to be concave and the dorsal surfaces frequently have cortex on them.

Retouched pieces

Apart from the conventional artefacts described below some flakes have retouch or chipping on their edges, although it is not always certain whether this is deliberate. Four of the flakes do seem to have abrupt nibbling retouch along their edges including 1442; and 1418 a blade-like segment of muddy coloured greeny-grey mat appearance with irregular retouch, which is rounded or worn in parts particularly on the distal end (Fig. 7.2). A calcined blade fragment (1229) from F792 has inverse retouch towards the distal end.

Scrapers

There are four scrapers, finds numbers 1411, 1431, 1433 and 1444, all from pits with Neolithic pottery (Figs. 7.2 and 7.3). Three are made on flakes of pebble flint and FN 1431 is also burnt; the fourth (FN 1444) is on dark grey flint and is finely worked with pressure retouch at a considerably less abrupt angle compared to those on the pebble flint flakes; its proximal end has been truncated and it has a slightly concave longitudinal profile. Of the scrapers made on pebble flint two are thick and abruptly retouched and the scraper retouch extends along the left edge and distal end forming a rounded but not particularly regular contour; on FN 1431 the retouch is undercut and on the distal end and right side (the intersection of

which form a sharp corner) and the butt end; FN 1411 has a battered proximal end suggesting that it may have been a split pebble. The third scraper, FN 1433, has only minimal retouch.

Oblique arrowhead

A fine oblique arrowhead, FN 1214, was recovered from a small cut, 634, at the top of post-hole 792 (Fig. 7.1). It is of Green's (1984) oblique type (Clark 1934 Type F). It is made on a flake of mid-brown-grey semi-translucent flint similar to scraper FN 1444. The retouch is executed bifacially along the two shorter edges. The longer edge (the right side of the flake) is only retouched on the dorsal surface. The proximal end of the flake has been abruptly retouched on both edge and forms a robust point.

Triangular point

A small, fairly thick flake of mid brown semi-translucent flint (FN 1037), $30 \times 18 \times 6.5$ millimetres, probably struck from a polished tool, has been abruptly retouched along both edges which converge to form a sharp, thickish point (Fig. 7.1). The proximal end has been truncated. The original form of the polished tool cannot be reconstructed and the possibility that this gloss was caused by rubbing in a haft cannot be entirely discounted but the polish is very high and striations on the polish on the dorsal face diagonal to the axis of the artifact are observable at $\times 20$ magnification.

Fabricators

A fragment of a fabricator, FN 1243, was recovered from post-hole 792 (Fig. 7.1). It has been heated and made on the fragment of large flake (the original flake would

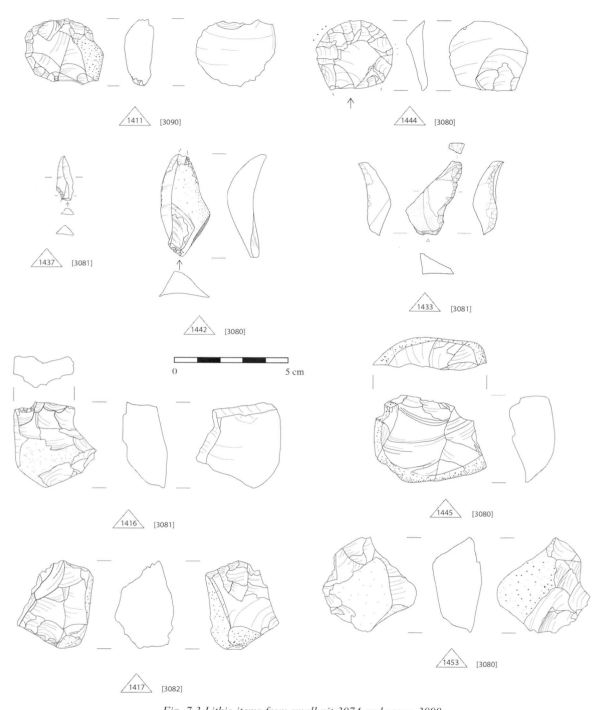

1411 [3090]

1444 [3080]

1437 [3081]

1442 [3080]

1433 [3081]

0   5 cm

1416 [3081]

1445 [3080]

1417 [3082]

1453 [3080]

Fig. 7.3 Lithic items from small pit 3074 and scoop 3090

have been far larger than any present in the debitage, though similar to the burnt flake fragments from the same feature) has been worked to a point with semi-invasive scale flaking on both sides. The pointed end is flaked on all surfaces and appears worn, although is damaged by heat and is slightly patinated. The right edge is crushed. There is also a red deposit on the pointed end visible under 10× magnification which may be ochre. The wear and the presence of ochre are typical of the wear caused by leather working. Another fabricator, FN 1380, is a largish triangular sectioned flake of mid grey flint with thick fresh cortex. Both edges have been abruptly retouched and converge at an abruptly retouched rounded point. It has no macroscopic signs of wear (Fig. 7.1).

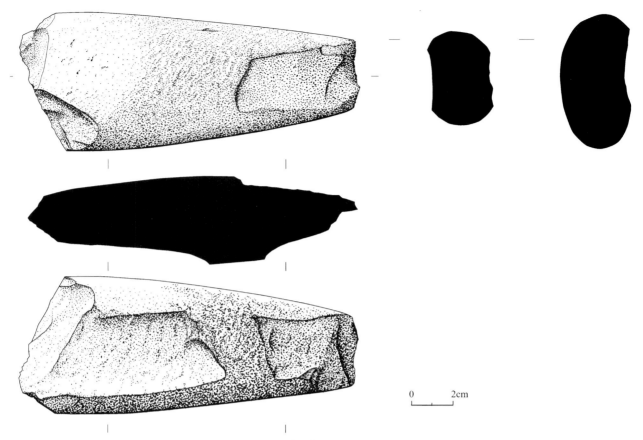

0   2cm

Fig. 7.4 Sandstone axe FN1462

Microlith and notched blade

A single microlith (FN 1156) was recovered from post-hole 3219/332 (Fig. 7.1). It is made on a blade of light brown semi-opaque flint. It has been shaped by abrupt retouch on its left edge to form an isosceles triangle and is early Mesolithic in date. A bladelet (FN 1437) from a pit with Neolithic pottery has broken across a retouched notch may be a failed attempt to snap a blade. Two further bladelets FN 1303 and FN 685 may originate from Mesolithic activity.

Large calcined pieces

In addition there are a number of fragments of a large flake or flakes which conjoin but which have been burnt and shattered by the heat (Fig. 7.5). They were all found in different contexts in a post-hole in the inner palisade (feature 792) (Table 7.2). Several refits were made and allow an idea of the size of the original piece of the largest piece (find numbers 1335+1336+1231) which now measures some 60 millimetres in length and 48 millimetres in width. The other two fragments (find numbers 1360+1279 and 1368 + 1353) are shorter but of similar width and thickness. No joins were made between the two groups but it is possible that they are part of a single object. No original edges of this object survive but there is no indication of retouch on the fragments. The original piece would have been exceptionally large for the assemblage.

There is also a large fragment of a core which has been heavily calcined (FN 1275).

Stone axehead

A fragment of a large axehead of coarse sandstone (FN 1462) was found in post-hole 4110 at the intersection of the middle ring of the palisaded enclosure and the timber cursus (Fig. 7.4). The axe has been pecked and ground into shape and has been polished towards the blade end where it becomes slightly concave. At approximately mid-point the pecking is coarser, possibly to seat it in the haft. Although the axe is broken at both ends it still measures some 165 × 74 × 45 millimetres and the complete axe is likely to have been *c.* 180–190 millimetres in length. It is not possible to obtain details of either the butt or the blade but in cross-section the axe is a rounded oval shape the sides being only slightly flattened. The butt end has been flaked away longitudinally, and the blade end irregularly broken in a similar way to the Group VI axe from Warehouse 37, Girvan (Becket and MacGregor 2013: Fig 5.3). The breakage appears to have been deliberate rather than through use (cf Coles 2011a: 144).

I am grateful to Amanda Edwards (SEAS, University of Manchester) for identifying the raw material from which this axe was made. She describes it as "a coarse wacke sandstone. This means that the sediment grains are between 0.5 and 2mm in diameter and consist of a mixture of quartz, feldspar and rock fragments. The rock also has a finer grained matrix between the grains making up more than 15% of the rock volume, this means it can be called a greywacke". Although not formally attributed to a group it is very similar to Group XXVII described by Fenton, which outcrops in Wales, the Lake District and the southern uplands of Scotland (Fenton 1988: 99ff; fig 18).

This rock type is frequently used to manufacture axe hammers and battle axes (Fenton 1988: table 33) but the list of identifications in *Stone Axe Studies Volume Two* (Clough and Cummins 1988) suggests that occasionally axes of this group and greywacke more generally are found in the north of England.

Contexts of the lithics

As noted above in Table 7.1 the lithics have a very restricted spatial distribution and only occur in a limited number of features; this is probably because the original ground surface has been destroyed in recent times rather than reflecting a real situation, but it does mean that there is no general assemblage to compare the lithics from the features with.

The artefacts from the pits and the palisade are in some respects complementary and in other ways contrasting as post-hole 792 and pit 3074 indicate. Both features have a relatively high proportion of retouched material; both feature 792 and feature 3074 have artefacts made of dark grey, non-local flint: a scraper in 3074 and an oblique arrowhead and two flakes in 792. Both these artefacts are highly finished. The non-local flint from which they are made contrasts markedly with rest of the flint within these features. The composition of the two assemblages is also different, for example the flint in 3074 includes items related to core reduction and scrapers whereas 792 has flakes and two fabricators and is the only feature with calcined material (but see feature 084).

Post-holes

Feature 792

The flint from feature 792 comes from several different contexts within the feature (Table 7.2 and Fig. 7.1) perhaps suggesting different episodes of deposition. The oblique arrowhead is from context 634 which is a small cut feature inserted into the top of the post-hole, and is the only lithic find from this context and probably is not

Fig. 7.5 Refitting burnt flake fragments from feature 792

associated with the rest of the artefacts. Only one flake and a calcined chip come from the original cut (contexts 654 and 651 respectively). Nothing was recovered from the primary fill; some calcined artefacts were recovered from contexts 867 and 967 and the fabricator 1380 comes from context 951. No lithic artefacts were recovered from context 952. The majority of the artefacts come from context 685 including a core, FN1234, two early stage flakes, FN 1283 and FN 1253, and five other small flakes, two of which are of non-local flint, and a fabricator FN 1243 (which is made of similar sized flint to the calcined pieces (below) and has itself been subjected to heat), as well as the bulk of the calcined flint.

The deposition of calcined flint in the post-hole is particularly interesting. The calcined flint consists of a large number of tiny fragments or chips, some chunks (including a probable core) and 46 flake fragments. Some of these fragments are large and were clearly part of large flakes (Fig. 7.5); it has been possible to rejoin some of the pieces (Fig. 7.5). The joining pieces come from several contexts although all have a component from context 685. It would seem that this flint was subjected to intense heat somewhere on the site and deposited in the post-hole in different episodes.

Other post-holes in the inner palisade

The contents of feature 084 seem to represent core reduction and includes a small pebble, a small core, an early stage flake of dark grey flint, a flake from a changed orientation core and splintered edge and a trimming flake as well as a calcined chip. There are no retouched pieces.

Other post-holes have only occasional flakes of flint, apart from feature 319/332 which as two very small flakes (both under 15 millimetres in length) and a microlith (FN 1156) (Fig. 7.1).

Pits with Neolithic pottery: 3074, 3112 and 050

These are all small, relatively shallow features.

3074 is the more interesting assemblage with four cores and three scrapers as well as flakes, some possibly retouched. There are two layers: one from the earliest fill of the pit (context 3080) and the other from 3081 above it. Both have similar compositions. One of the scrapers (FN 1444) from the primary fill is a finely worked, pressure-flaked scraper of good quality dark grey flint. The other two are made of gravel flint and are much more abruptly retouched, probably using a hard hammer.

3112 is a single context and also contains a core (FN 1420) and a scraper (FN 1431), as well as a blade segment of matt fine material (possibly chert) of muddy brown colour with fine retouch on both edges, although the right is damaged. The edges towards the distal end are rounded, probably through use. There is also a 'slice' of a pebble with a battered end and edge.

The lithics in *050* are all flakes and appear to represent a much more random accumulation of artefacts.

Miscellaneous features

Feature 032
This feature contained a single pointed object (FN 1037). It is made on the distal part of a flake from a ground and polished object of mid-brown flint. The sides have been abruptly retouched to form a sharp point at the distal end.

Feature 4110
The deposition of the large stone axe in the unusually large post-hole at the junction of the middle post-ring and the earlier cursus could of course be fortuitous, but various circumstances suggest that it was deliberate and

so highly significant. The axe itself is large, its breakage appears to have been deliberate and it is the only item (apart from a flake) of material culture to have been found in the post-holes of the middle circle. Perhaps it was a way of marking the break between the old cursus and the new circle. It is perhaps surprising that there no other axes or fragments were recovered given the amount of timber that must have been worked and the axes and fragments known from the area (Coles 2011a: 143).

Discussion

As we have seen the lithics from Dunragit indicate Mesolithic and Late Neolithic activity (the majority) and have a number of interesting aspects including the use of different raw materials, their depositional contexts, as well as selection of artefacts within some features. Mesolithic activity suggests that the site must have had a long standing significance; this situation is not unique – a scalene microlith was recovered from Meldon Bridge (Ballin 1999) and construction of Megalithic tombs in sites where Mesolithic activity is well known (Healey and Green 1984; Saville 1990).

The numbers of lithic artefacts are low, but lithic artefacts are sometimes sparse in timber circles and palisaded enclosures, so it may not be remarkable (Gibson 1994: 178; 1999: 73). The possibility that the artefacts had independent use-lives elsewhere and were only subsequently gathered together for deposition in the post-holes should also not be discounted (cf. Donahue 1999).

The juxtaposition of different types of raw material is of interest as much for what is missing as for what is present. Pebble flint makes up the greater part of the assemblage and was almost certainly collected from Luce Sands (Coles 2011a; 2011b). A smaller 'exotic' component (the grey-brown flint) was probably acquired in the form of finished artefacts although the occasional flake of similar flint suggests some working of this material on site. The use of such flint is not unknown in other late Neolithic contexts where good flint is not easily available (see for example a discussion of the situation in Yorkshire: Thorpe and Richards 1984). Other exotic raw materials include the axe of greywacke. The absence and artefacts of pitchstone and axes of Group VI material is surprising given that they are common in the area (Coles 2011a). Only one of the latter has been recorded from Dunragit (TT74/07 Treasure Trove in Scotland). However, the chronological relationships between the assemblages also needs to be assessed in case the accounts for the difference.

The highly calcined and fragmented objects in post-hole 792 seem to relate to a deliberate act of destruction and perhaps transformation, and this is not unknown elsewhere in Grooved Ware assemblages (Jackson and Ray 2012: 157).

8

CREMATED BONE

Jacqueline I. McKinley
(reports submitted 1999 and 2004)

Introduction

Cremated bone from two contexts at Dunragit, each representing the remains of an unurned burial, was subject to analysis. Both were dated via radiocarbon analysis of bone samples, one (context 227, from post-hole 215) returning a Late Neolithic date and the other (context 2025, from grave 2042) a Middle Bronze Age date (see Chapter 10 for dating information). The post-hole formed part of the 'eastern arc' of the inner post-ring (Figs. 3.5 and 3.71). The later grave was flanked by post-holes 2028 and 2036 in Trench E (Figs. 3.101 and 3.105)

Methods

The remains of the Middle Bronze Age burial 2025 (subsequently also allocated a find number 1404), were lifted as a block for excavation by the writer. This was undertaken in a series of four 20 millimetre spits to enable the formation process of the deposit to be ascertained in greater detail. The fills were floated to allow the recovery of any charred plant remains, and wet-sieved to 1 millimetre fraction-size.

Analysis followed the writer's standard procedure for the examination of cremated bone (McKinley 1994a: 5–21; 2004a). Age was assessed from the stage of skeletal and tooth development (Beek 1983; McMinn and Hutchings 1985; Scheuer and Black 2000) and the patterns and degree of age-related changes to the bone and teeth (Brothwell 1972; Buikstra and Ubelaker 1994).

Sex was ascertained from the sexually dimorphic traits of the skeleton (Bass 1987; Buikstra and Ubelaker 1994).

Late Neolithic burial remains 227 (Fig. 8.1)

The bone is in relatively poor condition, the cortical surface being worn and of the chalky appearance indicative of burial in an acid microenvironment. Some trabecular bone is present but it is probable, given the hostile nature of the burial conditions, that there will have been some post-depositional loss of trabecular bone e.g. elements of axial skeleton and articular surfaces (McKinley 1997a: 245).

The 300.1 grammes of cremated bone recovered represents the remains of a subadult/adult female of more than 16 years of age. A small quantity (c. 13 grammes) of the bone derived from a sheep or sheep-sized mammal. No pathological lesions were observed.

The bone is uniformly the buff-white colour indicative of a high degree of oxidation (Holden et al. 1995a; 1995b). Characteristic dehydration fissuring with occasional slight crazing on some of the lower limb shafts demonstrates that the bone was burnt green/fresh. The quantity of bone recovered represents a maximum of c. 30% of the expected weight of bone from an adult cremation (McKinley 1993), probably more in the region of 19%, though – as observed above – it is possible that a small proportion of trabecular bone may have been lost due to adverse soil conditions. Most of the bone (c. 84%) was recovered from the 10 millimetre sieve fraction, and the maximum fragment size is 64.8 millimetres; there is no evidence to suggest deliberate fragmentation of bone prior to burial (McKinley 1994b). Fragments from all areas of the skeleton were included in the burial with no evidence to suggest deliberate selection of any specific elements.

The inclusion of animal remains, representative of pyre goods, in cremation burials is a common characteristic of the rite; for example, an average of *c.* 15% of Bronze Age burials from a sample of 31 cemeteries examined by the writer contained cremated animal bone, most commonly parts of sheep and pig (McKinley 1997b; 2000). Data for the Neolithic has not been systematically collated but pig was found in two of the six burials from Sarn-y-Bryn, Powys (Stead 1994); immature animal bone was found in one burial from Llandegai Henge A, Gwynedd (McKinley 2004b); there are records of only one of the burials from the large assemblage (*c.* 165 burials) at Dorchester-on-Thames containing cremated animal bone (red deer antler; Zeuner 1951); and none was found amongst the bone from the *c.* six burial remains from Imperial College, Middlesex (McKinley forthcoming). A potential for regional variation in the inclusion of animal remains on the pyre within this period would require a more comprehensive survey and probably a consistent re-analysis of some of the material.

The very small quantity (0.5 grammes) of charcoal recovered with the burial probably represents an incidental inclusion of pyre debris.

Cremated bone recovered from Neolithic contexts in much of the British Isles seems to often take the form of relatively small quantities of scattered remains from within long barrows/cairns, e.g. the *c.* 200 small fragments (no weight given but probably 100–150 grammes) representing parts of an adult and a child from the north entrance of the Hazleton North Long Cairn (Saville 1990: figs. 120 and 136; Rogers 1990), or the 32.7 grammes from disparate contexts at Geirisclett, North Uist (McKinley 1999). What is unclear in these cases is whether only small quantities of bone were ever included in these deposits or if some was 'removed' or disturbed during the 'curation' commonly indicated in Neolithic long barrows and cairns (e.g. see Saville 1990; Whittle 1991). An argument in favour of the latter is indicated by the recovery of a substantial (1692 grammes), compact heap of cremated bone from the NE chamber in the West Kennet long barrow (Lisowski 1962) which contained remains from two adults; animal bone was mentioned but it is unclear if this was cremated and part of burial deposit. In other locations the range of weights recovered appears consistently greater, lending weight to the hypothesis of probable manipulation of the material within the chambered cairns. For example, a range of 236.1–1266.1 grammes, mean 670.6 grammes, was recovered from the burials at Imperial College (McKinley forthcoming), with variable but relatively comparative averages record from each of the sites at Dorchester-on-

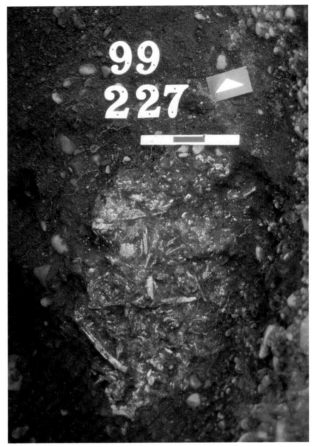

Figure 8.1 Cremation 227

Thames (906.6 grammes Site II, 493.5 grammes, 504.2 grammes and 754.9 grammes from Sites IV–VI; Weiner 1951, excluding weights of <75 grammes which were clearly either very disturbed or not burials as such).

Middle Bronze Age unurned burial 1404/2025 (Fig. 8.2)

The grave cut survived to the relatively shallow depth of *c.* 0.10 metres (Fig. 8.2). A few fragments of cremated bone were evident at surface level, but most survived as a concentration in the lower 0.08 metres of the grave cut. It is unlikely that much, if any bone, had been removed from the deposit as a result of disturbance. The visual condition of the cremated bone was relatively good, though some fragments from the upper half of the burial were slightly worn and chalky in appearance. Trabecular bone – most prone to disintegration in burial conditions adverse to good bone survival (McKinley 1997a: 245; Nielsen-Marsh *et al.* 2000) – is relatively well represented; this suggests limited loss of bone from the deposit due to post-depositional disintegration.

The 728.5 grammes of bone recovered represent the

Figure 8.2 Cremation 1404

remains of a *c.* 25–45 year old adult, probably female, and a small quantity (*c.* 2.2 grammes) of cremated bone from a medium/large sized mammal. Several minor pathological lesions were observed including those indicative of mild periodontal disease (gum infection) in the mandible; slight porotic *cribra orbitalia* (believed to be linked with childhood iron deficiency anaemia; Molleson 1993; Robledo *et al.* 1995) in the right orbital vault (uni-lateral); the early stages of osteoarthritis (Rogers and Waldron 1995: 32–46) in the right temporo-mandibular joint (uni-lateral); and slight osteophytes (irregular growths of new bone along joint margins; Rogers and Waldron 1995: 20–31) in a minimum of one lumbar vertebra. Two small wormian bones, most probably from the lambdoid suture, were also identified.

The bone was almost universally white in colour – with only one fragment of slightly grey skull vault – indicative of full oxidation (Holden *et al.* 1995a; 1995b). The weight of bone recovered represents *c.* 45% of the expected weight of bone from an adult cremation (McKinley 1993), and falls within the average range of weights recovered from Bronze Age cremation burials (McKinley 1997b: 137, 142). The weight is considerably greater than that from the earlier burial 227 but the bone from the latter was in poorer condition and some of that originally deposited may not have survived excavation (see above).

The majority of the bone was recovered from the 10 millimetre sieve fraction (*c.* 68%) and the maximum fragment size is 69 millimetres. There are a number

of factors which may affect the size of cremated bone fragments the majority of which are exclusive of any deliberate human action other than that of cremation itself (McKinley 1994b), and there is no indication of deliberate fragmentation of bone prior to burial. As is generally observed within the mortuary rite, elements from all four major skeletal areas were included in the burial, with no apparent bias towards particular elements or areas. Fragments of six tooth roots and nine of the small bones of the hands and or/feet were recovered; the relatively common inclusion of these small skeletal elements may reflect a collection procedure which included raking-off the upper levels of the burnt-out pyre to recover bones rather than hand collection of individual fragments from the surface, thereby enhancing the chance of recovering such small bones.

Pyre goods, in the form of a small quantity (2.2 grammes) of cremated animal bone was recovered from spit 3 of the burial deposit. The tradition is relatively common in all periods within which the mortuary rite was practised (see above for further discussion).

Fragments of bone from different parts of the burial deposit – spits 1 and 2, 2 and 4, and 1 and 4 were found to join. This suggests that the bone was mixed during collection from the pyre – which could have occurred as a result of the raking process suggested above – and/or during/at the point of burial. It is most probable that the burial was made in an organic container, which it could have been placed in during collection from the pyre or transferred to prior to burial.

Details of cremated bone

Context 227

SKULL: Molar root fragment.
Mandible: right distal body fragment with molar socket.
Fragment anterior ramus border.
Fragments left and right petrous temporals, W1 = 10.7
millimetres. Left zygomatic tubercle with articular
tubercle and mandibular fossa fragment. Fragment left
malar body.
Vault; 30 small fragments, frequently single plates. 1a =
2.5 millimetres.

AXIAL SKELETON: Thoracic; 2 articular processes
and fragment minimum 1 other.
Rib; 5 fragments shaft.
Innominate; 3 fragments ilium including left auricular
surface and greater sciatic notch with angle tending
obtuse.

UPPER LIMB: Fragments humerus (3) and radius (2)
shaft.
Ulna; fragment trochlear notch. Fragment (?right) proximal shaft with very small tuberosity, faint bluish/green
discolouration. 5 fragments shaft.
Fragment very small hook of hamate. 3 fragments metacarpal shaft. Fragments 2 proximal phalanges heads
with shafts, and 5 middle phalanges heads with shafts.
Middle phalanx proximal articular surface, unclear if
fused or not.

LOWER LIMB: Femur; 17 fragments shaft. 2 fragments
distal articular surface.
Fragments tibia (3) and fibula (12) shaft.
Fragment very small intermediate cuneiform.

AGE: older subadult/adult
SEX: female
ANIMAL: 13.0 grammes. Sheep and sheep size; includ-
ing fragments of femur and ?tibia (PS).
INCLUSIONS: Charcoal wt. 0.5 grammes
CONDITION: Worn with heavily chalky appearance.
Classic dehydration fissuring with slight crazing on
some lower limb shafts.

FN 1404; context 2025

spit 1; upper 20mm, taken to create flat surface
SKULL: Incisor root fragment. Premolar root fragment.
Mandible – right anterior ramus border fragment (buccal).
Maxilla; body fragment.
Fragment sagittal crest. Fragment articular fossa. Fragment ?medium-sized pointed mastoid process. Fragment
orbital vault. Right lateral supra-orbital fragment (joins
fragment in spit 2) medium margin. Small fragment left
lateral so (joins fragment in spit 4); medium/narrow

margin. Left medial supra-orbital fragment with foramen
and notch (joins fragment in un.no. bag) moderate margin.
Vault; 30 relatively thin fragments; 1a = 3.3 millimetres (1
slightly grey). 2 small wormian bones; 16 × 7 millimetres
& 11 × 7 millimetres .

AXIAL SKELETON: Cervical; articular process pair.
Thoracic; fragments 2 articular processes, 2 spinal
processes.
Thoracic/lumbar; 2 small fragments body with slight
marginal osteophytes (angled).
Rib; 8 fragments shaft.
Innominate; fragment acetabulum.

UPPER LIMB: Scapula; fragment left coronoid process.
Fragments humerus (4) and ulna (1) shaft.
Fragments minimum 1 metacarpal head with neck. 2
fragments proximal/middle phalanges shafts.
LOWER LIMB: Fragments femur (8) and fibula (7) shaft.
Small fragment calcaneum anterior articular surface.
COMMENT: some fragments have slight worn appear-
ance.

spit 2
SKULL: Fragments ?maxillary molar root.
Mandible – anterior body fragment with small spines
with incisor and left canine sockets; ?pointed mental
protuberance. Small fragments labial distal body with
minimum 1 molar socket – slight periodontal disease.
Maxilla – small fragment distal palate with molar socket.
Fragment mastoid process. Right zygomatic tubercle
(chalky). Right medial supra-orbital fragment (joins spit
1); narrow/moderate margin. Broad left malar process.
Left mandibular fossa & articular tubercle. Left and
right postglenoid tubercles with external auditory meati.
Sphenoid fragment.
Vault; 32 small fragments; 1a = 3.3 millimetres. Sutures
up to half fused.

AXIAL SKELETON: Cervical; lamina fragment.
Thoracic; fragments 2 articular processes.
Lumbar; fragments minimum 1 body, slight marginal
osteophytes. Fragments 2 articular processes.
Rib; 8 fragments shaft.
Innominate; ilium body fragment.

UPPER LIMB: Scapula; 2 small fragments glenoid fossa.
Body fragment.
Fragments humerus (5), radius (9) and ulna (4) shaft.
Metacarpal head with shaft fragment. Distal phalanx
shaft fragment.
LOWER LIMB: Femur; fragment head with notch. 10
large fragments shaft.
Fragments tibia (5) and fibula (5) shaft.
Talus fragment.

COMMENT: some long bone slightly worn & chalky appearance.

spit 3
SKULL: Fragments minimum 1 maxillary & 1 mandibular tooth root.
Mandible – fragment sigmoid notch and small fragment distal body with socket.
Maxilla – right distal palate & body fragment with minimum 2 molar sockets. Right anterior body fragment with minimum 3 sockets. Anterior left fragment with canine & I2 sockets.
Small fragment petrous temporal. Superior portion right nasal bone. Fragment minimum right malar body. Articular tubercle; flattened profile with slight pitting and osteophytes on anterior margins. Small fragment mastoid process. Articular fissure.
Vault; 33 fragments, 1a = 3.7 millimetres ; sutures open – 2/3rd fused.

AXIAL SKELETON: Cervical; fragments 2 articular processes, spinal fragment.
Thoracic; fragments minimum 2 articular processes.
Rib; 10 fragments shaft.
Innominate; small fragment greater sciatic notch, angle unclear but tending obtuse.

UPPER LIMB: Humerus; head fragment. 10 fragments shaft. Fragments distal articular surface.
Fragments radius (2) and ulna (5) shaft.
2 fragments metacarpal shaft.

LOWER LIMB: Femur; head fragment. 10 fragments shaft.
Tibia; fragment proximal condyle. Shaft fragment.
Fibula; 7 fragments shaft.
ANIMAL: Long bone fragment from medium/large-sized mammal (slightly chalky
than other bone). 1.6 grammes

spit 4
SKULL: Fragments minimum maxillary molar root.
Mandible – left anterior body fragment (joins spit 2) with premolar and 1 molar sockets.
Right lateral supra-orbital (joins spit 1) with orbital vault, very slight pitting in central area. 2nd small supra-orbital fragment also joins that from spit 1. Small fragment medial supra-orbital with narrow margin & foramen. Fragments small, pointed right mastoid process. Nasal

process fragment.
Vault; 23 small fragments 1a = 2.8 millimetres. Sutures open. Few shelly fragments.

AXIAL SKELETON: Cervical; body fragment with articular process pair. Spine fragment.
Thoracic; fragments minimum 4 articular processes.
Rib; 10 fragments shaft.

UPPER LIMB: Fragments humerus (4), radius (2) and ulna (2) shaft.

LOWER LIMB: Fragments femur (4), tibia (3) and fibula (4) shaft.
    Proximal phalanx head with shaft fragment.

unspec.
SKULL: Right nasal process & inferior fragment left. Medial supra-orbital fragment (joins above) with slight-mild ridge (2).
Vault; 20 fragments, 1a = 3.5 millimetres, sutures open.

AXIAL SKELETON: Axis; fragment right arch with articular surfaces
Rib; shaft fragment.
Innominate; fragments acetabulum.

UPPER LIMB: Scapula; left & right acromion necks.
Humerus; 2 fragments shaft, distal articular surface fragment.
Radius; small fragment head. 2 fragments shaft.
Ulna 2 fragments shaft.
LOWER LIMB: Femur; 2 fragments head. 5 fragments shaft with gracile linea aspera.
Tibia; proximal condyle fragment.
Fibula; 4 fragments shaft.

ANIMAL: ??fragment. 0.6 grammes

AGE: adult *c*. 25–45 yr.
SEX: ?female
PATHOLOGY SUMMARY: cribra orbitalia – min. right; osteoarthritis – temporo-mandible (min. 1 side); periodontal disease – slight mandibular; osteophytes – minimum 1 lumbar; morphological variation – wormian bones.
ANIMAL: *c*. 2.2 grammes medium/large mammal
CONDITION: some bone in upper spits slightly worn and chalky.

SOIL MICROMORPHOLOGY OF POST-HOLE FILLS FROM DUNRAGIT

Helen Lewis

Introduction

In 1999 block samples for soil micromorphological study were taken from a number of post-hole features excavated during the Dunragit palisaded enclosure investigations. The samples taken were chosen to represent a variety of post-hole fills, and the aim of doing soil micromorphology was to gather as much information as possible about a selection of the features, and thus the site, which were greatly truncated by post-depositional land use and erosion. Block samples were taken from features in the inner and middle post-rings, and smaller post-holes linked with the middle post-ring (see this volume, Chapter 3).

Thin sections were made from these samples by Julie Boreham, then at the McBurney Laboratory of the University of Cambridge Department of Archaeology, following the method outlined by Murphy (1986). They were described following the guidelines of Bullock *et al.* (1985) using a Nikon Eclipse LV100Pol microscope, in plane polarized (PPL) and cross polarized (XPL) light. All percentages and frequency descriptions below represent proportion of visible area at macroscopic and microscopic scales. Munsell colours in this summary refer to macroscopic descriptions of thin sections under normal ambient light following Munsell Color (2009); colours here have been done on the fine fabric, excluding gravels. It is normal for there to be some variation with the field descriptions due to the much thinner layer of sediment examined, the fact that it is impregnated with resin, and the light source under which each context was described.

Post-hole fills

The post-hole features were found cut into glacial outwash gravels (see this volume, Chapter 3) and sands, buried by a shallow topsoil profile only. These gravels also made up a great part of many post-hole fills across the site, comprising mainly 1–3cm sized rounded to subangular mixed gravels and sands. Samples were taken from Trench A, in a field under pasture at the time, but previously cultivated (see this volume, Chapters 1–3). Soil blocks were taken from the features and fills listed in Table 9.1; field descriptions and interpretations follow those used in Chapter 3. Context information for three of the sample sets was lost between sampling date and

Table 9.1 Contexts sampled for soil micromorphology

Area of Site	Feature number	Context number	Sample numbers
Inner post-ring	084	079, 082, 085	014, 015, 016
Inner post-ring	087	037, 218, 014	011, 012
Inner post-ring (E arc)	215	214, 249, 250	021, 022
Middle post-ring	099	201–2, 204–6, 208, 210–12	013A&B, 017, 018
Middle post-ring	035	012, 034	004, 005

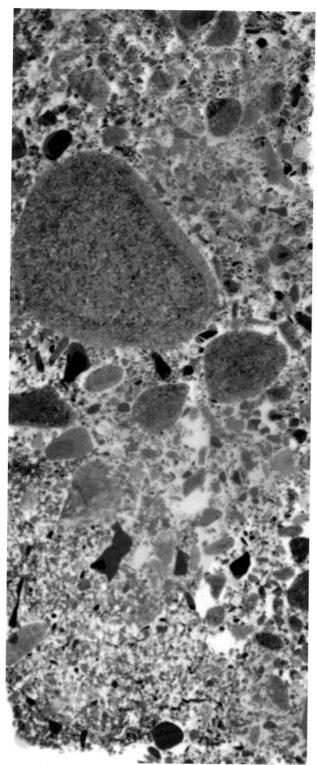

Figure 9.1 Soil micromorphological sample 015

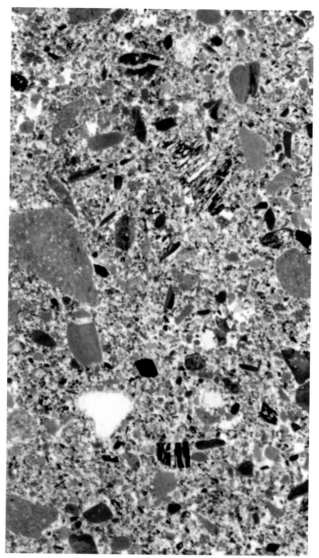

Figure 9.2 Soil micromorphological sample 011A

The Inner post-ring – Feature 084, contexts 079, 082 and 085 (Fig. 3.48)

Context 079 was a post-pipe fill, and 082 a packing fill of post-hole 084. Context 079 was described in the field as dark brown loamy sand, overlying context 081, a loose, brown sand layer. The latter overlay context 082, described as dark reddish-brown firm loamy sand, overlying context 086, a dark brown, loose sandy gravel fill (see Chapter 3).

Context 079 in thin section comprises dark brown (7.5YR 3/3) loamy sand with frequent rounded and subangular gravels up to 3 centimetres in size visible macroscopically; about 40% of the thin section is made up of gravel. The gravels have a steep diagonal or vertical orientation, presumably related to being part of a steep fill. The c:f ratio of the deposit is 75:25 (very coarse sand 35%, coarse sand 20%, medium sand 15%, fine sand 5%, very

analysis date; however, it has been possible to tentatively re-identify them from the section drawings, which had the sample numbers noted on them (see Figs. 3.48, 3.68, 3.72 and 3.80).

fine sand 5%, silt 10%, clay 10%). The soil component has a mixed structure, with loose crumb peds (mainly <500µm in size), sometimes pellet, in packing pores, representing the activity of soil fauna; these are also weakly coalesced into poorly developed angular blocky structure (1–2 centimetres) in between gravels. This aggregation appears to reflect mainly the packing of the deposit, rather than any obvious soil formation factor. Porosity varies from *c*. 20% where gravels and coarse sands are fewer, to about 40% where these are more frequent; this is made up mainly of packing pores, although there are rare cracks and channels (50–150µm × 100–400µm, unaccommodated) in the peds seen. The related distribution of the soil component is also mixed, with open and close porphyric related distribution in blocky zones, and chitonic to enaulic related distribution elsewhere. The groundmass is stipple speckled to undifferentiated, very dark reddish brown (PPL) and very dark brown to black (XPL). These characteristics are related to strong amorphous organic and moderate iron staining. In rare coatings where clay is visible, it is orange (PPL and XPL), moderately birefringent, and 'dirty'; the groundmass in general reflects a great deal of leaching, disturbance and bioturbation. Occasional charcoal fragments, mainly up to *c*. 3 millimetres in size are also visible macroscopically. Microscopically, charcoal is the dominant organic component (ranging from 100–1000µm in size), with small amorphous organic fragments (up to *c*. 200µm) also found. Altogether, organic components total <5% of the context in thin section. Most grains and gravel fragments have fine coatings of organic-stained clay and microaggregates. There are occasional rounded dense zones of the main fabric (*c*. 400µm in size), which appear to relate to soil faunal activity. The occasional charcoal inclusions are the only cultural inclusions.

Context 082 is less iron-stained than context 079; indeed, the Munsell colour of the soil in the thin section is very dark greyish-brown (2.5Y 3/2), at variance from that recorded in the field (dark reddish-brown; see Chapter 3). This fill is also distinct macroscopically from 079 by its relatively fine nature, with only *c*. 10% of the thin section comprising gravels, and most of these being 1 centimetre sized or smaller, and by its moderate occurrence of charcoal inclusions, mainly 0.2–0.6 millimetre in size. This increase in charcoal makes the organic component rise slightly, to about 5% of the thin section, although there is no increase in the frequency of smaller charcoal fragments. There are also no macroscopically-visible peds, unlike 079 which had weak blocky structure; in 082 the same type of fine microaggregates are seen as in 079, in packing pores and coatings, but these are not coalescing into larger aggregates. Porosity in 082 is uniformly around 25–35% packing pores. The c:f ratio is 85:15 (very coarse sand 30%, coarse sand 30%, medium sand 15%, fine sand 10%, very fine sand 5%, silt 5%, clay 5%), representing the relatively more sandy nature

of this fill, and the relative reduction in the proportion of fine soil fraction. The combination of relatively less and smaller gravels and relatively more sand could represent some aspect of sorting; whether that means that this fill came from a finer original deposit than 079 or it became better sorted within the post-hole is unknown. The related distribution is chitonic. All other components are as described in 079; the moderate charcoal inclusions are the only cultural indicators.

Two further contexts are seen in thin section 015. The upper 5 centimetres, context 078, comprise a dark reddish-brown (5YR 3/2) gravel-rich loamy sand with fine crumb and intergrain microaggregate structure, and porosity of *c*. 30% (packing pores). The c:f ratio is 70:30 (very coarse sand 20%, coarse sand 25%, medium sand 15%, fine sand 10%, very fine sand 5%, silt 10%, clay 15%). There is an enaulic related distribution, with close porphryic related distribution in crumb peds. The groundmass is very dark brown (PPL), very dark reddish-brown (XPL), and stipple-speckled, with granostriation. Organic components comprise <5% of the visible area. These are mainly amorphous angular and subangular fragments, from 100–3000µm in size; some of the larger ones appear to be charcoal. Most grains are coated with microaggregates and/or brown clay (PPL & XPL) similar to the main fabric. The context is moderately organic- and iron-stained.

The boundary between the two contexts is marked by a diagonal (30°) slope where the overlying loose gravelly soil changes to the underlying dense, relatively gravel-free fill (Fig. 9.1).

The lower context, 085, is a dark brown (7.5YR 3/4) sandy loam with fine crumb structure (<4 millimetres), with microscopic zones of very fine angular blocky (<500µm peds) and interpedal microaggregate. Porosity is *c*. 20%, mainly packing pores, but also interpedal cracks (10 × 400–500µm). The c:f ratio is 55:45 (very coarse sand 10%, coarse sand 20%, medium sand 10%, fine sand 15%, very fine sand 15%, silt 15%, clay 15%). Organic components make up 5% of the context, and these are mainly fragments of charcoal (100–1000µm), and occasional iron-stained organic tissues of the same size range. The groundmass is dark reddish-brown (PPL & XPL), stipple speckled. There are frequent coatings of grains and rock fragments; these are mainly <20µm thick, light orange to brown (PPL), yellow (XPL) and of moderate birefringence. Sometimes these are 'dusty' and organic stained. Grains are also frequently coated with microaggregates.

The inner post-ring – Feature 087, contexts 037, 219 and 014 (Fig. 3.48)

In sample 012, context 037 is very similar to context 082 in regard to its soil component; however it is extremely gravelly, with subangular to angular gravels (1–3 centimetres in size) making up about 60% of the thin section. These are oriented horizontally to slightly dipping (20%), with an increase in diagonal downward inclination with depth. The latter probably relates to the context being a 'steeply-pitched post-pipe' (see Chapter 3), but this pitch is not strongly reflected in gravel orientation in the thin section. Soil crumb aggregates make up the remainder of the sediment, being distributed mainly in packing pores, and also as grain and rock fragment coatings, as in the contexts described above. Porosity is about 30% (packing pores). As in context 082, there is moderate charcoal found in 037, again mainly in a relatively large fraction (for thin sections) of 0.2–1 centimetres in size. The c:f ratio is 75:25 (very coarse sand 25%, coarse sand 20%, medium sand 25%, fine sand 10%, very fine sand 5%, silt 10%, clay 10%); most of the fine fraction is found in grain coatings and intergrain microaggregates. All other components are as described for context 084.

Sample set 011A&B is rather different from the others; initially it was thought that the numbering might represent context 011 from Feature 024, a small circular post-hole (this volume, Chapter 3), but it is clear from the section drawing (Fig. 3.48) that it came from the upper part of the profile of post-hole 087, between contexts 014 and 218. Sample 011 is relatively charcoal-rich relative to the other samples studied here. However, it is not so rich in charcoal that one would conclude *in situ* burning of a post, and there is no wood ash or burnt sand to suggest that either.

The thin sections appear to represent one context (014), which is a dark reddish brown (5YR 3/3) sandy loam, although there is some gravel sorting seen with depth (the lower 4cm comprise about 50% gravels 0.3–1 centimetres in size), which could represent a separate context (218). For the most part gravel makes up about 25% of the context, and ranges in size from *c*. 0.4–1.5 centimetres. There is no obvious orientation visible. The structure of the sediment is very fine crumb (<3 millimetres) to apedal, with channels visible in some places (*c*. 5000μm diameter in size), and mixed with intergrain microaggregate structure. Porosity in general is 25–30%, but increasing with depth to *c*. 30–35%; mainly this is packing pores, with channels as noted. The c:f ratio is 65:35 (very coarse sand 10%, coarse sand 30%, medium sand 15%, fine sand 10%, very fine sand 10%, silt 15%, clay 10%). The groundmass is mixed, reddish brown (PPL & XPL) and very dark reddish brown (PPL), undifferentiated (XPL), showing both amorphous iron and organic staining, and is stipple speckled and granostriated. There is an enaulic related distribution, and most grains are coated with microaggregates; some grains also have clay coatings, which appear similar to the main groundmass. Organic components make up 5–10% of the profile; these are primarily charcoal, and usually

of a relatively large size grade (0.3–1.2cm in size) (Fig. 9.2); finer charcoal makes up <5% of the context and is usually 50–300μm in size, and usually found in zones near the larger fragments.

The inner post-ring (eastern arc) – Feature 215, fills 214, 249, 250; cut 217 (Fig. 3.68)

Context 214 represents the main fill of the post-pull within Feature 215 post-hole. It was described in the field as comprising several tip lines, including lines of gravel, thought to represent the collapse of sediment into the post-pull; one of these lines of gravel was substantial enough to be given a separate context number (249) (see Chapter 3).

In thin section there are four layers (described in the field as 'tip lines') visible. The upper layer comprises 3 centimetres of dark brown soil (7.5YR 3/4) with subrounded gravels 1–2.5 centimetres in size making up about 45% of the visible area. This layer does not have an overall downward orientation, being only slightly inclined to horizontal for the most part. The layer has a granular structure with *c*. 30% porosity (packing pores) and a mixed gefuric and enaulic related distribution. Most of the fine soil material occurs as intergrain microaggregates and as grain coatings. The c:f ratio is 80:20 (very coarse sand 10%, coarse sand 40%, medium sand 20%, fine sand 10%, very fine sand 5%, silt 5%, clay 10%). Organic components are <2%, mainly amorphous and <300μm in size. The groundmass is granostriated, with stipple speckled groundmass seen in microaggregates; it is light reddish brown (PPL), orange to very dark reddish brown (XPL), and iron-stained. There are no obvious cultural inclusions.

The second layer is 1–2 centimetres thick and is made up primarily of fine gravel (0.3–1 centimetre sized), oriented downwards with a 30° slope, and sand. The colour is the same as the layer described above, although there is more black gravel present. The structure is granular, with occasional intergrain microaggregates, and the context has an enaulic to gefuric related distribution. Porosity is *c*. 25% (packing pores). The c:f ratio is 85:15 (very coarse sand 10%, coarse sand 50%, medium sand 15%, fine sand 10%, very fine sand 5%, silt 5%, clay 5%). Organic components are <2%, mainly angular amorphous fragments (<300μm) in size; there is no obvious charcoal. The groundmass is orange to dark reddish brown (PPL), dark reddish-brown to amorphous (XPL), and is granostriated. All grains have coatings of clay and/or microaggregates.

The third layer is a 1 centimetre thick layer of sand, with the same fine fraction colour as above, and is largely gravel-free. It has an intergrain microaggregate structure and *c*. 25% porosity (packing pores), and a chitonic related distribution. The c:f ratio is 75:25 (very coarse sand 15%, coarse sand 35%, medium sand 20%, fine sand 5%, very fine sand 10%, silt 5%, clay 10%). Organic matter comprises <5% of the visible area, and is mainly amorphous particles (<200μm) and modern plant tissues; there is no obvious charcoal. The groundmass is dark reddish-brown (PPL & XPL), granostriated and amorphous. Most grains have coatings of clay and/or microaggregates.

The fourth layer (context 249) comprises about 50% angular and subrounded gravel (0.5–1.5 centimetres) with a 30° downward orientation. The structure of this layer is granular and intergrain microaggregate, with *c.* 25–35% porosity (packing pores). The c:f ratio is 70:30 (very coarse sand 25%, coarse sand 30%, medium sand 10%, fine sand 5%, very fine sand 10%, silt 10%, clay 10%). Organic matter is primarily charcoal (<500μm in size), and makes up <5% of the visible area. The fine groundmass is reddish-brown (PPL), very dark reddish-brown to undifferentiated (XPL); where clay coats grains, this is sometimes orange in XPL, but very 'dusty'. The groundmass is mixed, primarily being granostriated, but also stipple speckled where intergrain microaggregates occur, and is iron stained.

Relationships described in the field suggest that cut number 217, which is the post-pull cut inside feature 215, should be represented in the samples, physically occurring between contexts 214 and 250, although this sequence does not represent their true stratigraphic matrix. The post-pull cut appears to be represented in thin section by a change in density. At the base of context 249 is a change in sediment density, with a change from *c.* 30% porosity (base of 249) to about 40–50% porosity (upper 250). The line of this boundary slopes downward on the same orientation as context 249 gravels, and this appears to mark cut 217. In thin section this boundary is not represented by any major change in components or texture, but simply by a lower porosity.

Context 250 is a secondary packing fill, a brown (10YR 5/3) sand and gravel layer, in feature 215, predating the post-pull feature. This fill is distinguished macroscopically from those above by a more random organisation of gravel, and a generally smaller gravel size (<1 centimetre, usually 0.4–0.6 centimetres). Gravel makes up about 20–25% of the visible area; the remainder is pore space (40–50%, packing pores) and soil. The structure is granular. No mottles were noted in thin section, although these were recorded in the field. The soil c:f ratio is 85:15 (very coarse sand 10%, coarse sand 50%, medium sand 15%, fine sand 10%, very fine sand 5%, silt 5%, clay 5%. The latter occurs primarily as grain coatings and in dispersed intergrain microaggregates). Organic components represent <2% of the visible area; these are mainly charcoal fragments <500μm in size, with rare recent plant tissues, and are found loose in pore spaces. The fine groundmass is orange to medium

brown (PPL), very dark reddish-brown (XPL), and mainly granostriated. There is a gefuric related distribution. This is a strongly leached coarse sand layer with gravel inclusions.

The nature of these lower fills, both within and underneath the post-pull feature, suggest strong leaching of the sediments, and some possible size-sorting based on this, i.e. it is not certain that they are 'tip lines' *per se*, which imply small dumps or erosion of the sides, but more likely that they acquired the 'lensing' seen post-depositionally through processes related to leaching. The deposits of origin for these fills were evidently primarily coarse sands, but the finer fraction variation suggests that certain layers have seen leaching out of most fine materials. Where there is soil proper, as opposed to grain coatings, this is always as intergrain microaggregates, representing bioturbation by soil fauna. It is uncertain whether this soil component represents the original nature of the fills, as it could have been moved by fauna from above (or below) to the pore spaces in between the sand grains and gravels. There are only rare, small charcoal fragments found, and it is possible that these have moved into this feature from elsewhere through bioturbation.

In both sets of samples 021 and 011 the charcoal is all of a relatively large size grade (for thin section studies), suggesting that it did not travel far and that it has not seen a lot of degradation since it was deposited. In neither case is *in situ* burning indicated.

The middle post-ring – Feature 099, fills 201, 202, 204, 205, 206, 208, 210, 211, 212 (Fig. 3.72)

Context 201 was one of the later fills of a large post-hole (Feature 099); in thin section 013 this is represented by 2–3 centimetres of dark yellowish-brown loamy sand with frequent gravel (mainly 1 centimetre size, but up to 3 centimetres). This deposit has weakly developed crumb structure (up to 1 centimetre), comprised of coalesced microaggregates as described previously, and with frequent coatings of the main fabric on sand grains, again as previously described. Porosity is 20%, mainly packing pores between microaggregtes, sand grains and crumb peds. The c:f ratio is 70:30 (very coarse sand 20%, coarse sand 30%, medium sand 10%, fine sand 10%, very fine sand 5%, silt 10%, clay 15%). The groundmass is stained with amorphous organic matter and iron oxide, and is reddish-brown to very dark reddish-brown (PPL), very dark reddish-brown (XPL). All other components are as previously described for the other post-hole fills (above), with one exception: organic components are <2% (mainly amorphous fragments) and no charcoal was noted in this layer in the thin section.

Underlying context 201 is context 202, a fine layer

of loamy sand, which is distinguished in thin section primarily by its loose, open structure and lack of gravels above the 1 centimetre size. Porosity is about 40%, packing pores, and the main structure is intergrain microaggregate. The c:f ratio is 65:35 (very coarse sand 15%, coarse sand 15%, medium sand 20%, fine sand 15%, very fine sand 10%, silt 10,% clay 15%), and gravel <1cm in size makes up about 45% of the total visible area. Gravels in this layer are oriented diagonally downward at 50° to the horizontal. A further distinction, and one which may relate to the colour designation in the field of 'light reddish-brown' (see Chapter 3) is the presence of less organic staining in this layer. Although much of the fine groundmass is stained as described for context 201, clay coatings on sand grains and rock fragments in 202 are frequently not as heavily stained with amorphous organic matter; these are reddish-brown (PPL) and orange to very dark reddish-brown (XPL), up to 50μm thick and 'dusty' to 'dirty', representing disturbance of the fine groundmass. This means that in addition to the usual stipple speckled fabric, this layer also has a grano-striated fine fabric. It is unclear whether this relative lack of amorphous organic matter relates to the origin of the fill or post-depositional soil formation processes – the latter is likely, possibly related to the relatively low density (increased leaching) of this fill layer. There is also some potential manganese precipitation in this layer, in small zones (up to 200μm in size). This layer has <5% organic matter, mainly tiny amorphous inclusions ('punctuations'); there is no clear charcoal.

Under 202 is context 204, a sandy loam layer described as having collapsed in to the post-hole (see Chapter 3) which is dark brown to dark reddish-brown (10YR 3/2, 5YR 2.5/2) macroscopically in thin section. This description is also somewhat different from that made in the field (dark greyish-brown – *ibid.*). The fill is gravel-rich in the upper 4cm (gravel 0.5–2 centimetres making up about 30% of the visible area), and relatively dense compared to overlying 202, with apedal (channel) structure comprised of coalesced microaggregates, and 15–20% porosity (mainly packing pores, with occasional channels 200–1000μm diameter, rarely 3000μm). The upper boundary with context 202 is distinctly marked by a diagonal line between areas of varying density (less dense 202-more dense 204), and a line of gravel. This diagonal orientation is also seen in gravels lower in the layer. As in all the other fills described above, microaggregates are frequently found as coatings on grains and rock fragments in an enaulic to gefuric related distribution, but where coalesced there is a close porphyric related distribution. The c:f ratio is 65:35 (very coarse sand 20%, coarse sand 20%, medium sand 15%, fine sand 10%, very fine sand 5%, silt 15%, clay 15%). The soil fabric is strongly stained with amorphous organic matter and with iron oxide, and is very dark reddish-brown (PPL), very dark reddish brown to undifferentiated (XPL), with

a stipple speckled groundmass. As previously described, there are clay coatings on most grains, and here /3) they are mainly strongly organic stained. Organic components remain low (<5–10%, mainly 'punctuations'); occasional charcoal fragments (<400μm, rarely up to 1000μm) are included in this proportion.

At the base of context 204 is a layer of similar soil material, but with gravels oriented diagonally in the opposite direction at a slope of 40–50° to the horizontal; these appear to mark the surface of context 205. Context 205 comprises a dark brown (10YR 3/3) layer with apedal to poorly developed subangular blocky structure, with frequent gravels (up to 1.5 centimetres) at its upper and lower boundaries. The c:f ratio of this layer is 75:25 (very coarse sand 10%, coarse sand 20%, medium sand 25%, fine sand 20%, very fine sand 5%, silt 10%, clay 10%). This fill contains occasional to moderate charcoal, with organic components *c.* 10% (mainly charcoal up to *c.* 0.8 centimetres in size). This makes it somewhat different from the other fills of this post-hole, and more similar to context 082 (discussed above) in this regard; these are also oriented in the same manner as the gravel, and appear to be part of the dumped layer (i.e. not post-depositionally transported). Porosity is about 15–20%, mainly packing pores, even in between the poorly developed peds, and there are rare modern root remains in some places. The soil fabric is reddish-brown (PPL) and undifferentiated (XPL), with a stipple speckled groundmass. In this case the fabric seems coated with amorphous sesquioxides, and is not as organic-stained as described previously. In rare locations there are 100μm (maximum) sized 'clean' red (PPL) and undifferentiated (XPL) clay coatings and cappings on grains.

Underlying 205 in this post-hole fill sequence is layer 206, a dark brown (7.5YR 3/4) sandy (clay) loam with poorly developed blocky structure made of coalesced microaggregates; microaggregates also coat most grains and rock fragments. Porosity is 15%, mainly channels (300–500μm × 1000–10,000μm, unaccommodated) and packing pores. The c:f ratio is 60:40 (very coarse sand 10%, coarse sand 20%, medium sand 25%, fine sand 10%, very fine sand 10%, silt 20%, clay 20%). Between the structure and texture, this fill appears to have seen strong influence of soil formation processes related to faunal and floral activity. The groundmass is strongly iron stained, strong reddish-brown (PPL), very dark reddish-brown (XPL) and stipple speckled. Organic components make up about 5% of the visible area. These are mainly very small angular amorphous fragments (<100μm) and 'punctuations'; none is clearly charcoal. There is one fragment of possible bone; this is iron-stained and 500 × 300μm in size.

Underlying this sequence was fill 208, one of a number of deposits filling the post-void (see Chapter 3). This layer is reddish-brown (5YR 4/4) sand with about 50% mixed angular and subrounded gravels (0.5–1 centimetre in size).

Porosity is about 40% (packing pores with occasional channels and chambers, up to 7000μm in diameter), and the structure is mixed crumb (<1 centimetre), granular and intergrain microaggregate. The c:f ratio is 75:25 (very coarse sand 10%, coarse sand 30%, medium sand 25%, fine sand 10%, very fine sand 5%, silt 10%, clay 10%). The groundmass is stipple speckled, brown (PPL), very dark reddish brown (XPL), and there is a mixed close porphyric and enaulic related distribution. Organic components are <5%, mainly small angular amorphous fragments (<300μm); there is no obvious charcoal. The fine fabric is organic- and iron-stained.

Fill 211 may have represented a layer of packing slipped into the post void (this volume, Chapter 3). It is made of fine gravels (<1 centimetre in size) and dark reddish-brown sand (5YR 3/2). This is relatively densely packed compared to many other sand contexts, with 20–25% porosity (packing pores), and has a granular structure with interpedal microaggregates, and an enaulic related distribution. The c:f ratio is 80:20 (very coarse sand 10%, coarse sand 35%, medium sand 25%, fine sand 10%, very fine sand 5%, silt 5–10%, clay 5–10%). The groundmass is dark reddish brown (PPL), very dark reddish-brown (XPL) and stipple speckled. There are frequent coatings made of the main fabric on grains. Organic components are <5%, mainly amorphous angular fragments (<500μm), including very rare charcoal, and 'punctuations'. The fine fabric is very strongly stained with amorphous organic matter and iron.

The primary fill of feature 099 is context 212, described as representing the initial 'silting in' of the feature (see Chapter 3). It is made of about 40% gravel, mainly subrounded and around 1 centimetre in size, with no clear orientation pattern. The structure is very intergrain microaggregate, with 40% porosity (packing pores). The c:f ratio is 75:25 (very coarse sand 10%, coarse sand 25%, medium sand 25%, fine sand 15%, very fine sand 10%, silt 5%, clay 10%), making this a sand deposit. The groundmass is reddish-brown (PPL), very dark reddish-brown to undifferentiated (XPL) and stipple speckled, with frequent grain coatings of microaggregates. Organic components are as in Fill 211, but with rare possible charcoal fragments up to *c.* 1000μm in size. There are moderately occurring grain coatings with brown (PPL), yellowish-brown (XPL) clay *c.* 10μm thick and 'dusty'.

The middle post-ring – Feature 035, fills 012, 034 (Fig. 3.80)

Fill 012 is a post-pipe in a deep, narrow post-hole (Feature 035; this volume, Chapter 3), comprising dark brown (7.5YR 3/2) soil with moderate mixed gravel inclusions (angular to rounded, 0.5–1.5 centimetres). The fill has

a mixed structure, with zones of apedal (channel) and zones of crumb aggregates (<0.5 centimetres). Porosity is 15–20% in the apedal zones (packing pores and channels 200–500μm in diameter, <2 centimetres long). The c:f ratio is 50:50 (very coarse sand 5%, coarse sand 20%, medium sand 10%, fine sand 15%, very fine sand 10%, silt 20%, clay 20%), making this one of the few fills studied here that are truly loamy (sandy clay loam). There is an open prophyric related distribution, and organic components make up about 5% of the visible area. These are mainly very dark brown, amorphous organic fragments <300μm in size, and only rarely with cellular structure. There is extremely rare charcoal (<500μm), which increases slightly in occurrence with depth. The groundmass is reddish-brown (PPL), very dark reddish-brown (XPL), and stipple-speckled to undifferentiated, with iron staining. There are frequent grain coatings made of the main soil matrix, and of clay; rarely, the latter are laminated, orange (PPL) and dark brown to amorphous (PPL). Besides the rare charcoal mentioned, there are no obvious cultural inclusions. The fill appears to be a soil by its structure and texture; perhaps this fill has become integrated into the modern topsoil.

The underlying material (context 034) comprises about 25% subrounded and elongated angular gravels (mainly 1–3 centimetres in size), with the remainder made up of brown (7.5YR 4/2) sand and *c.* 30% porosity (packing pores). The structure is granular and intergrain microaggregate, with frequent 200–5000μm sized microaggregates and zones of coalesced microaggregates. These are also found as coatings on most of the grains present. The c:f ratio is 75:25 (very coarse sand 15%, coarse sand 20%, medium sand 30%, fine sand 10%, very fine sand 10%, silt 5–10% , clay 5–10%). Organic components comprise <5%, mainly amorphous fragments <400μm in size, with rare charcoal of the same size. The groundmass is reddish brown (PPL), very dark reddish-brown (XPL), and granostriated with zones of stipple speckled. There are frequent grain coatings, as mentioned above, and the main groundmass is stained with amorphous organic matter and iron oxide.

Discussion

This study of post-hole fills from Dunragit has not provided a lot of new information about the site, despite its aims. However, it was important to carry out this exercise due to the extremely truncated nature of the site, and the fact that very few post-holes have seen soil micromorphological study, or even detailed archaeological investigation, despite the existence of experimental comparatives (e.g. Reynolds 1994), and the importance of post-holes on prehistoric sites of many kinds.

Charcoal amounts varied between post-hole fills; in no case, however, were they high enough to suggest *in situ* burning of a post, nor were any other burning indicators noted, and thus they do not contradict the site-based models of posts being pulled out (this volume, Chapter 3). Fill 037 was the fill of a post-pipe in post-hole Feature 087; this fill, along with those sampled in 011 and 021 are relatively richer in charcoal than the others sampled, although, again, none are as charcoal-rich as one might expect from the *in situ* burning of a post, and there are no other expected indicators of burning (wood ash, burnt soil). While wood ash may be leached away, *in situ* burning should have at least produced some oxidized soil. The charcoal seen in the various fills appears to relate more to the origin of the fill material than post burning or post-depositional processes; *i.e.* charcoal inclusions appear to be inclusions of the pre-depositional fill material, and not moved into the fills from other contexts. This is particularly the case where charcoal follows the same alignment as gravels, and where charcoal is relatively large and intact. Charcoal fragments do not appear to be size- or otherwise sorted within each post-hole, unlike the gravels, sands and fine fraction, which do show size sorting possibly related to settling, bioturbation and leaching. Perhaps some origin soils or sediments making up those fills that are relatively rich in charcoal came from locations near hearths, hearth rake-out or midden deposits with burnt remains. It is also possible that the fills with more charcoal in them originally came from sediments or soils in areas in proximity to burnt posts (e.g. the post-defined cursus – see Chapter 3).

With one exception of a possible tiny bone fragment in context 206, the only cultural micro-indicators within the fills are the charcoal inclusions. No fragments of pottery, clay, wood ash, burnt soil or even subsoil aggregates were found within the fills examined. The lack of subsoil (e.g. B horizon) fragments would not be surprising if the soil was essentially the same thin topsoil level as it is today, but the lack of fabrics representing other activities on the site is quite odd. In pits it is common to find small fragments of such materials included in fills, which often represent dumped material from other parts of the site, and it is possible to use these inclusions to interpret nearby activities. This has also been seen from the few

other soil micromorphological studies of post-hole fills. For example, heterogeneous fills were described through soil micromorphology of post-holes by Macphail and Crowther (2006) at White Horse Stone, Kent, and these, in combination with geochemical results, could be related to activities on site.

Besides charcoal, the fills from the Dunragit post-holes are essentially culturally 'clean' topsoil (and leached topsoil materials) and sedimentary deposits. This might seem to suggest that very few types of activities or events happened on the site, with wood (perhaps post) burning being the only one represented in thin section. A limited range of activities, such as seen here, could be interpreted in a number of ways. For example, a lower frequency of cultural micro-indicators is often found near walls and in corners within structures, as well as with interpreted short-term occupation or use of a site (for a summary of use-of-space indicators see, for example, Matarazzo *et al.* 2010; Milek and French 2007; Goldberg and Macphail 2006, Chapters 10–11). Charcoal in post-hole features is also not the most indicative of indicators. For instance, while those posts with larger and more frequent charcoal inclusions at Dunragit may represent a closer proximity to a burning area (e.g. a hearth), post-holes may contain charcoal from post-preparation, i.e. posts may be charred before construction, so may not indicate later uses of the structure at all.

The charcoal seems to represent material within the surrounding soils and deposits, which found its way into the post-holes through post-packing when the posts were erected, through backfilling when the posts were extracted, and/or through erosion while the post-holes were open. I find the lack of other materials to be surprising on such a large and important site, and the post-packing scenario seems the best explanation to me. That would suggest that the charcoal within the fills mainly represents activities occurring before or around the time of post erection. This could include the charring of post ends before post erection. When the posts were standing in their packed post-holes, it would be difficult for additional materials to arrive in their fills. After the posts were pulled out, or rotted *in situ*, backfilling, where seen, used immediately available topsoil (with gravel inclusions) that had not seen significant cultural deposition.

RADIOCARBON DATING AND BAYESIAN MODELLING

Derek Hamilton and Julian Thomas

Introduction

The radiocarbon dating strategy for Dunragit was intended to determine the absolute date of the main elements of the cursus monument and palisaded enclosure, and to provide an estimate of the duration of the Late Neolithic phase of activity in the monument complex. Necessarily, this strategy was an opportunistic one, given subsoil conditions in which unburned bone did not survive. In practice the dateable samples were restricted to wood charcoal and cremated human bone. In the former case, most of the material submitted was derived from short-life species, although two samples of oak charcoal were employed. One of these gave a clearly anachronous result for the context from which it was recovered, and the material would appear to have been residual. A total of nine radiocarbon dates were obtained from the site, and their full details including contextual information are tabulated here (Table 10.1). There results were used by Dr Derek Hamilton to construct a Bayesian statistical model for the site, and the outcome is discussed below.

The radiocarbon dates and Bayesian Analysis

Derek Hamilton

A total of nine radiocarbon measurements are available on samples recovered from features associated with or near the Neolithic cursus and enclosure at Dunragit, Galloway, Scotland. All the samples were single-entities (Ashmore 1999) of short-lived charcoal, charred plant material, or cremated human bone and were submitted to the Scottish

Universities Environmental Research Centre (SUERC) to be measured by Accelerator Mass Spectrometry (AMS).

The charcoal and charred plant material was pretreated following Stenhouse and Baxter (1983), while the cremated bone was pretreated following the method of Lanting *et al.* (2001). All the samples were combusted as described in Vandeputte *et al.* (1996) with the graphite targets prepared and measured following Naysmith *et al.* (2010). The SUERC laboratory maintains rigorous internal quality assurance procedures, and participation in international inter-comparisons (Scott 2003) indicate no laboratory offsets; thus validating the measurement precision quoted for the radiocarbon ages.

The radiocarbon results are given in Table 10.1. These are conventional radiocarbon ages (Stuiver and Polach 1977), quoted according to the international standard set at the Trondheim Convention (Stuiver and Kra 1986), and calibrated with the internationally agreed curve of Reimer *et al.* (2013) using OxCal v4.2 (Bronk Ramsey 1995; 1998; 2001; 2009). The date ranges in Table 1 have been calculated using the maximum intercept method (Stuiver and Reimer 1986), and quoted with the endpoints rounded outward to 10 years. The probability distributions seen in Figures 10.1–10.3 were obtained by the probability method (Stuiver and Reimer 1993).

Methodological approach

A Bayesian approach has been adopted for the interpretation of the chronology (Buck *et al.* 1996). Although the simple

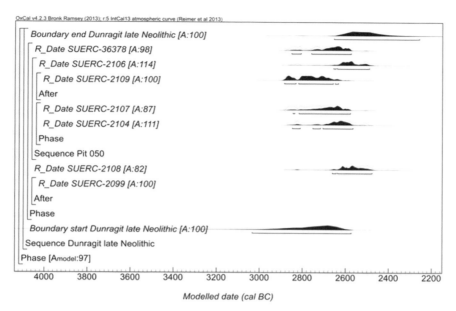

OxCal v4.2.3 Bronk Ramsey (2013); r:5 IntCal13 atmospheric curve (Reimer et al 2013)

Boundary end Dunragit late Neolithic [A:100]
R_Date SUERC-36378 [A:98]
R_Date SUERC-2106 [A:114]
R_Date SUERC-2109 [A:100]
After
R_Date SUERC-2107 [A:87]
R_Date SUERC-2104 [A:111]
Phase
Sequence Pit 050
R_Date SUERC-2108 [A:82]
R_Date SUERC-2099 [A:100]
After
Phase
Boundary start Dunragit late Neolithic [A:100]
Sequence Dunragit late Neolithic
Phase [Amodel:97]

4000   3800   3600   3400   3200   3000   2800   2600   2400   2200

Modelled date (cal BC)

Figure 10.1 Chronological model for the later Neolithic activity associated with the enclosure at Dunragit

calibrated dates are accurate estimates of the dates of the samples, this is usually not what archaeologists really wish to know. It is the dates of the archaeological events represented by those samples, which are of interest. In the case of Dunragit, it is the overall chronology of the Neolithic activity centred around the cursus monument and enclosure – when did the dated activity begin; when did it end; and for how long did it take place – that is under consideration, and not always the dates of any individual samples. The dates of this activity can be estimated not only using the absolute dating information from the radiocarbon measurements on the samples, but also by using any the stratigraphic relationships between samples and the general phasing.

Fortunately, methodology is now available which allows the combination of these different types of information explicitly, to produce realistic estimates of the dates of archaeological interest. It should be emphasised that the *posterior density estimates* produced by this modelling are not absolute. They are interpretative *estimates*, which can and will change as further data become available and as other researchers choose to model the existing data from different perspectives.

The technique used is a form of Markov Chain Monte Carlo sampling, and has been applied using the program OxCal v4.2. Details of the algorithms employed by this program are available from the on-line manual or in Bronk Ramsey (1995; 1998; 2001; 2009). The algorithm used in the model described below can be derived directly from the model structure shown in Figure 10.1.

The samples and the model

Four excavated features were dated at Dunragit that were associated with the later Neolithic enclosure. A total of seven results are available from post-pits and other features associated with the inner and middle post-ring, along with one cremation burial (Fig. 10.1).

One result (SUERC-2099) is available from a fragment of oak from the upper fill (010) of post-hole 027 in the middle post-ring of the enclosure. The date is included here as providing a *terminus post quem* for the formation of the context, though the result is approximately 3000 radiocarbon years earlier than expected and is most likely a residual piece of material in this context, rather than suffering from an 'old wood' offset. Two features related to the inner post-ring of the enclosure were dated. SUERC-2108 is a result on a fragment of hazel charcoal from the primary fill (244) of the first-phase post-hole 063. The hazel is thought to be from the fuel used to char the end of the post prior to burial.

There are four results from pit 050, associated with the inner post-ring, and the pit contains internal stratigraphy. Two results (SUERC-2104 and -2107) are available on a fragment of hazel charcoal and a charred hazelnut shell, respectively, from the basal fill (049). From above this there is a third result (SUERC-2109) on a fragment of oak charcoal recovered from fill (048). Since the oak was not identified as a short-lived specimen (i.e. sapwood or roundwood), the result has been treated here as providing a *terminus post quem* for the formation of the context. The final fill (004) produced a result (SUERC-2106) on a fragment of hazel charcoal.

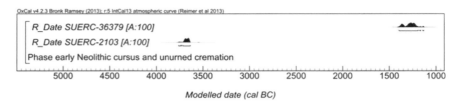

Figure 10.2 Calibrated radiocarbon dates for samples from a post and a Bronze Age cremation

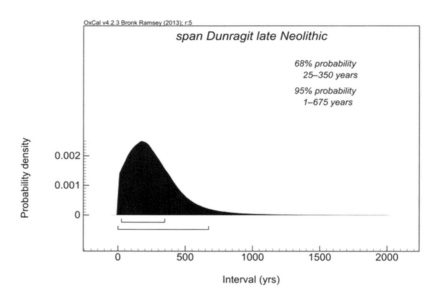

Figure 10.3 Probability distribution for later Neolithic activity associated with the Dunragit enclosure

Finally, there is a single result (SUERC-36378) on cremated bone from a discrete deposit (227) at the base of the secondary recut 217 within post-hole 215. The deposit appears to have been placed following the removal of the post.

There are two other results that are not from the later Neolithic, and which are not formally modelled (Fig. 10.2). SUERC-2103 is on a fragment of hazel charcoal from fill (013) of post-hole [040], which formed part of the post-defined cursus monument. The second result (SUERC-3679) is on cremated bone from an unurned cremation (2025) in gave [2042]. The grave pit shared an alignment with the cursus monument, but the result is Bronze Age in date.

Results

The model for the dated activity in the later Neolithic associated with the enclosure has good agreement between the radiocarbon dates and the archaeology (A_{model}=97).

The model estimates that the dated activity began in *3035–2570 cal BC* (*95% probability*; Fig. 10.1; *start Dunragit Late Neolithic*), and probably in *2835–2620 cal BC* (*68% probability*). The activity may have spanned as many as *675 years* (*95% probability*; Fig. 10.3; *span Dunragit Late Neolithic*), and probably *25–350 years* (*68% probability*). The activity ended in *2655–2255 cal BC* (*95% probability*; Fig. 10.1; *end Dunragit Late Neolithic*), and probably in *2615–2445 cal BC* (*68% probability*).

Discussion

The low number of measurements, combined with the overall paucity of stratigraphy, has resulted in a model that is likely to overestimate the start, end, and duration of activity (Steier and Rom 2000). The five radiocarbon measurements from the later Neolithic enclosure activity that were not treated as *termini post quos* were subjected to a chi-square test, which indicates that are not significantly different (T'=8.8; ν=4; T'(5%)=9.5: Ward and Wilson

1978). These measurements could be the same actual age, which further suggests that the period of activity is likely shorter rather than longer.

Implications

Julian Thomas

The results of the radiocarbon dating and statistical analysis are broadly in line with contemporary expectations for the kinds of structures and artefacts represented at Dunragit. The single date for the post-defined cursus monument falls in the thirty-seventh or thirty-eighth century cal BC, and is comparable with date ranges for similar structures at Nether Largie (Cook, Ellis and Sheridan 2010: 174), Bannockburn (Rideout 1997: 52), Castle Menzies (Halliday 2002), Holm and Holywood North (Thomas 2007a). Necessarily, many of the determinations from these sites have come from oak charcoal from the posts, and as a result may be artificially old. It is probably best to agree with Ashmore (2007: 249–50) that post-defined cursus monuments most likely date to the horizon between 3800 and 3600 BC. This, however, would make them some of the earliest Neolithic monuments in Scotland, constructed shortly after the regional commencement of the period (Whittle, Healy and Bayliss 2011: 804). It follows that they may have been implicated in the formation of Neolithic communities in the Scottish lowlands, by whatever process.

The Dunragit palisaded enclosure was perhaps constructed at some time between the twenty-ninth and the twenty-seventh century cal BC, and used for a period of 25 to 350 years, ending before the twenty-fifth century cal BC. Given the small number of dates that these estimates are based upon, and the even smaller number of archaeological features from which the samples were derived, it would not be wise to make too much of this result. None the less, it is significant that on this evidence the Dunragit enclosure was precisely contemporary with that at Forteviot, and overlapped with that at Blackshouse Burn (Noble and Brophy 2011b: 74). As Noble and Brophy argue, it is possible that the Scottish palisaded enclosures fit into a distinct horizon, perhaps 2800 to 2600 BC, and comparable with the floruit of palisaded enclosures in Scandinavia. Elsewhere, the enclosures at Hindwell in Powys and Greyhound Yard in Dorset are broadly contemporary, although those at West Kennet in Wiltshire and Mount Pleasant in Dorset were appreciably later, and might represent a separate 'wave' of enclosure building. The date of 2869 to 2580 cal BC for the cremation burial in post-hole 215 is consistent with an emerging pattern in which cremation appears to have dominated the archaeologically visible funerary practices of mainland Britain in the period between 3100 BC and 2400 BC (Parker Pearson 2012: 322).

Aside from the enclosure, the Dunragit Late Neolithic determinations are significant in that they date an assemblage of Grooved Ware. Grooved Ware seems to have emerged in the Orkney Islands in the later part of the fourth millennium BC (Cowie and MacSween 1999: 54), possibly building on local traditions of decorated, round-based pottery. Early Orcadian Grooved Ware appears to have been dominated by incised decoration, often forming parallel sets of wavy lines, to which arrangements of dots and chevrons may be added. Plastic decoration, including decorated cordons, was progressively added, becoming heavy and elaborate by the middle of the third millennium. In Orkney, Ireland and the British mainland, Grooved Ware incorporates a series of motifs that were ultimately derived from Irish passage tombs art in its 'intermediary' stage between the earlier 'depictive' and later 'plastic' styles, dating to around 3100 to 2900 BC (Brindley 1999b: 135). These include alternately filled squares and triangles, running lozenges, zig-zag and herringbone lines, conjoined balanced motifs, and spirals. Grooved Ware in Orkney, Ireland and Britain developed in parallel, sharing some elements of form and design, while taking on a regionalised character. Wainwright and Longworth (1971: 236–43) defined three sub-styles of Grooved Ware that applied to mainland Britain (in addition to the 'Rinyo' style of Orkney): Clacton, Woodlands, and Durrington Walls. Garwood (1999: 157) has recently suggested that the former two of these were actually a single tradition, with the incised and grooved decoration of Clacton giving way to the plastic cordons of Woodlands over time. The difficulty with this scheme is that at the Scottish site of Balfarg Riding School, Woodlands style pottery occurred as early as any of the Clacton assemblages that Garwood cites in the south of Britain (Henshall 1993: 106). Yet Garwood may be correct to draw a basic distinction between the smaller tub-shaped vessels of Clacton and Woodlands, and the larger buckets with closed mouths of the Durrington Walls style, which are more often associated with monumental structures, and particularly henge enclosures. It is also arguable that the Durrington Walls style is more remote from the Orcadian Grooved Ware.

As Jones (1997: 90) argues, these different sub-styles have tended to merge and break down to a certain extent as more material has gradually accumulated, and are perhaps less easy to apply in mainland Scotland than in southern England. None the less, there is a sense in which separate groups of potters appear to have manufactured Grooved Ware within a particular tradition, which may have remained stable over considerable periods of time. If the Dunragit Grooved Ware assemblage broadly fits into the Durrington Walls style, its date in the twenty-eighth to twenty-sixth century or so is unremarkable. While appreciably earlier than the material from the southern henges of Durrington Walls, Mount Pleasant or Woodhenge, the date is comparable with those from

Table 10.1. Radiocarbon dates from Dunragit

Code	Radiocarbon age	$\delta^{13}C$ VPDB	Material
SUERC-2103	4890±35 BP	-26.30	Charcoal
Calibrated date (95.4% probability)	3760–3630 cal BC		

Piece of hazel charcoal (Sample 1052) from well within fill 013 of post-hole of post-defined cursus monument (cut no. 040), which pre-dated the Late Neolithic enclosure. Post-hole cut into natural gravel. It is suggested that oak charcoal in this context represents burnt post stump, and that the hazel was burned in the same episode – possibly brushwood used in burning the upright. This short-life material should therefore give an accurate date for *destruction* of the timber monument. However, it is equally possible that the sample had been burned and incorporated into the packing deposit at the time when the cursus was being constructed.

Code	Radiocarbon age	$\delta^{13}C$ VPDB	Material
SUERC-2099	7535±35 BP	-25.90	Charcoal
Calibrated date (95.4% probability)	6460–6250 cal BC		

Piece of oak charcoal (Sample 1105) well sealed in uppermost fill (010) of large post-hole of middle post-ring of Later Neolithic enclosure (cut 027). Fill probably represented post-pipe of post that had rotted out. Fill may have been material that tumbled into the post void as the timber rotted out, perhaps from original packing material, but possibly from overlying soil; in either case charcoal may have been residual.

Code	Radiocarbon age	$\delta^{13}C$ VPDB	Material
SUERC-2104	4085±35 BP	-26.30	Charcoal
Calibrated date (95.4% probability)	2870–2490 cal BC		

Piece of hazel charcoal (Sample 1055) from fill 048 of a large pit 050 near innermost ring of Later Neolithic enclosure. Feature produced numerous sherds of Grooved Ware. Pit was cut into natural gravel, fill 048 sealed by upper layers of fill. Context represents part of deliberate backfill containing what seem to be placed deposits of material culture. Backfilling presumably prompt, and extensive range of charcoal from the context probably relates to this event.

Code	Radiocarbon age	$\delta^{13}C$ VPDB	Material
SUERC-2106	4055±35 BP	-24.80	Charcoal
Calibrated date (95.4% probability)	2860–2460 cal BC		

Piece of hazel charcoal (Sample 1063) from uppermost fill 004 of large pit 050 cut into natural gravel near innermost ring of Later Neolithic enclosure. Feature produced numerous sherds of Grooved Ware, fill 004 represents part of deliberate backfill containing what seem to be placed deposits of material culture. Backfilling presumably prompt, and extensive range of charcoal from the context probably relates to this event.

Code	Radiocarbon age	$\delta^{13}C$ VPDB	Material
SUERC-2107	4150±35 BP	-29.30	Nutshell
Calibrated date (95.4% probability)	2880–2600 cal BC		

Hazel nutshell (Sample 1141) from layer of fill (049) in large pit 050 near innermost ring of Later Neolithic enclosure. Feature produced numerous sherds of Grooved Ware. It was cut into natural gravel, sealed by upper layers of fill. Context represents part of deliberate backfill containing what seem to be placed deposits of material culture. Backfilling presumably prompt, and extensive range of charcoal from the context probably relates to this event.

Code	Radiocarbon age	$\delta^{13}C$ VPDB	Material
SUERC-2108	4025±35 BP	-25.30	Charcoal
Calibrated date (95.4% probability)	2630–2460 cal BC		

Piece of hazel charcoal (Sample 024 Bag A) from primary gravel fill 244 of first-phase post-hole (063) of the inner ring of Later Neolithic enclosure. Post-hole cut into natural gravel, fill 244 sealed by later layers of fill. Material integral to gravel packing around post-pipe, and thus deposited as part of initial construction of the monument. Oak charcoal in post-hole formed compact mass, which appeared to represent a plank, or outer surface of a post.

Code	Radiocarbon age	δ¹³C VPDB	Material
SUERC-2109	4175±45 BP	-27.30	Charcoal

Calibrated date (95.4% probability)   2890–2600 cal BC

Piece of oak charcoal (Sample 1134) from fill 048 of large pit (050) cut into natural gravel near innermost ring of Later Neolithic enclosure. Feature produced numerous sherds of Grooved Ware. Fill part of deliberate backfill containing what seem to be placed deposits of artefactual material. Backfilling presumably prompt, extensive range of charcoal from context probably related to this event.

Code	Radiocarbon age	δ¹³C VPDB	Material
SUERC-36378	4125±30 BP	-24.4	Cremated bone

Calibrated date (95.4% probability)   2869–2580 cal BC

Cremated bone from single Neolithic context recovered as undisturbed, discrete deposit (227) concentrated within *c*. 0.20 × 0.40 m area at base of secondary recut (217) within large post-hole (215) forming part of the second inner palisade ring. Deposit had apparently been made subsequent to deliberate removal of the post (217). Post-hole cut into natural gravel, and sealed by topsoil. Sample consisted of cremated bone, which had been placed into crater created by removal of large post from post-hole. The 300.1 g of cremated bone recovered represented remains from older subadult/adult (>16 yr) female; 13 g of bone was from sheep or sheep-sized mammal.

Code	Radiocarbon age	δ¹³C VPDB	Material
SUERC-36379	3025±35 BP	-23.4	Cremated bone

Calibrated date (95.4% probability)   1397–1132 cal BC

Remains of an unurned cremation burial 2025, made in grave cut 2042, lifted as a block. 2042 cut into natural gravel, sealed by topsoil. Grave formed one element of a complex of features which shared an alignment with early Neolithic cursus. Sample consisted of cremated bone, which had been placed into the pit/grave, which in turn was flanked by two large post-holes.

Trelystan, Barford Farm, Firtree Field and Wyke Down (Garwood 1999: 157). Perhaps more significantly, the single date associated with the Durrington Walls style assemblage from Hillend in Clydesdale, of 3340–2890 cal BC (95% probability: Beta-73955) is slightly earlier than those from Dunragit. The latter, then, does not stand out as in any way exceptional.

11

DISCUSSION

Julian Thomas

The post-defined cursus monument

The post-built cursus monument at Dunragit strat-igraphically preceded the Late Neolithic palisaded enclosure (Fig. 11.1). Furthermore, it is dated by a piece of hazel charcoal from post-hole 040 to 3760–3630 cal BC, at 2σ (SUERC-2103). The burnt hazel fragment may have entered the post-hole as part of the material used to burn the structure down, having entered the post void as the upright burned out. In this case the date would relate to the destruction of the cursus, but the sample could also possibly have been a stray piece of charcoal that was incorporated into the post packing at the time of construction. So the date might indicate either the beginning or the end of the life of the timber monument. In either case, the date places it into the same broad horizon as a number of similar structures, all located in lowland Scotland (Fig. 11.2). Pit- and post-defined cursus monuments have been identified as a relatively distinct class of structures in recent years (Brophy 1999: 125–7). While the often very large cursus monuments enclosed by banks and ditches, such as the Dorset Cursus and the Greater and Lesser Stonehenge Cursuses, are more familiar to archaeology, they generally date to the latter half of the fourth millennium BC (Thomas 2006: 230; Thomas *et al.* 2009). These are dispersed through much of the lowlands of Britain, with examples also known from Ireland (Harding and Barclay 1999). Linear enclosures composed of timber uprights or discrete cut features, with straight or rounded terminals, appear to be earlier in date, are generally less than 500 metres in length, and are more constrained in their geographical distribution. Although

they were much larger than the roofed timber halls of the primary Neolithic, the post-built cursuses in particular have often been compared with these structures. Both were constructed of oak timbers, both had a rectilinear plan, and both had frequently been destroyed by fire, apparently deliberately (Noble 2006: 69; Thomas 2006: 236). A further structural similarity is that several post-built cursuses, including Milton of Guthrie, Balneaves Cottage and Douglasmuir, were internally divided by a number of transverse partitions (Brophy 1999: 127). These compare with the internal screens or walls within a number of timber halls, such as Claish and Balbridie (Fairweather and Ralston 1993; Barclay, Brophy and MacGregor 2002: 107).

Furthermore, the isolated axial uprights inside the halls of Claish, Warren Field and Balbridie, which may have had no structural role, also have parallels amongst the post-defined cursuses. Indeed, large isolated axial posts have also been identified inside the rather later unroofed rectilinear enclosures of Lattleour and Balfarg Riding School 2 (Barclay and Maxwell 1998; Barclay and Russell-White 1993), which Brophy (2007: 91) identifies as structures that draw on the 'architectural vocabulary' of the timber halls. Clearly, the presence of massive timber uprights inside rectangular and trapezoidal structures was a recurring and significant theme in the Early Neolithic architecture of Britain, and arguably one that was related to the use of pairs of enormous oak uprights to frame the mortuary structures found beneath earthen long barrows (Thomas 2013: 328). In each case the wooden upright took on a focal role, connected with the gathering together of the living or dead members of a community.

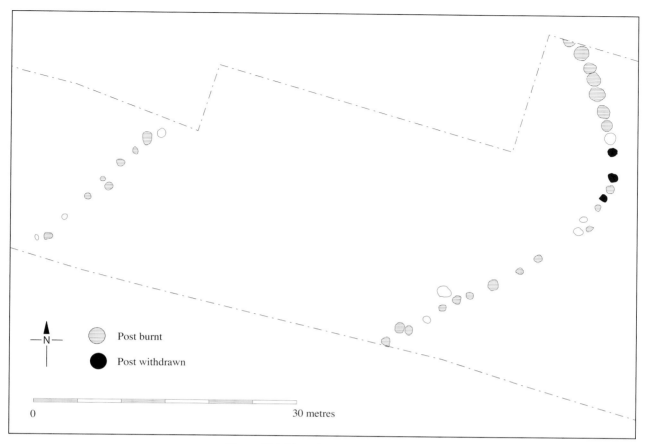

Post burnt

Post withdrawn

0   30 metres

Figure 11.1 Plan of the Dunragit cursus

The raising of the post might then be conjectured to be associated with an assertion of collective identity, as is the case with the erection of house-posts in many non-western societies (Fox 1993: 157). At Douglasmuir in Angus one of the two compartments that made up the overall structure contained a large, axially set pit (context BEA), which had at some point held a wooden post (Kendrick 1995: 32). Similarly, the cursus at Holywood North near Dumfries contained a very large post set within the apex of its northern terminal (Thomas 2007a: 174). This post had been renewed on a number of occasions, and perhaps deliberately burned more than once before the timber cursus was enclosed within a bank and ditch. The post-cursus itself had been built and destroyed on at least four separate occasions, individual posts having been withdrawn or burnt. In the final phase, the majority of the posts were set alight, before the traces of the structure were enclosed within the surrounding ditch and thereby rendered comparatively inaccessible (Thomas 2007a: 237). A hazelnut shell from one of the post-pipes of the timber enclosure gave a date of 3778–3698 cal BC (SUERC-2115). The same feature produced sherds of Carinated Bowl pottery, while fragments of a thicker, heavy-rimmed vessel came from the ditch, confirming its later date (Thomas 2007a: 237).

In the case of the Dunragit cursus, there were subtle hints of the varied activities that had taken place before and during construction. Some of the post-holes contained layers of silting or collapsed gravel from the edges of the features, while in other cases the packing deposits had seemingly been inserted shortly after the post-hole had been dug. Some of these deposits had doubtless been generated by the activity of manoeuvring heavy timbers into their sockets and holding them in place whilst backfilling had begun. However, in some cases it seems that the post-holes had stood open for some while before the posts were put in place. Equally, some of the post-holes (for instance, feature 3158) revealed traces of burning that had taken place *before* the post had been inserted. It is possible that this was related to the clearing of the site immediately prior to the construction of the cursus, with vegetation in particular being burnt off in order to create a large open area, or with the preparation of the posts for erection. Some features may actually have been earlier than the main series of cursus post-holes. These include feature 4254, which may have been cut by cursus post-hole 4093. It is not clear whether this feature was a post-hole or simply a pit, but it provides a further indication that some form of activity took place on the site before the post cursus was set up. Indeed, the

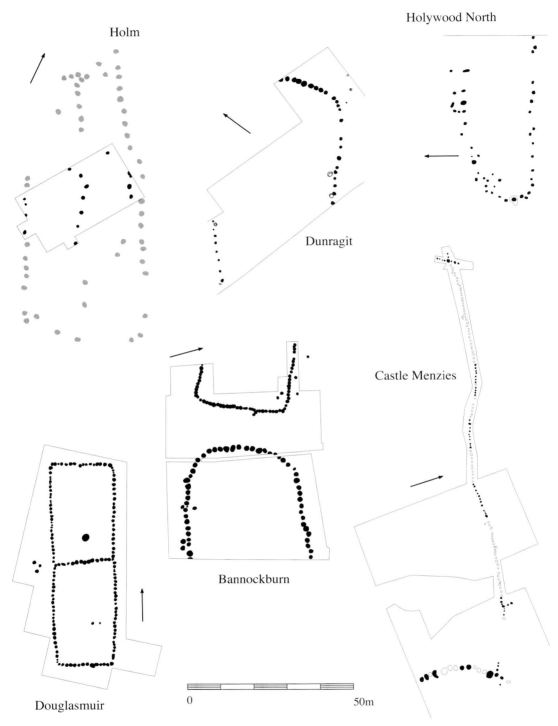

Figure 11.2 Comparative plans of pit and post cursus monuments

recovery of a small number of Mesolithic stone tools from the excavations confirms that the site had been frequented over a long period (see Chapter 7). A cursory look at the descriptions of the cursus post-hole fills in Chapter 3 reveals that they had quite diverse individual histories, involving digging, silting, collapse, post emplacement,

packing with gravel, sand and stones, settling, collapse, rotting, burning, withdrawal, the slipping and slumping of the packing deposits, and silting into the tops of the features. So although the cursus was an integral structure, its construction and use were made up of innumerable actions that were not entirely standardised. At least one of the post-holes, 091/393, held two different posts, and these may have been sequential or may have stood simultaneously. It is as well to remember that the construction of the cursus may have been a relatively messy process, played out over a period of weeks or months, with the builders struggling to achieve the desired result using earth, gravel, stone and wood, as well as their own skills and bodily capacities. Timbers must have been felled, dressed, and dragged to the site using ropes and perhaps rollers or rails. There would have been accidents, mishaps and injuries. As McFadyen points out, prehistoric monuments were 'building sites' (2006: 96), where a series of overlapping and more or less coordinated activities took place.

The obvious contrast between bank and ditch cursuses on the one hand and post-defined structures on the other lies in their temporal characteristics. While the sides of the ditch of the former would erode rapidly over the first few winters after construction, leading to the accumulation of a rapid silting in the ditch, a stabilisation would eventually occur leaving the monument as an enduring presence in the landscape. It is for this reason that William Stukeley was able to identify the two cursus monuments near Stonehenge (Thomas *et al.* 2009: 40). A post-built structure, however, would be virtually erased once the timbers had rotted away, and this process would have been accelerated by the burning out of the uprights. The distinction is therefore one between wooden monuments that were more or less temporary, and which may have been created in order to provide the settings for specific events or activities before being purposefully destroyed, and earth and turf structures, which were intended to be retained as a permanent mark on the land. Such features were often incorporated into later divisions of the landscape, with their banks preserved as hedge-lines or field-walls (Loveday 2006: 39). This contrast harmonises with differences in the architectural organisation of the two kinds of structures. Pit- and post-cursus monuments had a discontinuous perimeter, which defined an enclosed area but did so in a way that was essentially permeable. They could therefore be entered, while the ditched monuments were less accessible. Indeed, many of them had no entrances at their terminals, prompting the suggestion that they may not have provided a formal setting for procession, and may actually have commemorated processions or other activities that had taken place at some time in the past. Indeed, the interior of a ditched cursus may have been reserved for metaphysical beings, or even cursed, which would account for the general lack of internal structures and the paucity of small finds from the ditches (Johnston 1999: 44).

However, it must be admitted that amongst the pit and post cursus monuments the degree of deliberate destruction and reconstruction is quite variable. At Holm Farm near Dumfries, what appeared from the air as a confused mass of cut features resolved on excavation into a series of separate phases of a rectilinear or trapezoidal enclosure, each superimposed upon the last (Thomas 2007a: 244). Each phase of building had been followed by extensive burning, to the extent that the timbers were burned to charcoal deep into their sockets. Some individual post-holes held as many as three or four separate post stumps, suggesting that attempts had been made to re-establish the enclosure on its original site on a number of occasions. However, given that only charred fragments remained, the monument repeatedly shifted its position across the flat gravel river terrace. Evidently, the activity at Holm was recurrent and episodic. Five radiocarbon dates on oak sapwood, lacking tyloses, may be relatively accurate, and indicate a period of use over some decades within the thirty-eighth century BC (Ashmore 2007: 249). At Cowie Road, Bannockburn, near Stirling, two separate trapezoidal enclosures were set end to end. One of these was defined by uprights posts, and the other by pits, which showed evidence for repeated recutting, and a phase in which the pits were lined with stone, as well as intense burning (Rideout 1997: 36). The pit-bounded Enclosure 1 was apparently the earlier of the two, and the second phase of activity within the pits produced radiocarbon dates in the interval 4000–3800 cal BC. However, these determinations were made on oak charcoal, possibly from heartwood, and may not be entirely reliable (Ashmore 2007: 250). None the less, the pits produced sherds of Carinated Bowl pottery, indicating that the enclosure was probably in use during the earlier part of the fourth millennium BC. A slightly different form of post cursus was found at Castle Menzies in Perthshire, where an enclosure 130 metres long, with sinuously curving sides terminated at its eastern end by a concave façade (Halliday 2002: 14). The structure had been neither burned nor recut, but a series of radiocarbon dates gave a range of 4040–3660 cal BC.

The deliberate burning of the Dunragit timber cursus is therefore in line with the evidence from a number of other sites. At Dunragit the evidence for burning includes not only the charcoal of the posts themselves, but also burnt stones in the fills, and the cut edges and subsoil surfaces surrounding post-holes scorched by the heat. As an observation, it seemed that the effects of the heat were most pronounced upon fills and bands in the natural gravel that were more clayey, as opposed to stony. In several cases, the remains of the burned posts were angled toward one side of the post-hole. This might suggest that they had been pulled over before combustion, or perhaps more likely that the charred stumps of the posts had been pulled out after burning, leaving only the very base of the post *in situ*. This may have been because the posts were less thoroughly burned below ground level, and an attempt was being made to remove all traces of the monument. About 70% of the posts that were excavated in 1999 to 2002 had been burnt, and of the remainder some had apparently been left to rot away, while others had been withdrawn. This combination of burnt posts, removed posts and rotted posts was also observed at the Nether Largie cursus in Kilmartin Glen (Cook, Ellis and Sheridan 2010: 194). It may be significant that those posts at Dunragit that had definitely been withdrawn, features 3028, 3033 and 3040, were concentrated in the immediate area of the possible entrance at the northeast corner of the cursus, at the point where the post-holes began to be larger and more closely spaced (see Fig. 11.1). It is conceivable that the posts that bracketed the entrance were particularly significant, and they might even have been decorated in some way. Their physical removal suggests that they may have been re-used, perhaps as part of some other structure. The digging-out and withdrawal of posts immediately prior to the destruction of a large timber structure finds a parallel in the Early Neolithic timber hall at Warren Field in Aberdeenshire, where the two large timbers that had stood at either end of the building interior were removed before burning took place, and deposits including numerous sherds of pottery and cereal grains placed in the resulting craters (Murray, Murray and Fraser 2009: 39). In both cases, the implication is that the decommissioning and destruction of the structure was carefully executed.

The burnt posts and the northern terminal at Dunragit make up a very coherent plan for the cursus, but a further problem is raised by the many post-holes that are found on broadly the same alignment, either running alongside the cursus or beyond its northeasterly termination. A scatter of these were present in Trench F (features 3069, 3084, 3110 and 3147), and more in Trench E. When these were first discovered it was presumed that they represented later features that had been 'tacked on' to the established orientation of the monument, perhaps centuries after its construction. This is certainly the case with cremation burial pit 2042, and its two deep flanking post-holes 2028 and 2036, which appear to date to the Middle Bronze Age. Despite its late date, it seems that the cremation burial was positioned to reference the cursus monument. It is interesting that the two post-holes between which it was bracketed were so much deeper than the other features that were related to the cursus. The implication is that they were intended to hold especially tall uprights, which would draw attention to the location of the burial. In a sense, the two posts had a role that was comparable with a barrow mound, although they had a much clearer orientation than the round mounds of the Bronze Age. In general terms, this arrangement would find a parallel in the immediate environs of the Dorset Cursus, where the alignment of the Ogden Down timber avenue and the organisation of the cremation burials in the Down Farm Pond Barrow both referenced the position of the cursus (Barrett, Bradley and Green 1991: 132; Green 2000: 114). However, results from some recent cursus excavations in Scotland have some bearing on how the rest of these

features might be interpreted. As we have already seen, the post settings at Holm Farm did not all conform to the same overall plan, although they did follow the same broad alignment (Thomas 2007a: 242). At Holywood North, too, the observed plan of post-holes was actually a composite of three or more phases of construction, which did not all precisely overlap (Thomas 2007a: 234). It is therefore conceivable that some of the various post-lines that share the orientation of the Dunragit cursus were actually separate iterations of the cursus itself, whether earlier or later than the most coherent version of the structure. It is possible that these features were set up in a relatively piecemeal and sporadic fashion and had an essentially commemorative character, if they post-dated the 'main' phase of construction, use and destruction of the cursus, which was evidently more monumental in character than the more northerly post arrangements.

The variation in size amongst the cursus post-holes excavated in Trench F was of particular interest. Both in diameter and in depth they appeared to be graded, becoming larger from south to north. Moreover, the packing stones wedged around the post-bases became steadily more numerous and more massive, suggesting that the uprights that they were intended to keep in place were themselves larger. Precisely how tall these posts were is difficult to guess, as the depth of subsoil that has been lost to erosion is unknown, but at a conservative estimate we might suggest that the uprights in the side of the cursus might have been 2–3 metres in height, rising to 4–5 metres at the terminal. This elaboration of the terminal has many parallels within the overall cursus tradition. In the case of the greater Stonehenge Cursus, Patricia Christie (1963) noted that the cursus ditch was wider and deeper at the Fargo terminal, presumably in order to provide for a more substantial bank. Even today, the Thickthorn terminal of the Dorset Cursus is a massive structure, which resembles the long barrows that surround it, and the same may have been true of the cursus terminal at Rudston excavated by Greenwell (1877: 254). At Upper Largie, the broadest and deepest of the post-holes occurred at the southern terminal, representing a very precise parallel for the situation at Dunragit (Cook, Ellis and Sheridan 2010: 194). As we have mentioned already, the post-defined cursus at Castle Menzies had a distinct concave façade, composed of 16 post-holes (Halliday 2002: 11). These were considerably larger than the features forming the sides of the structure. In this particular case there is a clear comparison to be made with the post-façades associated with many earthen long barrows, which serve to separate the forecourt area from the space occupied by the mortuary structure. Evidently, post-defined cursus monuments shared with both long barrows and timber halls the simple geometry of being a linear structure with a 'front' and a 'back' as well as an 'inside' and an 'outside'. The façade served the function of defining a focal area at one end of the monument.

The excavation of Trench J in 2002 added some important refinements to the understanding of the cursus. Surprisingly, it was found that the western side of the structure was not parallel with the eastern, and the two sides appeared to be converging toward the south. The most likely explanation for this phenomenon is that the cursus enclosure was slightly trapezoid, with the northern terminal being rather broader than the rest of the structure. In this respect it recalls the plans of some of the long mounds of northern Europe (e.g. Pospieszny 2010: 151), although no specific relationship with these is suggested. The expanded terminal also evokes parallels with some other Scottish cursus monuments, such as Balneaves (Brophy 1999: 126), while a more general level of similarity can be suggested with the western end of the Stonehenge Cursus (RCHM 1979: 14). It also further enhances the importance that we can attribute to the northern façade of the cursus, for as well has having graded, taller posts, it seems that the structure will have been wider here than throughout most of its length, drawing further attention to the point of entry into the enclosed space.

This brings us to the important point that the northern terminal of the Dunragit timber cursus was penetrated by at least one entrance. As we have noted above, recent discussions of cursus monuments as ceremonial avenues or route-ways (e.g. Tilley 1994; Johnston 1999) have been queried on the grounds that it may not have been possible to enter some of these linear enclosures at their ends. The banks and ditches of the Dorset Cursus and Greater Stonehenge cursuses are unbroken at the terminals, for instance, and this would have rendered any kind of solemn procession down the length of the monument impractical. Yet at Dunragit, access to the enclosure would have been afforded by the northern entrance. The southwestern end of the cursus is not visible on the aerial photographs of the site, so the full extent of the monument is unknown. However, it is likely to have been 200 or 300 metres, and perhaps more. If the cursus had served as part of an axis of movement, it would have taken people down from Challoch Hill, across the Freuch, and onto the higher ground behind Stoneykirk to the southwest. The cursus effectively describes a line between Challoch Hill, which is the highest point locally, and the northern part of the Rhins of Galloway. We have seen in Chapter 2 that there was some Mesolithic occupation in the Luce Sands area, while evidence for primary Neolithic activity (in the form of fine Carinated Bowl pottery) is also present, if sparse. The only other Early Neolithic structures locally are the chambered cairns at Mid Gleniron, which are potentially a little later in date than the cursus. The Dunragit cursus might then be understood as a foundational statement of some kind, an assertion of human presence in the landscape, which paved the way for subsequent developments. In this respect it is very comparable with the Nether Largie timber cursus, which appears to have been the first monumental structure in the Kilmartin Glen, where a sequence of cairns, stone circles and standing stones developed over further centuries (Cook, Ellis and Sheridan 2010: 195).

The recognition of the existence of the cursus demonstrates that the Late Neolithic palisaded enclosure was built in a location that had already been of significance for generations. To some extent this can be attributed to the peculiarities of the location. The relatively flat expanse of outwash gravel at Dunragit is unlike the landscape further to the east, where the hills rise abruptly from the sea. It also represents a 'skirt' of more well-drained land before the topography drops into the damp low country of the Freuch, immediately to the south and west. A further locational factor lies in the position of Dunragit at the confluence of a series of natural route-ways: northward up the valley of the Water of Luce, east and west along the Galloway coast, and northwest to Loch Ryan. If we were to argue that the monuments represented a gathering point for dispersed and potentially mobile communities, Dunragit would provide an ideal position. However, we could also suggest that the gradual, accretional development of the significance of the place is an important consideration. The earlier excavations at the Pict's Knowe, Holywood and Holm have all demonstrated the ways in which particular locations can gather meaning over time, so that a series of episodes of construction and performance may be attracted to the same place, over a period of many centuries (Thomas 2007a). One might argue that one of the particular characteristics of Neolithic monumentality in the Scottish southwest is the way in which short-lived (and indeed even deliberately destroyed) monuments contributed to complex histories of place, maintained through memory and tradition. Even though their physical traces might have been ephemeral, these locations were evidently incorporated into traditions of collective memory.

The Late Neolithic palisaded enclosure

An extensive stretch of each of the two innermost post-rings of the Late Neolithic enclosure was excavated in Trenches A, AA, F and J (Fig. 11.3), while the outermost ring was sampled in Trench E. The investigation of such a large portion of the enclosure provided the opportunity to explore the diversity of the component elements of the monument, and to consider the structural history of the site as a whole. The development of Late Neolithic monument complexes in locations that had already been frequented in the Earlier Neolithic and even earlier is a pattern that can be discerned throughout much of northern and western Britain (Noble 2006: 142). Existing structures might serve as precedent for new centres, and this was especially clear in the case of palisaded enclosures,

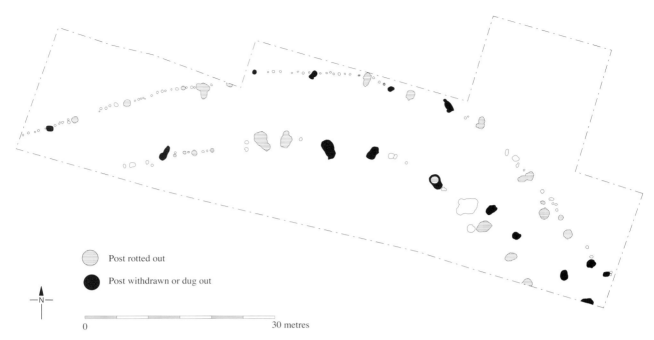

Figure 11.3 Plan of the inner two rings of the Dunragit palisaded enclosure, as excavated, showing rotted and withdrawn posts

which often occur amidst clusters of both earlier and later monuments. In Scotland, both Blackshouse Burn and Leadketty are juxtaposed to smaller enclosures, which might potentially have causewayed ditches, while the construction of the Meldon Bridge enclosure was preceded by extensive pit-digging and deposition (Speak and Burgess 1999: 12). The relationship between the enclosure and cursus at Dunragit is paralleled by that between the Marne Barracks palisaded enclosure and the Scorton cursus near Catterick in Yorkshire (Hale, Platell and Millard 2009: 266; Topping 1982). In the Walton Basin of Radnorshire, the two palisaded enclosures at Hindwell and the further example at Walton were located in an area that had been defined by the positions of the Womaston causewayed enclosure and the Hindwell and Walton Green cursus monuments (Jones 2009: 36–8). Like Dunragit, several of these other complexes developed on favourable routes across the landscape, as demonstrated by the position of Blackshouse Burn in a natural hollow between surrounding hills (Lelong and Pollard 1998: 48).

Sites enclosed by palisades of upright timbers are a characteristic feature of the European Neolithic. From the first appearance of the Neolithic north of the Alps and Carpathians with the *Linearbandkeramik*, sites with fences or palisades were constructed, as at Köln-Lindenthal in Germany and Darion in Belgium (Meyer 2002: 59). In many cases these fences were paired with a ditch and integral to an upcast bank. A more formal expression of the palisade idea emerged with the rondels of central Europe in the Lengyel period, circular ditched enclosures with four entrances and one or more concentric

internal palisade slots (Andersen 1997: 155; Turek 2012: 186). Timber palisades also formed integral elements of the causewayed enclosures of the Scandinavian TRB, as with Sarup, and the Michelsberg, as with Mayen, Urmitz, Thieusies and Bazoches (Andersen 1997: 196; Svensson 2002: 29). However, it is significant that more substantial enclosures defined purely by arrangements of posts were generally a later development. In Zealand, Scania and Bornholm, a series of large palisaded enclosures date to the period between 2900 and 2500 BC, the final TRB and the Battle Axe Culture (Larsson 2012: 110; Svensson 2002: 38). These sites vary between two and six hectares in extent, and can have single or multiple palisades, composed of posts set either in post-holes or in trenches (Fig. 11.4). As with some of the British examples, the uprights were sometimes not contiguous with each other, but set a little way apart (Larsson 2012: 116). These sites were often purposefully destroyed by burning, and have produced evidence for both domestic occupation and activities such as deliberate deposition and the manufacture of flint axes, with flakes from axes having been deposited into post-holes at the same time as the posts were erected at Dösjöbro (Larsson 2012: 117). A concentration of four such enclosures has recently been investigated in the immediate vicinity of Malmö (Brink and Hydén 2006). The relatively simultaneous development of large palisaded enclosures in Britain, Ireland and Scandinavia is an intriguing phenomenon, which prompts speculation concerning the relative significance of cultural influence and parallel social processes between regions. In both areas, the development of these sites coincided with that of new inter-regional

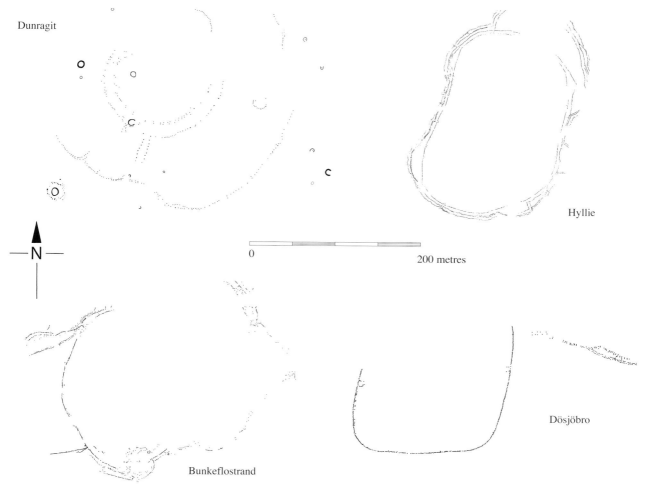

Figure 11.4 Dunragit compared with Scandinavian palisaded enclosures

assemblages and patterns of interaction (Grooved Ware and the Battle Axe complex). This may imply the emergence of new social imperatives, requiring new kinds of organised spaces for social interaction. Notably, though, the Scandinavian enclosures rarely achieved the degree of conspicuous monumentality found with some of the British examples, such as Mount Pleasant, Hindwell II and West Kennet (Fig. 11.6). Some of these structures enclosed vast areas, while others were simply massively constructed, using huge tree-trunks for uprights.

Palisades also formed part of the 'architectural vocabulary' that was in use in Britain and Ireland from the start of the Neolithic. In Ireland there are a number of fenced enclosures of Early Neolithic date, including Knowth, Lyle's Hill and Thornhill (Eogan and Roche 2002: 24). Some of these are associated with domestic occupation. In Britain there are fewer of such fenced sites, although palisades are sometimes found as constructional elements within causewayed enclosures. Enclosures at Orsett and Haddenham had palisades, while at Crickley Hill a palisade slot was integral to the stone rampart (Dixon 1988: 76). Major palisaded enclosures without ditches were therefore an innovation of the Later Neolithic, in Britain as much as in Scandinavia, although they were one that drew upon and elaborated architectural devices that were already in use (Whittle 1997a: 158). As such, they are best understood as part of a suite of inter-related architectural forms that came to be distributed through Britain in the earlier third millennium BC, including cellular houses with central hearths, timber circles and 'four-poster' arrangements of wooden uprights (Noble, Greig and Millican 2012: 160; Pollard 2009; Thomas 2010: 8). This can be seen as part of a more general pattern of the dispersal of new cultural elements from north to south during this period (Sheridan 2004: 33). This architecture made use of earthfast posts and stakes in order to create spaces that were used for a variety of different purposes, from domestic dwellings to ceremonial gathering and veneration. At one end of the scale were small dwelling structures like those at Trelystan (Britnell 1982) and Wyke Down (Green 2000: 75), while more massive constructions that may not have

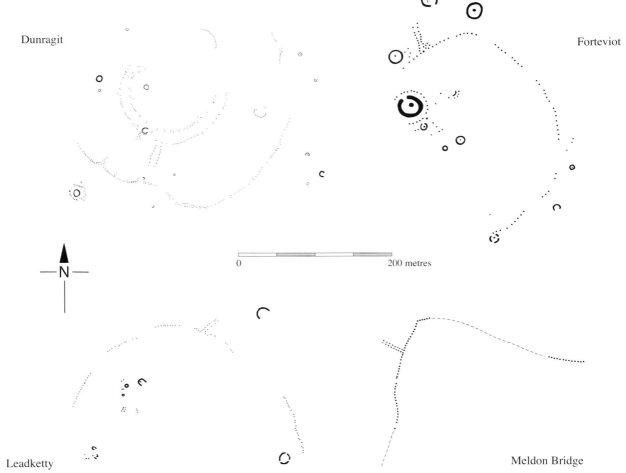

Dunragit

Forteviot

—N—

0   200 metres

Leadketty   Meldon Bridge

Figure 11.5 Comparative plans of Late Neolithic palisaded enclosures in Scotland

been roofed but which share a similar spatial ordering are known at Durrington 68 (Pollard 1995), the Knowth timber circle (Eogan and Roche 1994) and the Northern Circle at Durrington Walls (Wainwright and Longworth 1971: 41). Later Neolithic timber architecture therefore spans (or disregards) any division that we might wish to construct between 'ritual' and 'everyday', and indeed it is possible that some of these structures may have been used for occupation and ceremonial at different points in their histories, or simultaneously.

Very often both palisade enclosures and focal structures of various kinds were found together, as at Ballynahatty in County Down, where a four-post setting ringed by two circles of uprights was located inside a larger enclosure (Hartwell 1998: 39). Although these elements were not always mutually associated, it is arguable that the overall unity of the series can be attributed to its connection with the idea of the house and the household (Thomas 2010: 9). In other words, the basic structure of a setting of freestanding timbers surrounded by a ring of stakes or posts (sometimes of 'square in circle' pattern) is

ultimately derived from an idealised dwelling. Thus in the Western Enclosures at Durrington Walls in Wiltshire small house-like structures were surrounded by circular palisades of posts, and in one case fronted by a façade of large posts, which may have been capped by lintels (Thomas 2007b: 152). Arguably, this monumentalisation of the house, and the identification of the 'household' as a model for social organisation, was connected with the spread of Grooved Ware out from northwest Scotland and into the rest of Britain and Ireland. At many palisaded sites in Britain and Ireland, the primary cultural association of Late Neolithic post architecture is with Grooved Ware, from Greyhound Yard and West Kennet to Knowth, Ballynahatty, Bettystown and Balgatheran (Grogan and Roche 2002: 25). Whether the structures are ones that appear to have been occupied, or much larger timber circles or 'shrines', there appears to be an emerging pattern in which centrally-positioned focal features and entrances received relatively dense deposits of pottery, flint and animal bone, while surrounding palisades, post arrangements or walls contained few or no finds (see, for example, Ó Drisceoil 2009). The spatial organisation of the Dunragit enclosure, which endured through two phases of construction, was therefore one that had much in common with a series of other structures with which it shared a cultural association.

Alex Gibson has argued that the Neolithic palisaded enclosures of Britain can be divided into three broad groups, and that this classification has chronological implications (1998: 71). Firstly, there are enclosures defined by a series of separate post-holes, often spaced some distance apart, as with Walton, Leadketty, Forteviot, Dunragit and Meldon Bridge (Type 1). All of the sites that have entrances formed by external avenues of posts belong to this category, and it is notable that all of the Scottish enclosures fall into this group (Noble and Brophy 2011b: 61). Secondly, there are sites at which the post-holes are more closely spaced, and even intersect with one another, as at Greyhound Yard and Marne Barracks (Type 2). At Hindwell II the post-holes were contiguous, but the ramps used to erect the posts were distinct from one another. Finally, in a small number of cases the separate post-holes were replaced by a continuous palisade trench (Type 3). The best-known examples of this final category are Mount Pleasant and West Kennet, and in the latter case the lack of post-ramps was accommodated by digging one side of the slot less vertically to enable the posts to be tilted into place (Whittle 1997a: 151). Although there is doubtless some overlap, Gibson argues that the Type 2 sites date to between 2800 and 2600 BC, with Type 1 a little earlier, and Type 3 dating to 2500–2100 BC (Gibson 2002: 6; Whittle 1997a: 160). This suggests that over time the palisaded enclosures were more robustly constructed, with larger posts set increasingly close together. The process was one of escalating monumentality, in which greater effort was invested in creating more impressive structures, but also one in which the interior of the enclosure became progressively more secluded. At Blackshouse Burn in Lanarkshire this process can be seen in microcosm, with a stone bank being inserted between two concentric rings of posts, and eventually being enhanced after the posts had rotted out (Lelong and Pollard 1998: 41).

Some of the British palisaded enclosures were very large indeed. The biggest was Hindwell II, which contained an area of 34 hectares, while Meldon Bridge and Walton were each around 8 hectares in extent (Gibson 1998: 73). However, when compared with causewayed enclosures it is notable that large areas of the interiors of many of these sites are featureless, a situation paralleled in many of the Scandinavian enclosures (Gibson 2002: 13). The outer ring of the palisaded enclosure at Dunragit contained an area of around 7 hectares, and the innermost about 1.5 hectares, so it was of comparatively modest size. However, the presence of three concentric rings of palisades at Dunragit is quite unusual. Marne Barracks, Hindwell I and Enclosure 1

at West Kennet all had multiple palisade rings (Hale, Platell and Millard 2009: 268; Jones 2011: 14; Whittle 1997a: 55), but the contrasting character of the various circuits at Dunragit stands out as being distinctive, and of particular interest. Revealing its significance is problematic, for it depends upon the detailed evaluation of the episodes of digging, post insertion, recutting, withdrawal, deposition and replacement that took place within particular contexts. The interpretation of the stratigraphic histories of individual features on the basis of their excavation and the perusal of their sections is of course fraught with difficulty, and this is especially the case with post-holes. Reynolds and Barber (1984: 99) have pointed out that after the decay of the upper part of a post and the collapse of the stump, the heartwood of the timber often rots out, so that material from ground-level can enter the post core while the outer edge of the timber still survives. As a result, what are sometimes interpreted as recuts in the tops of post-hole features may be no more than a product of the natural process of decay and settling. Despite this reason for caution, there is a strong indication that the stratigraphic sequences of the post-holes in the inner post-ring at Dunragit are rather different (and more complex) from those in the middle and outer post-rings. In many cases the post-holes of the inner ring were two-phase features, containing either a replacement post or a recut holding a placed deposit of some kind, while in the easternmost portion of the excavated area two distinct series of post-holes existed side by side. Where two separate sets of post-holes were present, there was less indication of re-cutting, other than in the case of the deep post-removal cut containing a cremation burial deposit in post-hole 215. The implication is that the innermost post-ring at Dunragit was a two-phase structure, while the outer two rings were only single-phase. This evidence for renewal and reconstruction is unusual amongst the British palisaded enclosures. For instance, at Meldon Bridge, only one post (EO3) demonstrated replacement (Speak and Burgess 1999: 109). For the most part the life histories of these sites were governed by the time that it took for their posts to decay, although there are strong indications that even in a state of decrepitude and disrepair they retained their importance.

Gibson (1998: 76) argues that the British palisaded enclosures were structures that ringed an area with an impermeable boundary, to which access was severely restricted. None the less, their locations and certain aspects of their architecture argue against their having been used for defensive purposes. Very often they were positioned in low country overlooked by hills, as is the case with Dunragit. The avenue entrances present at many of these sites, defined by two lines of posts set narrowly apart, lead outward from the enclosures, and would have been of little help for defence. However, they share with the massive pairs of entrance posts at Mount Pleasant the feature of limiting access to the interior

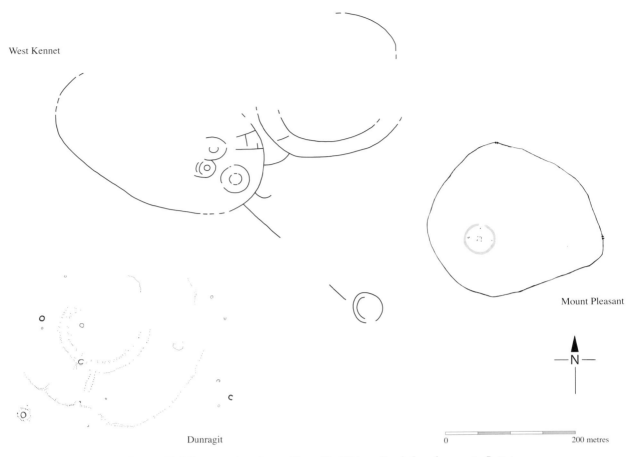

West Kennet

Mount Pleasant

—N—

Dunragit

0   200 metres

Figure 11.6 Comparative plans of Late Neolithic palisaded enclosures in Britain

(Wainwright 1979: 50). These 'gunsite' entrances are found at Dunragit, Forteviot, Leadketty, Meldon Bridge and Walton, and only at the former is the avenue set radially in relation to the enclosure (Gibson 2002: 6) (Fig. 11.5). This suggests that the normal pattern was one in which the view into the interior of the enclosure was occluded until any person entering had almost come to the end of the avenue. The exceptional arrangement at Dunragit was probably determined by the relationship between the enclosure and the Droughduil mound, toward which the entrance is directly aligned (see below). The Dunragit entrance structure remains unexcavated, but the aerial photographs suggests that it was around 35 metres in length, by comparison to the 27 metres at Meldon Bridge (Speak and Burgess 1999: 24). As at that site, it is possible that the posts in the entrance structure were larger than those elsewhere in the enclosure. At Forteviot the entrance passage was 35 metres long and 4–5 metres wide, and composed of especially large post-holes over 1 metre deep. It is estimated that they might have held uprights that were 6 metres tall and up to 0.9 metres in diameter (Noble and Brophy 2011a: 793).

The palisaded enclosure: post-hole histories

The larger post-holes of the three rings at Dunragit generally appear to have had ramps to facilitate the insertion and erection of the timbers. Heavy wooden posts would simply have been rolled into place and toppled into their sockets using the ramps, before being pulled upright and packed in place. It has to be remembered that all of the features investigated were severely truncated, owing to the erosion of the subsoil, and that as a consequence all of the post-ramps observed will have been deeper and longer than they appeared on excavation, while shallower examples had probably been removed altogether. For the most part, the post-ramps were much more pronounced in the innermost ring, which may have been composed of larger and taller posts. The latter would obviously have been more cumbersome, and the larger ramps would have helped in placing them in their sockets, although the greater expenditure of effort involved in digging the inner ring post-holes may also have been important, as a form of conspicuous investment of labour. The direction of the ramps was not consistent, although it was not as clearly varied as at Meldon Bridge, where Speak and

Burgess argue that the diversity aided the structural integrity of the palisade (1999: 19). In addition to the complex histories of recutting and post-removal evident in many of these post-holes, there is also the question of burning. There is a debate in the literature concerning the charring of timbers before their erection, and whether this does or does not enhance their survival in the ground by limiting fungal growth (see, for example, Morrell, Miller and Schneider 1999: 11; Watts 2004: 70). At Hindwell II, for instance, it is argued that the posts had been partially burned before insertion (Gibson 1998: 69), while at Marne Barracks it is suggested that some of the posts had been burned *in situ* (Hale, Platell and Millard 2009: 268). Similarly, the palisade at Mount Pleasant appears to have been subject to a combination of burning, removal and decay (Wainwright 1979: 54), a situation that was paralleled at Forteviot (Noble and Brophy 2011b: 78–9).

The posts at West Kennet may have been burned above ground level, with charcoal later falling into the voids left by the rotting post stumps. None of these appear to have been withdrawn (Whittle 1997a: 158). At Meldon Bridge, all the posts are considered to have rotted out (Speak and Burgess 1999: 20). Burnt material in the bases of the post-holes was argued to arise from trimming of the posts before insertion, and was not *in situ* burning (Speak and Burgess 1999: 19).

The situation at Dunragit is far from clear (see Table 11.1). Many posts connected with the palisaded enclosure showed no signs of burning whatever, while some contained charred post-bases or other burnt material. In some cases these took the form of a U-shaped line of charcoal in the bottom of the post-pipe. If these had been charred before insertion, the remainder of the post may have rotted out from above, and from the inside outwards.

Table 11.1 Details of post-holes of the palisaded enclosure

Inner Post-Ring: posts of the western part of the circuit

319/332	Two separate posts, sequence unclear	230	Post possibly withdrawn?
579/619	579 post dug out, deposition in post-removal/recut 619	255	Post possibly withdrawn?
594	Charred post stump, probably rotted out	310	Post rotted out
		532	Post possibly withdrawn?
756/449	756 Post withdrawn; 757 rotted out, possibly charred	656	Post possibly withdrawn?
792	792 post dug out, recut 950 contained placed deposit	690	Post rotted out
		860	Post possibly withdrawn?
825/826	826 rotted out; 825 charred and rotted out	896	Post withdrawn
		898	Post rotted out
4018	Post rotted out	3024	Post rotted out
4029	Post rotted out	4047	Post rotted out
4145/4173	4145 charred and possibly rotted, then recut; 4173 post probably withdrawn, or perhaps no second post	4053	Post rotted out
		4110	Post rotted out
4230	Post rotted out	4172	Post rotted out
4243	Post rotted out	4204	Post rotted out

Western Arc of the Inner Post-Ring

		4260	Post withdrawn
063	Carbonised wood present; post rotted out		

Middle Post-Ring: lesser post-holes

084	Post rotted out	035	Post rotted out
087	Post rotted out	285	Post rotted out

Eastern Arc of the Inner Post-Ring

		798	Post rotted out
046	Post withdrawn	907	Post rotted out

Outer Post-Ring

054/057	Post withdrawn		
215	Post dug out, cremation burial deposit in recut	2046	Post rotted out
		2049	Post rotted out
306	Post withdrawn	2054	Post rotted out

Middle Post-Ring

		2073	Post rotted out
027	Post rotted out	2097	Post burned out
099	Post rotted out		

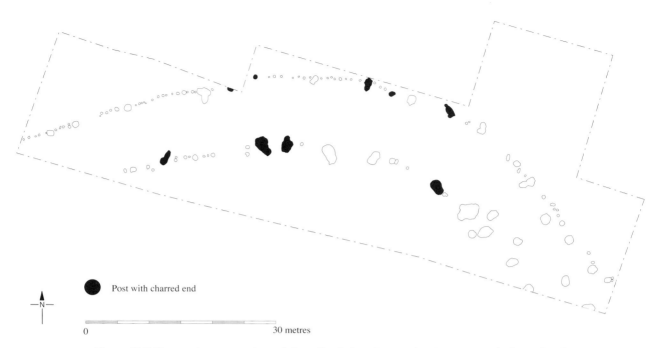

Post with charred end

N

0   30 metres

Figure 11.7 The two innermost rings of the palisaded enclosure, showing posts with charred ends

As a consequence, soil and gravel would have fallen down into the post void, and the packing of the post-hole would then have slumped inward. This was probably the case in features 532, 594, 690, 756/449, 825/826, 860, 896 and 4145/4173. In a few cases, the evidence is more in line with posts having burned *in situ*, as with features 4264 and especially the outer ring post-hole 2097, in Trench E. But even in these examples, the burning is not as clear as in the case of the cursus posts (see above). Yet in either case it is mystifying why only a minority of posts should have been either fire-treated or burned out. One possibility is that the construction of different parts of the enclosure may have been the prerogative of different social segments or work-gangs, who may have had slightly different ways of working and preparing the timbers. It is therefore potentially quite significant that the traces of charred post stumps in both the inner and middle post-rings were concentrated in the central portion of the excavated area, largely within Trench AA (Fig. 11.7). This would suggest that the same group of people had been responsible for constructing adjacent stretches of the inner and the middle post-rings. The further implication is that specific social entities each built and maintained a radial segment of the enclosure. A similar pattern has been suggested at the great henge monument of Durrington Walls in Wiltshire, where the chalk bank appears to have been constructed in a series of separate sections, each distinguished from the next by a number of marker features (Parker Pearson 2012: 115).

Pointing to the diversity of the treatment of individual posts at Forteviot and Dunragit, Noble and Brophy (2011b: 78) argue that the separate life histories of the

timbers concerned would have been of some consequence. Something similar has previously been proposed by Mike Pitts (2001) in discussing the results of his investigation of the timber setting at Sanctuary on Overton Hill in north Wiltshire, an element of the Avebury monumental complex. Here Pitts was able to identify small patches of sediment in some of the post-holes that had not been removed by the Cunningtons' excavation in 1930 (Cunnington 1931). The multiple episodes of packing that these documented implied that each individual post-hole had contained a series of different timber uprights, which had been removed and replaced on a number of occasions. Pitts argued on this basis that particular timbers had been 'circulated' from place to place, either within the monument, or within the wider landscape. It potentially follows from this argument that as well as representing utilitarian building material, timbers gained value from having been used in particular places and as elements of particular structures. A parallel argument has been made in relation to the wooden members of houses within Neolithic tell settlements in southeast Europe, which were sometimes recovered in charred condition following the burning of buildings, and incorporated into new structures (Chapman 1999). The implication is that these timbers were redolent of ancestral occupation, and drew the influence of past generations into the new dwelling. This recalls Nancy Munn's discussion of the manufacture of canoes on Gawa Island in the Solomon Sea. Munn points out that the importance and value of the canoe depends on the appearance of the wood, and the location of the tree from which is has been cut (1986: 129). It is conceivable that in a similar manner, rather than

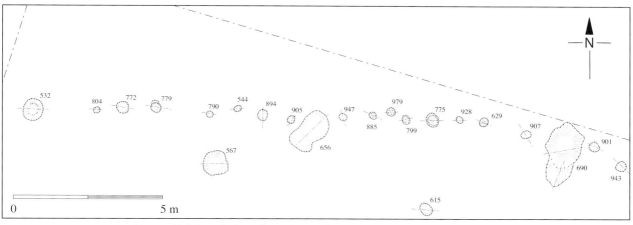

Figure 11.8 Detail plan of post-holes of the middle post-ring in Trench AA

all of the timbers within the palisade enclosure having been equal, and having been understood as no more than inert matter suited to construction, they may each have had quite distinct meanings and biographies. Particular posts may have been cut down and brought to the site by different families or clans, from groves or forests that would have had distinct associations of their own. Just as the bluestones were brought to Stonehenge from west Wales, when equally suitable materials were available closer to hand, and just as stone axes were quarried from relatively inaccessible locations in the west of Britain and circulated to areas which had perfectly good flint for making functionally equivalent tools, it should not be assumed that all of the Dunragit posts were sourced locally, or from a single site. Some timbers may have previously been used in other structures of some kind, while their felling and dragging to the site might have been accompanied by adventures, ceremonies, feasts, gatherings or mishaps. All of these factors might have served to individuate specific wooden uprights, creating conditions under which they would have been dealt with in different ways as the enclosure was constructed, used, and came to be decommissioned, or fell into disuse and disrepair.

Table 11.1 provides some salient details of the histories of individual posts, principally relating to the question of whether they had been removed by rocking or digging out, or whether they had been allowed to rot away *in situ*. In many cases, particularly those of the smaller posts, the post-hole fill was homogeneous and uninformative, and these features are omitted from the table.

Given the apparent diversity of form and construction among the three post-rings at Dunragit, the question must arise of whether all three represented continuous boundaries. Amongst some palisaded enclosures, there were gaps between the uprights. Thus the 0.7 metre diameter posts at Hindwell II were separated by intervals of 0.7–0.9 metres (Gibson 1999: 14). Similarly, the timbers at Greyhound Yard would have been about 1

metre apart from each other (Woodward, Davies and Graham 1984: 101). It is conceivable that these closely set posts were joined by shuttering or walling of a kind that had left no archaeological trace. But equally, it is possible that as with the sarsen stones at Stonehenge, a discontinuous barrier was sufficient to interrupt vision and the flow of sound between interior and exterior. At Meldon Bridge the large uprights were separated by appreciable gaps, similar to those at Dunragit, but these were interspersed by smaller post-holes set forward from the bigger post-holes. It is reasonable to interpret these as a post-and-panel arrangement, in which horizontal members spanned the spaces between the large posts, and were held in place by the smaller ones (Speak and Burgess 1999: 105). Yet at Dunragit the situation is rather different. In the middle post-ring there are anything up to eight small post-holes between the large ramped post-pits (Fig. 11.8). These were often positioned on the forward site of the bigger posts (although sometimes not in a precise line), and might have functioned in the same way as the Meldon Bridge posts, retaining horizontal elements. Yet these would have had to be rather long in order to span the distance between the larger posts, and it is just as likely that the small uprights formed the skeleton of a fence, perhaps of wattle, stabilised by the major uprights. In either case, it is probable that the middle ring did represent a continuous barrier of some kind, although perhaps more of a screen or wall than a fortification.

The evidence for the outermost ring is more ambiguous, for only a small section of the palisade was investigated, crossing the corner of Trench E in an area where the degree of erosion and truncation of the subsoil had obviously been very severe indeed. Smaller features were none the less observed as well as substantial post-holes, and it is probable that this was also an unbroken fence or palisade. But in the case of the innermost ring the presence of lesser posts is difficult to demonstrate over much of the observed circuit. In trenches A and

AA, taking account of the cluster of small post-holes that can be attributed to the later prehistoric round house (see below), there were very few lesser post-holes amongst the large ramped features. This pattern is particularly noteworthy when one considers that two consecutive series of large post-holes had been dug in this area. Only in part of Trench J was a line of smaller post-holes identified as part of the inner post circuit. This evidence can be interpreted in a number of different ways. Firstly, it may be that smaller posts had been present around the entire inner circuit, and have been lost to subsoil erosion. This is possible, but it is difficult to explain why inner ring post-holes should have been destroyed in areas where middle ring posts survived. Secondly, it is possible that the innermost post-ring was never a true palisade, and was effectively a circle of large freestanding uprights. Only in small areas, such as part of Trench J, did patches of screening or arrangements of smaller uprights occur. Significantly, in this area the entire character of the post-ring was different from elsewhere, for there were very few large post-holes in Trench J at all. Criticising this hypothesis, Gibson (2002: 8) argues that the inner ring could have been a continuous barrier, with horizontal, pegged timbers between the uprights, in a fashion comparable with Meldon Bridge. However, if the innermost ring had been of post-and-panel construction, pairs of small post-holes comparable with those at Meldon Bridge might have been expected between the large post-pits. Moreover, it is difficult to explain why this form of construction should have been used to create a continuous palisade around (part of) the innermost ring when a different method was used elsewhere, with multiple lesser uprights between the large posts. It is relevant to note that recent excavations at Forteviot have detected no smaller posts whatever between the major uprights, although again, these might have been lost to erosion (Noble and Brophy 2011a: 800).

The interpretation preferred here is that the innermost ring represented a colossal timber circle, around 120 metres in diameter, but that the two outer rings were effectively fences, composed of large posts at roughly 5 metre intervals, with smaller posts, much closer together, placed in between. The inner ring (the post circle) had had two distinct phases of construction. Some of the posts had been replaced, a few may have been retained from the first phase, and others had been dug out without a second post being inserted. In these latter cases, some form of deliberate deposit had often been placed in the recut or crater from which the post had been removed. While some posts survived from the first into the second phase of the timber circle, there may also have been entirely new post-holes. In Trench A, where the two phases did not coincide spatially, new posts were certainly added, probably represented by the 'western arc' of post-holes (see below). The single post in post-hole 594 may have formed an element of both phases of the circle, or may

even have been a new addition in the second phase, while recut post-holes such as 579/619 and 792 probably had no second post added. This almost certainly means that the number and arrangement of the posts making up the large timber circle were quite different in its two phases of existence. Furthermore, it may also be that the post circle was not entirely regular throughout its circuit, as is the case with some stone circles. We have already noted that in part of Trench J, some smaller post-holes appear to have been present in the inner ring, and indeed, the 'major' post-holes in this area were not particularly large. Post-holes 4018 and 4029 seemed to be 'intermediate' in size, and aside from the large post-hole 4145/4173 this stretch of the inner ring in the immediate vicinity of the eastern side of the cursus appeared a little messy, or even 'botched'. Further, few of the features in this part of the inner ring other than 4145/4173 (and the presence of a second post in 4145/4173 itself is not absolutely clear) gave the impression of having been either replaced or recut. Some of these features may have formed part of both iterations of the monument, or may have only been present in one, so that extensive gaps may have existed between the posts in one or other phase.

One important finding of the Dunragit excavation, then, was that the monument as a whole was somewhat irregular, with posts of different thickness inserted into post-holes that had been dug to different depths and with different morphologies, which subsequently developed and were treated in distinctive and individual ways. At different times during the site's development, the spaces between the posts of the inner ring may have varied in size. In this respect, the Dunragit enclosure contrasts with the rather more careful, precise and regular construction of other Grooved Ware related monumental post architecture, such as the Southern Circle at Durrington Walls (Wainwright with Longworth 1971: 23–38). The latter was a few centuries later in date than Dunragit, and was perhaps connected with a larger scale of social organisation. But it is interesting to speculate whether the internal structural diversity and general 'scruffiness' at Dunragit might be a consequence of its construction by a number of different social units whose overall coherence and coordination was limited, and who adhered to rather different ways of doing things. We have already raised this possibility in relation to the charring of the ends of timbers, which may have been concentrated in particular radial segments of the enclosure perimeter. The more general variation in construction is a further hint that the monument was created by a loose aggregation of semiautonomous social units, rather than a tightly integrated hierarchical entity.

By contrast with the innermost post-ring, each of the two outer rings was a single-phase construction, and while the middle ring was broadly circular the outer had an undulating, scalloped plan. The entrances of the two outermost post-rings did not respect each other, so that it

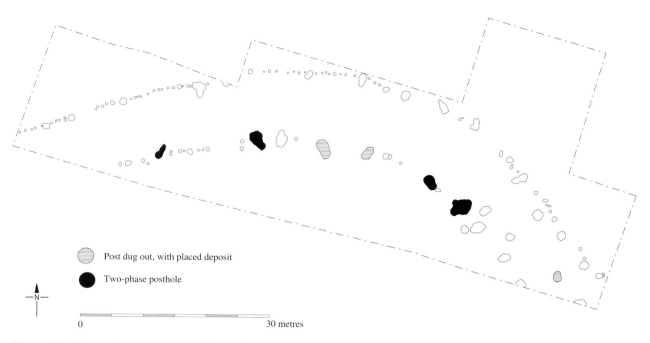

Figure 11.9 The two innermost rings of the palisaded enclosure, showing posts that had been dug out, and two-phase post-holes

would not have been possible to pass from the outside to the interior of the enclosure in a straight line, had the two been contemporary. Further, the entrance to the middle ring was the elaborate and monumental post-avenue discussed above, which as we have noted was aligned on the Droughduil mound, while the outer ring had two quite different entrances, which were simple gaps in the post-lines. If the outer two post-rings had been in existence at the same time, it would not have been possible to view the mound through the post-avenue (or indeed, to view the interior of the enclosure from the top of the mound), or to progress directly between the post-avenue and the mound. All of this suggests that the two outer post arrangements were *not* contemporary, and that the monument as a whole was rebuilt on at least one occasion. In each phase it consisted of the same essential structure: a timber circle surrounded by a single continuous fence or palisade. The implication is that between the first and second phase the overall size of the enclosure changed, although it is not clear whether the larger or the smaller fence was the earlier. Although post-avenue entrances tend to be associated with what may be the earliest of the British palisaded enclosures, this is has no definitive bearing on the internal sequence at Dunragit.

The post-holes of the innermost ring were appreciably larger than those of the outer two rings, and it is possible that the greater size of the uprights of the timber circle reflected their focal status at the centre of the monument. In Chapter 3 above we noted that some of the two-phase posts of the innermost ring appeared to have been withdrawn before their sockets were recut, while some of the posts that were subsequently inserted

were eventually left to rot out (see Table 11.1) (Fig. 11.9). This is not an entirely clear pattern: for instance, the first post in post-hole 825/826 may have rotted out before the feature was recut and the second post inserted, while in post-hole 4145/4173 the trace of the burnt sides of the first post could indicate *either* that the post had rotted, or that the burnt material was left behind when the semi-rotted post was withdrawn. None the less, the overall tendency suggests that the primary posts in these features could have been equivalents to the 'eastern arc' of inner ring posts, which had mostly been withdrawn (Fig. 11.10). It is also notable that with the exception of feature 252, the post-holes of the 'eastern arc' were rather shallow, representing only the bases of features that had originally been deeper, but which had been subject to erosion. It is plausible that some of the posts that had been set in these earlier, quite shallow sockets had collapsed or slipped from the vertical, and that as a result the second phase post-holes had uniformly been cut to a greater depth. Conversely, the posts that were inserted following recutting were often left to rot away, a pattern paralleled by the 'western arc' of post-holes. Although these observations are based on equivocal evidence, it is clearly significant that almost all of the outer ring post-holes that were investigated had rotted out, while about 45% of the excavated middle ring posts had been withdrawn. The different treatment of the posts in the outer two rings adds some weight to the notion that they were not contemporary, and that one succeeded the other. If we accept these arguments, it may be that the first phase of the innermost post-ring was contemporary with the middle ring (where there was an appreciable quantity

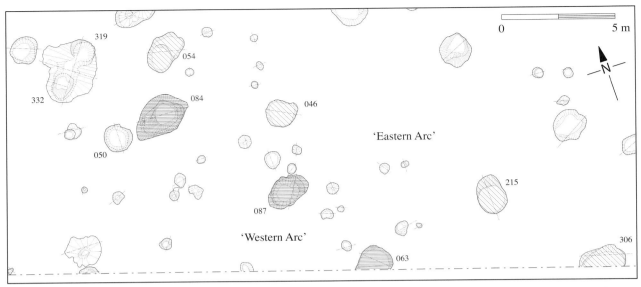

Figure 11.10 Detail of the 'eastern' and 'western arcs' of inner ring post-holes of the Late Neolithic enclosure in Trench A

of post removal), while the second phase was paired with the outer ring (largely rotted). In this scenario, the fundamental pattern of a large timber circle surrounded by a palisade or fence was maintained in both phases, but the overall footprint of the structure became larger between the two. Although this interpretation is preferred, it should be noted that a different interpretation is also possible. It was noted in the course of excavation that the sandy fills of the primary cuts of the inner post-ring were similar to the 'western arc' post-holes, while the darker, moister fills of the recuts were more comparable with those of the 'eastern arc'. On the basis that the distinction between withdrawn primary posts and rotted-out recut posts is not a categorical one, we could construct an alternative argument in which the 'western arc' posts were earlier. This being the case, the presumption that the middle ring posts were withdrawn before being replaced by the outer ring might begin to break down. The significance of these arguments is that depending upon which version of events we choose the overall size of the enclosure changed from smaller to larger (middle to outer ring), or vice versa, over time. So, either the monument expanded to admit a larger group of people (and/or livestock), or its reduction in size might indicate increasing restriction on those granted access.

However, irrespective of the precise details of the sequence, it is probable that in both of the two phases of construction the inner post-ring represented the core of the structure, enclosed and secluded by a continuous outer boundary. This being the case, the contrast between the large post-holes of the inner ring and the smaller ones of the two outer rings is instructive. We might say that the middle and outer ring features seemed more 'functional'. They were sometimes ramped, but they were no larger than required to hold a substantial timber,

and consequentially more diminutive than the inner ring post-holes. With the one exception of a fine ground stone axe (see below) they contained no structured deposits, or indeed any other cultural material at all, beyond two sherds of Grooved Ware and a flint flake. The implication of this contrast is that the timber circle represented the symbolic focus of the monument, the uprights of which were significant in and of themselves, while the fence or palisade was the perimeter of the site, and had the role of regulating access and vision into the interior. We might compare this arrangement to the relationship between the earthen bank and the internal features with a large henge monument, which would have a similar concentric ordering of space. Indeed, one of the consequences of the ditch being set on the inner side of the bank amongst henge monuments would have been that the contents of the ditch were more visible and accessible from the inside than the outside of the enclosure.

The palisaded enclosure: construction and investment of effort

Unquestionably, both phases of the Dunragit enclosure represented a substantial investment of labour, although perhaps not on the same scale as some of the other Late Neolithic palisaded enclosures in Britain. We have noted already that the wavering, scalloped plan of the outer post-ring is rather less regular than other enclosures, while the size, spacing and morphology of the major post-holes were more diverse than at some other sites. Only at Meldon Bridge did a similar degree of variability manifest itself (Speak and Burgess 1999: 15). The outer post-ring at Dunragit had a diameter of roughly 290 metres, and thus a circumference of 911 metres. In the excavated portion there was approximately one major post in every 3.6 metres of the perimeter. By extrapolation, this would indicate a total of around 253 posts. The middle post-ring had a diameter of 125 metres, a circumference of 393 metres, and with one post every 6.9 metres in the excavated portion would have had a total of the order of 57 posts. The innermost ring had a diameter of 105 metres, and a circumference of 330 metres. In the excavated area, major posts were identified every 5.8 metres around the circumference, also giving a projected total of 57 posts (although it seems probable that the number differed between the two phases of construction). While it is acknowledged that the spacing of the posts was highly irregular, it is none the less interesting that the number of posts calculated for the two innermost rings is equal. This perhaps echoes the evidence that we have already cited indicating that the construction of distinct radial segments of the enclosure may have been the responsibility of different social groups – each might have been charged with contributing a certain number of posts to each of the rings. For the most part the post-holes at Dunragit were spaced at wider intervals than those at other comparable palisaded enclosures. At Meldon Bridge, the posts were 3–4.4 metres apart (Speak and Burgess 1999: 15), while those at Forteviot were 4–5 metres apart (St Joseph 1978).

These figures suggest that the numbers of larger posts employed in the construction of the Dunragit enclosure would have been 114 for the phase involving the middle post-ring, and 310 for that incorporating the outer post-ring, although the number would have been slightly smaller in whichever was the later phase, as the number of posts added to the innermost ring appears to have declined. To this can be added the 20 or so posts of the entrance avenue, and the numerous rather smaller uprights that stood in between the large timbers in the outer two rings, and in places within the innermost ring. Much more wood would have been employed if horizontal members had been employed at any point. Despite this, the quantities of material employed at Dunragit would have been considerably less than the 2000 posts employed at Marne Barracks, the 1600 at Mount Pleasant, the 2800 at West Kennet 1, or the 1400 at Hindwell II (Hale, Platell and Millard 2009: 282). It is difficult to estimate the diameter of the posts used at Dunragit, as the post-pipes were generally slumped and disrupted, and there was evidently much variation. However, it appears that the lager posts were of the order of 40–50 centimetres in diameter. These would have been significantly smaller and lighter than the 1 metre diameter posts at Greyhound Yard (Woodward, Davies and Graham 1984: 101). The timbers at Dunragit were similar in size to those at Meldon Bridge, where it is estimated that the posts would have taken about a century to rot away (Speak and Burgess 1999: 109). Depending on which of

the possible interpretations of the sequence we choose to adopt, this might given an indication of the period of time that elapsed between the two constructional phases of the enclosure. Whittle (1997a: 154) notes that oak trees are commonly 21–30 metres tall, so that a number of posts could have been acquired from a single tree. Given the severely eroded character of the subsoil at Dunragit it is difficult to evaluate the original depth of the post-holes, which then might be used to estimate the lengths of the posts. Even the lengths of the surviving post-ramps do not appear to provide a reliable guide to post length. However, at Meldon Bridge Speak and Burgess argue that the posts were of the order of 3.5–4 metres long. If the Dunragit posts were of this size, five or six could have been acquired from a single tree. Each phase of construction might then have required no more than 60 trees. If 150 oak trees grow in a hectare of forest (Whittle 1997a: 154), it is evident that the construction of the Dunragit enclosure would not have had a catastrophic effect on local woodland, even if the posts had been acquired from a single local area. However, the work involved in felling and dressing these timbers, and building the monument would have been considerable, and would presumably have required the labour of an appreciable number of people. It is likely that these would have been drawn from a wider area than the immediate environs of the site, and this supports the idea that the structure may have been built and used by a number of distinct social groups.

The palisaded enclosure: depositional practice

We have noted that the inner ring post-holes in particular had a series of different individual sequences of development. Some posts had been left to rot out, while others had been withdrawn, and other post-holes had been recut. This picture is further complicated by the recognition that the withdrawal of posts could take two distinct forms. In some cases, posts had apparently been rocked out of their sockets, with the effect that the packing and other fills became displaced and homogenised, and any trace of a post-pipe was removed. Occasionally, fragments of the charred end of a post might have been left behind, and sometimes what were apparently lenses of backfill had been introduced to the feature. Most of the post-holes of the 'eastern arc' of the inner ring (046, 054, 306) took this form, in which lenses of mixed, slipped and disturbed packing material were surmounted by settling and silting deposits, which post-dated the removal of the post. By contrast, in a minority of cases the stump of the post had actually been dug out, resulting in a distinct cut feature or crater, the clearest example being post-hole 215. As an observation, it may be that this 'digging out' was more likely to occur in deeper post-holes, where the post-stump was more firmly embedded in the earth. Where digging out took place, the feature may subsequently have been treated differently from those post-holes from which the upright had simply been withdrawn. The practice of 'digging out' was effectively a kind of recutting, and where it took place some form of purposeful deposition generally followed. Indeed, there were three cases in which the primary use of the post-hole to contain a timber upright had been followed by a major recutting event and an episode of deposition, and it may be that none of these post-holes had ever contained a second post. If this were the case, then the number of posts that made up the timber circle of the innermost ring during its second phase may have been smaller than in the first, although it is equally possible that these recuttings did not take place until after the circle had been rebuilt, or even that some of the single-phase post-holes were added to the circuit in the second phase (see below).

These examples of the removal of a post and the introduction of cultural material into the resulting cavity evoke the complicated issue of 'structured deposition'. Over the past 30 years, there has been continuing debate over the character of deposits that have apparently been deliberately introduced into the archaeological record, often with some degree of formality, and which seem to have been particularly characteristic of the Neolithic and Early Bronze Age in Britain and Ireland (e.g. Garrow 2006; Richards and Thomas 1984; Thomas 1999: 62–88; Thomas 2012a). One difficulty has always lain in the recognition that material culture patterning is undoubtedly generated by relatively unstructured everyday activities that may embody no particular meaning, but that 'odd deposits' involving clearly placed and arranged materials are not infrequently encountered on archaeological sites. There is consequentially a potential danger of over-interpreting the archaeological evidence, and seeking deep symbolic meanings in every pit, post-hole and artefact assemblage (Garrow 2012: 105). However, it is just as dangerous to establish a clear-cut dichotomy between 'odd deposits' and 'average practice', and imagine that we can sort the archaeological evidence into either one category or the other (Thomas 2012b: 126). In practice, in may be more helpful to imagine a continuum between the most random processes that generate archaeological patterning, which may not necessarily involve human agency at all, and the rare and spectacular deposits in which rich and complex materials have been carefully arranged to convey a particular message. Many funerary deposits, for example, would fall at the more complex and meaningful end of the spectrum, with a body laid out in a grave surrounded by objects that may have had either personal or social significance. Somewhere between the two poles are more difficult instances, in which the patterned character of the archaeological evidence has been generated not by the conscious effort to express a specific meaning, but

by the routine observation of established social norms. Thus where a particular animal species is considered unclean or defiled, its remains may be kept separate from other animal bones as an unevaluated aspect of everyday practice. For the people concerned this is just 'the way that things are done', rather than a matter for deliberation. The difficulty for archaeologists lies in distinguishing the degrees of complexity and formality implicit in particular deposits, and seeking to identify the extent to which some might qualify as special, significant, and potentially open to deeper interpretation. In the case of the Dunragit Late Neolithic enclosure we are faced with a variety of archaeological contexts that might be located in different positions on the scale between random accumulation and deliberate placement. Where one or two abraded sherds of Grooved Ware occur in a middle ring post-hole, we may feel confident in identifying them as stray and accidental inclusions in the packing fill. Yet the small pits containing more numerous pieces of Grooved Ware within the cursus boundary in Trench F would seem to suggest something a little different, while the burial of the cremated remains of a woman with burnt fragments of a small animal in post-hole 215 was evidently a very careful and purposeful act. It is with these considerations in mind that we can address the range of potential 'structured deposits' at Dunragit.

All of the examples of post removal having been followed by an elaborate depositional episode of some kind were identified within the inner post-ring, a feature which points once again to the special or focal character of the inner posts, in contrast with the 'mundane' outer fences. We might go so far as to say that the posts of the inner ring 'attracted' formal or symbolically freighted acts, including acts of deposition. One of the particular problems of a site in which all of the cut features represent separate and unrelated sequences, stratigraphically linked only by the topsoil covering them and the gravel below, is that it is very difficult to identify any degree of synchroneity or correlation between events that took place within different features. So we cannot know whether these post removals and depositions were essentially episodic, played out over a century or more, or whether there was a distinct temporal horizon during which a series of partially rotted post-stumps were pulled or dug out, backfilling took place, and new sockets were dug in preparation for the renewal of the monument. Either of these two scenarios has its attractions. As we have argued already, we can imagine a radical reconstruction of the enclosure, in which all of the surviving posts were toppled or dug out, and all of the resulting cavities were backfilled, before an entirely new set of uprights was erected, some of them inserted into recuts in the earlier features. But alternately, we could consider a less thoroughgoing version of the rebuilding, in which the replacement of the middle ring palisade by the outer (or perhaps vice-versa) was matched by a piecemeal

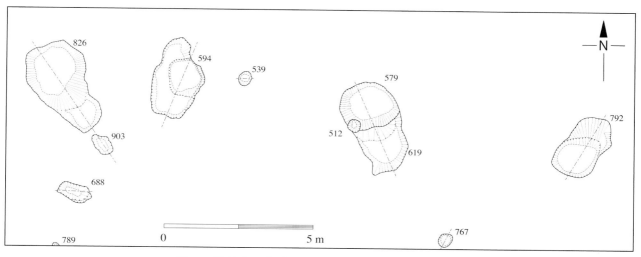

Figure 11.11 Detail of inner ring post-holes in Trench AA

episode of 'maintenance' on the inner circle. Some posts might have been left standing, others rocked out and replaced, while the recutting and backfilling of some post-holes may have taken place at other times entirely. The one part of the excavated portion of the site where replacement certainly took place on a significant scale was to the east, in Trench A, where we have argued that the 'eastern arc' of post-holes was probably superseded by the 'western arc'.

One of the 'eastern arc' post-holes that had been deeper than the others contained a post that was dug out. Deposit 227, representing the cremated remains of a young woman and fragments of burnt bone from a sheep-sized animal, was placed into post-hole 215 following the removal of the post. Arguably, then, the insertion of the cremation burial deposit had taken place as part of the process by which the timber circle was reconfigured and renewed. The deposition of human remains at this juncture might indicate that the rebuilding of the circle was conducted in honour of a recently deceased person, even as part of their funeral. Alternatively, the deposit might be identified as dedicatory in character, and the body understood as being subsidiary to a monument that was connected with the collective identity of a larger group. But in either case, the person's memorability was secured by physically incorporating them into the fabric of the monument. A similar insertion of cremated human remains into the space left by a removed post was observed at Forteviot, in the entrance avenue (Noble and Brophy 2011b: 79). Two of the other placed deposits at Dunragit also fell within the main body of the inner post-ring, in post-holes that may not have received a replacement post. A number of possible interpretations of this phenomenon suggest themselves. It might be that the deposit served as an equivalent or substitute for the second post, or as a form of compensation or exchange for the opening of the earth and the removal of the post

stump. But equally, each act of deposition might simply have taken advantage of the digging of the post-removal pit to provide a suitable receptacle. Finally, each deposit might have commemorated a particular event or person, and the conspicuous absence of a particular post within the timber circle would then have served as a 'negative marker', drawing attention to the presence of the buried material. Depending on whether the replacement of the timber circle was a distinct event or a more protracted process, the other deposits inserted into post-holes may have been broadly contemporary with the cremated bone in post-hole 215, or rather later. Soil micromorphology results from this post-hole demonstrated that charcoal fragments in some of the layers were of unusually large size grade. This is interpreted as indicating that the burnt fragments had not travelled far, and had not been subject to significant attrition before they entered the feature (see Chapter 9). The implication is that they were derived from an episode or episodes of burning that had taken place nearby, and perhaps not long before the post-hole was backfilled. One possibility is that the pyre on which cremation had taken place had been close to the inner post-ring.

Post-hole 792 had contained a single post, which was subsequently removed by a major recut, which penetrated to the base of the original feature (Fig. 11.11). Only minimal traces of the original packing were left *in situ*, on the ramped side of the post-hole. The recut contained a series of distinct layers and lenses of backfill. It is possible that this recut had held a second post at some point, and that the lower fills (966 to 867) represented the displaced packing of an upright that had been withdrawn. However, economy of hypothesis argues that the recut removed the stump of the first post, and that subsequent layers were simply backfill. Feature 792 contained a great quantity of material culture, concentrated in the upper part of the profile. A couple of small fragments of flint were present in the primary packing, and isolated pieces of flint or pottery in layers 867, 951 and 967. However, the great mass of the material was recovered from contexts 653 and, particularly, 685. Each of these two layers contained multiple sherds from a series of Grooved Ware vessels, although the greater quantity was in 685. 685 also produced far the greatest quantity of flint, including a core, two early stage flakes, several smaller flakes and a fabricator, as well as a further core and 46 flake fragments that had been subjected to intense heat. In total, this feature contained more than half of the flint from the entire site (see Chapter 7). It is possible that the pottery sherds in 653 had been displaced from earlier layers, and that a single cultural deposit had at some point been placed in 685. Indeed, although calcined flints were found in several different contexts, they seem to have derived from a small number of objects, which were for the most part concentrated in 685 (see Chapter 7). In other words, the material from the different layers was derived from a single original assemblage rather than a series of separate sources.

The dark, greasy, burnt organic material of layer 685 had a texture that was quite unlike that of other deposits on the site. This seemed very like the kind of fill that is often found in isolated Neolithic pits containing deliberate cultural deposits (Thomas 1999: 64). Although there was little indication that the pottery and flint had been arranged in any formal manner, it is very probable that the artefacts and their dark organic matrix had been purposefully redeposited from elsewhere. Quite possibly it had come from a surface midden, or had been scraped up from the vicinity of a hearth. As such, whatever meaning it held was likely restricted to the general connotations of domesticity, occupation, gathering, consumption and conviviality, although it might equally have been derived from a particular episode of assembly and the sharing of food. However, the presence of a large number of seemingly purposefully burnt items of good quality flint is an interesting aspect of this deposit. It does suggest the conspicuous wastage of a valuable material, while the activity of placing large items of flint on an open fire is one that might be both spectacular and dangerous, if fragments exploded and spalled. While the redeposition of this assemblage may have been no more 'structured' than the tossing of a mass of burnt soil and artefacts into the top of an open post-hole, it none the less merits comparison with the deposits in post-holes 215 and 579/619. At a later stage, a further small, bowl-shaped recut was dug into the surface of the ramp of feature 792. It was lined with a deposit of virtually pure charcoal, 627, and within the subsequent fill 634, one of the finest artefacts from the site was discovered, an oblique flint arrowhead of Late Neolithic date, made from translucent grey-brown flint. In all probability the little pit was dug with the purpose of depositing this item in mind, and it may be that this represented a form of

veneration, adding to the sequence of significant events that was by then embodied in the post-hole. As such, its relationship with post-hole 792 is comparable with that between pit 050 and post-hole 084 (see below).

579/619 was an exceptionally complex feature, with an elaborate history. There is little doubt that the activities that contributed to its formation were both significant and resist a straightforward explanation, yet they were also rather different from most instances of 'structured deposition' that have been reported for the British Neolithic. As in the case of post-hole 792, the recutting of this feature was very extensive, and while some of the primary packing survived, there was no clear evidence than a second post had ever been inserted. The primary post-hole had been almost entirely scoured out, although much of the original ramp was intact, and its fill contained four sherds of Grooved Ware. A further fragment from the same vessel was found on top of the small mound of clean sand that had been deposited on the base of the emptied post-hole. It is to be presumed that this sherd was encountered in the course of recutting the feature and set aside for re-deposition, although the fact that it was in fresher condition than the sherds from the ramp suggests otherwise. Further pieces of the same pot were also found in pits 3074 and 3112 (see below). Both the sherd and the sandy mound were subsequently covered by a mass of oak charcoal, which contained minute fragments of burnt bone and burnt sand grains. Apparently a fire had been burned in a sandy place, and cremation or cooking had taken place. Given that prehistoric pyres have been identified on Luce Sands, as at Cowie's Site J (see Chapter 2 above) it is tempting to speculate that the person buried in post-hole 215 had been cremated on the sands, and their bones and pyre debris had been deposited in two separate post-holes of the inner ring. However, it seems that the burnt bone in 579/619 is more likely to have been animal than human, so it is possible that the two deposits relate to different episodes, although the presence of the burnt bone of a possible sheep in 215 should not be overlooked. Like 792, 579/619 seems to have been backfilled with a series of lenses of material thrown in from different directions, before stabilising and finally silting. The charcoally layer 603 occupied a similar position in the stratigraphy as 685 in post-hole 972, but it contained none of the same dense cultural material. The striking difference between the two post-holes, then, was that while the cultural deposit in 792 occurred halfway up the profile, as part of the process of backfilling, the significant events in 579/619 had taken place on the bottom of the recut.

The deposits in 215, 579/619 and 792 could all be contemporary, and might be understood as a means of commemorating the timber circle and its individual posts. If no second post had ever stood in 579/619 or 792, it is an open question whether the removal of the primary post stumps from these features formed part of the preparation

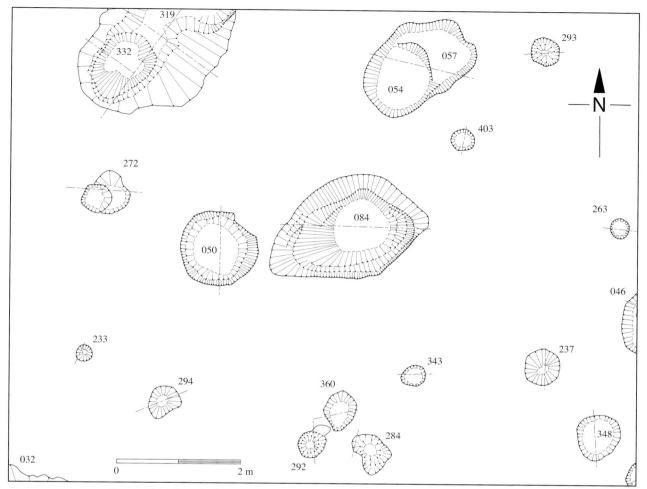

Figure 11.12 Detail of inner ring post-hole 084 and pit 050 and their setting in Trench A

for the rebuilding of the circle, or whether these posts had survived into the second phase and were dug out at a later stage. In the case of 215, it is much more certain that the digging out of the post and the deposition of the cremated remains took place at the end of the first phase, when the 'eastern arc' of the inner post-ring was probably replaced by the 'western arc'. We have argued that the burial of the deceased person in the backfilled post-hole served to establish a connection between them (and presumably their surviving kin) and an important location. Yet while post-hole 215 formed an element of the 'eastern arc', another post-hole containing significant cultural materials was found in the 'western arc', and is particularly difficult to interpret. Feature 084 appeared to represent a single-phase post-hole, within which the post rotted from its core outward, resulting in an unusual v-profiled post-pipe section. The feature contained numerous pottery sherds, which were concentrated in the uppermost fills, 003 and 077, although individual pot fragments were found deeper into the profile, and even in the primary packing. The mechanisms by which the pottery became dispersed through the fills of 084 are difficult to discern, although

the process of rotting-out was doubtless involved. It may also be that post-depositional processes displaced individual fragments. The picture is further complicated by the intimate relationship between 084 and 050, the small pit located immediately to the west of the post-hole, just beyond the post-ramp (Fig. 11.12). 050 produced 44 sherds from six Grooved Ware vessels, four of which were also represented amongst the pottery in 084. It may be that the two features were contemporary, and were filled at the same time from a common source, whether as a by-product of activities that had taken place nearby, or from a surface midden. Alternatively, 050 might have been dug and filled at a time when some form of disturbance of the fill of 084 took place. 050 might then have had the status of a commemorative deposit, a form of veneration. Finally, it is possible that sherds and other material from the surface became incorporated in 084 as the post rotted out. This would not easily explain why sherds were found in the primary packing of the feature however. None the less, there were some differences between the lithic assemblages from the two features. While 050 contained a random selection of struck flakes, 084 produced a series of items connected with primary core reduction, including core fragments and a trimming flake. If this material represents a more coherent assemblage related to a distinct stage within the lithic reduction sequence, and if the processes affecting lithics and ceramics in these contexts were related, it is possible that the artefacts in 084 were deposited in the aftermath of a specific event, while those from 050 were a more general accumulation of ambient and curated material.

Mention of feature 050 introduces the theme of deposition in pits. 050 contained sherds from the same vessels as post-holes 084 and 054, as well as the shallow Beaker-related feature 032, while pits 3074 and 3112, located further to the north, contained sherds from the same vessels as the ramp of post-hole 579/619 and the recut in post-hole 792. This may mean that these features were broadly contemporary, although sherds might have entered any of these features after a period of curation. Grooved Ware pits often have highly structured contents, and they are sometimes understood as the consequence of 'tidying up' after episodes of occupation, or as commemorative deposits in significant locations (Garrow 2006: 80). But rather than features that post-dated the main activity at the enclosure, the pits at Dunragit seem to have been intimately connected with the cutting, filling and recutting of the post-holes. We have seen that this is particularly the case with 050, which was closely juxtaposed with post-hole 084, as well as containing fragments from the same pottery vessels. Pits 3074 and 3112 were rather small features (even allowing for subsoil erosion), and yet it is probable that the deposition of material in them was quite significant. It may also be of some importance that these two features were located within the northern terminal of the cursus, given that there is a recurring pattern of Grooved Ware pits being dug in and around much earlier monuments and structures, including causewayed enclosures and timber halls (e.g. Pryor 1998: 111; Hey, Mulville and Robinson 2003: 86). One further pit that may be worthy of some consideration was 032, a very shallow feature that contained the only Beaker pottery from the site. This was undoubtedly the last surviving fragment of what must originally have been a more substantial, if shallow, pit. Grooved Ware and Beaker pottery were recovered from the uppermost of three fills, and it is highly probable that more extensive cultural material had been lost in the erosion of this deposit. There have been numerous finds of Beaker pottery from the Luce Bay area (see Chapter 2), and while its presence in 032 may be fortuitous, it may also be an example of the very common practice of the deliberate introduction of Beaker-age material into monuments of earlier date (Clarke, Cowie and Foxon 1985: 88).

In Trench J, the most westerly part of the palisaded enclosure to be investigated, we have seen that the major posts of the middle post-ring were relatively scarce, and that the distinction between major and minor posts was not as clear as elsewhere. This is interesting, for as we have also noted, in this part of the site the *inner* ring post-holes were smaller, and there seem to have been some very small posts as well. Once again, this supports the notion that distinct groups of people may have built different parts of the enclosure in slightly different ways. Most of the middle ring post-holes in Trench J, such as 4260, 4047 and 4204, lacked post-ramps. However, this need not mean that the main timber uprights were any smaller in this area, and the differences in constructional technique could be interpreted in terms of the activity of separate work-gangs. However, one of the more substantial middle ring posts in Trench J stood out as quite distinct from the others. This was 4110, a deep post-hole with a ramp on the western side. This was by some margin the largest middle ring post-hole that was investigated in all four seasons of work at Dunragit. Importantly, this feature cut one of the post-holes of the cursus monument, 4157, and this represents the only example of the physical intersection of the two major Neolithic monuments observed at Dunragit. This stratigraphic relationship gave the reassuring confirmation that the cursus (presumably Earlier Neolithic in date) was earlier than the enclosure. But the relationship had a more interesting dimension, for feature 4110 contained a large polished stone axe (FN 1462). The axe is of a coarse, gritty wacke sandstone, and the cutting edge had been broken off from it, perhaps deliberately (see Chapter 7). Thus, this feature is quite unusual, in that it is both the only post-hole of the middle ring of this size, and the only one to contain any significant item of material culture, aside from two sherds of Grooved Ware and a single flint flake.

That this feature should be located at the precise point where the enclosure cuts across the cursus seems unlikely to have been a matter of chance. It is possible that the larger post and the deliberately deposited axe were a means of acknowledging or commemorating the relationship between the new monument and the old. The burning of the upright timbers of the Dunragit cursus implies that it was short-lived, yet at precisely the point where its western side intersected with the middle post-ring of the enclosure, an unusually large post-hole containing an unusually impressive artefact was located. This argues that the post-hole and its contents represented an explicit acknowledgement of the presence of the earlier monument. Now, it may be that the outline of the cursus was somehow recalled over a period of some centuries, but it is perhaps more likely that the collective memory of the structure was imprecise, and that it was the digging of post-hole 4110 into 4157 that alerted the builders of the enclosure that they had encroached on the earlier monument. Fill 4155 was very dark and contained a great deal of charcoal, and this is likely to have been recognised by the person who originally dug feature 4110, even if they had been doing so with an antler pick. It is plausible that although it was deliberately intended to build the palisaded enclosure in the same location as the cursus, the act of digging directly into the cursus post-hole was an inauspicious one. The deposition of the axe in post-hole 4100 might therefore have represented a form of reparation or penance for the damage done to the already ancient structure. The relationship between features 4100 and 4157 underlines the point that the earlier existence of the cursus may have been a factor influencing the location of the Dunragit enclosure. This kind of relationship with a cursus is shared by certain henges. At Thornborough and Maxey the henge lay directly over the cursus (Vatcher 1960; Harding 2013; Pryor 1984), but there are also close henge-and-cursus associations at Rudston, Dorchester and Llandegai, not to mention Stonehenge and Durrington Walls (Atkinson, Piggott and Sandars 1951; Dymond 1966; Houlder 1968; RCHM 1979). An earlier form of monument may have provided precedent and legitimacy for a later one.

The insertion of cultural material and cremation burials into post-removal craters, the creation of pit deposits, and the relationship between the enclosure and the cursus all point to the way in which the structure was freighted with memory. Noble and Brophy (2011b: 80) argue that palisaded enclosures might initially have been constructed with a particular gathering or event in mind, but that subsequently they would gradually have fallen into dilapidation and decay. It may be that the burning and removal of individual posts did not all take place at the same time, even if the replacement of the inner post-ring had been a single, coordinated episode. The various acts of deposition, including the digging and filling of a number of pits, would then have punctuated the period over which the enclosure was descending into disarray. A specific gap in a post-line might then be understood to mark the place where a cremated body had been placed, or where the pots employed in a memorable feast had been buried. Increasingly, the enclosure would have taken on the character of a kind of 'theatre of memory', so that activities that took place were contextualised in relation to past happenings and their physical traces. This emphasis on remembering past events and persons might not only have been the means by which performances and ceremonies that took place inside the enclosure achieved sanction and validity. The monument may also have progressively become a repository for the collective history of an extended social group, or series of groups.

The palisaded enclosure: architecture and social action

Given that it was composed of a combination of large wooden uprights and impermeable fences or screens, an important aspect of the palisaded enclosure at Dunragit is the way in which it provided opportunities for people

to gather, to stand in relation to one another, and to move and process within defined areas, while at the same time restricting both movement and vision. In this respect the monument was related to a variety of other Later Neolithic architectural forms, including timber and stone circles, avenues, houses and henge monuments. However, it has been argued that at many henge monuments the bank and ditch represent late structural elements, added as an act of closure or sanctification after activity at the site had ceased (Gibson 2010: 244). From this point of view, the internal ditch and external bank that characterise henge monuments can be explained as a means of containment, 'keeping something in' where other kinds of enclosures from causewayed camps to hillforts are generally understood as excluding outsiders or attackers. A henge enclosure might be constructed around a timber circle, a house, or even an auspicious location where some important happening had taken place, but which had left no physical trace. Pollard (2012: 104) offers several examples of sites that began as settlements or temporary occupations, but which eventually took on a sacred or ceremonial character, as they were enclosed within a henge bank and ditch. In these cases, the residues of domestic activity may have taken on a kind of spiritual power than needed to be harnessed and contained. Ultimately, this means that rather than a henge being a particular kind of monument, 'henging' was a practice, something that happened to places and structures of a variety of different kinds (Brophy and Noble 2012: 32). It would follow from this that our analysis of how henges might have been used should focus less on the bank and ditch themselves than on the architectural elements that they enclosed, since these will often have operated in isolation prior to the closing event. While the entrances to henge monuments would have enabled pre-existing architecture to be 'visited', the conditions under which this would have taken place were transformed by the creation of the enclosure.

If henging could be applied to different *kinds* of sites, it is open to question whether palisaded sites with and without henge-style ditches were fundamentally similar or different monuments. At Mount Pleasant in Dorset, a very substantial palisaded enclosure was constructed inside a henge monument. According to the excavator, the timber enclosure was considerably later than the henge bank and ditch, having been constructed in the twenty-second century BC (Wainwright 1979: 239). However, Whittle (1997a: 158) disputes the chronology of the palisade. The two radiocarbon dates from the Mount Pleasant palisade were on charcoal and antler, the former from the upper part of one of the post-pipes, the latter from the packing (Wainwright 1979: 58–9). Whittle draws attention to the mixed character of the fills in the palisade trench, and suggests that the palisade and the henge ditch might actually have been contemporary (1997a: 160). If we are ready to accept that the Mount

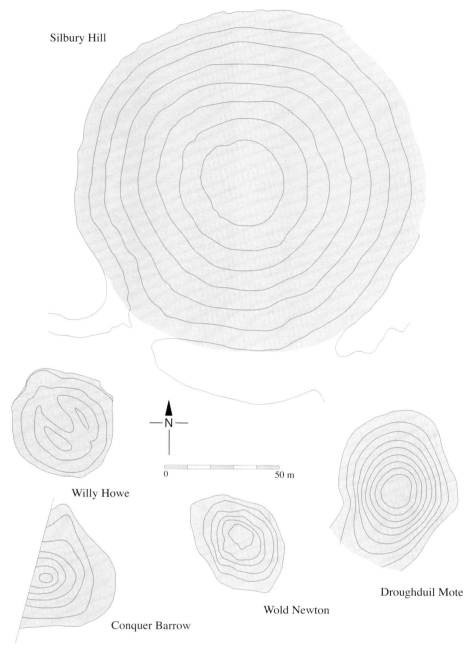

Silbury Hill

Willy Howe

Conquer Barrow

Wold Newton

Droughduil Mote

Figure 11.13 Comparative plans of large prehistoric mounds

Pleasant palisade was not a Beaker-era monument, but formed part of the Grooved Ware-associated activity on the site, comparable with the similar monuments at West Kennet, then we might go so far as to argue that the palisade was actually primary, and the ditch and bank an addition. Just as at other sites, then, the Mount Pleasant enclosure might have been 'henged' after it fell out of use. An important argument against this, however, is that while the palisade enclosure had only two entrances, the henge enclosure had four, two of which correspond with those in the palisade. At Greyhound Yard in Dorchester,

a massive ring of ramped wooden posts was surrounded by a very minimal ditch (Woodward, Davies and Graham 1984; 1993). It is unclear whether the ditch was dug at the same time as the post-holes, or whether it too represented a closing statement enacted when the use of the enclosure was discontinued. Either of these sites might be understood as a 'henge monument', or as a palisaded enclosure that had been 'henged'.

Depending upon how we read the sequences at these two sites, we might choose to see Dunragit as similar to or different from each. Arguably, it might be more profitable to address the entire suite of Late Neolithic architectural forms as an interrelated whole, rather than sorting them into a series of mutually exclusive types, particularly if we wish to consider the place of these forms within their landscapes, and the ways in which they were occupied and moved through. At Dunragit as at other sites some spaces were secluded, while others afforded enhanced visibility for numbers of people. This suggests that these structures were used for performances that involved some acts or events that were highly secretive, and others that were intended to be witnessed by many persons. Some of these spaces could accommodate large congregations, others would only admit a small minority of a population. Indeed, one of the most important aspects of these sites was that they probably represented large expanses of ground that had been cleared of trees and vegetation (Noble and Brophy 2011b: 80). As massive clearances they would have afforded the opportunity for very large numbers of people to come together in mutual visibility. If pre-state societies are characterised by face-to-face relations, such an opportunity would have been of critical importance to generating a sense of collective identity and shared purpose.

We have argued already that the Dunragit enclosure was distinguished by an organisation of space in which a central large timber circle served as a focus of attention, which was contained within a continuous fence or palisade. This spatial order was reflected in patterns of deposition, which were focused on the post-holes of the inner post-ring. The same pattern was apparently indicated by the results of the micromorphological analysis of sediments from the post-holes of the two innermost post-rings. Notably, charcoal fragments were quite scarce in the post-holes of the middle ring, features 099 and 035. By contrast, appreciable quantities of charcoal came from the fills of the inner ring post-holes 084, 215 and especially 087. We have seen already that in the case of post-hole 215 the charcoal fragments were relatively large and unabraded, and it may be that the pyre for the cremation burial in that feature had burned nearby. In any case, it is possible that fires (whether culinary or funerary) were concentrated within the inner post-ring. Helen Lewis (this volume, Chapter 9) suggests that one of the sources of ambient charcoal in the enclosure may have been the preparation of posts for erection. Given that a number of posts did indeed have charred tips, this is almost certainly part of the answer. However, this alone does not explain the disparity between the inner and the middle post-rings. Moreover, the charcoal often seems to be especially dense in the silting deposits in the upper parts of the post-hole profiles. While other micro-indicators of human activity were scarce in the post-hole fills, it none the less seems plausible that groups of people gathered together inside the enclosure cooked feasts over open fires, and perhaps also cremated their dead within the space defined by the great timber circle.

However, social and spatial division was as important as gathering together. At West Kennet in Wiltshire the two large palisaded enclosures were accompanied by four smaller concentrically organised structures, set both inside and outside of the palisades (Whittle 1997a: 61). The Forteviot palisaded enclosure is the focus for a group of ring-ditches and small henges, two of the latter having external post circles (St Joseph 1978; Brophy and Noble 2012). Excavation has demonstrated that in one case the post circle preceded the henge, and enclosed a Neolithic cremation cemetery (Noble and Brophy 2011a: 795). These features resemble a structure located immediately to the southwest of the Dunragit enclosure, and not yet investigated at the time of writing (Fig. 1.6). It is unfortunate that our Trenches C and D were relatively inconclusive, for it would be useful to know more about the lesser structures associated with the palisaded enclosure. At Meldon Bridge, there was an Early Bronze Age cremation cemetery located inside the enclosure (Speak and Burgess 1999: 24). This kind of later appropriation of Neolithic monuments is a familiar pattern (Bradley 2002). It is likely that some of the ring-ditch features associated with palisaded enclosures are later funerary monuments. Others, though, were spaces that were integral to the Late Neolithic architecture, and they potentially have more to tell us about the practices that were engaged in at these sites. As suggested above, the large open space of the palisaded enclosure, and the substantial gatherings that it would have admitted were probably complemented by smaller and more exclusive spaces. One such may have been the summit of the Droughduil mound.

Droughduil Mote

Although its name seems to suggest otherwise, Droughduil Mote would be morphologically uncharacteristic for a medieval castle mound, as it lacks the flattened profile of local examples such as Motte Slapp at Sandhead or Druchtag near Port William, as well as having an unusually low-lying location. It is possible that the identification of the site as a castle mound was informed by the imperative to find 'missing' medieval defences in lowland Scotland during the twentieth century. In some cases, this resulted in the re-interpretation of structures that had previously been described as tumuli (Linge 1987: 23). When the aerial photographic plot of the Dunragit complex was projected onto the map of the area the relationship between the mound and the palisaded enclosures could readily be appreciated: the avenue-like entrance of the middle ring aligned almost precisely on the mote. This might have been entirely fortuitous, but there is a recurring connection between large, flat-topped prehistoric mounds and Late Neolithic enclosures. Silbury Hill, for instance, lies close to both the Avebury henge and the West Kennet palisade enclosures (Whittle 1997a: 5). At Knowlton in Dorset, a very large round barrow stands amongst a group of henges of varying sizes. The Hatfield Barrow, a colossal round mound, originally lay within the great henge at Marden in the Vale of Pewsey (Wainwright 1971). The Conquer Barrow stands on (or has been incorporated into) the bank of the Mount Pleasant henge in southern Dorset, adjacent to the palisade enclosure that lies within the earthwork and seemingly post-dates it (Wainwright 1979). The modified natural hilltop of Castle Hills, near to the palisaded enclosure at Marne Barracks, Catterick in Yorkshire, may be another example (Hale, Platell and Millard 2009: 267).

Another locational factor that Droughduil Mote has in common with the large mounds of known or presumed Neolithic date lies in their proximity to water. Silbury Hill is situated close to Swallowhead Springs, and its huge ditch often fills with water in winter, while the Hatfield Barrow and its surrounding enclosure are adjacent to the River Avon (Barber *et al.* 2010: 165). The Marlborough Mound, now securely dated to the mid-third millennium BC, is located within a bend in the River Kennet (Leary *et al.* 2013: 156). Droughduil Mote today sits within a loop in Piltanton Burn, which runs out to sea through Luce Sands. However, the work of Tipping, Smith and Jordan (this volume, Chapter 5) has demonstrated that the mound is virtually surrounded by estuarine deposits. Throughout the period from the mid-sixth to the mid-third millennia BC the sea-level was relatively stable, and appreciably higher than today. During high tides, the area between the Droughduil mound and the Dunragit enclosure, the Whitecrook Basin, would have filled with water, which would have entirely drained at the lowest tides. At times, the mound would have appeared to stand on a small island, when viewed from the enclosure. This recurring connection with water may simply have reflected the importance of inter-regional contacts that were mediated by rivers and the sea during the Later Neolithic, but they might also have had a symbolic or cosmological significance. Indeed, it has been noted that the ditches of henge monuments would often have contained standing water, so that the Droughduil mound may effectively have been set within a barrier that was equivalent to a henge ditch (Richards 1996: 332).

Recent work at Silbury Hill has highlighted the complexity and protracted duration of its construction, which may have taken several generations to complete. The implication of this is that the final form of the monument may have been arrived at in the course of building, rather than having been predetermined or 'designed' (Leary 2010: 148). Silbury began as a small gravel mound, which was enclosed within a stake circle that was itself infilled with turves and clayey soil. The growing mound was contained within a series of chalk banks, and a large surrounding ditch, which was possibly causewayed, and comparable with those at Stonehenge

and Flagstones in Dorset, and perhaps that at Duggleby Howe as well (Leary and Field 2010: 106; Kinnes *et al.* 1983). Eventually, after several episodes of recutting and renewal, this ditch was engulfed by the chalk mound, and a new and more massive ditch dug to contain the final structure. Other large Late Neolithic mounds may also have had elaborate structural histories. The Great Barrow at Knowlton is surrounded by two separate concentric ditches, probably representing distinct phases of construction, and it is possible that the mound stands within a former henge monument (Barber *et al.* 2010: 155). So at both Silbury and Knowlton the presence of a cut boundary seems to have been of considerable importance. All of this ostensibly makes the absence of any surrounding ditch at Droughduil all the more remarkable. Arguably, our initial research design was too much influenced by what was already known about Late Neolithic mounds, but the failure of any of the test-pits radiating from the mound to identify a ditch (despite being cut to a depth of 2 metres in some cases) is none the less a significant finding. As we have already suggested, it may be that the position of the mound on a sandy eminence that was periodically cut off from the Dunragit enclosure by standing water may have obviated the need for a ditch. It appears that the mound was built of material scraped up from the surface, and the presence of laminated deposits at the foot of the construction suggests that this was heaped onto the natural topography. However, there is no particular reason to suppose that this need have taken place as a single operation, and it is entirely possible that a more invasive cutting into the mound material, as opposed to simply exposing the mound surface, might reveal considerable structural complexity. Like Silbury, the Droughduil mound may have been quite different in character at different stages in its development.

The oval plan of the mound, with a long axis running from north to south, is not immediately obvious on the surface. It may be more likely that this was a consequence of the topography, and the way that the mound emerged from the underlying natural sandy knoll, than that it was designed in this way in advance. In any case, the flat-topped mound is not dissimilar from a series of large prehistoric barrows in western Scotland, if rather larger (Linge 1987: 24). The surface that now presents itself is composed of a series of deposits of wind-blown sand, reflecting the same processes of erosion and deposition that results in the ceaseless movement of the dunes to the south. It was surprising that the removal of the first of these deposits revealed a mass of stone, tumbling from the summit down the side of the mound. This material proved to have been derived from the cairn on the summit of the mound, which is now entirely invisible. The construction of the cairn was revealing: it was composed of a core of large rounded boulders beneath a mass of more angular stones, and appeared to be bounded within a kerb. As such, it was very similar indeed to Mid Gleniron A, which is reasonably securely dated to the Early Bronze Age (Corcoran 1969b: 91). The tiny fragments of burnt bone and the two flint scrapers found amongst the stones of the Droughduil cairn suggest that much the same date may apply here. A similar conclusion is indicated by the OSL date of 1810±240 BC from the thick layer of wind-blown sand that sealed the cairn. That so much stone had collapsed down the side of the mound probably indicates that the cairn was originally quite tall, and would have represented a highly conspicuous feature in its elevated position.

It was the multiple deposits of wind-blown sand, as well as the collapsed stone, that were responsible for the preservation of the original profile of the mound, and perhaps for enhancing its stability. The sand that lay stratigraphically beneath the cairn peeled off to reveal the much more densely packed sand of the mound surface. It was quite remarkable that this surface should form a series of shallow steps. One immediate suspicion might be that the mound had been landscaped in historic times, as happened at the Marlborough Mound during the seventeenth century (Whittle 1997a: 170). However, the steps were securely stratified beneath the cairn material. If the cairn was prehistoric, then the steps could not be later, and the same attribution is supported by the suite of OSL dates from wind-blown sand contexts. Individual spot samples gave very encouraging results: the second millennium date from beneath the cairn, and a date of 2640±400 BC from sand within one of the ledges, for instance. But more impressive was the coherent sequence of dates from the laminated sands at the foot of the mound. Here, six results ran in chronological order, from a determination of 1200 BC immediately below the cairn collapse in succession back to the mid-third millennium BC. While the high standard deviation means that we should not view this as in any sense a precise determination, it is at least a broad indication that the Droughduil mound fits into the same general chronological horizon as the Dunragit enclosure, rather than the twelfth or thirteenth century AD.

While the surface beneath the wind-blown sand was pure, hard-packed sand, it is to be presumed that at one time some kind of revetment must have existed, whether of timber of turf. None the less, it is curious that no trace of such a revetment survived. Although three distinct steps were revealed, the increasing depth of the wind-blown sand deposits further down the mound had the consequence that the entire mound surface was not revealed, and this means that further steps may have existed. Indeed, little was revealed of the skirt of the mound, and the laminated deposits mentioned above were encountered outwith the area of the mound as it is visible on the present-day land surface. The pitch of these deposits from east to west suggests that they may have built up after the construction of the mound, as loose sand was washed off its surface and accumulated below. The flat top and stepped sites

of the mound invite comparison with Silbury Hill, and recent work at that site makes the comparison a legitimate one. The construction of Silbury Hill began in the later third millennium BC, and until recently, working with the materials from Atkinson's excavations, it was possible to argue that construction was played out over several hundreds of years (Bayliss, McAvoy and Whittle 2007: 27). However, the high quality evidence recovered from the reinvestigation in 2007 facilitated a more precise dating of the site, which suggests that Silbury was built over the period between 2450 and 2350 BC (Leary and Field 2012: 112). This places the monument firmly at the end of the Late Neolithic and the beginning of the Beaker era, shortly after the main stone phase at Stonehenge and the principal activity at Durrington Walls. If the Droughduil mound had indeed been contemporary with the Dunragit enclosure, in the second quarter of the third millennium BC, it would then have been a little earlier than Silbury – and the latter might actually have drawn inspiration from it. Other large mounds associated with Late Neolithic monumental complexes may have been of comparable date, and may actually have predated the henge monuments with which they were juxtaposed. The ditch of the Conquer Barrow, for instance, produced a date in the earlier third millennium BC, and rather than being perched on top of the bank of the Mount Pleasant henge, might have been accommodated into the form of the later enclosure (Barber *et al.* 2010: 159). However, the stepped profile of the Droughduil mound might equally profitably be compared with some of the passage graves of southern Brittany, such as the Table des Marchand and Quéric-la-Lande (L'Helgouach 1965: 27). In either case, it is possible that the Droughduil mound was deliberately constructed in such a way as to refer to distant places, which only a few of its builders and users might ever have visited.

Discussing Silbury Hill, John Barrett once argued that a flat-topped mound might have represent a raised platform, which would allow a privileged group of people to stand in an elevated position in relation to a congregation gathered in an enclosure, such as the Avebury henge (1994: 31). In the case of Silbury this interpretation may be compromised by the possibility that the top of the mound might have been truncated by later activity (Leary 2010: 147). However, in relation to Droughduil the argument may be considerably more powerful. A person or group standing on top of the mound would have been silhouetted against the sky from the point of view of anyone positioned inside the Dunragit enclosure, with only the sand dunes and the sea behind them. Moreover, seen from the centre of the enclosure they would have been framed by the entrance avenue of the middle post-ring. Further, at particular times this view would have taken in the volatile tidal waters of the Whitecrook Basin, separating the mound from the enclosure.

The Dunragit/Droughduil complex suggests a complementary role for enclosures and large mounds in the third millennium BC. It is conceivable that the mound did serve as an elevated location from which a pre-eminent group could observe a congregation gathered in the enclosure, while achieving recognition for their authority. Equally, the alignment of the middle ring entrance could have served to define a pattern of movement between the two structures. Of course, at particular times this passage would have involved passing through or over standing water in the Whitecrook Basin. This suggests two things. Either the tidal conditions may have laid down temporal conditions when it was appropriate to move between the two monuments, or the crossing of water may actually have been a significant element in any activities that united the two structures. We can compare this situation with the recent discussion of the relationship between Stonehenge and Durrington Walls in Wiltshire. Here, the discovery of the avenue that connects the Durrington Walls henge with the River Avon has demonstrated that the two monuments were integrated through a pattern of movement that incorporated the river itself (Parker Pearson 2012: 156). At midsummer and midwinter, people (or indeed metaphysical entities, such as the spirits of the recently deceased) may have been intended to process from the southern timber circle at Durrington to the Stonehenge stones, or vice-versa, following the route of the river. Similarly, the henge monument of the Pict's Knowe near Dumfries was located on a small sandy island in a low-lying valley bottom. As at Droughduil/Dunragit, higher sea-levels in the Neolithic and Bronze Age would have had the consequence that the henge was surrounded by a saltmarsh (Thomas 2007a: 142). In all of these examples, moving between and gaining access to Late Neolithic monuments involved passage through or over water. It seems probable that the presence of standing or moving bodies of water influenced the location of these structures, deliberately creating conditions under which the use of the monuments would involve encounter with water. In effect, the natural topography was incorporated into monumental architecture. This might simply have been a means of heightening the physical experience of the place, but it might equally have carried the connotations of transformation or purification, so that a person would arrive at a mound or enclosure in a different spiritual state from the one in which they had set out (Strang 2004: 92). In the case of Dunragit and Droughduil, passing out of the enclosure along the entrance passage, and walking down into the Whitecrook Basin and then through the water before climbing the mound might have been understood as a journey of transition or initiation.

It is also possible that very large round mounds, not necessarily with any funerary role, formed another element in the suite of cultural innovations that developed in the north some time before they were adopted in southern England. The inspiration for such mounds might have been found either in the passage grave tradition or the large earthen round mounds of Scotland and Yorkshire (Gibson and Bayliss 2010; Sheridan 2010). Grooved Ware, small cellular houses and their larger, non-domestic derivatives, and palisaded enclosures are all implicated in a set of inter-regional developments that seem to have germinated in the north and west, and are yet to be fully explained (Thomas 2010: 6). We will discuss these issues further below.

We have argued that the Droughduil was a prehistoric mound rather than a medieval motte. Strikingly, there is no evidence that the site was even re-used as a castle mound. There was not a single medieval artefact recovered from the 2002 excavation. This can be compared, as an example, with the modest investigation of the motte at Roberton on Clydesdale, which produced very considerable quantities of medieval pottery, largely jugs of southern Scottish white quartz-tempered wares (Haggarty and Tabraham 1982: 58). In contrast with the absence of medieval activity, an entirely unexpected aspect of the work at Droughduil was the discovery of the small building of eighteenth or nineteenth century date in Trench H, on the summit of the mound. It is possible that this had some functional purpose connected with the agricultural use of the immediate landscape. However, several large glass bottle bases were recovered from the upper part of the cairn collapse, and this suggests a more recreational use. It seems probable that the building was a small folly, used by the local gentry for social gatherings, and selected for the panoramic views that it would have commanded across Luce Sands and the bay (in older editions of the Ordnance Survey maps for the area, the woodland surrounding the mound today is absent). In any case, there can be little doubt over the date of its destruction by Robert Broadfoot. What is less clear is the reason for the demolition, although the structure may simply have become dilapidated and dangerous.

At a more practical level, the significance of the Droughduil mound lies in demonstrating that there is potentially an element of our monumental landscapes that has been underestimated. It is tempting to speculate whether other sites that have been identified as castle mounds might have had an earlier origin, even potentially having been re-used in the medieval era.

Dunragit/Droughduil as a Late Neolithic monumental complex

The Dunragit enclosure, the Droughduil mound and the other attendant structures together represent one of the characteristic 'monumental complexes' of the Late Neolithic, in which a series of diverse architectural forms are clustered together in a landscape. These monuments are generally understood to have been constructed in ways that referred or responded to one another, so that although there may have been no original plan that was played out through the process of building, there is a sense in which the whole gradually gained a degree of coherence or unity. In some parts of Britain, distinct concentrations of monuments had begun to emerge toward the end of the fourth millennium BC (Richards and Thomas 2012). Much later, by the middle of the third millennium BC it seems clear that in some cases a deliberate attempt was being made to impose an overall order, often in the form of a single pattern of movement, onto groups of monuments that had built up in a more haphazard fashion (Gillings *et al.* 2008: 201). The imperative to draw together significant aspects of a landscape within a single experiential or conceptual frame might encompass not only existing monuments, but also residues of former occupations and outstanding topographic features. These tendencies are most developed in the great Wessex complexes of Avebury, Cranborne Chase and Stonehenge/Durrington, in the Boyne valley of Ireland, and on the mainland of Orkney, but the urge to knit together the traces of past activity with distinctive landforms was widespread. Gillings and colleagues (2008: 220) point to the considerable variability in the scale and rate of development of these monumental foci in different parts of Britain and Ireland. They argue that the greater long-term stability of societies in Wessex and Orkney may have enabled them to consistently organise the construction of monumental works. Other interpretations are possible, however: the scale of social networks, the structure of social relations, or the character of authority might all have varied between regions.

Ultimately these arguments can be traced to Colin Renfrew's discussion of the role of emerging social hierarchies in the development of monumental landscapes in Neolithic Wessex (1973). Renfrew contended that groups of large monuments represent emerging centres of political power. Across the centuries of the Neolithic there was a degree of continuity in the function of monuments, in that they reflect the ability of nascent elites to mobilise labour, creating permanent centres that facilitate exchange and redistribution. Increasing levels of social organisation enabled progressively greater quantities of labour to be recruited from within growing populations (Renfrew 1973: 542). This was manifested in the gradual change from earthen long barrows to causewayed enclosures, henge enclosures, and finally a suite of mega-monuments including Silbury Hill and the stone phases at Stonehenge. Monuments became larger, fewer in number, and more centralised, echoing the change from small, acephalous communities to consolidated chiefdoms. In this way, the distribution of monumental structures provided an index of both the scale and the territorial organisation of Neolithic societies. An important criticism of this view is that it renders monuments as the products or outcomes

of the functioning of social systems, which are then understood as having an existence which is prior to and separate from the material world (Barrett 1994: 160). An alternative is to see monument building as a medium through which social relationships are both reproduced and transformed. It is also possible that Renfrew's model exaggerates the degree of centralised monitoring and control of a population that elites can achieve in pre-state societies (Barrett 1994: 161).

If internal social evolution, driven by economic intensification and population growth is one way in which we might explain the emergence of monument complexes during the later Neolithic, another lies in external contacts between regions. Addressing artefactual assemblage variation throughout the British Neolithic, Richard Bradley drew attention to the distinctive character of the Grooved Ware complex. Bradley pointed out that Grooved Ware ceramics were shared by regions whose later Neolithic archaeology might otherwise be quite diverse (1982: 35). Grooved Ware pots were not used exclusively in monumental contexts, but Bradley suggested that their use might have been the prerogative of pre-eminent persons, and served as a means of social exclusion. The pots themselves were not exchanged between regions, but the decorative motifs that they bore were circulated between spatially-discrete elites, as part of a system of 'ranked spheres of exchange' in which the monopolisation of access to particular goods and symbols places a restriction on the achievement of high social standing (Bradley 1982: 36). Bradley and Chapman (1986: 128) would later note that a number of 'core areas' with substantial monument complexes within Britain and Ireland were linked by the presence of either Grooved Ware or passage graves, and suggested that maritime contacts may have connected otherwise autonomous communities.

Building on these views, it is possible to argue that the Grooved Ware complex was composed of a series of media that had been extracted from the domestic context and elaborated or magnified. We have noted already that Grooved Ware is intimately connected with a suite of architectural forms that are ultimately based upon the small cellular houses of Orkney (Bradley 2001: 89). Transforming the spatial order of the house into timber circles, palisade enclosures and shrines, and transforming domestic vessels into large, elaborately decorated pots used for collective consumption are argued to be aspects of the creation of an 'imagined community', in which the model of the household is applied to a larger emerging political entity (Thomas 2010: 1). A place for collective gathering, such as the Dunragit enclosure, presented as a 'great house' might then be understood as a means of forging the collective identity of a new social unit. Significantly, many of the aggregation sites of the Later Neolithic are characterised by the consumption of food on a prodigious scale (Parker Pearson *et al.* 2011). The sharing of food and drink, of course, represent a means of enhancing social solidarity, and can foster a sense of shared identity, which might easily be expressed in terms of the membership of a household (Dietler and Hayden 2001). The acidic soils at Dunragit have not preserved the meat bones which might otherwise have littered the site, and the ceramic assemblage is of modest scale when compared to those from Durrington Walls or Mount Pleasant. None the less, the Grooved Ware vessels from Dunragit show extensive evidence of sooting, and some sherds retain organic residues, indicating that they had been extensively used for the preparation and serving of food. But as well as meeting within this space the construction of the monument itself might have been a means of drawing in a dispersed population and establishing bonds of sociality amongst them. Speculatively, we have argued at a number of points in this volume that aspects of the building of the enclosure betray idiosyncrasies that might be related to slightly different traditions of working. Rather than a single homogeneous population, the Dunragit site may have been created by a number of semiautonomous groups, and formed the instrument of their temporary or permanent integration. Palisaded enclosures in Scotland have to date yielded few artefactual finds, and Dunragit is atypical in having produced a Grooved Ware assemblage. None the less, it is reasonable to connect these structures with a new mode of social organisation that was emerging in northern Britain in the earlier third millennium BC.

It has been noted that discussion of 'core areas' in the Neolithic has tended to relegate Scotland to a comparatively peripheral status (Barclay 2001: 14). The recognition of the palisaded enclosures of Scotland does something to redress this impression, demonstrating the emergence of a series of regional centres in the period between 2800 and 2600 BC (Noble and Brophy 2011b: 74). We have noted that the Dunragit complex lies at the confluence of a series of natural routeways: northward up the valley of the Water of Luce, east and west along the Galloway coast, and northwest to Loch Ryan. Much the same can be said of Forteviot, which is situated on the principal route between Loch Tay and the west (Noble and Brophy 2011a: 788). This perhaps strengthens the case that these complexes did not preside over stable political entities with bounded territories, but were located in relation to the seasonal movements of semi-mobile communities, perhaps also attracting pilgrims from further afield. A similar conclusion has been arrived at in Wessex, where strontium isotope analysis of cattle jaws recovered from the settlement that predated the henge bank at Durrington Walls indicate that animals had been brought to the site from a considerable distance. Most of the cattle had been reared off the chalk, and two specimens had come from either Wales or the southwest peninsula (Parker Pearson *et al.* 2009; Balter 2008: 1704).

The development of monument complexes in Neolithic Scotland may thus have been a means by which aspiring elites sought to draw in dispersed and mobile populations, binding them into more enduring social relationships. Such a group might not have been in a position to unilaterally command the construction of monuments, and might have had to rely on a combination of debts, favours, obligations, gifts and oratory in order to persuade others to take part. Such an enterprise would have been risky, and might easily have failed (see Richards 2013: 119–23). But in the process, architectural conditions for the exercise of social authority and the maintenance of collective history and identity were created. While the Scottish palisaded enclosures share a 'family resemblance' their precise histories are rather diverse. The Dunragit enclosure was built on the site of the cursus, and activity in the Early Bronze Age is only hinted at by the presence of a number of ring-ditches on the site, the single cremation burial in Trench E, and the cairn on top of the Droughduil mound. At Meldon Bridge the sequence began with pit digging and the deposition of Impressed Ware pottery, but a cremation cemetery succeeded the enclosure (Speak and Burgess 1999: 15). Forteviot was different again, the enclosure being built around an existing cremation cemetery, which was itself later enclosed within a small henge monument. Finally, an Early Bronze Age dagger grave was inserted into the interior of the henge (Noble and Brophy 2011a: 799). These idiosyncratic sequences of events point to an important feature of the Scottish monuments complexes: the interaction of the local with the supra-regional. Noble and Brophy (2011b: 80) have recently pointed to the use of natural materials and topographic features in the construction of palisaded enclosures. Wooden posts were set upright, and it is possible that these were still visibly tree-like, even in some cases inverted and with their roots still attached, as in the case of the massive central post of the 'Seahenge' timber circle at Holme-Next-the-Sea (Brennand and Taylor 2003: 15). Thus, say Noble and Brophy, the enclosures may have seemed like enormous clearances ringed by trees. Equally, at Meldon Bridge and Leadketty, rivers or streams were employed to form part of the boundary of the enclosure. At Dunragit, as we have seen, the tidal Whitecrook Basin was integral to the overall layout of the complex. What all this suggests is that these structures were radically embedded in their landscapes, apparently emerging from the earth rather than imposed upon it. But the paradox is that in employing exotic forms of monumental architecture (such as the Droughduil mound) and artefacts (notably Grooved Ware, with its motifs derived from passage grave art) these complexes combined this embedding with references to distant places and persons.

Complexes like that at Dunragit brought together the local and the distant, the past and the present, the social collectivity in the enclosure and the sub-groups who could occupy privileged locations. In this way they betray the

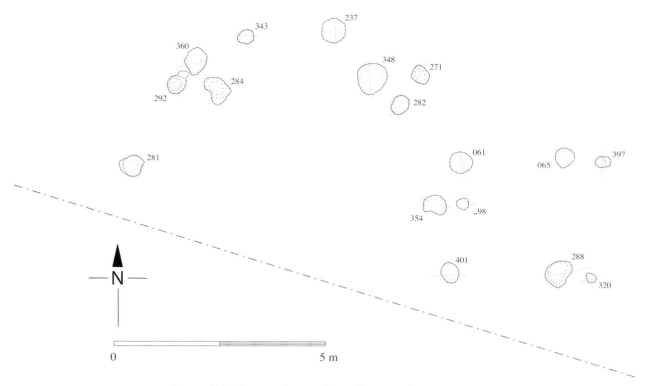

Figure 11.14 Later prehistoric house from Trench A at Dunragit

same urge toward incorporation and integration that has been identified in the monumental landscapes of southern Britain (Gillings *et al*. 2008: 210). Judging purely by the number of posts employed in the construction of the Dunragit enclosure the amount of labour invested in it does not compare with the monumental foci or Wessex and Orkney. None the less, the rebuilding of the inner post-ring indicates that it remained of importance over an appreciable period of time. The presence of the cursus, and the dense concentrations of Impressed Ware pottery on Luce Sands, tell us that it did not spring into the landscape *ex nihilo*. What remains unclear is the degree to which its builders retained a shared identity over the decades following its construction. We saw in Chapter 2 that Luce Bay attracted significant concentrations of Beaker pottery and Early Bronze Age metalwork, but their broader context remains to be explored.

Later occupation

One unexpected feature of the excavations at Dunragit was the discovery of two round houses of apparent late prehistoric date within Trenches A and E, and a possible third in Trench D. This is of note because to date finds of round houses in the southwest of Scotland

have primarily been concentrated in enclosures of one kind or another (Banks 2002: 28). This undoubtedly reflects the comparative archaeological neglect of the region, and points to the potential for the discovery of unenclosed Bronze and Iron Age settlements. None of the round houses identified at Dunragit was complete. That in Trench A was composed of 17 post-holes, and was roughly eight metres in diameter. It had two concentric rings of post-holes, the outer of which was more extensive, and a porch-style four-post entrance. Only nine post-holes of the house in Trench E survived, but it was essentially similar in structure to the Trench A house, with a slightly smaller diameter of about seven metres. The putative structure in Trench D was composed of an arc of four post-holes in the northwest corner of the trench, although it is possible that some of the other small features in this cutting were associated. The diameter of this structure would have been about 5 metres. None of the structures produced any particularly significant finds (one possible chert flake, a fragment of burnt bone and three pieces of burnt clay), and in this respect they are consistent with much of the later prehistoric archaeology of the southwest. Few Iron Age sites have produced many artefacts, whether owing to the loss of bone objects to acidic soil conditions, or a general paucity of pottery and metalwork in the west (Banks 2002: 31).

In the absence of artefacts or other datable material

it is difficult to be precise about the date of the Dunragit buildings. They are similar in size and layout to Iron Age houses at Dryburn Bridge in East Lothian, but they lack the ring-ditch which is a characteristic element of many structures of the period (Harding 2004: 71). The Dunragit houses fit into the typical range of Iron Age round house diameters in northern Britain, of 6–15 metres (Cunliffe 1991: 286). The orientation of their entrances toward the east or southeast is typical of later prehistory as a whole. The comparative regularity of the outer post-ring in each building, and the lack of a central post-hole, suggests the use of ring-beam construction. In all probability the walls of the houses would have been made from hazel or birch hurdle screens, which would have been covered in daub. Recent excavations at Kintore in Aberdeenshire have produced a series of round houses of Bronze and Iron Age date. Of the eight Late Bronze Age houses at Kintore, RH14 compares well with the Dunragit examples, having two concentric rings of posts and a porch, although it also had an internal ring-ditch (Cook and Dunbar 2008:

103). The six Middle Iron Age houses were smaller and simple, although some had porch entrances (Cook and Dunbar 2008: 115). In terms of the typology employed at Kintore, the Dunragit structures would represent Type 5 round houses, with a post-ring, no ring-ditch, and a separate four-post entrance (Cook and Dunbar 2008: 321). The presence of these relatively complex entrances may be significant, since they are not present in all buildings of the period. It has been suggested that the elaboration of the house entrance during the first millennium BC was a means of conspicuous display, drawing attention to the importance of a particular household (Parker Pearson 1996). If so, it is interesting that unenclosed houses like those at Dunragit should have such entrances, if they represented independent households rather than elements of more corporate social groups. If the structure in Trench D was a third house, it is interesting that these buildings were widely dispersed across the excavated area, and this possibly has some significance for later prehistoric settlement in southwest Scotland.

BIBLIOGRAPHY

Admiralty Hydrographic Department 1996 *Admiralty Tide Tables: European Waters Including the Mediterranean Sea, vol. 1.* Taunton: Hydrographer of the Navy.

Alexander, D. and Armit, I. 1992 Excavations at Wellbrae (parcel 249), Strathclyde Region. *North Western Ethylene Pipeline 2 Report 16.* Edinburgh: Centre for Field Archaeology.

Andersen, N.H. 1997 *The Sarup Enclosures: Sarup Vol. 1.* Moesgard: Jysk Arkeologisk Selskab.

Armit, I., Cowie, T. and Ralston, I. 1994 Excavation of pits containing Grooved Ware at Hillend, Clydesdale District, Strathclyde Region. *Proceedings of the Society of Antiquaries of Scotland* 124, 113–27.

Ashmore, P.J. 1999 Radiocarbon dating: avoiding errors by avoiding mixed samples. *Antiquity* 73, 124–30.

Ashmore, P.J. 2007 Radiocarbon dates from the Pict's Knowe, Holywood and Holm. In: J. Thomas, *Place and Memory: Excavations at the Pict's Knowe, Holywood and Holm Farm, Dumfries and Galloway, 1994–8,* 248–59. Oxford: Oxbow.

Atkinson, R.J.C., Piggott, C.M. and Sandars, N. 1951 *Excavations at Dorchester, Oxon.* Oxford: Ashmolean Museum.

Ballin, T.B. 1999 Lithic assemblage. In: S. Speak and C.B. Burgess, Meldon Bridge, Peebleshire. *Proceedings of the Society of Antiquaries of Scotland* 129, 81–93.

Balter, M. 2008 Early Stonehenge pilgrims came from afar, with cattle in tow. *Science* 320, 1704–5.

Banks, I.B.J. 2002 Always the bridesmaid: the Iron Age of south-west Scotland. In: B. Ballin Smith and I.B.J. Banks (eds.) *In the Shadow of the Brochs: The Iron Age in Scotland,* 27–34. Stroud: Tempus.

Barber, M., Winton, H., Stoertz, C., Carpenter, E. and Martin, L. 2010 The brood of Silbury? A remote look at some other sizeable Wessex mounds. In: J. Leary, T. Darvill and D. Field (eds.) *Round Mounds and Monumentality in the British Neolithic and Beyond,* 153–73. Oxford: Oxbow Books.

Barclay, G.J. 2001 'Metropolitan' and 'parochial'/'core' and 'periphery': a historiography of the Neolithic of Scotland. *Proceedings of the Prehistoric Society* 67, 1–18.

Barclay, G.J. 2009 Introduction: a regional agenda? In: K. Brophy and G. Barclay (eds.) *Defining a Regional Neolithic: The Evidence from Britain and Ireland,* 1–4. Oxford: Oxbow.

Barclay, G.J., Brophy, K. and McGregor, G. 2002 Claish, Stirling: an early Neolithic structure in its context. *Proceedings of the Society of Antiquaries of Scotland* 132, 65–137.

Barclay, G.J. and Maxwell, G.J. 1998 *The Cleaven Dyke and Littleour: Monuments in the Neolithic of Tayside.* Edinburgh: Society of Antiquaries of Scotland.

Barclay, G.J. and Russell-White, C.J. 1993 Excavations in the ceremonial complex of the fourth to second millennium at Balfarg/Balbirnie, Glenrothes, Fife. *Proceedings of the Society of Antiquaries of Scotland* 123, 43–210

Barrett, J.C. 1994 *Fragments from Antiquity.* Oxford: Blackwell.

Barrett, J.C., Bradley, R.J. and Green, M. 1991 *Landscape, Monuments and Society: The Prehistory of Cranborne Chase.* Cambridge: Cambridge University Press.

Bass, W.M. 1987 *Human Osteology.* Springfield: Missouri Archaeological Society.

Bayliss, A., McAvoy, F. and Whittle, A. 2007 The world recreated: redating Silbury Hill in its monumental landscape. Antiquity 81, 26–53.

Beadsmoore, E., Garrow, D. and Knight, M. 2010 Refitting Etton: space, time and material culture within a causewayed enclosure in Cambridgeshire. *Proceedings of the Prehistoric Society* 76, 115–34.

Becket, A and MacGregor, G. 2012 Big pit, little pit, big pit, little pit… pit practices in Western Scotland in the fourth millennium. In: H. Anderson-Wymark and J. Thomas (eds.) *Regional Perspectives on Neolithic Pit Deposition: Beyond the Mundane,* 51–62. Oxford: Oxbow.

Beek, G.C. van 1983 *Dental Morphology: An Illustrated Guide.* Bristol: Wright PSG.

Bradley, R.J. 1982 Position and possession: assemblage variation in the British Neolithic. *Oxford Journal of Archaeology* 1, 27–38.

Bradley, R.J. 1997 *Rock Art and the Prehistory of Atlantic Europe.* London: Routledge.

Bradley, R.J. 2001 The birth of architecture. In: W.G. Runciman (ed.) *The Origin of Human Social Institutions,* 69–92. London: British Academy.

Bradley, R.J. 2002 *The Past in Prehistoric Societies.* London: Routledge.

Bradley, R.J. and Chapman, R. 1986 The nature and development of long-distance relations in later Neolithic Britain. In: C. Renfrew and J.F. Cherry (eds.) *Peer Polity Interaction and Socio-Political Change,* 127–36. Cambridge: Cambridge University Press.

Brennand, M. and Taylor, M. 2003 The survey and excavation of a Bronze Age timber circle at Holme-next-the-sea, Norfolk, 1998–9. *Proceedings of the Prehistoric Society* 69, 1–84.

Brindley, A. 1999a Irish Grooved Ware. In: R. Cleal and A. MacSween (eds.) *Grooved Ware in Britain and Ireland,* 23–35. Oxford: Oxbow.

Brindley, A. 1999b Sequence and dating in the Grooved Ware tradition. In: R. Cleal and A. MacSween (eds.) *Grooved Ware in Britain and Ireland,* 133–44. Oxford: Oxbow.

Brink, K. and Hydén, S. 2006 *Citytunnelprojektet: Hyllie Vattentorn*

– Delområde 4 och Palissaden – Delområde 5: Rapport över Arkeologisk Slutundersökning. Malmö: Malmö Kulturmiljö.

Britnell, W. 1982 The excavation of two round barrows at Trelystan, Powys. *Proceedings of the Prehistoric Society* 48, 133–202.

Bronk Ramsey, C. 1995 Radiocarbon calibration and analysis of stratigraphy: the OxCal program. *Radiocarbon* 37, 425–30.

Bronk Ramsey, C. 1998 Probability and dating. *Radiocarbon* 40, 461–74.

Bronk Ramsey, C. 2001 Development of the radiocarbon calibration program. *Radiocarbon* 43, 355–63.

Bronk Ramsey, C. 2009 Bayesian analysis of radiocarbon dates. *Radiocarbon* 51, 337–60.

Brophy, K. 1999 The cursus monuments of Scotland. In: A. Barclay and J. Harding (eds.) *Pathways and Ceremonies: the Cursus Monuments of Neolithic Britain and Ireland,* 119–29. Oxford: Oxbow.

Brophy, K. 2000 Excavations at Milton of Rattray, Blairgowrie. *Tayside and Fife Archaeological Journal* 6, 9–18.

Brophy, K. 2007 From big house to cult house: Early Neolithic timber halls in Scotland. *Proceedings of the Prehistoric Society* 73, 75–96.

Brophy, K. and Noble, G. 2012 Henging, mounding and blocking: the Forteviot henge group. In: A. Gibson (ed.) Enclosing the Neolithic: Recent Studies in Britain and Europe, 21–36. Oxford: British Archaeological Reports s2440.

Brothwell, D. R. 1972 *Digging Up Bones.* London: British Museum (Natural History).

Buck, C.E., Cavanagh, W.G. and Litton, C.D. 1996 *Bayesian Approach to Interpreting Archaeological Data.* Chichester: John Wiley & Sons.

Buikstra, J.E. and Ubelaker, D. H. 1994 *Standards for Data Collection from Human Skeletal Remains.* Fayetteville: Arkansas Archaeological Survey Research Series 44.

Bullock, P., Federoff, N., Jongerius, A., Stoops, G., Tursina, T. and Babel, U. 1985 *Handbook for Soil Thin Section Description.* Wolverhampton: Waine Research Publishers.

Burgess, C.B. 1976 Meldon Bridge: a Neolithic promontory complex near Peebles. In: C. Burgess and R. Miket (eds.) *Settlement and Economy in the Third and Second Millennia BC,* 151–79. Oxford: British Archaeological Reports.

Callander, J.G. 1911 Notice of the discovery of two vessels of clay on the Culbin sands, one containing wheat and the second from a kitchen midden, with a comparison of the Culbin sands and the Glenluce sands and of the relics found on them. *Proceedings of the Society of Antiquaries of Scotland* 45, 158–81.

Callander, J.G. 1929 Scottish Neolithic pottery. *Proceedings of the Society of Antiquaries of Scotland* 63, 29–98.

Callander, J.G. 1933 A short cist containing a Beaker at Newlands, Oyne, Aberdeenshire, and sundry archaeological notes. *Proceedings of the Society of Antiquaries of Scotland* 67, 228–43.

Chapman, J. 1999 Deliberate house-burning in the prehistory of Central and Eastern Europe. In: A. Gustafsson and H. Karlsson (eds.) *Glyfer och Arkeologiska Rum – En Vänbok till Jarl Nordbladh,* 113–26. Göteborg: Göteborg University.

Cherry, P. and Cherry, J. 1997 Two late Mesolithic sites in the Luce Bay area. *Transactions of the Dumfries and Galloway Natural History and Antiquarian Society* 72, 109.

Christie, P. 1963 The Stonehenge Cursus. *Wiltshire Archaeological Magazine* 58, 370–82.

Clark, J.G.D. 1934 Derivative forms of the petit tranchet in Britain. *Archaeological Journal* 91, 34–58.

Clarke, D.L. 1970 *Beaker Pottery of Great Britain and Ireland.* Cambridge: Cambridge University Press.

Clarke, D.V., Cowie, T. and Foxon, A. 1985 *Symbols of Power at the Time of Stonehenge.* Edinburgh: HMSO.

Clough, T. and Cummins, W. 1988 *Stone Axe Studies, Volume Two.* London: Council for British Archaeology.

Coles, D. 2011a Shining water, shifting sand: exotic lithic material from Luce Sands, southwest Scotland. In: A. Saville (ed.) *Flint and Stone in the Neolithic Period,* 139–52. Oxford: Oxbow.

Coles, D. 2011b A welter of flint chips: experimental knapping to investigate local flint from Luce Sand, Wigtownshire. *Lithics* 32, 22–28.

Coles, J. 1963 New aspects of the Mesolithic settlement of south-west Scotland. *Transactions of the Dumfries and Galloway Natural History and Antiquarian Society* 41, 67–97.

Coles, J. 1965 Bronze Age metalwork in Dumfries and Galloway. *Transactions of the Dumfriesshire and Galloway Natural History and Antiquarian Society* 42, 61–98.

Cook, M. and Dunbar, L. 2008 *Rituals, Roundhouses and Romans: Excavations at Kintore, Aberdeenshire 2000–2006.* Edinburgh: Scottish Trust for Archaeological Research.

Cook, M., Ellis, C. and Sheridan, A. 2010 Excavations at Upper Largie Quarry, Argyll & Bute, Scotland: new light on the prehistoric ritual landscape of the Kilmartin Glen. *Proceedings of the Prehistoric Society* 76, 165–212.

Corcoran, J.W.X.P. 1969a Excavation of two chambered cairns at Mid Gleniron Farm, Glenluce, Wigtownshire. *Transactions of the Dumfriesshire and Galloway Natural History and Antiquarian Society* 46, 29–90.

Corcoran, J.W.X.P. 1969b Excavation of two burial cairns at Mid Gleniorn Farm, Glenuce, Wigtownshire. *Transactions of the Dumfriesshire and Galloway Natural History and Antiquarian Society* 46, 91–9.

Corcoran, J.W.X.P. 1972 Multi-period construction and the origins of the chambered long cairn in western Britain and Ireland. In: F. Lynch and C. Burgess (eds.) *Prehistoric Man in Wales and the West,* 31–63. Bath: Adams and Dart.

Cormack, W.F. 1970 A Mesolithic site at Barsalloch, Wigtownshire. *Transactions of the Dumfries and Galloway Natural History and Antiquarian Society* 47, 63–80.

Cormack, W. F. and Coles, J. 1968 A Mesolithic site at Low Clone, Wigtownshire. *Transactions of the Dumfries and Galloway Natural History and Antiquarian Society* 45, 44–72.

Cowie, T. 1993 A survey of the Neolithic pottery of eastern and central Scotland. *Proceedings of the Society of Antiquaries of Scotland* 123, 13–41.

Cowie, T. 1996 Torrs Warren Sands, Galloway: a report on archaeological and palaeoecological investigations undertaken in 1977 and 1979. *Transactions of the Dumfriesshire and Galloway Natural History and Antiquarian Society* 71, 11–105.

Cowie, T. and MacSween, A. 1999 Grooved Ware from Scotland: a review. In: R. Cleal and A. MacSween (eds.) *Grooved Ware in Britain and Ireland,* 48–56. Oxford: Oxbow.

Cummings, V. 2001 *Landscapes in Transition? Exploring the Origins of Monumentality in South-West Wales and South-West Scotland.* PhD Thesis, University of Cardiff.

Cunliffe, B. 1991 *Iron Age Communities in Britain.* London: Routledge.

Cunnington, M.E. 1931 The 'Sanctuary' on Overton Hill, Near Avebury. *Wiltshire Archaeological and Natural History Magazine* 45, 300–35.

Davidson, J.M. 1952 Report on some discoveries at Glenluce Sands, Wigtownshire. *Proceedings of the Society of Antiquaries of Scotland* 86, 43–69.

Dietler, M. and Hayden, B. 2001 Digesting the feast: good to eat, good to drink, good to think. An introduction. In: M. Dietler and B. Hayden (eds.) *Feasts: Archaeological and Ethnographic Perspectives on Food, Politics, and Power,* 1–20. Tuscaloosa: University of Alabama Press.

Dixon, P. 1988 The Neolithic settlements on Crickley Hill. In: C. Burgess, P. Topping, C. Mordant and M. Madison (eds.) *Enclosures and Defences in the Neolithic of Western Europe,* 75–88. Oxford: British Archaeological Reports s403.

Donahue, R. 1999 Microwear analysis of the flint artefacts from Upper Ninepence. In: A. Gibson, *The Walton Basin Project: Excavation and Survey in a Prehistoric Landscape 1993–7,* 100–11. York: Council for British Archaeology.

Dymond, D.P. 1966 Ritual monuments at Rudston, East Yorkshire, England. *Proceedings of the Prehistoric Society* 32, 86–95.

Edwards, K. 1996. The contribution of Tom Affleck to the study of the Mesolithic of southwest Scotland. In: T. Pollard and A. Morrison (eds.), *The Early Prehistory of Scotland,* 108–22. Edinburgh: Edinburgh University Press.

Eogan, G. and Roche, H. 1994 A Grooved Ware wooden structure at Knowth, Boyne Valley, Ireland. *Antiquity* 68, 322–30.

Eogan, G. and Roche, H. 2002 Irish palisade enclosures – a long story. In: A. Gibson (ed.) *Behind Wooden Walls: Neolithic Palisaded Enclosures in Europe,* 24–7. Oxford: British Archaeological Reports s1013.

Evans, C. 1988 Monuments and analogy: the interpretation of causewayed enclosures. In: C. Burgess, P. Topping, C. Mordant and M. Maddison (eds.) *Enclosures and Defences in the Neolithic of Western Europe,* 21–46. Oxford: British Archaeological Reports s403.

Fairweather, I. and Ralston, I.B.M. 1993 The Neolithic timber hall at Balbridie, Grampian Region, Scotland: the building, the date, the plant macrofossils. *Antiquity* 67, 313–24.

Feachem, R.W. 1956 Iron Age and early medieval monuments in Galloway and Dumfriesshire. Transactions of the Dumfriesshire Galloway Natural History and Antiquarian Society 33, 58–65.

Fenton, M.B. 1988 The petrological identification of stone battle-axes and axe-hammers from Scotland. In: T.H. McK Clough and W.A. Cummins (eds.) *Stone Axe Studies Volume 2,* 92–132. London: Council for British Archaeology Research Report 67.

Fox, J.J. 1993 Memories of ridgepoles and crossbeams: the categorical foundations of a Rotinese cultural design. In: J.J. Fox (ed.) Inside Austronesian Houses: Perspectives on Domestic Designs for Living, 140–79. Canberra: Australian National University.

Garrow, D. 2006 *Pits, Settlement and Deposition during the Neolithic and Early Bronze Age in East Anglia.* Oxford: British Archaeological Reports 414.

Garrow, D. 2012 Odd deposits and average practice. A critical history of the concept of structured deposition. *Archaeological Dialogues* 19, 85–115.

Garwood, P. 1999 Grooved Ware in southern Britain: chronology and interpretation. In: R. Cleal and A. MacSween (eds.) *Grooved Ware in Britain and Ireland,* 145–76. Oxford: Oxbow.

Gibson, A. 1982 *Beaker Domestic Sites: a Study in the Domestic Pottery of the Late Third and Early Second Millennia BC in the British Isles.* Oxford: British Archaeological Reports 107.

Gibson, A. 1994 The excavation of the Sarn-Y-Bryn-Caled cursus complex Welshpool, Powys, and the timber circles of Great Britain and Ireland. *Proceedings of the Prehistoric Society* 60, 143–24.

Gibson, A. 1998 Hindwell and the Neolithic palisaded sites of Britain and Ireland. In: A. Gibson and D. Simpson (eds.) *Prehistoric Ritual and Religion,* 68–79. London: Sutton.

Gibson, A. 1999 *The Walton Basin Project.* London: Council for British Archaeology Research Report 118.

Gibson, A. 2002 The later Neolithic palisaded sites of Britain. In: A. Gibson (ed.) *Behind Wooden Walls: Neolithic Palisaded Enclosures in Europe,* 5–23. Oxford: British Archaeological Reports s1013.

Gibson, A. 2010 Excavation and survey at Dyffryn Lane henge complex, Powys, and a reconsideration of the dating of henges. *Proceedings of the Prehistoric Society* 76, 213–48.

Gibson, A. and Bayliss, A. 2010 Recent work on the Neolithic round barrows of the Great Wold Valley, Yorkshire. In: J. Leary, T. Darvill and D. Field (eds.) *Round Mounds and Monumentality in the British Neolithic and Beyond,* 72–107. Oxford: Oxbow Books.

Gillings, M., Pollard, J., Wheatley, D. and Peterson, R. 2008 *Landscape of the Megaliths: Excavation and Fieldwork on the Avebury Monuments, 1997–2003.* Oxford: Oxbow.

Goldberg, P. and Macphail, R.I. 2006 *Practical and Theoretical Geoarchaeology.* Malden: Blackwell.

Green, H.S. 1984. Flint Arrowheads: Typology and Interpretation. *Lithics* 5: 19–39

Green, M. 2000 *A Landscape Revealed: 10,000 Years on a Chalkland Farm.* Stroud: Tempus.

Greenwell, W. 1877 *British Barrows: A Record of the Examination of Sepulchral Mounds in Various Parts of England.* Oxford: Clarendon.

Grogan, E. and Roche, H. 2002 Irish palisaded enclosures – a long story. In: A. Gibson (ed.) *Behind Wooden Walls: Neolithic Palisaded Enclosures in Europe,* 24–7. Oxford: British Archaeological Reports s1013.

Haggarty, G, and Tabraham, C. 1982 Excavation of a motte near Roberton, Clydesdale, 1979. *Transactions of the Dumfriesshire and Galloway Natural History and Antiquarian Society* 57, 51–63.

Hale, D., Platell, A. and Millard, A. 2009 A Late Neolithic palisaded enclosure at Marne Baracks, Catterick, North Yorkshire. *Proceedings of the Prehistoric Society* 75, 265–305.

Halliday, S. 2002 Excavations at a Neolithic enclosure at Castle Menzies, Aberfeldy, Perthshire. *Tayside and Fife Archaeological Journal* 8, 10–18.

Harding, D.W. 2004 *The Iron Age in Northern Britain: Celts and Romans, Natives and Invaders.* London: Routledge.

Harding, J. 2013 *Cult, Religion, and Pilgrimage: Archaeological Investigations at the Neolithic and Bronze Age Monument Complex of Thornborough, North Yorkshire.* London: Council for British Archaeology.

Harding, J. and Barclay, A. 1999 An introduction to the cursus monuments of Neolithic Britain and Ireland. In: A. Barclay & J. Harding (eds.) *Pathways and Ceremonies: the Cursus Monuments of Britain and Ireland,* 1–10. Oxford: Oxbow Books.

Hartwell, B. 1998 The Ballynahatty complex. In: A. Gibson and D. Simpson (eds.) *Prehistoric Ritual and Religion,* 32–44. London: Sutton.

Healey, E. and Green, H.S. 1984 The lithic industries. In: W.J. Britnell and H.N. Savory, *Gwernvale and Penywyrlod: Two Neolithic Long Cairns in the Black Mountains of Brecknock,* 113–132. Cardiff: Cambrian Archaeological Association.

Henshall, A. 1993 The Grooved Ware: vessels P41–82. In: G. Barclay and C.J. Russell-White, Excavations in the ceremonial complex of the fourth to second millennium BC at Balfarg/Balbirnie, Glenrothes, Fife. *Proceedings of the Society of Antiquaries of Scotland* 123, 94–108.

Hey, G., Mulville, J. and Robinson, M. 2003 Diet and culture in southern Britain: the evidence from Yarnton. In: M. Parker Pearson (ed.) *Food, Culture and Identity in the Neolithic and*

Early Bronze Age, 79–88. Oxford: British Archaeological Reports S1117.

Hodder, I. 1999 *The Archaeological Process: An Introduction.* Oxford: Blackwell.

Holden, J.L., Phakley, P.P. and Clement, J.G. 1995a Scanning electron microscope observations of incinerated human femoral bone: a case study. *Forensic Science International* 74: 17–28.

Holden, J.L., Phakley, P.P. and Clement, J.G. 1995b Scanning electron microscope observations of heat-treated human bone. *Forensic Science International* 74: 29–45.

Houlder, C. H. 1968 The henge monuments at Llandegai. *Antiquity* 42, 216–21.

Jackson, R and Ray, K. 2012 Place, presencing and pits in the Neolithic of the Severn-Wye Region. In: H. Anderson-Wymark and J. Thomas (eds). *Regional Perspectives on Neolithic Pit Deposition: Beyond the Mundane,* 144–170. Oxford: Oxbow.

Johnston, R. 1999 An empty path? Processions, memories and the Dorset Cursus. In: A. Barclay and J. Harding (eds.) *Pathways and Ceremonies: the Cursus Monuments of Neolithic Britain and Ireland*, 39–48. Oxford: Oxbow.

Jones, A.M. 1997 Ceramics. In: T. Pollard, Excavation of a Neolithic settlement and ritual complex at Beckton Farm, Lockerbie, Dumfries and Galloway. *Proceedings of the Society of Antiquaries of Scotland* 127, 89–96.

Jones, A.M. 2002 *Archaeological Theory and Scientific Practice.* Cambridge: Cambridge University Press.

Jones, N.W. 2009 Womaston Neolithic causewayed enclosure, Powys: survey and excavation 2008. *Archaeologia Cambrensis* 158, 19–42.

Jones, N.W. 2011 *Excavations at Hindwell, Radnorshire, 2010–11.* Welshpool: Clwyd-Powys Archaeological Trust.

Kendrik, J. 1995 Excavation of a Neolithic enclosure and an Iron Age settlement at Douglasmuir, Angus. *Proceedings of the Society of Antiquaries of Scotland* 125, 29–67.

Kinnes, I.A., Schadla-Hall, T., Chadwick, P. and Dean, P. 1983 Duggleby Howe reconsidered. *Archaeological Journal* 140, 83–108.

L'Helgouach, J. 1965 *Les Sépultures Mégalithiques en Armorique.* Rennes: University of Rennes.

Lanting, J.N., Aerts-Bijma, A.T. and van der Plicht, J. 2001 Dating of cremated bone, *Radiocarbon*, 43(2A), 249–54.

Larsson, L. 2012 Mid Neolithic enclosures in southern Scandinavia. In: A. Gibson (ed.) Enclosing the Neolithic: Recent Studies in Britain and Europe, 109–23. Oxford: British Archaeological Reports s2440.

Leary, J. 2010 Silbury Hill: a monument in motion. In: J. Leary, T. Darvill and D. Field (eds.) *Round Mounds and Monumentality in the British Neolithic and Beyond*, 139–52. Oxford: Oxbow Books.

Leary, J., Canti, M., Field, D., Fowler, P., Marshall, P. and Campbell, G. 2013 The Marlborough Mound, Wiltshire. A further Neolithic monumental mound by the River Kennet. *Proceedings of the Prehistoric Society* 79, 137–64.

Leary, J. and Field, D. 2010 *The Story of Silbury Hill.* London: English Heritage.

Lelong, O. and Pollard, T. 1998 The excavation and survey of prehistoric enclosures at Blackshouse Burn, Lanarkshire. *Proceedings of the Society of Antiquaries of Scotland* 128, 13–53.

Linge, J. 1987 Re-discovering a landscape: the barrow and motte in north Ayrshire. *Proceedings of the Society of Antiquaries of Scotland* 117, 23–32.

Lisowski, F.P. 1962 Report on the cremations from the West Kennet long barrow. In: S. Piggott, *The West Kennet Long Barrow, Excavations 1955–56*, 90–94. London: HMSO.

Longworth, I., Ellison, A. and Rigby, V. 1988 *Excavations at Grimes Graves, Norfolk, 1972–1976. Fascicule 2: The Neolithic, Bronze Age and Later Pottery.* London: British Museum.

Loveday, R. 2006 *Inscribed Across the Landscape: The Cursus Enigma.* Stroud: Tempus.

Lucas, G. 2012 *Understanding the Archaeological Record.* Cambridge: Cambridge University Press.

Lynch, F.M. and Musson, C. 2004 A prehistoric and early medieval complex at Llandegai, near Bangor, North Wales. *Archaeologia Cambrensis* 150, 17–142.

MacGregor, G., Donnelly, M., Glendinning, B., Johnstone, L. and Taylor, K. 1996 *Excavations at Fox Plantation.* Glasgow: GUARD.

MacHaffie, F.G. 2001 *Portpatrick to Donaghadee: The Original Short Sea Route.* Stranraer: Stranraer and District Local History Trust.

Macphail, R. and Crowther, J. 2006 The soil micromorphology, phosphate and magnetic susceptibility from White Horse Stone, Aylesford, Kent (WHS98). CRTL Specialist Report, London and Continental Railways. Available online through ADS at http://ads.ahds.ac.uk/catalogue/adsdata/arch–335–1/dissemination/pdf/PT2_Spec_Reps/06_Palaeoenvironment/ENV_research_reports/ENV_Geoarch/ENV_GEO_Text/ENV_Micromorph_WHS_text.pdf?CFID=573996&CFTOKEN=39545028 (accessed Nov. 2011)

Mann, L. 1903 Report on the excavation of prehistoric pile-structures in Wigtownshire. *Proceedings of the Society of Antiquaries of Scotland* 37, 370–415.

Matarazzo, T., Berna, F. and Goldberg, P. 2010 Occupation surfaces sealed by the Avellino eruption of Vesuvius in the Early Bronze Age village of Afragola in southern Italy: a micromorphological analysis. *Geoarchaeology* 25, 437–466.

McFadyen, L. 2006 Material culture as architecture. *Journal of Iberian Archaeology* 8, 91–9.

McInnes, I.J. 1964 The Neolithic and Bronze Age pottery from Luce Sands, Wigtownshire. *Proceedings of the Society of Antiquaries of Scotland* 97, 40–81.

McKinley, J.I. 1993 Bone fragment size and weights of bone from modern British cremations and its implications for the interpretation of archaeological cremations. *International Journal of Osteoarchaeology* 3: 283–287.

McKinley, J.I. 1994a *The Anglo-Saxon cemetery at Spong Hill, North Elmham Part VIII: The Cremations.* Dereham: East Anglian Archaeology No. 69.

McKinley, J.I. 1994b Bone fragment size in British cremation burials and its implications for pyre technology and ritual. *Journal of Archaeological Science* 21: 339–342.

McKinley, J.I. 1997a The cremated human bone from burial and cremation-related contexts. In: A.P. Fitzpatrick, *Archaeological Excavations on the Route of the A27 Westhampnett Bypass, West Sussex, 1992, Volume Two*, 55–72. Salisbury: Wessex Archaeology Report No. 12.

McKinley, J.I. 1997b Bronze Age 'barrows' and the funerary rites and rituals of cremation. *Proceedings of the Prehistoric Society* 63, 129–45.

McKinley, J.I. 1999 Report on the cremated bone from Geirisclett Chambered Tomb, North Uist (unpublished report for Edinburgh University Field Unit).

McKinley J.I. 2000 Human Bone and Funerary Deposits. In: K.E. Walker and D.E. Farwell *Twyford Down, Hampshire Archaeological investigations on the M3 Motorway from Bar End to Compton, 1990–93*, 85–119. Winchester: Hampshire Field Club Monograph 9.

McKinley, J.I. 2004a Compiling a skeletal inventory: cremated human bone. In: M. Brickley and J.I. McKinley (eds.) *Guidelines to the Standards for Recording Human Remains*, 9–12. London: British Association for Biological Anthropology and Osteoarchaeology and Institute for Field Archaeology.

McKinley, J.I. 2004b Appendix 5: Llandegai Henge A: report on cremated bone from cremation circle. In: F. Lynch and C. Musson, A prehistoric and early medieval complex at Llandegai, near Bangor, North Wales. *Archaeologia Cambrensis* 150, 127–129.

McKinley, J.I. forthcoming Human bone and cremation rite. In: A.B. Powell, A. Barclay, L. Mepham and C. Stevens, *Landscape History: the Development of Communities in the Colne Valley. Imperial College Sports Ground and RMC Land, Harlington*. Salisbury: Wessex Archaeology

McMinn, R.M.H. and Hutchings, R.T. 1985 *A Colour Atlas of Human Anatomy.* London: Wolfe Medical Publications.

Meyer, M. 2002 Palisaded enclosures in the German Neolithic. In: A. Gibson (ed.) *Behind Wooden Walls: Neolithic Palisaded Enclosures in Europe,* 59–92. Oxford: British Archaeological Reports s1013.

Milek, K.B. and French, C.A.I. 2007 Soils and sediments in the settlement and harbor at Kaupang. In: Skre, D. (ed.) *Kaupang in Skiringssal*, 321–360. Aarhus: Aarhus University Press.

MoLAS 1994 *Archaeological Site Manual: Museum of London Archaeological Service* (third edition). London: Museum of London.

Molleson, T.I. 1993 The human remains. In: D.E. Farwell and T.I. Molleson, *Poundbury Volume 2, The Cemeteries,* 142–214. Dorchester: Dorset Natural History and Archaeological Society.

Morrell, J.J., Miller, D.J. and Schneider, P.F. 1999 *Service Life of Treated and Untreated Fence Posts.* Corvallis: Oregon State University Forestry Publications Office.

Morris, R. 1979 *The Prehistoric Rock Art of Galloway and the Isle of Man.* Poole: Blandford Press.

Morrison, A. 1968 Cinerary urns and pygmy vessels in south-west Scotland. *Transactions of the Dumfriesshire and Galloway Natural History and Antiquarian Society* 45, 80–140.

Munn, N. 1986 *The Fame of Gawa: A Symbolic Study of Value Transformation in a Massim (Papua New Guinea) Society.* Durham: Duke University Press.

Munro, A. 2014 Dunragit road works unearth ancient treasure trove. *The Scotsman* 14th May 2014.

Munsell 2009 *Munsell Soil Colour Charts 2009 Edition.* Grand Rapids: Munsell Colour.

Murphy, C.P. 1986 *Thin Section Preparation of Soils and Sediments.* Berkhamsted: AB Academic Publishers.

Murray, H.K, Murray, J.C. and Fraser, S. 2009 *A Tale of Unknown Unknowns: A Mesolithic Pit Alignment and a Neolithic Timber Hall at Warren Field, Crathes, Aberdeenshire.* Oxford: Oxbow.

Murray, J. 1981 The stone circles of Wigtownshire. *Transactions of the Dumfriesshire and Galloway Natural History and Antiquarian Society* 56, 18–30.

Naysmith, P., Cook. G., Freeman. S., Scott E.M., Anderson, R., Dunbar, E., Muir, G., Dougans, A., Wilcken, K., Schnabel, C., Russell, N., Ascough, P., and Maden, C. 2010 ^{14}C AMS at SUERC: improving QA data from the 5 MV tandem AMS and 250 kV SSAMS. *Radiocarbon* 52, 263–71.

Nielsen-Marsh, C., Gernaey, A., Turner-Walker, G., Hedges, R., Pike, A. and Collins, M. 2000 The chemical degradation of bone. In: M. Cox and S. Mays (eds.) *Human Osteology in Archaeology and Forensic Science,* 439–454. London: GMM.

Noble, G. 2005 Ancestry, farming and the changing architecture of the Clyde cairns of south-west Scotland. In: V. Cummings and A. Pannett (eds.) *Set in Stone: New Approaches to Neolithic Monuments in Scotland,* 25–36. Oxford: Oxbow.

Noble, G. 2006 *Neolithic Scotland: Timber, Stone, Earth and Fire.* Edinburgh: Edinburgh University Press.

Noble, G. and Brophy, K. 2011a Ritual and remembrance at a prehistoric ceremonial complex in central Scotland: excavations at Forteviot, Perth and Kinross. *Antiquity* 85, 787–804.

Noble, G. and Brophy, K. 2011b Big enclosures: the later Neolithic palisaded enclosures of Scotland in their Northwest European context. *European Journal of Archaeology* 14, 60–87.

Noble, G., Greig, M. and Millican, K. 2012 Excavations at a multi-period site at Greenbogs, Aberdeenshire, Scotland. *Proceedings of the Prehistoric Society* 78, 135–72.

Ó Drisceoil, C. 2009 Archaeological Excavations of a Late Neolithic Grooved Ware Site at Balgatheran, County Louth. *Journal of the County Louth Archaeological and Historical Society* 27, 77–102.

Orton, C., Tyers, P. and Vince, A. 1993 *Pottery in Archaeology*. Cambridge: Cambridge University Press.

Parker Pearson, M. 1996 Food, fertility and front doors in the first millennium BC. In: T. Champion and J.R. Collis (eds.) *The Iron Age in Britain and Ireland: recent Trends,* 117–32. Sheffield: Sheffield Academic Press.

Parker Pearson, M. 2012 *Stonehenge: Exploring the Greatest Stone Age Mystery.* London: Simon and Schuster.

Parker Pearson, M., Chamberlain, A., Jay, M., Marshall, P., Pollard, J., Richards, C., Thomas, J., Tilley, C. and Welham, K. 2009 Who was buried at Stonehenge? *Antiquity* 83, 23–39.

Parker Pearson, M., Cleal, R., Marshall, P., Needham, S., Pollard, J., Richards, C., Ruggles, C., Sheridan, A., Thomas, J., Tilley, C., Welham, K. et al. 2007 The age of Stonehenge. *Antiquity* 81, 617–39.

Parker Pearson, M., Pollard, J., Richards, C., Thomas, J., Welham, K., Albarella, U., Chan, B., Marshall, P. and Viner, S. 2011 Feeding Stonehenge: feasting in Late Neolithic Britain. In: G. Aranda Jimenez, S. Monton-Subias and M. Sanchez Romero (eds.) Guess Who's Coming to Dinner: Commensality Rituals in the Prehistoric Societies of Europe and the Near East, 73–90. Oxford: Oxbow.

Penney, S. 1975 Unpublished finds from Luce Sands, Wigtownshire. *Transactions of the Dumfriesshire and Galloway Natural History and Antiquarian Society* 51, 14–17.

Piggott, S. 1954 *The Neolithic Cultures of the British Isles.* Cambridge: Cambridge University Press.

Piggott, S. and Powell, T.G.E. 1949 The excavation of three Neolithic chambered tombs in Galloway, 1949. *Proceedings of the Society of Antiquaries of Scotland* 83, 103–61.

Pitts, M. 2001 Excavating the Sanctuary: new investigations on Overton Hill, Avebury. *Wiltshire Archaeological and Natural History Magazine* 94, 1–23.

Pollard, J. 1995 The Durrington 68 timber circle: a forgotten Late Neolithic monument. *Wiltshire Archaeological and Natural History Magazine* 88, 122–5.

Pollard, J. 2009 The materialization of religious structures in the time of Stonehenge. *Material Religion* 5, 332–53.

Pollard, J. 2012 Living with sacred spaces: the henge monuments of Wessex. In: A. Gibson (ed.) Enclosing the Neolithic: Recent Studies in Britain and Europe, 93–107. Oxford: British Archaeological Reports s2440.

Pospieszny, L. 2010 The Neolithic landscapes of the Polish lowlands. In: A.M. Larsson and L. Papmehl-Dufay (eds.) *Uniting Sea II: Stone Age Societies in the Baltic Sea Region*, 147–70. Borgholm: Opia.

Prehistoric Ceramics Research Group 1997 *The Study of Later

Prehistoric Pottery: General Policies and Guidelines for Analysis and Publication. Chelmsford: Prehistoric Ceramics Research Group Occasional Papers 1/2.

Pryor, F.M. 1984 Personalities of Britain: two examples of long-term regional contrast. *Scottish Archaeological Review* 3, 8–15.

Pryor, F.M. 1998 *Etton: Excavations at a Neolithic Causewayed Enclosure Near Maxey, Cambridgeshire, 1982–7.* London: English Heritage.

RCHM 1979 *Stonehenge and its Environs.* Edinburgh: Edinburgh University Press.

Reid, R.C. 1952 Dunragit. *Transactions of the Dumfriesshire and Galloway Natural History and Antiquarian Society* 29, 155–6.

Reimer, P.J., Bard, E., Bayliss, A., Beck, J.W., Blackwell, P.G., Bronk Ramsey, C., Buck, C.E., Cheng, H., Edwards, R.L., Friedrich, M., Grootes, P.M., Guilderson, T.P., Haflidason, H., Hajdas, I., Hatté, C., Heaton, T.J., Hoffmann, D.L., Hogg, A.G., Hughen, K.A., Kaiser, K.F., Kromer, B., Manning, S.W., Niu, M., Reimer, R.W., Richards, D.A., Scott, E.M., Southon, J.R., Staff, R.A., Turney, C.S.M., and van der Plicht, J. 2013 IntCal13 and Marine13 radiocarbon age calibration curves 0–50,000 years cal BP. *Radiocarbon* 55(4), 1869–87.

Renfrew, C. 1973 Monuments, mobilisation and social organisation in Neolithic Wessex. In: C. Renfrew (ed.) *The Explanation of Culture Change,* 539–558. London: Duckworth.

Reynolds, N. and Barber J.W. 1984 Analytical excavation. *Antiquity* 58, 95–102.

Reynolds, P.J. 1994 The life and death of a post-hole. *Interpreting Stratigraphy* 5, 21–25.

Richards, C.C. 1996 Henges and water: towards an elemental understanding of monumentality and landscape in late Neolithic Britain. *Journal of Material Culture* 1, 313–36.

Richards, C.C. 2013 *Building the Great Stone Circles of the North.* Oxbow: Windgather.

Richards, C.C. and Thomas, J.S. 1984 Ritual activity and structured deposition in later Neolithic Wessex. In: R. Bradley and J. Gardiner (eds.) *Neolithic Studies,* 189–218. Oxford: British Archaeological Reports.

Richards, C.C. and Thomas, J.S. 2012 The Stonehenge landscape before Stonehenge. In: A. Jones, J. Pollard, M. Allen and J. Gardiner (eds.) *Image, Memory and Monumentality: Archaeological Engagements with the Material World,* 28–42. Oxford: Oxbow.

Rideout, J. 1997 Excavation of Neolithic enclosures at Cowie Road, Bannockburn, Stirling, 1984–5. *Proceedings of the Society of Antiquaries of Scotland* 127, 29–68.

Ritchie, J.N.G. 1970a Beaker pottery in south-west Scotland. *Transactions of the Dumfriesshire and Galloway Natural History and Antiquarian Society* 47, 123–46.

Ritchie, J.N.G. 1970b Excavation of the chambered cairn at Achnacreebeag. *Proceedings of the Society of Antiquaries of Scotland* 102, 31–55.

Ritchie, J.N.G. and Shepherd, I.A.G. 1973 Beaker pottery and associated artifacts in south-west Scotland. *Transactions of the Dumfriesshire and Galloway Natural History and Antiquarian Society* 50, 18–36.

Robledo, B., Trancho, G.J., and Brothwell, D. 1995 *Cribra Orbitalia*: health indicator in the late Roman Population of Cannington (Sommerset [sic.], Great Britain). *Journal of Palaeopathology* 7, 185–193.

Roe, F.E.S. 1967 The battle-axes, mace-heads and axe-hammers of south-west Scotland. *Transactions of the Dumfriesshire and Galloway Natural History and Antiquarian Society* 44, 57–80.

Rogers, J. 1990 The human skeletal material. In: A. Saville, *Hazleton North: The Exacavation of a Neolithic Long Cairn of the Costwold-Severn Group,* 182–98. London: English Heritage.

Rogers, J. and Waldron, T. 1995 *A Field Guide to Joint Disease in Archaeology.* Chichester: Wiley.

St. Joseph, J. K. 1978, Air reconnaissance: recent results, 44. *Antiquity* 52, 1978, 47–50.

Saville, A. 1990 *Hazelton North: The excavation of a Neolithic long carin of the Cotswold-Severn Group.* London: English Heritage.

Scheuer, L. and Black, S. 2000 *Developmental Juvenile Osteology.* London: Academic Press.

Scott, E.M. 2003 The Third International Radiocarbon Inter-comparison (TIRI) and the Fourth International Radiocarbon Intercomparison (FIRI) 1990–2002: results, analysis, and conclusions. *Radiocarbon* 45, 135–408.

Scott, J.G. 1969 The Clyde cairns of Scotland. In: T. Powell, J. Corcoran, F. Lynch and J.G. Scott (eds.) *Megalithic Enquiries in the West of Britain,* 175–222. Liverpool: Liverpool University Press.

Scottish Natural Heritage 2006 *Luce Bay and Sands Special Area of Conservation: Advice Under Regulation 33 (2).* Edinburgh: Scottish Natural Heritage.

Selwyn, S.M. 1976 *The Archaeology of Luce Bay: A Synthesis, Mesolithic to Bronze Age.* Edinburgh: University of Edinburgh MA Dissertation.

Sharples, N. 2000 Antlers and Orcadian rituals: an ambiguous role for red deer in the Neolithic. In: A. Ritchie (ed.) *Neolithic Orkney in its European Context,* 107–16. Cambridge: McDonald Institute.

Sheridan, A. 2004 Going round in circles? Understanding the Irish Grooved Ware 'complex' in its wider context. In: H. Roche, E. Grogan, J. Bradley, J. Coles and B. Raftery (eds.) *From Megaliths to Metals,* 26–37. Oxford: Oxbow.

Sheridan, A. 2005 Pitfalls and other traps… why it's worth looking at museum artefacts again. *The Archaeologist* 58, 20–21.

Sheridan, A. 2006 Creating (and using, amending and reacting to) appropriate dwellings for the dead in Neolithic Scotland. *Journal of Iberian Archaeology* 8, 103–25.

Sheridan, A. 2010 Scotland's Neolithic non-megalithic round mounds: new dates, problems and potential. In: J. Leary, T. Darvill and D. Field (eds.) *Round Mounds and Monumentality in the British Neolithic and Beyond,* 28–52. Oxford: Oxbow Books.

Simpson, D.D.A. 1965 Food vessels in south-west Scotland. *Transactions of the Dumfriesshire and Galloway Natural History and Antiquarian Society* 42, 26–50.

Sissons, J.B. 1974 The Quaternary of Scotland: a review. *Scottish Journal of Geology* 10, 311–337.

Smith, D.E., Wells, J.M., Mighall, T., Cullingford, R.A., Holloway, L.K., Dawson, S. and Brooks, C.L. 2003a Holocene relative sea levels and coastal changes in the lower Cree Valley and estuary, SW Scotland, UK. *Transactions of the Royal Society of Edinburgh: Earth Sciences* 93, 301–331.

Smith, D.E., Haggart, B.A., Cullingford, R.A., Tipping, R.M., Wells, J.M., Mighall, T.M. and Dawson, S. 2003b Holocene relative sea level changes in the lower Nith Valley and estuary. *Scottish Journal of Geology* 39, 97–120.

Smith, D.E., Cullingford, R.A., Mighall, T.M., Jordan, J.T. and Fretwell, P.T. 2007 Holocene relative sea level changes in a glacio-isostatic area: new data from south-west Scotland, United Kingdom. *Marine Geology* 242, 5–26.

Smith, D.E., Hunt, N., Firth, C.R., Jordan, J.T., Fretwell, P.T., Harman, M., Murdy, J., Orford, J.D. and Burnsdie, N.G. 2012 Patterns of Holocene relative sea level change in the North of Britain and Ireland. *Quaternary Science Reviews* 54, 58–76.

Speak, S. and Burgess, C.B. 1999 Meldon Bridge: a centre of the third millennium BC in Peebleshire. *Proceedings of the Society of Antiquaries of Scotland* 129, 1–118.

Stead, S. 1994 Cremated bone. Fiche 14–21 in: A. Gibson, Excavations at the Sarn-y-bryn-caled cursus complex, Welshpool, Powys, and the timber circles of Great Britain and Ireland. *Proceedings of the Prehistoric Society* 60, 143–223.

Steier, P. and Rom, W. 2000 The use of Bayesian statistics for ¹⁴C dates of chronologically ordered samples: a critical analysis. *Radiocarbon* 42, 183–98.

Stell, G. 1996 *Exploring Scotland's Heritage: Dumfries and Galloway.* Edinburgh: The Stationary Office.

Stenhouse, M.J. and Baxter, M.S. 1983 ¹⁴C reproducibility: evidence from routine dating of archaeological samples. *PACT* 8, 147–61.

Stevenson, H.B.K 1946 Jottings on early pottery. *Proceedings of the Society of Antiquaries of Scotland* 80, 141–3.

Strang, V. 2004 *The Meaning of Water.* Oxford: Berg.

Stuiver, M. and Kra, R.S. 1986 Editorial comment. *Radiocarbon,* 28, ii.

Stuiver, M. and Polach, H.A. 1977 Reporting of ¹⁴C data. *Radiocarbon,* 19, 355–63.

Stuiver, M. and Reimer, P.J. 1986 A computer program for radiocarbon age calibration. *Radiocarbon* 28, 1022–30.

Stuiver, M. and Reimer, P.J. 1993 Extended ¹⁴C data base and revised CALIB 3.0 ¹⁴C calibration program. *Radiocarbon* 35, 215–30.

Svensson, M. 2002 Palisaded enclosures – the second generation of enclosed sites in the Neolithic of northern Europe. In: A. Gibson (ed.) *Behind Wooden Walls: Neolithic Palisaded Enclosures in Europe,* 28–58. Oxford: British Archaeological Reports s1013.

Thomas, J.S. 1999 *Understanding the Neolithic.* London: Routledge.

Thomas, J.S. 2006 On the origins and development of cursus monuments in Britain. *Proceedings of the Prehistoric Society* 72, 229–41.

Thomas, J.S. 2007a *Place and Memory: Excavations at the Pict's Knowe, Holywood and Holm Farm, Dumfries and Galloway, 1994–8.* Oxford: Oxbow.

Thomas, J.S. 2007b The internal features at Durrington Walls: investigations in the Southern Circle and Western Enclosures, 2005–6. In: M. Larsson and M. Parker Pearson (eds.) *From Stonehenge to the Baltic,* 145–58. Oxford: British Archaeological Reports s1692.

Thomas, J.S. 2010 The return of the Rinyo-Clacton folk? The cultural significance of the Grooved Ware complex in Later Neolithic Britain. *Cambridge Archaeological Journal* 20, 1–15.

Thomas, J.S. 2012a Introduction: beyond the mundane? In: H. Anderson-Wymark and J.S. Thomas (eds.) *Regional Perspectives on Neolithic Pit Deposition: Beyond the Mundane,* 1–12. Oxford: Oxbow.

Thomas, J.S. 2012b Some deposits are more structured than others. *Archaeological Dialogues* 19, 124–7.

Thomas, J.S. 2013 *The Birth of Neolithic Britain: An Interpretive Account.* Oxford: Oxford University Press.

Thomas, J.S., Marshall, P., Parker Pearson, M., Pollard, J., Richards, C., Tilley, C. and Welham, K. 2009 The date of the Greater Stonehenge Cursus. *Antiquity* 83, 40–53.

Thorpe, I.J. and C. Richards 1984 The decline in ritual authority and the introduction of Beakers into Britain. In: R. Bradley and J. Gardiner (eds.) *Neolithic Studies: A Review of Some Current Research,* 67–84. Oxford: British Archaeological Reports 133.

Tilley, C. 1994 *A Phenomenology of Landscape.* London: Berg.

Toolis, R. 2005 *A75 Dunragit, Dumfries and Galloway: Archaeological Watching Brief.* Loanhad: AOC Archaeology.

Topping, P. 1982 Excavation at the cursus at Scorton, North Yorkshire, 1978. *Yorkshire Archaeological Journal* 54, 7–21.

Turek, J. 2012 The Neolithic enclosures in transition. Tradition and change in the cosmology of early farmers in Europe. In: A. Gibson (ed.) Enclosing the Neolithic: Recent Studies in Britain and Europe, 185–201. Oxford: British Archaeological Reports s2440.

Vandeputte, K., Moens, L. and Dams, R. 1996 Improved sealed-tube combustion of organic samples to CO_2 for stable isotope analysis, radiocarbon dating and percent carbon determinations. *Analytical Letters* 29, 2761–73.

van Hoek, M. 1986 The prehistoric rock art of Galloway. *Transactions of the Dumfries and Galloway Natural History and Antiquarian Society* 61, 20–40.

Vatcher, F. de M. 1960 The Thornborough cursus, Yorkshire. *Yorkshire Archaeological Journal* 38, 425–45.

Vergès, J.M. and Ollé, A. 2011 Technical microwear and residues in identifying bipolar knapping on an anvil: experimental data. *Journal of Archaeological Science* 38, 1016–1025.

Wainwright, G.J. 1971 The excavation of a late Neolithic enclosure at Marden, Wiltshire. *Antiquaries Journal* 51, 177–239.

Wainwright, G.J. 1979 *Mount Pleasant, Dorset: Excavations 1970–71.* London: Society of Antiquaries.

Wainwright, G.J. and Longworth, I.H. 1971 *Durrington Walls: Excavations 1966–1968.* London: Society of Antiquaries.

Ward, G.K. and Wilson, S.R. 1978 Procedures for comparing and combining radiocarbon age determinations: a critique. *Archaeometry* 20, 19–32.

Warren, G. 2006 Chipped stone tool industries of the earlier Neolithic in Eastern Scotland. *Scottish Archaeological Journal* 28, 27–47.

Watts, S.M. 2004 *Practicing Primitive: A Handbook of Aboriginal Skills.* Layton, Utah: Gibbs Smith.

Weiner, J.S. 1951 Cremated remains from Dorchester. In: R.J.C. Atkinson, C.M. Piggott and N.K. Sandars, *Excavations at Dorchester, Oxon,* 129–41. Oxford: Ashmolean Museum.

Whitelaw, C.E. 1932 Donations to the museum. *Proceedings of the Society of Antiquaries of Scotland* 66, 1–32.

Whittle, A. 1991 Wayland's Smithy, Oxfordshire: excavations at the Neolithic tomb in 1962–63 by R.J.C. Atkinson and S. Piggott. *Proceedings of the Prehistoric Society* 75, part 2, 61–101.

Whittle, A. 1997a *Sacred Mound, Holy Rings: Silbury Hill and the West Kennet Palisade Enclosures.* Oxford: Oxbow.

Whittle, A. 1997b Moving on and moving around: Neolithic settlement mobility. In: P. Topping (ed.) *Neolithic Landscapes,* 14–22. Oxford: Oxbow.

Whittle, A., Healy, F. and Bayliss, A. 2011 *Gathering Time: Dating the Early Neolithic Enclosures of Southern Britain and Ireland.* Oxford: Oxbow.

Williams, J. 1970 Neolithic axes in Dumfries and Galloway. *Transactions of the Dumfriesshire and Galloway Natural History and Antiquarian Society* 47, 111–22.

Woodward, P.J., Davis, S.M. and Graham, A.H. 1984 Excavations at Greyhound Yard car park, Dorchester, 1984. *Proceedings of the Dorset Natural History and Archaeological Society* 106, 99–106.

Woodward, P.J., Davis, S.M. and Graham, A.H. 1993 *Excavations at the Old Methodist Chapel and Greyhound Yard, Dorchester, 1981–1984.* Dorchester: Dorset Natural History and Archaeological Society.

Zeuner, F.E. 1951 Cremations. In: R.J.C. Atkinson, C.M. Piggott and N.K. Sandars, *Excavations at Dorchester, Oxon,* 124–7. Oxford: Ashmolean Museum.

INDEX

Numbers in italics indicate pages with illustrations